# THE RISE OF PRUSSIA 1700–1830

We work with leading authors to develop the
strongest educational materials in history,
bringing cutting-edge thinking and best
learning practice to a global market.

Under a range of well-known imprints, including
Longman, we craft high-quality print and
electronic publications which help readers to understand
and apply their content, whether studying or at work.

To find out more about the complete range of our
publishing, please visit us on the World Wide Web at:
www.pearsoneduc.com

# THE RISE OF PRUSSIA
## 1700–1830

Edited by
### PHILIP G. DWYER

Longman

An imprint of **Pearson Education**

Harlow, England · London · New York · Reading, Massachusetts · San Francisco
Toronto · Don Mills, Ontario · Sydney · Tokyo · Singapore · Hong Kong · Seoul
Taipei · Cape Town · Madrid · Mexico City · Amsterdam · Munich · Paris · Milan

**Pearson Education Limited**
Edinburgh Gate
Harlow
Essex CM20 2JE

and Associated Companies around the world

*Visit us on the World Wide Web at:*
www.pearsoneduc.com

**First published 2000**

ISBN   0–582–29268–9 PPR
      0–582–29269–7 CSD

**British Library Cataloguing-in-Publication Data**
A catalogue record for this book is available from the British Library

**Library of Congress Cataloging-in-Publication Data**
The rise of Prussia: rethinking prussian history, 1700–1830 / edited by Philip G. Dwyer.
    p.  cm.
    Includes bibliographical references and index.
    ISBN 0–582–29268–9 (pbk.) — ISBN 0–582–29269–7 (cased)
    1. Prussia (Germany)—History—Frederick William I, 1713–1740.   2. Prussia
(Germany)—History—1740–1815.  3. Prussia (Germany)—History, Military.  4.
Nationalism—Germany—Prussia—History—19th century.  5. Church and
state—Germany—Prussia—History—18th century.  I. Dwyer, Philip G.

DD395.R58  2000
943′.05—dc21                          00–057560

10 9 8 7 6 5 4 3 2 1
04 03 02 01 00

Typeset by 35 in Baskerville MT 11/13pt
Produced by Pearson Education Asia Pte Ltd.
Printed in Singapore

# CONTENTS

# LIST OF MAPS AND TABLES

## MAPS

## TABLES

# LIST OF PRUSSIAN RULERS

| *Rulers* | *Reign* |
|---|---|
| Frederick William, the Great Elector (1620–1688) | 1640–1688 |
| Elector Frederick III, King Frederick I from 1701 (1657–1713) | 1688–1713 |
| King Frederick William I (1688–1740) | 1713–1740 |
| King Frederick II, the Great (1712–1786) | 1740–1786 |
| King Frederick William II (1744–1797) | 1786–1797 |
| King Frederick William III (1770–1840) | 1797–1840 |
| King Frederick William IV (1795–1861) | 1840–1861 |
| King William I, Kaiser William I from 1871 (1797–1888) | 1861–1888 |
| Kaiser Frederick III (1831–1888) | 1888 |
| Kaiser William II (1859–1941) | 1888–1918 |

# PREFACE

The purpose of this collection of essays and its companion, *Modern Prussian History, 1830–1947*, is to offer an overview of key themes in Prussian history over long periods of time. Specialists have approached their subjects from new perspectives, incorporating recent research which often questions traditional interpretations. Although distinct and separate, the two volumes are in many ways complementary. An essay taken in isolation, from either volume, will probably not give the reader very much of an insight into why Prussia developed the way it did. A combination of essays taken together, however, will throw light on long-term trends in Prussian – and by extension German – history. The resulting picture shows that Prussia was much more complex, diverse and in some respects less reactionary than traditional interpretations would have it.

These essays also give an indication of the wealth and diversity of work that has been carried out on Prussia over the last few decades. A number of them review Prussia's rise to power and the problems that its kings faced in asserting themselves on both the domestic and the foreign political fronts. This is a fairly standard approach: historians have generally thought in terms of foreign policy, the administration and the army when discussing the rise of Prussia. However, there is a tendency for Prussia's regional, ethnic and religious diversity to be glossed over in general texts that make sweeping assertions about what 'Prussia' was, and what it was to be 'Prussian'. Prussia's emergence as a leading European power, which was by no means straightforward nor inevitable, cannot be adequately understood without reference to its diverse social, economic and cultural structures. A number of essays in this collection consequently examine questions that are often neglected in the traditional political narratives: religion, intellectual history, the economy, and the development of a specifically Prussian culture and society, both urban and rural. They are all intimately linked in one way or another to the development and expansion of the centralized state. An attempt is thus made to integrate political history into a broader social framework.

Historians have never agreed on when Prussian history begins and when it ends. Stefan Berger's contribution in this volume discusses the various dates offered by historians and points out how differing interpretations of Prussian history were often related to specific political agendas. The dates chosen for this collection have been defined primarily by a desire to stay within the modern era. As such, 1701, the year when Frederick, Elector of Brandenburg-Prussia, crowned himself king in Königsberg, seems like the most practical date to start with. It was much easier to find a terminating point – 1947, when the Allies officially dissolved the state of Prussia. It was thought that 1830 would be an appropriate halfway point between these two dates. Despite its apparent arbitrariness, 1830 marks a new departure in Prussian history. By that stage, the liberal Reform Movement, which began in 1807 and which was born in military defeat at the hands of Napoleon, had petered out and the conservative forces around the throne had reasserted their position of power. The 1830s also saw the founding of the first conservative weekly newspaper, the *Berliner Politisches Wochenblatt*, and the creation of a Customs Union, the *Zollverein*. In other words, an old force (the nobility) was finding new ways to express itself, while new forces (economic and political) were coming onto the scene which would eventually vie with traditional social and political structures. The tensions these forces created are some of the issues explored in *Modern Prussian History, 1830–1947*.

This collection of essays is the end result of a collective effort and I am deeply indebted to all the contributors, not only for their unfailing co-operation and support, but for the patience with which they have borne the delays that inevitably attend this type of collection. Two people in particular, however, stand out above the others – Hamish Scott, who gave unstintingly of his time and advice when this book was just an idea, and Andrew MacLennan, formerly of Addison Wesley Longman, for his enthusiasm, energy and encouragement during the early stages of this project. It has seen the light of day largely as a result of their help. Thanks to Heather McCallum, who took up the project midstream. I should also like to thank Bill Hagen, Dennis Showalter, Tim Hochstrasser and Narelle Parkinson for their help and advice at various stages of the project. Renate Oakley helped me with the translations from German into English. I am also happy to acknowledge, at a time when research money is difficult to come by, the support of the Research Management Committee at the University of Newcastle and the Deutsche Akademische Austauschdienst for providing financial assistance towards the completion of this and its companion volume. Their generous support has made the project possible.

*Philip G. Dwyer*

# ABOUT THE CONTRIBUTORS

**Stefan Berger** is Professor of History at the University of Glamorgan, Wales. He is the author of *The British Labour Party and the German Social Democrats, 1900–1931* (Oxford, 1994, German transl. Bonn, 1997), *The Search for Normality: National Identity and Historical Consciousness in Germany since 1800* (Oxford, 1997), and *Social Democracy and the Working Class in the Nineteenth and Twentieth Century Germany* (London, 1999). He is currently working on a cultural history of German nationalism for Edward Arnold.

**Christopher Clark** is a Fellow and Lecturer in Modern European History at St Catharine's College, Cambridge. He is the author of *Politics of Conversion. Missionary Protestantism and the Jews in Prussia, 1728–1941* (Oxford, 1995) and *William II* (London, 2000). He has published widely in the field of Prussian and German history.

**Philip Dwyer** is Lecturer in Modern European History at the University of Newcastle, Australia. He is the editor of *Modern Prussian History, 1830–1947* (London, 2000), and author of a number of articles on Prussian foreign policy during the Napoleonic era. He is currently working on a study of Charles-Maurice de Talleyrand for Longman's 'Profiles in Power' series, as well as editing a collection of essays entitled *Napoleon, France and Europe: A Reassessment.*

**Karin Friedrich** is Lecturer in History at the School of Slavonic and East European Studies, University College, London. She is the author of *The Other Prussia. Royal Prussia, Poland and Liberty, 1569–1772* (Cambridge, 2000) as well as several articles on the Polish Prussian Enlightenment, religious conflict in Poland-Lithuania, the history of ideas, and the history of early modern Cracow and Prague. She contributed a chapter on 'Intellectual and Cultural Trends' in pre-unification Germany in Mary Fulbrook (ed.), *German History Since 1800* (London, 1997). She is currently working on a two-volume *History of the Prussian Lands*, from the fifteenth to the twentieth centuries for Pearson Education.

**Rodney Gothelf** recently received his Ph.D. in Modern History from the University of St Andrews, Scotland, where he specialised in the rise of the modern state. He has taught at St Andrews, Scotland and at the University of Notre Dame, Indiana. He is currently working on a manuscript about the operation of provincial government during the reign of Frederick William I, 1713–1740.

**Matthew Levinger** is Assistant Professor of Modern European History at Lewis & Clark College in Portland, Oregon. He is the author of *Enlightened Nationalism: The Transformation of Prussian Political Culture, 1806–1848* (Oxford, 2000), and several articles on political culture in revolutionary France and nineteenth-century Prussia. He is currently at work on a study of German nationalism since the fall of the Berlin Wall.

**Edgar Melton** is Associate Professor of History at Wright State University, Dayton, Ohio. He studied Russian history under Marc Raeff at Columbia University, where he received his doctorate. He has held numerous research fellowships, and was a Mellon Faculty Fellow at Harvard in 1989/90. His articles on Russian and German history have appeared in *Past & Present*, *Journal of Modern History*, *German History*, and other scholarly journals. He has also contributed chapters to several books published by Longman, including H. M. Scott (ed.), *The European Nobilities in the Seventeenth and Eighteenth Centuries*, 2 vols (London, 1995), and Tom Scott (ed.), *The Peasantries of Europe from the Fourteenth to the Eighteenth Centuries* (London, 1998). He is presently completing a study of a serf estate in early nineteenth-century Russia.

**Hagen Schulze** is Chair of Modern German and European History at the Friedrich Meinecke Institute at the Freie University of Berlin. His previous books include *Nation-Building in Central Europe* (1987), *The Course of German Nationalism: From Frederick the Great to Bismarck, 1763–1867* (Cambridge, 1991), *States, Nations and Nationalism: From the Middle Ages to the Present* (Oxford, 1996) and *A New History of Germany* (1998).

**H. M. Scott** is Senior Lecturer in Modern History at the University of St Andrews. He is the author (with Derek McKay) of *The Rise of the Great Powers 1648–1815* (London, 1983), *British Foreign Policy in the Age of the American Revolution 1763–1783* (Oxford, 1991) and numerous articles on eighteenth-century international history, and the editor of *Enlightened Absolutism: Reform and Reformers in Later Eighteenth-Century Europe* (London, 1990) and *The European Nobilities in the Seventeenth and Eighteenth Centuries*, 2 vols (London, 1995). He is currently completing a study of *The Emergence of the Eastern Powers 1756–75*. He is co-editor of the 'Cambridge Studies in Early Modern History'.

**Dennis Showalter** is Professor of History at The Colorado College, Colorado Springs. He is the author of *Railroads and Rifles: Soldiers, Technology and the Unification of Germany* (London, 1975), *What Now? Der Stürmer in the Weimar Republic* (Hamden, CT, 1982), *Tannenberg: Clash of Empires* (Hamden, CT, 1991), and *The Wars of Frederick the Great* (London, 1996), as well as numerous articles and chapters on war and the German army.

**Johan van der Zande** has taught in the Netherlands and at the University of California, Santa Barbara. He is the author of *Bürger und Beamter: Johann Georg Sulzer, 1739–1799* (Stuttgart, 1986), and the editor (with Richard H. Popkin) of *The Skeptical Tradition Around 1800: Skepticism in Philosophy, Science, and Society* (Dordrecht/Boston/London, 1998). He has published several articles on German popular philosophy and is currently writing a study of German philosophy between Wolff and Kant.

# Acknowledgements

We are grateful to the following for permission to reproduce copyright material:

Table I.1 from André Corvisier, *Armées et sociétés en Europe de 1494 à 1789* (Paris, 1976), p. 126, Presses Universitaires de France; all maps adapted from H. W. Koch, *A History of Prussia* (1978), reproduced with permission from Pearson Education Limited.

Whilst every effort has been made to trace the owners of copyright material, in a few cases this has proved impossible and we take this opportunity to offer our apologies to any copyright holders whose rights we may have unwittingly infringed.

# The rise of Prussia

PHILIP G. DWYER

In the seventeenth and eighteenth centuries, Prussia rose out of obscurity to become one of the most powerful countries in Europe. Prussia's rise took time, but it occurred over a relatively short period by contemporary standards. In 1640, there was no kingdom of Prussia at all, only the Electorate of Brandenburg, linked to disparate patches of land that were difficult to administer and even more difficult to defend. Moreover, the Electorate suffered from poor soil, declining trade and a sparse population. Its territory was often at the mercy of marauding mercenaries; this was especially the case during the Thirty Years' War. This was hardly the stuff out of which a great power was likely to be made.

The domestic and military reforms carried out by, first, the Great Elector, then Frederick III (King Frederick I from 1701), and further developed by the so-called soldier king, Frederick William I (ruled 1713–40), changed all of that. In the face of continuing military conflicts and the economic disruptions which marked the closing decades of the seventeenth century, Frederick III/I saw the need for a modern, highly trained army to protect the state.[1] To support it, he had to completely refashion both the political and the economic structures of the Electorate, emulating the absolutism of Louis XIV along the way. He transformed his state into a kingdom in 1701 and was largely responsible for the features that were to become characteristic of Prussia during the eighteenth and part of the nineteenth centuries.

---

1 See Derek McKay, 'Small-power diplomacy in the age of Louis XIV: the foreign policy of the Great Elector during the 1660s and the 1670s', in Robert Oresko, G. C. Gibbs and H. M. Scott (eds), *Royal and Republican Sovereignty in Early Modern Europe: Essays in Memory of Ragnhild Hatton* (Cambridge, 1997), pp. 189 and 191. My thanks to Dennis Showalter and Brendan Simms for their comments on various drafts of this chapter.

When Frederick II came to the throne in 1740, Prussia was on a par with its two German neighbours, Saxony and Hanover, with which it was competing for leadership in North Germany. That is, it was a second- or even a third-rate power. The economic and military reforms that had been carried out over the last two or three decades were then rudely put to the test during the Seven Years' War (1756–63). They enabled Frederick II to withstand assaults from Austria, France and Russia, whose combined populations outnumbered that of Prussia by more than fifteen to one.[2] Quite unexpectedly, Prussia emerged as a major player on the inter- national scene; it did so by defeating France at the battle of Rossbach in November 1757, and Austria one month later at the battle of Leuthen. Austrian defeats were fairly run-of-the-mill, but the rout of a major French army, especially since it had enjoyed numerical superiority, was a very different affair and it accordingly made a tremendous impact on con- temporary opinion. By the end of the Seven Years' War, and largely as a result of its military achievements, Prussia had entered the exclusive club of great powers, but at a tremendous cost. As Frederick the Great put it, Prussia was like 'a man with many wounds who has lost so much blood that he is on the point of death'.[3] He spent much of the rest of his reign consolidating his military and territorial gains in a Europe that, fortunately for Prussia, was relatively calm. Its membership in the club of great powers seemed confirmed when, in 1787, Frederick the Great's successor, Frederick William II, marched into Holland and conquered it in a matter of weeks, accomplishing what Louis XIV had in vain attempted over a period of years.

Prussia's great-power status, however, was flawed; its power base too fragile. It had neither the population nor the economic resources, let alone the geographical coherency, needed to carry out the obligations which came with its enhanced political stature. This is perhaps no better illus- trated than by the events that occurred during the French Revolutionary and Napoleonic wars. After a somewhat dismal performance during the War of the First Coalition, Prussia withdrew into the relative isolation of neutrality and was not shaken out of it until her interests were directly threatened by Napoleon's encroachments in northern Europe. When Prussia decided to stand up to France by going to war in 1806, its army, which had once been the envy of Europe, virtually collapsed after one major encounter

---

2  Richard L. Gawthrop, *Pietism and the Making of Eighteenth-Century Prussia* (Cambridge, 1993), p. 1.
3  Cited in C. B. A. Behrens, *Society, Government and the Enlightenment: The Experiences of Eighteenth-Century France and Prussia* (London, 1985), p. 81.

at Jena-Auerstedt (14 October 1806). Prussia's fate was subsequently decided on a raft in the middle of the Neva river near a town called Tilsit where, in July 1807, Napoleon met with Alexander I of Russia. The King of Prussia, Frederick William III, was left standing in the rain on the banks of the river waiting to learn his fate.

Napoleon's treatment of Frederick William III was significant. At Tilsit, Prussia was reduced to a rump state, but it came away determined to reform itself in order to regain its place as a great power in the European system. The reforms that were consequently carried out gave Prussia that chance. By the time Napoleon was exiled to St Helena in 1815, Prussia had, through its role in defeating France and after haggling at the negotiating tables at the Congress of Vienna, not only regained its former boundaries, but had added substantial new territories to its kingdom. It had survived the eighteenth century and was now prepared to lurch into the nineteenth, if not entirely reformed, then at least better prepared to meet the exigencies of the modern world than it had been before the advent of the French Revolution.

The story of Prussia's rise and rise, of its fall and its rise again is a familiar one. In telling it, historians have generally focused on a range of factors that help explain the reasons for Prussia's long-term success: the organizing and military genius of Prussia's rulers who together reigned for a period of almost one hundred and fifty years;[4] the efficiency of the Junker-officered army and the introduction of a system of recruitment based on the local canton; the Prussian state's massive expenditure on the army; the relative decline of Prussia's neighbours in north Germany (especially Sweden and Poland) as well as the decline of imperial influence in Germany; the reforms that were pushed through at various stages of Prussia's history; and finally, sheer good luck. All of these traditional elements are discussed in a number of essays collected for this book, but it is clear that the rise of Prussia was by no means as linear as many historians have believed.[5] A number of factors were nevertheless fundamental in shaping Prussia's political, social and economic development – geography, religion, the centralization of state power, the army and foreign policy.

---

4  Frederick William, the Great Elector (1640–1688), Frederick III/I (1688–1713), Frederick William I (1713–1740) and Frederick II (1740–1786). All of them were sane and able-bodied. This was a remarkable record of continuity and stability without which the House of Hohenzollern might not have been so successful.

5  Gawthrop, *Pietism*, esp. chs 2 and 3, for example, challenges the assumption of an essential continuity in Prussian history between the mid-seventeenth and the late eighteenth centuries.

# The disparate nature of the Prussian state

One of the most important elements to take into consideration when explaining the development of the Prussian state and which in large part determined policy, especially foreign policy, was the disparate nature of 'Prussia' as a geographic, political entity. The rise of Prussia can be understood only in terms of the country's geopolitical position in the heart of Europe. The work of Rodney Gothelf, Hamish Scott, Dennis Showalter and Hagen Schulze, as well as my own, all point to this. At the end of the eighteenth century, the distance between the western and the eastern extremes of the monarchy exceeded 1,000 kilometres. In between, a solid block of German territories separated the western lands from the main body of the state.

This lack of geographical integrity was remarkable even by contemporary standards. The heterogeneous character of the state was reflected in the titles that preceded the Prussian king's name. He was Margrave of Brandenburg, Duke of Pommern, Magdeburg and Cleves, Prince of Minden and Halberstadt, Count of Mark and Ravensburg and Prince of Neuchatel, to name but the most important. Not only were these territories spread over a large area of northern Europe, but Prussia enjoyed no natural boundaries that helped protect it from outside aggression. Furthermore, Prussia was not a uniquely German state, but rather a religious and political hybrid, a non-national state – although not to the extent that Austria was. This was especially the case after Protestant Prussia annexed parts of Catholic Poland in 1772, 1793 and 1795, but there were also enormous differences in social, economic and political traditions between provinces which also contained other ethnic and religious minorities (Danes and Lithuanians, for example).

The disparate nature of 'Prussia' as a state made the establishment of monarchical authority difficult if not problematic. It was under Frederick William I, one of the least understood kings in Prussian history, that a number of institutional and social changes were made in an attempt to draw the scattered provinces together, and to reduce the autonomy of the nobility. The end result was a state system that essentially remained intact until the defeat of the Prussian army by Napoleon in 1806, lending the state an extraordinary degree of institutional continuity throughout most of the eighteenth century. However, as Rodney Gothelf shows in his chapter on the beginnings of Prussian absolutism, the establishment of the king's authority was not as complete as the traditional historical interpretation has made out. Not only did Prussia's extraordinary geographical diversity intervene to complicate and even impede the smooth running of the king's centralizing initiatives, but so, too, did the opposition of local ruling elites to this process. This opposition was partly the result of religious friction between two Protestant confessions. The Prussian monarchy and its administration was largely Calvinist (its bureaucrats were often of Dutch or French origin), and it inevitably ran into the opposition of entrenched local elites who were largely Lutheran and who were jealous of protecting their privileges. Mainly, however, the opposition of the nobility was an attempt to impede the encroachment of the state.

# Religious and intellectual movements: Pietism and the Enlightenment

All of this was possible because of the manner in which the Prussian state was tailored to meet the needs of the army. Most aspects of Prussian society were obliged to conform to the overriding needs of the state. Social forces were deliberately harnessed by the state towards the same ends, or provision was made to accommodate social or religious groups and movements that in other countries became centres of opposition to the state. This was especially the case for religion.

Prussia in the seventeenth and eighteenth centuries was a centre of religious toleration, its rulers extending invitations to persecuted Protestants in Germany and the rest of Europe. For example, the Great Elector, Frederick William, invited over 20,000 French Huguenots to settle in Prussia after Louis XIV revoked the Edict of Nantes in 1685. Christopher Clark's chapter on the Pietist movement in Prussia suggests that one of the reasons why its rulers were prepared to support other religious, especially Protestant, confessions was that toleration was 'objectively' built into the Prussian state. That is, the Prussian court was Calvinist in a largely orthodox Lutheran population (with Catholic minorities after the annexations of Silesia and Poland) and was consequently obliged to adopt a policy of peaceful coexistence. This is not to say that friction between the Calvinist state and the Lutheran population did not exist, especially towards the end of the seventeenth century, nor between Catholics and Protestants after the second and third partitions of Poland. But by the beginning of the eighteenth century, not only had toleration prevailed as official policy, but the monarchy had learnt to use religion, in the shape of the Pietist movement, to enhance its own political and cultural authority. There is, in other words, a direct connection between politics and religion in eighteenth-century Prussia.

The Pietist movement in Prussia originated as an attempt to reform the Lutheran church from within. The person generally regarded as the father of Pietism, Philipp Jakob Spener (1635–1705), was a pastor in Frankfurt-am-Main who supported the idea of 'conventicles' (small groups within the established church which met for Bible reading, prayer and discussion), and who exhorted people to practise piety in their everyday life. His views, summarized in his major work, *Pia Desideria*, formed the basis of the Pietist movement. Spener's ideas attracted widespread support, not only among the clergy but among the laity as well. In 1694, he played an important role in the foundation of the University of Halle, where the theological faculty became a major centre of Pietist doctrine. As a result of his growing fame, he was eventually appointed to a post in Berlin.

The other key figure in the movement, Spener's admirer and friend, August Hermann Francke (1663–1727), founded a number of institutions which provided social services, such as charities for the poor, orphanages, schools, and even a publishing house. In doing so, Pietism, which bore a close resemblance to Puritanism in England, began to play a central role in the construction of auxiliary state institutions. What started out as a missionary movement opposed by the official state church soon became absorbed into the workings of the Prussian government. A partnership developed which was mutually beneficial, especially to the state. This was in part possible because of the nature of Prussian court society. Instead of attracting and rewarding a newly domesticated court nobility, as in France, the Prussian state devoted the major proportion of its revenues to military expenditure (see Hagen Schulze's contribution). Consequently, court culture in Prussia, unlike other European courts, was committed to military service, discipline and a rather prudish morality. Contemporary Pietists did not understand the political motives behind such a style of government, but as a result felt more disposed towards working hand-in-hand with the state.

Co-operation between the monarchy and the Pietist movement reached a peak during the reign of Frederick William I when it was used in the support of specific domestic policies. During this period, most of Prussia's civil servants, clergymen and officers were trained in schools run by Pietists. By the 1730s, a Pietist education was an essential prerequisite for those wanting to enter state service. It was this development – that is, the alliance between Pietism as ideology and the state – which has led Richard Gawthrop to postulate that Frederick William I came to see policy in Pietist terms, and which has led Mary Fulbrook to suggest that Pietism was central to the successful establishment of the absolutist state.[6]

In this manner, in Prussia, religion became an instrument of social control, but the movement also left its mark on the corporate ethos of the

---

6  Gawthrop, *Pietism*, pp. 11–12, 211–14, and 271; Mary Fulbrook, *Piety and Politics. Religion and the Rise of Absolutism in England, Württemberg and Prussia* (Cambridge, 1983), pp. 9 and 164–7. For a discussion on why Pietism never became an explosive doctrine and was absorbed into the Prussian political mainstream, see ibid., 'Religion, revolution and absolutist rule in Germany and England', *European Studies Review* 12 (1982), 301–21.

state and the army. In practical terms, Pietism inculcated in the common people habits of orderliness. The Prussian clergy as a whole, less worried about the salvation of the souls of their congregations than about establishing an 'enlightened' state, advocated virtues that were important for the maintenance of the state.[7] Pietist chaplains and instructors also instilled a heightened sense of discipline in the lower ranks of the army. This factor may help explain the relatively low desertion rates of Prussian troops during the Silesian wars.[8] Schooling was another area in which the influence of the movement made itself felt and in which the characteristics which became specifically associated with the Prussian 'system' – discipline, self-denial, obedience, deference to authority – were inculcated.[9] Although one should be wary about the degree to which rules and regulations, overwhelmingly religious in character, were effective in bringing about obedience and discipline, Pietism seems to have made a significant contribution to the consolidation of the absolutist state.

By the time Frederick II came to the throne in 1740, however, the influence of Pietism had begun to wane; he was not particularly sympathetic to a movement that had enjoyed his father's support. At the same time, another cultural/intellectual trend was starting to excite educated Prussian minds and for which Pietism had helped prepare the way – the Enlightenment, or more precisely its German variant, the *Aufklärung*. Under Frederick II, Berlin, along with Halle, Königsberg, Breslau and Frankfurt-an-der-Oder, became a leading centre of the Enlightenment often associated with his reign. The king's admiration for a number of French *philosophes* in particular (the correspondence between Voltaire and the king was extensive) for a long time led to the belief that the principles of the Enlightenment prevailed in Prussia. One of Germany's greatest exponents of the Enlightenment, Christian Wolff, who was expelled from Halle in 1723 by Frederick William I, was lured back seventeen years later by Frederick II. Indeed, Frederick II, along with Catherine II of Russia and Joseph II of Austria, is usually referred to as an 'enlightened despot', although there is a debate about the relationship between these rulers and the movement.

Johan van der Zande, on the other hand, believes that, contrary to traditional interpretations, Frederick II did not have much to do with the

---

7   This is the view of Günter Birtsch, 'The Christian as subject: the worldly mind of Prussian Protestant theologians in the late Enlightenment period', in Eckhart Hellmuth (ed.), *The Transformation of Political Culture: England and Germany in the Late Eighteenth Century* (London, 1990), pp. 309–26.

8   Gawthrop, *Pietism*, p. 228.

9   For the influence of Pietism on compulsory schooling in Prussia, see James van Horn. Melton, *Absolutism and the Eighteenth Century Origins of Compulsory Schooling in Prussia and Austria* (Cambridge, 1988), esp. ch. 2.

Enlightenment.[10] The impetus for reform in these countries, he argues, was political; it was part of the process of consolidating monarchical state power that had begun at the end of the seventeenth century. Frederick II never let Enlightenment principles interfere with what he considered to be his primary function – the strengthening of the state under his personal control.

This said, van der Zande approaches the topic from an entirely different perspective. He explores the other face of the Enlightenment by focusing on the creation of a specific body of knowledge by various thinkers, and the development of a number of institutions which helped foster the emergence of a public sphere in eighteenth-century Prussia. He traces the origins of what he refers to as a 'science of man' – the study of human nature – which began to dominate Enlightenment thinking in the second half of the eighteenth century and whose ideas were expressed in journals designed to reach wider reading audiences. This was part of an 'enlightenment sociability' which helped create a public sphere independent from and critical of the state (although this did not have political consequences until well into the nineteenth century). A whole generation of Prussian bureaucrats, teachers and intellectuals was trained in the spirit of Kantian rationalism. The Enlightenment was also expressed in various institutions such as the Berlin Academy of Sciences, coffee houses, societies like the *Mittwochsgesellschaft* (Wednesday Society) and the *Montagsclub* (Monday Club), or prominent journals like the *Berlinsche Monatschrift* or the *Allgemeine Deutsche Bibliothek*.[11] To this extent, the social forms of the Enlightenment in Prussia were no different to what was going on in other parts of Europe. The types of issues discussed and their consequences were, however.

## The rural and urban environment

There were, of course, other factors regulating the relationship between the monarchy on the one hand, and the people on the other. In order to sustain the links between the monarchy and the nobility, a compromise was reached.

---

10  In contrast to the interpretation put forward by T. C. W. Blanning, 'Frederick the Great and the Enlightenment', in H. M. Scott (ed.), *Enlightened Absolutism. Reform and Reformers in Later Eighteenth-Century Europe* (London, 1990), pp. 265–88, who believes that the Enlightenment had a discernible influence on Frederick's policies. On the controversial question of how faithfully Frederick II adhered to Enlightenment precepts, see Charles Ingrao, 'The Problem of "Enlightened Absolutism" and the German States', *Journal of Modern History* 58 (1986), 161–80.

11  For an account of Enlightenment society in Berlin, whose members were drawn mainly from the educated middle class, see Horst Müller, 'Enlightened societies in the metropolis: The case of Berlin', in Hellmuth (ed.), *The Transformation of Political Culture*, pp. 219–33.

In crude terms, in return for surrendering political power at the highest levels of government, the nobility was permitted to retain a number of socio-political privileges, which included their domination of the officer corps and the bureaucracy, control over government institutions at the local level, and, above all, their continued control over the peasantry.[12] The crown essentially bowed out of interfering in peasant–noble relations. However, since the peasant soldier and the noble officer were the two most significant elements in the army, and the army was fundamental for the survival of the Prussian state, Prussia's kings attempted to preserve and protect both the peasantry and the nobility. A series of royal decrees (1709, 1714, 1739, 1749) sought to protect peasants from excessive service demands from their lords in order to facilitate the smooth recruitment of peasants into the army. Peasant-tilled land, for example, could not be bought by the bourgeoisie or the nobility – this was known as *Bauernschutz*.[13] Noble land, on the other hand, could not be bought or sold to non-nobles, while struggling land-owners were provided with financial assistance. Nobles were forbidden to travel abroad without royal consent and requests to do so, except, of course, on official business, were consistently rejected. Noble officers could not even marry without the king's consent and, under Frederick II at least, requests were commonly refused; in most regiments, only between one-sixth and one-seventh of officers were married.[14] The interests of the individual were always secondary to those of the state.

The end result of these arrangements was a reciprocal relationship of dependency between the monarchy and the nobility. In this manner, the Prussian kings achieved something that the French monarchs were never able to do – overcome the opposition of a potentially unruly nobility by making them dependent on the crown for their privileged status in society. This alliance between the Prussian monarchy and the nobility was to last intact, although in modified form, right up to the end of the nineteenth century.

This was not always smooth running. It is clear from Rodney Gothelf's contribution that tensions almost continually existed between the monarchy and the nobility on the one hand, and the nobility and the peasantry on the other. Edgar Melton's chapter on the rural economy in East Elbia and the

---

12  For a discussion of the socio-political relations between noble and peasant, see Robert Berdahl, *The Politics of the Prussian Nobility: The Development of a Conservative Ideology 1770–1848* (Princeton, NJ, 1988), esp. chs 1 and 2; and Hanna Schissler, 'The social and political power of the Prussian Junkers', in Ralph Gibson and Martin Blinkhorn (eds), *Landownership and Power in Modern Europe* (London, 1991), pp. 99–110.

13  Otto Büsch, *Military System and Social Life in Old Regime Prussia 1713–1807: The Beginnings of the Social Militarization of Prusso-German Society* (New Jersey, 1997), pp. 46–7.

14  Christopher Duffy, *The Army of Frederick the Great* (Newton Abbot, 1974), p. 46.

feudal relationship between lord and peasant supports that view. Within the feudal organization of rural society, the noble was dependent on the peasant for his labour, while the peasant owed his lord labour services of various kinds. The relationship, however, was often a coercive one and was often resented by the peasantry. If, for example, the estate owner pushed the peasant for more or better work, the peasant was likely to respond by various strategies, which sometimes included sabotage. Melton cites the case of peasants who, when forced to cart hay or manure for their lord, would drive so recklessly that most of the content would be lost before they reached their destination. If the reaction on the part of the landlord was punitive, it would further poison relations between the lord and peasant. The unrest fostered by labour services was so pronounced that reform became an urgent political issue for the Prussian government. Moreover, traditional relations between peasant and lord in the last third of the eighteenth century were being undermined by changing economic conditions (the feudal estate was being converted into a modern estate based on wage-labour).[15] After 1807, when a concerted effort was made to dramatically transform Prussian agriculture, the nobility lost its monopoly over estate ownership, as a result of which the Prussian countryside, especially in East Elbia, began to see the emergence of a capitalist agriculture (to which, one might add, the old rural elites adapted themselves quite well).

If the relationship between the monarchy, the nobility and the peasantry was not always as smooth as tradition would have it, this does not mean to say that there was *only* opposition to the centralizing state. As Karin Friedrich shows in her chapter on the development of the Prussian town, urban elites, including the nobility, often found common ground on which to work. As much as historians might know about a few major urban centres, conditions in other towns, especially in Polish Prussia, have aroused little interest until quite recently. Karin Friedrich's contribution helps rectify this imbalance and adds another, all too often neglected, dimension to Prussian history by taking Polish Prussia into consideration. In doing so, she points to the importance of recognizing the dual roots of Prussia's history in both the Polish and the German contexts, and underlines the fact that Prussia, for

---

15 Hartmut Harnisch, 'Peasants and markets: the background to the agrarian reforms in feudal Prussia East of the Elbe, 1760–1807', in Richard J. Evans and W. R. Lee (eds), *The German Peasantry: Conflict and Community in Rural Society from the Eighteenth to the Twentieth Centuries* (London, 1986), pp. 37–70. On the breakdown of peasant–lord relations, see William W. Hagen, 'The Junkers' faithless servants: peasant insubordination and the breakdown of serfdom in Brandenburg-Prussia, 1763–1811', ibid., pp. 71–101.

much of its history, was 'facing both ways'.[16] Towns in Polish Prussia, for example, preserved political links with Warsaw throughout the eighteenth century, thus demonstrating, according to Friedrich, the willingness of Polish Prussian burghers to maintain a certain degree of political independence.

This, however, was a trend that towns found increasingly difficult to maintain as the eighteenth century progressed and as they were brought under the centralizing orbit of the monarchy. The development of the Prussian town was in part dictated by the administrative structures of the state. The creation of the General Directory in 1722, and the introduction of the canton system in 1733 (to which they were also subject) necessarily had an impact on the manner in which towns developed. So, too, did the introduction of an excise tax (essentially a tax on consumption) into all Prussian towns in accord with the centralizing initiatives carried out by Frederick William I and in an attempt to make the collection of taxes much more efficient. The moneys raised from this tax inevitably went into the state treasury and the army, and were never invested back into the provinces from whence they had come. The tax met with varying degrees of resistance in royal towns, but especially in those which were privately owned (more than half of Prussian towns were private – that is, they belonged to the nobility). It was one further means used by the state to interfere in almost every aspect of its citizens' lives, and it has generated a debate among historians as to how effective, or detrimental, such measures were in promoting the modernization and expansion of urban centres in eighteenth-century Prussia. Centres like Berlin and later Potsdam also received an additional – and, one might argue, artificial – impetus through the injection of large sums of money associated with the crown's building programme.

Apart from a few large urban centres like Königsberg (the largest in 1700 with a population of 40,000–45,000) and Berlin, most Prussian towns in the eighteenth century, especially in East Prussia, were very small; few towns exceeded 2,000 inhabitants. As the eighteenth century progressed, Berlin's population started to outstrip Königsberg; it grew from about 58,000 in 1730, to 113,000 in 1750, and to 145,000 on the eve of the French Revolution. It should be kept in mind, however, that the population figures for Berlin were bloated by the presence of military personnel. Depending on the period under consideration, the percentage of the population belonging to the military garrison usually varied between one-quarter and one-third of the overall population (approximately 14,000 in 1730, and 33,000 in 1789), and this did not include the families of military personnel. These figures

---

16  See Karin Friedrich, 'Facing Both Ways: New Works on Prussia and Polish–Prussian Relations', *German History* 15 (1997), 256–67.

could increase to as much as 50 per cent, as in the case of Potsdam where, in 1801, 9,000 soldiers lived alongside 18,000 civilians. As with the rest of Prussian society, where a symbiotic relationship existed between the military and the civilian population, the same could be said of the major urban/garrison centres.

This, as Friedrich points out, could have both beneficial as well as detrimental effects on the life of the city. When garrisons went off to war, for example, cities could find themselves depleted of a large proportion of their population overnight, with all the consequences that this would necessarily have on local markets. When garrisons were stationed in towns, their presence often proved to be a double-edged sword, providing an impetus to local economies, certainly, but also exacting arbitrary demands and even committing excesses on the civilian population that led to tensions between the two spheres. The tension was often compounded by the corrupt practices of local government officials over whom the town's burghers had no control. Indeed, the citizenry were completely excluded from participating in urban affairs at all levels. Moreover, towns like Berlin fell directly under the control of the General Directory. It was not until the urban reform regulations (*Städteordnung*) of 1808 that a certain number of rights – like control over trade, industry, the police and the judiciary – were transferred to the citizens in royal towns. Private towns were not brought under the administration of the state until much later in the nineteenth century, but the lack of participation in local politics in some towns in East Prussia and Silesia was so well ingrained that they asked to be made exempt from carrying through the reforms. Unlike the western provinces where there was already a tradition of local autonomy, political lethargy was to remain a characteristic of the burgher mentality in East Prussia for at least a generation or two.

## The state and the army

As happened so often in Prussia's history, the centralizing initiatives of the state – and this includes many of the domestic reforms which were introduced in the course of the eighteenth century – received their impetus from foreign policy. It was Frederick William I's desire for foreign-political independence on the international scene that led him to pursue a policy of self-sufficiency at home. It resulted in the reform of the administration, especially in matters of finance, carried out through the creation of a new administrative body known as the General Directory. This in turn enabled the king to carry out another major reform which had enormous consequences for the future development of Prussia: the army. The military system which was introduced under Frederick William I became one of the key means by which Prussia's society and economy were integrated into a more coherent whole. By the time Frederick William I died in 1740, the size of the army had more than doubled to over 80,000. By that time, one in twenty-five males was serving in the army, almost every nobleman was an officer in the army, and most of the Prussian state budget was devoted solely to the purpose of maintaining it.

In his chapter on the development of the Prussian state, Hagen Schulze demonstrates that the growth of the army inevitably had consequences for the manner in which both Prussian society and its political structures developed. This was especially the case for a country which was not rich in either human or natural resources. In many respects, Prussia could hardly afford to maintain an army, let alone one that was eventually to become as powerful as the largest European great power. The other European states – France, Austria, Russia and Britain – had achieved great-power status in part because of the size of their territories, their relatively large populations and the natural wealth of their kingdoms. Prussia had none of these things and achieved recognition of its position by stretching its resources to the limit, and this over lengthy periods of time.

As the eighteenth century progressed, due to the dependence of the state on the army for its survival, the military took precedence over every aspect of Prussian life. Recruitment was based upon the 'canton system' introduced in 1733 by Frederick William I. Each regiment was allocated a defined district or canton for recruitment comprising 5,000 households within which all males, from childhood on, were obliged to register on the rolls. Literally every peasant was potentially also a soldier. Every aspect of civil society was assigned a military function. As Otto Büsch pointed out in his now-classic work on the origins of the Prussian military system, this was a specifically Prussian phenomenon.[17] The Prussian military organization thus became the most efficient of its time. It was also the vehicle by which Prussia increased its status within the European states-system. The canton system was replaced by conscription towards the end of the Napoleonic wars and the creation of a people's militia, the *Landwehr*, which was eventually incorporated into the active army (see Dennis Showalter's contribution), but the army continued to fulfil a socializing function, this time by creating a bond between the monarchy and the nation (see Matthew Levinger's contribution).

---

17   Büsch, *Military System and Social Life in Old Regime Prussia*, p. xv.

Table I.1    Relative troop strengths of the European powers[18]

| Country | Year | Size of army | Population | Percentage of population |
|---|---|---|---|---|
| Prussia | 1740 | 80,000 | 2,200,000 | 3.6 |
| | 1760 | 260,000 | 3,600,000 | 7.2 |
| | 1786 | 194,000 | 5,700,000 | 3.4 |
| Austria | 1705 | 100,000 | 8,000,000 | 1.25 |
| | 1786 | 240,000 | 23,000,000 | 1.04 |
| France | 1710 | 300,000 | 20,000,000 | 1.5 |
| | 1738 | 140,000 | 22,000,000 | 0.64 |
| | 1760 | 280,000 | 24,000,000 | 1.17 |
| | 1789 | 180,000 | 26,000,000 | 0.69 |
| Great Britain | 1698 | 24,000 | 10,000,000 | 0.24 |
| | 1710 | 75,000 | 11,000,000 | 0.68 |
| | 1747 | 120,000 | 12,000,000 | 1.00 |
| | 1783 | 51,000 | 16,000,000 | 0.32 |
| Russia | 1705 | 220,000 | 14,000,000 | 1.57 |
| | 1796 | 300,000 | 36,000,000 | 0.83 |

There has been considerable debate about just how militarized Prussian society really was, but, as Hagen Schulze and Dennis Showalter pointedly remark, the figures speak for themselves. By the time Frederick the Great died in 1786, Prussia was the thirteenth largest state in Europe in terms of population; in terms of area the tenth largest; but in terms of the size of its army, it was the third largest in Europe. The figures in Table I.1 point to the overwhelming disparity between the size of the population of Prussia and the size of its army in comparison with other European states.

Throughout the second half of the eighteenth century, Prussia consistently maintained an army equivalent to about 4 per cent of the population.[19] It has been calculated that if other European powers had structured their military along the same lines as Prussia in 1740, then Austria would have had an army of 600,000 men and France an army of 750,000 men.[20] It is misleading to think, however, that all soldiers in the army were Prussian.

18   Source: André Corvisier, *Armées et sociétés en Europe de 1494 à 1789* (Paris, 1976), p. 126, Presses Universitaires de France. The figures on the size of European armies vary from study to study. For slightly different figures for different years to those quoted above, see John Childs, *Armies and Warfare in Europe, 1648–1789* (Manchester, 1989), p. 42.
19   Behrens, *Society, Government and the Enlightenment*, p. 88.
20   Ludwig Dehio, 'Der Zusammenhang der preußisch-deutschen Geschichte 1640–1945', in Otto Büsch (ed.), *Moderne Preußische Geschichte*, 3 vols (Berlin, 1981), iii, p. 1627.

On the contrary, half the army or more might be filled with non-Prussian professionals, with prisoners of war or with deserters from other armies.[21] Nevertheless, Prussia's disproportionately large force was all the more impressive in view of the scarcity of its economic resources in comparison to other European powers. More significant perhaps than the numbers of soldiers in relation to the size of the population of Prussia was the percentage of the nobility who were enlisted into the officer corps. As the army grew, so too did the number of officers needed to command it so that by 1806, it has been argued, the officer corps of 7,000–8,000 men represented over 90 per cent of the Prussian nobility.[22]

## Expansion and consolidation

The gradual but dramatic expansion of the army under Frederick William I may have led some of his neighbours to conclude that he was preparing for a large and extended military campaign outside his borders, but this was patently not the case. Not only was there no direct foreign threat to Prussia during the period when Frederick William I was building up the Prussian army to unprecedented levels, but the king was determined to pursue a policy of peace to consolidate his domestic reforms. It is misleading to assume that because Prussia had a disproportionately large army it was predisposed towards aggression on the international scene or that expansion was its primary objective. For two extended periods – from 1725 to 1740 and again from 1797 to 1812 (with the exception of 1806) – Prussia's kings did their utmost to stay out of the wars and crises that characterized European diplomacy during those years. Much of this depended on the character of the king, and on whether the international constellation was favourably disposed towards non-involvement. It was not until the death of Frederick William I in 1740 and the ascension to the throne of his son, Frederick II, that Prussia launched upon an aggressive expansionist foreign policy that was to become one of the characteristics of the 'Prussian system' and which saw Prussia emerge as an important state in Europe.

This is the subject of Hamish Scott's chapter on the rise of Prussia to great-power status in the first half of Frederick the Great's reign. At the

---

21  Gordon A. Craig, *The Politics of the Prussian Army, 1640–1945* (Oxford, 1955), p. 23.
22  Otto Büsch, 'Die Militarisierung von Staat und Gesellschaft', in Manfred Schlenke (ed.), *Preußen. Beiträge zu einer politischen Kultur* (Berlin, 1981), p. 55.

death of Frederick William I in 1740, Prussia had become an important regional power. Over the next twenty years, and as a result of the wars fought by Frederick II, Prussia emerged as a leading European power. This emergence was inaugurated by the Prussian invasion of Austrian Silesia in December 1740. Frederick II's reasons for invading Silesia can be summed up in two words – sheer opportunism. That is, the opportunity simply to seize these territories presented itself and was duly taken. The Prussian invasion of Saxony in August 1756, which precipitated the Seven Years' War, has also been interpreted as a blatant act of aggression. However, Hamish Scott seeks to explain it in other terms. He believes that the king was acting under the conviction that Prussia would be attacked the following year, possibly by three hostile foreign powers. It was, in other words, a pre-emptive strike. These two wars typify in many respects what Prussia is all about. On the one hand, we have an opportunistic war (the Silesian) designed to 'round off' Prussia's territories. On the other, Prussia's position in the middle of Europe, surrounded on all sides by potentially hostile and more powerful neighbours, placed it in an extremely vulnerable position. The only alternative to possible destruction was attack.

These two considerations played an important if not a determining role in the types of policy choices made. Later in life, towards the end of his reign, Frederick II reflected on his past actions and formulated a theoretical justification for them. There is a passage in his political testament which roughly reads: 'The first task of a prince is to survive [ . . . ] the second is to expand.' It became a maxim for all Prussian monarchs and throws light on another well-known dictum: 'a neighbouring country which rounds off our territory is a hundred times more important than a country which is separated from our borders'.[23] Indeed, Frederick II was probably most responsible for postulating a tradition that was accepted by his heirs, namely that he was prepared to expand at the cost of war. He considered all his neighbours more or less potential enemies, and to a certain extent he was perfectly right in assuming that most of his great-power neighbours meant him no good. As for the smaller states like Saxony, Polish Prussia, Swedish Pomerania, Mecklenburg and to a lesser extent Hanover, Frederick II and his successors coveted them with a frankness that justified other states' mistrust and hostility towards Prussia.[24]

---

23  Gregor Schöllgen, 'Sicherheit durch Expansion? Die Aussenpolitischen Lageanalysen der Hohenzollern im 17. und 18. Jahrhundert im Lichte des Kontinuitäts problems in der Preussischen und Deutschen Geschichte', *Historisches Jahrbuch* 104 (1984), 39.

24  Frederick II, 'Testament Politique, 1752: Rêveries politiques', in G. B. Volz (ed.), *Die politischen Testamente Friedrichs des Grossen* (Berlin, 1920), pp. 59–65.

The most important precondition for the absorption of territory was the acquiescence of one or more of the other continental powers. This is what occurred, for example, when Prussia acquired Polish territory in 1772, 1793 and 1795. In 1793, Russia was in total agreement with Prussia, while Austria, France and Britain were all powerless to oppose or even delay the partition. A similar set of favourable foreign international circumstances was to occur under Bismarck, allowing him to launch upon wars of expansion without running the risk of a prolonged or a general war. Opportunities for war, and consequently expansion, as Table I.2 demonstrates, were never lacking.

As can be seen from the table, Prussia participated in every major European war in the eighteenth and nineteenth centuries bar one – the Crimean War (1854–56) – as well as a number of minor European conflicts; in all, about twenty-four interventions of one type or another. There was nothing out of the ordinary about this; Britain, Russia and Austria were engaged in even more conflicts over the same period of time. What is unusual, however, is that Prussia was victorious (in that it always gained an addition of territory) in all but one major war – the War of the Fourth Coalition against France. This was remarkable odds for any power. The fact that, as a result of losing the war against Napoleonic France in 1806, Prussia came close to annihilation, lends weight to Hagen Schulze's argument that each conflict for Prussia was a matter of life and death. Dennis Showalter reminds us, however, that an essential goal of Prussian and later German policy and strategy was to keep wars from reaching that stage.[25] Prussia's monarchs – and that includes the somewhat erratic Frederick William II – accepted the necessity of a strategy of limited goals backed by credible force.

Also, Prussia was the aggressor in all but one of these wars (the last stage of the war against Napoleon in 1815, although one can legitimately argue that even though Prussia declared war on France in 1806, Napoleon was the real aggressor). This needs to be qualified. It would be misleading to think that Prussia was always intent on war, although there were occasions when its kings were blatantly expansionist. More often than not, however, the Prussians were anxious to avoid war, thus exposing themselves to undue danger. Nevertheless, all bar one of these wars (Prussia's participation in the Russian campaign of 1812, during which it was virtually a satellite state) were fought with specific territorial acquisitions in mind. This does not

---

25  Dennis E. Showalter, 'Total wars for limited objectives: an interpretation of German grand strategy', in Paul Kennedy (ed.), *Grand Strategies in War and Peace* (New Haven and London, 1991), pp. 106, 120.

Table I.2  Prussian participation in European wars, 1701–1871

| Year | War |
| --- | --- |
| 1701–13 | The War of the Spanish Succession (Prussian troops were deployed intermittently on the side of the Holy Roman Empire, Portugal, the Netherlands, England and Sardinia against France, Spain and Bavaria) |
| 1700–21 | The Great Northern War (Prussia participated in the war between 1713 and 1720 on the side of Russia, France, Denmark, Saxony and Hanover against Sweden, Poland and Turkey) |
| 1733–38 | The War of the Polish Succession (Prussia played a small part in the war on the side of Austria, Saxony and Russia against France, Spain, Sardinia and Bavaria) |
| 1740–48 | The War of the Austrian Succession (France, Prussia, Bavaria, Spain and Sardinia (which changed sides in 1743) against Austria, England, the Netherlands, Russia and Saxony). During its course Prussia also fought: |
| 1740–42 | The First Silesian War (against Austria), and |
| 1744–45 | The Second Silesian War (against Austria) |
| 1756–63 | The Seven Years' War (Prussia, England and Hanover against Austria, Russia, France, Saxony and Sweden) including what has been called the Third Silesian War in 1757 |
| 1772 | The First Partition of Poland (Russia, Prussia and Austria against the Polish Confederates) |
| 1778–79 | The War of the Bavarian Succession, also known as the 'Potato War' (Prussia against Austria) |
| 1780 | The First Armed Neutrality (Russia, Prussia, Sweden, Denmark, Austria and Portugal against England) |
| 1787 | The Invasion of Holland (Prussia and Britain against the Dutch Patriots) |
| 1792–95 | The War of the First Coalition (Austria, Prussia and Sardinia in 1792, joined a year later by England, the Netherlands, Spain, Portugal and Naples against France; Prussia withdrew in March 1795) |
| 1793 | The Second Partition of Poland (Russia and Prussia against Poland) |
| 1795 | The Third Partition of Poland (Russia, Prussia and Austria against Poland) |
| 1801 | The Second Armed Neutrality (Prussia, Russia, Sweden and Denmark against England; Prussia invaded Hanover) |

Table I.2  (*cont'd*)

| Year | War |
| --- | --- |
| 1806 | 'War' with England (declared when Prussia occupied the Electorate of Hanover, although no fighting took place) |
| 1806–7 | The War of the Fourth Coalition (Prussia, England, Saxony and Russia against France) |
| 1812–14 | The War of the Sixth Coalition (the French Empire, the Rheinbund and Prussia against Russia and England; Prussia went over to Russia and England after the retreat from Moscow and entered the Wars of Liberation |
| 1815 | The War of the Seventh Coalition (Prussia, England, Austria, Russia and various lesser powers against Napoleon) |
| 1848 | The 'Reichskrieg' (Reich War) (Prussian troops constituted part of a larger German force fighting Denmark over Schleswig) |
| 1864 | The War of the Danish Succession (Prussia and Austria against Denmark) |
| 1866 | The Seven Weeks' War (Prussia against Austria, Hanover, Hesse, Nassau and Frankfurt) |
| 1870–71 | The Franco-Prussian War (the North German Confederation, under Prussian domination, and the South German states against France) |

mean that Prussia went to war only with territorial gains in mind, but that at one stage or another territory became an important objective in whatever war was being fought.

There is nothing exceptional about Prussia's expansionist behaviour. If what Albert Sorel referred to as 'raison d'Etat' governed all states, then aggrandizement became the object of politics.[26] In other words, expansion and conquest were not peculiar to the Prussian state. The desire to control foreign space and resources was an attitude that prevailed in most eighteenth- and nineteenth-century states to one degree or another. Not only did Europe's statesmen generally consider it necessary to expand in order to survive, territories were considered just compensation for the cost of war outlaid by the winning power. The continued existence of the Prussian state through expansion was such an important element in Prussian politics that it became

---

26  Albert Sorel, *L'Europe et la Révolution française*, 8 vols (Paris, 1893–1912), i, p. 19: 'La raison d'Etat étant la règle, l'aggrandissement est l'objet de la politique.'

an ideological component of the 'Prussian system'. One of the premises of Frederick II's *Anti-Machiavel*, first published in 1740, was that only a large, strong state could secure the welfare of its subjects.[27] In all likelihood, this attitude was as prevalent at the end of the eighteenth as at the end of the nineteenth century, although to my knowledge the ideological continuity of Prussian foreign policy has yet to be demonstrated.

Periods of expansion alternated with periods of consolidation on the home front. This is the subject of Hamish Scott's chapter on a much-neglected period in Prussian history, from the conclusion of the Seven Years' War until Frederick II's death in 1786. These decades were so distinct from previous years that Scott introduces the notion of a 'second reign' of Frederick the Great. During this period, the king personally took control of almost all aspects of government, delegating less and less. One might even go so far as to say that, to use a modern idiom, he was a control freak and that everything had to be subordinated to his will.

This raises questions about the nature of the Prussian monarchy. While not all Prussian kings were personally strong, Prussia in the eighteenth and nineteenth centuries was a strongly personal monarchy. Despite the increasing complexity of bureaucracies, as the eighteenth century progressed an executive style of monarchy developed in which Prussia's kings strengthened their personal control over both domestic and foreign policy. They ruled through a team of secretaries and court favourites, thus bypassing the relevant ministers and their departments. This was especially the case towards the end of the eighteenth century during the reigns of Frederick William II and Frederick William III. It was only when the administration was reformed after 1807 that ministers were given powers that corresponded with their portfolios. Even then, however, there was a tendency for Frederick William III, and even later under Frederick William IV, to rely on favourites who were responsible to no one other than the king.[28]

To a great extent, the king lent his character not only to the outward appearance of the state – the decisions to make war and peace, for example – but also to its ability to function well or not. It is not surprising under these circumstances that the state's power and prestige could rise or fall

---

27 Quoted in Dennis Showalter, *The Wars of Frederick the Great* (London, 1996), pp. 32–3.

28 See Thomas Stamm-Kuhlmann, *König in Preußens großer Zeit. Friedrich Wilhem III. der Melancholiker auf dem Thron* (Berlin, 1992), pp. 416–24, 458–64; and David Barclay, 'The Court Camarilla and the Politics of Monarchical Restoration in Prussia, 1848–58', in Larry Eugene Jones and James N. Retallack (eds), *Between Reform, Reaction and Resistance. Studies in the History of German Conservatism from 1789 to 1945* (Oxford, 1993), pp. 123–56.

depending on the character of a particular monarch, quite independently of the foreign political circumstances or the resources at the state's disposal. It was this element which gave Prussia, at one and the same time, both its resilience and its weakness. Certainly at the beginning of the eighteenth century, the only thing holding together the widely separated territories of Brandenburg-Prussia was the person of the king. Rodney Gothelf demonstrates the extent to which Frederick William I interfered in every aspect of government, to the point of deciding on the amount of firewood that could be burnt by his officials in winter. So, too, did Frederick II, although he did so partly because he was convinced that he was surrounded by incompetency. Frederick William II (ruled 1786–97), on the other hand, could not have cared less about the minutiae of government and would have much preferred to while away his time chasing women rather than sitting in Cabinet meetings.

He did care, however, as I point out in my chapter, about controlling foreign policy. Neither Frederick II nor Frederick William II had political scruples, but Frederick II at least measured his lack of scruples with a good dose of prudence. Frederick William II, whose ambition knew no limits, did not understand that if his uncle had succeeded it was because his policies were limited to what was possible. Frederick William III (ruled 1797–1840), on the other hand, had little or no ambition other than the good of his people and was extremely reluctant to draw the sword on occasions when few other Prussian kings would have hesitated. In short, the character of the king and his personal preferences and attitudes helped shape Prussian policies and, therefore, the Prussian state and society.

The king's choices could be influenced by any number of factors, including his association with religious sects (Pietism in the case of Frederick William I), mystic sects (the Rosicrucians in the case of Frederick William II), and personal depression, a common occurrence among Prussia's kings. Common, too, were strained relations between the Crown Prince and the king (not always the father) which often resulted in the heir feeling obliged to prove himself worthy of the royal mantle – a tendency that sometimes translated into an aggressive, expansionist foreign policy and which may have been a factor in the behaviour of Frederick II, Frederick William II and, much later, William II. These are aspects of the decision-making process to which historians have paid scant attention, and yet they are probably much more important than, for example, domestic political factors like public opinion, or commerce, or financial considerations which simply did not come into the foreign-political equation until quite late in the nineteenth century. Prussian kings and their advisers did not need to take these factors into account when making foreign-policy choices. Foreign policy was exclusively the realm of the Prussian ruling elite.

# The French Revolution and Napoleon

Towards the end of his reign, Frederick the Great found the burdens of a governmental system which revolved almost exclusively around the person of the king increasingly difficult to bear. The inadequacies of this type of system became apparent in the years following the death of Frederick in 1786 when he was succeeded by two monarchs whose personalities and abilities were less than suited to absolute rule. In terms of foreign policy, it had potentially disastrous consequences. This is the subject of my own chapter, in which I examine Prussia's place in the European system before the French revolutionary wars of 1792 and how it coped with the threat of French hegemony under Napoleon. Focus here is placed on Prussia's foreign-political options (which were extremely limited) and the reasons why it made particular foreign-political choices. Contrary to most of the traditional literature, I argue that, although character and the personal preferences of the two monarchs concerned are important in understanding the types of choices pursued during these years, one also has to take into account the international system and Prussia's place in it. The upshot of my chapter is that Frederick William II was not as erratic, and Frederick William III was not as weak, as historians have generally made them out to be.

There are two historical approaches that I attempt to marry here. The first is an attempt to put the person of the king back into the monarchy. In many instances, in times of crisis and in the heat of the moment, the personal preferences of the king often took precedence over political considerations. Thus, Frederick William III's personal reluctance to go to war under any circumstances during the period between 1797 and 1805 is in part a reflection of his own peaceful character and is but one example of how that monarch's individual preferences could determine the course of Prussian history. In general terms, the character of the king determined, up to a point, the type of foreign policy that was pursued – that is, either passive or aggressive.

The second approach takes into consideration all those factors over which the king and his advisers had little or no control. Prussia's geography and the changing political circumstances, which varied enormously during these years, have to be taken into consideration. In 1797, for example, the revival of France and the elimination of the Polish buffer zone meant that the security needs of the Prussian monarchy were different than they had been at the beginning of Frederick the Great's reign. The main threat was no longer Austria; the fact is that Prussia was increasingly becoming the meat in a Franco-Russian sandwich. The foreign-political attitudes of Prussia's statesmen were shaped by the realization that Prussia lay in a particularly vulnerable position at the mercy of a hostile great-power alliance. This meant that the very existence of Prussia was dependent on how well its leaders played the military-diplomatic game. This is no better illustrated than by the Treaty of Tilsit in 1807 when Napoleon came to an agreement with Alexander I over the shape of Europe; Prussia not only lost much of its territory as a result, but virtually lost any semblance of independence. It did not regain its lost status until the defeat of Napoleon in 1814–15. The Congress of Vienna saw Prussia not only restored to its former territorial boundaries, but increase in size with the acquisition of the Rhineland provinces and part of Saxony. Prussia was meant to act as a bulwark on the Rhine against the threat of potential French expansionism in the future. The increase in territory, however, came with consequences that were not immediately foreseeable. Prussia was traditionally Protestant while the Rhine was Catholic. Prussia had maintained its monarchical conservatism intact, while the Rhine had been absorbed into the French imperium and had considerably more advanced legal and economic structures. In the nineteenth century, a disproportionate number of liberals and radicals (Marx and Engels are the most famous examples) were to be drawn from the Prussian Rhine. In terms of security needs, the virtual elimination of French influence in Germany after 1815 meant that Prussia's focus definitively shifted away from the east towards the west.

Historians have long argued that Frederick II's organization of the state and the army left a number of structural weaknesses that contributed to the defeat of the Prussian army at Jena-Auerstedt in 1806. In fact, Prussia was probably better equipped than its two eastern European rivals, Austria and Russia, to cope with the head-on collision with France. The problem Prussia faced, of course, apart from its own structural inadequacies, was the military genius of Napoleon which no power was adequately equipped to deal with. Hagen Schulze argues that the subsequent collapse of the Prussian state after defeat was necessary to break the structure of the old Prussian military state. Certainly, Jena-Auerstedt marks a rupture in Prussian history. It brought with it the end of the *Ancien Régime* in Prussia and, so the argument goes, gave the monarchy the necessary impulse to completely overhaul the state.

In fact, the impetus for reform existed well before.[29] The problem was that reforms were somewhat desultory and never carried far enough. Certainly, defeat and the obligation to pay a huge indemnity set by France at 120 million francs in 1810 made financial concerns of paramount importance and

---

29  For a review of the literature of reforming activity in Prussia before 1806, see Brendan Simms, *The Impact of Napoleon: Prussian high politics, foreign policy and the crisis of the executive, 1797–1806* (Cambridge, 1996), pp. 115–36.

set in motion initiatives to modernize the state and to emancipate the economy. But there was another aspect to the Reform Movement to which historians have paid scant attention and which is underlined in Matthew Levinger's analysis: the goal of national renewal also incorporated principles such as equality, national harmony and patriotism.

The defeat of the Prussian army in 1806 and the fate of the dynasty met with widespread indifference among civilians in Prussia. One of the probable reasons for this was that ordinary people were simply not involved, at any level, in the political life of the nation. One way of mobilizing the nation, then, was to create a constitution and a central representative body or parliament. It is well known that reformers like Stein and Hardenberg were convinced that the authority of the state could be restored only through some form of popular representation. This could come about only if citizens were 'free' and this in turn could only come about if economic reform radically altered the structure of Prussian society. Political and economic reform, then, were closely intertwined.

Matthew Levinger argues, however, that the ultimate aim of the reformers was not to limit the power of the monarch, but, on the contrary, to enhance it by fusing 'the will of the king with the will of the nation'.[30] That is, the reformers attempted to mobilize the 'nation' in a manner that would guarantee the internal harmony of Prussian society. Such a parliament, the Prussian reformers believed, was not meant to tell the king the wishes of the people; that would entail a degree of popular sovereignty that the conservative elites would not be willing to admit. It was meant to be a means through which the king could become acquainted with the wishes of the people. As Levinger points out, many of the political reforms proposed by Hardenberg and Stein were an attempt to reconcile these two contradictory forces – monarchical sovereignty and national representation. Hardenberg strove until his death in 1822 to establish a constitution and a parliament for Prussia, but he did so in the face of constant and determined conservative opposition, not only from the landed elites, but also within the high bureaucracy and from the circle of Frederick William III's informal advisers at court.[31]

The Reform Movement was not limited to the army and the administration. One of the foundations of the Prussian military state was the rural economy, which was a major source of income for both the nobility and the monarchy throughout the eighteenth century. During the course of the second half of the eighteenth century, Prussian estate owners became less dependent on their peasants' labour, a development which helped pave the

---

30  See also Matthew Levinger, 'Hardenberg, Wittgenstein and the Constitutional Question in Prussia 1815–22', *German History* 8 (1990), 257–77.
31  Berdahl, *The Politics of the Prussian Nobility*, pp. 123–54.

way for the success of the agrarian reforms in the early nineteenth century. The monarchy contributed to this trend by abolishing labour services on crown lands, also during the course of the second half of the eighteenth century. Frederick William III took a step further by abolishing serfdom on royal domains, well before the famous Emancipation Edict of 9 October 1807, which declared that there would be only 'free people' throughout the kingdom.[32] A series of laws was introduced between 1807 and 1821 which virtually ended the policy of *Bauernschutz* and enabled peasants to acquire land from either the monarchy or the estate owners. A significant minority had to buy their land and freedom at a very high price, but the vast majority paid a nominal sum to dissolve their obligations towards their feudal lords. By 1848, in East Elbia at least, 90 per cent of the peasants had gone through the system and acquired land.

The reforms naturally benefited the peasants, but they were also designed both to protect the privileges of the nobility and to enable them to acquire land at little or no expense. The lifting of the traditional state protection of the peasantry allowed the nobility to increase the size of their estates at the expense of the peasants. In East Elbia, the nobility received 85 per cent of common lands from the peasants (even if this did not prevent many nobles from going bankrupt) (see Edgar Melton's contribution). The East Elbian landowning nobility, or Junkers as they are commonly referred to, continued to enjoy a disproportionate share of power and authority in the state for most of the nineteenth century. The agrarian reforms nevertheless effectively removed any barriers to ownership of the land and, in this respect, although it took a great deal longer, Prussia was eventually able to achieve parity with its more advanced western neighbour, France, by the middle of the nineteenth century.

Schulze, Showalter, Levinger and Melton all point to the impact of 1807 and the Reform Movement on the course of Prussian history. As a result of the impetus of reform, Prussia began to shed its feudal past and began in many respects to become a progressive state, or at least as progressive as an absolutist-type state could become without introducing a central representative body. Universal military training and a civilian-officered reserve army (the *Landwehr*) were introduced; the peasants were legally free (the abolition of serfdom was decreed in 1807 and further implemented after 1815); the agrarian reforms, based on freedom of movement, made the old canton system of peasant recruits obsolete; Prussia enjoyed a fairly progressive legal code (the *Allgemeines Landrecht*) – even though it was introduced in 1794 – and an independent judiciary – although many vestiges of

---

32  Ibid., pp. 115–23.

patrimonial jurisdiction survived on noble landed estates; the schooling system was one of the most advanced in Europe; and the state enjoyed the benefits of an efficient bureaucracy that went hand in hand with this education system.

The government was also overhauled. When the Prussian foreign minister, August von Hardenberg, was dismissed from office at the insistence of Napoleon in October 1807 and was replaced by Karl Freiherr vom Stein, the latter went about trying to create a modern, bureaucratic state that was based on the principle of ministerial responsibility. After months of opposition to his proposals, Stein finally persuaded the king to dissolve his cabinet of personal advisers and to replace them with five ministers at the head of well-defined departments. The ministers had direct access to the king, which in itself was an enormous change. In theory, the king remained absolute; in practice, the ministers were now able to play a greater part in the formulation of policy and were responsible for carrying it out. It was the first step in the transformation of the Prussian state from an absolutist to what some historians have referred to as a bureaucratic monarchy.[33]

However, these reforms were not accompanied by general political reforms. Despite the fact that Frederick William III promised to grant a constitution on three separate occasions (1810, 1815 and 1820), the king ultimately decided that a parliamentary institution would undermine the power of the monarchical state.[34] Moreover, it has been argued that the military reforms contributed to and did not diminish the growth of Prussian militarism because the universal obligation of military service was separated from the universal right of political participation originally connected to it.[35] The tensions inherent in the Prussian state in the post-Napoleonic era were, therefore, never fully resolved and came to boiling point in the Revolution of 1848. What the reforms did do, however, was to place Prussia on the path towards modernization. By 1815, the precariousness of Prussia's place in the European system had been overcome, largely because of the settlement it reached at the Congress of Vienna. At the same time, the Reform Movement laid the social and political foundations that would lead to Prussia's industrialization. It was this which, over the next fifty years, was to enable Prussia to launch upon the struggle for supremacy in Germany and later in Europe.

---

33 James J. Sheehan, *German History 1700–1866* (Oxford, 1989), pp. 298–9, although this notion would benefit from further research.
34 For the history of Prussia's first 'constitutional conflict' see Berdahl, *The Politics of the Prussian Nobility*, pp. 182–98. Instead of a national parliament, provincial diets were created; they had only consultative powers.
35 Paul W. Schroeder, *The Transformation of European Politics 1763–1848* (Oxford, 1994), p. 594.

# CHAPTER ONE

# Prussia in history and historiography from the eighteenth to the nineteenth century

## STEFAN BERGER

Prussia has meant all things to all people. Its history is characterized by manifold contradictions, inconsistencies and extremes of interpretation which are mirrored in its historiography. At one end of the spectrum lie the historical concerns which underpinned Law No. 96 of the Allied Control Council for Germany of 25 February 1947 which officially ended Prussia's existence. Strongly influenced by British historiography on Prussia, notably by the writings of Geoffrey Barraclough (1908–1984) and A. J. P. Taylor (1906–1990), representatives of the British government pressed hardest for the dissolution of Prussia which, they argued, was the epitome of militarism, aggressiveness and illiberalism. It was a state so morally rotten that it could only be abolished. At the other end stood the mainstream of German historiography until and well beyond 1947 which was committed to defending the Prussian state. The extraordinary range of different interpretations of Prussian history has much to do with the baffling number of binary oppositions which have structured its historiography. In the seventeenth and eighteenth centuries, Prussia was a centre of religious tolerance while, in the nineteenth century, it ruthlessly suppressed Liberals, Catholics, Socialists and Poles. Prussia under Frederick II has been portrayed as an absolutist state, run by a brutal and unfeeling despot. But Frederick, the friend and admirer of Voltaire, also made Prussia one of the centres of the European Enlightenment. In the eighteenth century, Prussia divided the Reich, while in the nineteenth it emerged as the motor behind the unification of Germany. Prussia's reputation rested to no small degree on its army, and a 'social militarism' (Otto Büsch) came to penetrate every fibre of its society. But Prussia was also one of the earliest states in which the despotism of the absolute monarch had its limits in the rule of the law. The General Legal Code (*Allgemeines Landrecht*) of 1794 breathed the spirit of the Enlightenment and has been widely regarded as the most progressive and comprehensive legal code of its time, and yet Prussia remained, well into the twentieth century, one of the tightest feudal societies in Europe. Land of the darkest reaction to some, for others it was the modern state *par excellence*, in which 'reform from above' (Otto Hintze, 1861–1940) had prevented the excesses of the French Revolution. The technical, industrial and economic progress of Prussia in the nineteenth century seemed in blatant contradiction to its political and social 'backwardness'. Viewed through certain historiographic lenses, Prussia could be portrayed as a tyranny ruled by the traditional elite of reactionary Junkers. Change the prism only slightly, and Prussia re-appears as the very model of a progressive bourgeois state, in which the 'enlightened absolutism' of its rulers successfully modernized society and state. In the Weimar Republic, Prussia was the key pillar of Weimar demo-cracy. Until the so-called Prussia coup in 1932, it had been a bastion of the democratic parties and a model for SPD-Centre Party co-operation. At the same time, the political right successfully mobilized the spiritual herit-age of the 'old Prussia' against the 'new Republic' and thus undermined the Republic's legitimacy. The famous National Socialist postcard which portrayed Hitler next to Frederick II, Bismarck and Hindenburg was no coincidence. Prussianism, however facile, was an important weapon in the armoury of National Socialist propaganda. And yet, under the Nazis, the Prussian state and its administration was dissolved when the unitary state was created in 1934. Furthermore, Prussian Junkers formed an important part of the German resistance against Hitler. This list of antitheses could easily be prolonged, but the extraordinary range of views and opinions on Prussia over the whole period of its history should be clear by now.

There has never even been agreement among historians as to the proper definition and periodization of Prussian history. Many histories of Prussia begin with the history of the Teutonic Order which, in the course of the thirteenth and fourteenth centuries, created a state of their own in Prussia. This state was divided into two following the Second Peace of Thorn which ended the Thirteen Years' War in 1466. Only the eastern part remained under the administration of the Teutonic Knights who had to swear an oath of allegiance to the Polish king. The western parts became Royal Prussia and were directly incorporated into the territories of the Polish crown. In 1525, the last Grand Master of the Knights, Albrecht von Hohenzollern, converted to Lutheranism and secularized the country. He became the first Duke of Brandenburg-Prussia. It was on this Prussia and, in particular, on the House of Hohenzollern and their building of a power-ful state in the seventeenth and eighteenth centuries, that much German (and Anglo-Saxon) historiography has concentrated ever since. Yet the two Prussias continued to coexist until 1772–93, when Brandenburg-Prussia annexed Royal Prussia. It has been only recently that historians such as Klaus Zernack (*1931) and Karin Friedrich (*1963) have pointed to the importance of recognizing the dual roots of Prussian history. They have repeatedly demanded that historians of Prussia locate its history in the Polish and German contexts, in the history of the Polish–Lithuanian Commonwealth and the Holy Roman Empire. One can only underline their plea for a Prussian history that 'faces both ways'.[1] Historians have come to realize that the regional diversity of the Prussian lands presents them with formidable problems of interpretation. The different Prussian provinces were treated quite differently, even in the nineteenth century, for example, with regard to the right to self-administration. In several important ways, Prussia was badly divided. In terms of religion, two-fifths of its population were Catholic after 1815. Different Prussian provinces had different legal systems and social structures. So, for example, the traditions of the Rhineland remained, for the most part, completely at odds with the traditions of the Old Prussia east of the river Elbe.

An independent statehood of Prussia is still often dated to 1701, the year in which the Hohenzollern Duke of Brandenburg-Prussia was crowned king. In the eighteenth century, the foundations of the Prussian state were laid under Frederick William I and Frederick II. As late as 1978, Sebastian Haffner's (1907–1999) best-selling history of Prussia drew almost exclusive attention to eighteenth-century Prussian history, a time when Hohenzollern Prussia allegedly was 'the most modern state in Europe'.[2] If the starting-point for Prussian history is already contested terrain, the end-point finds historians even more divided. Some have followed the Prussian conservative critics of Bismarck's policies of unification in arguing that Prussia had come to an end in 1871. With the foundation of the German Reich, Prussia ceased to exist as an independent state. Others have fiercely debated whether the German Reich became Prussianized after 1871, resembling a kind of enlarged Prussia, or whether Prussia became Germanized (*Verreichlichung Preußens*). Today, a great number of historians of Prussia, including the editor of this collection, are willing to consider Prussian history until the formal dissolution of the state of Prussia by the Allied Control Council in 1947. Certainly, this seems justified with regard to the important role that the Prussian state (*Land*) played in the constitutional set-up of both Imperial Germany and the Weimar Republic, and also with regard to National

---

1   Thus the formulation of Karin Friedrich, 'Facing both ways: new works on Prussia and Polish–Prussian relations', *German History* 15 (1997), 267. See also Klaus Zernack, 'Preußen als Problem der osteuropäischen Geschichte', *Studia Historica Slavo-Germanica* 6 (1977), 31–48.
2   Sebastian Haffner, *Preußen ohne Legende* (Hamburg, 1978), p. 21.

Socialist attempts to exploit the myth of Prussia for Nazism's political aims. In the following, I hope to be able to demonstrate how different historical interpretations of Prussian history were often mixed up with specific political agendas as well as with methodological and theoretical debates about the nature of history and historical enquiry.

# Prussian historiography in the eighteenth century

The roots of the idea of writing the 'official' history of Brandenburg-Prussia can be traced back to the reign of Frederick William (1640–1688) who employed a number of court historians, among whom Samuel von Pufendorf (1632–1694) was the most famous. While subsequent Prussian kings continued the tradition of encouraging an officially sanctioned view of their state, it was the lack of a coherent history of Brandenburg-Prussia which ultimately made Frederick II reach for his pen and publish the *Mémoires pour Servir à l'Histoire de Brandebourg* (1746). Following the example of Voltaire's *Siècle de Louis XIV*, its first part consisted of Brandenburg's diplomatic and military history, while its second part dealt in some detail with what might be termed the cultural history of customs and traditions. The focus on the interests of the Prussian state was combined with the espousal of anti-Polish sentiments. The latter were to have direct political implications after Brandenburg-Prussia annexed Western Prussia in 1772. Frederick taxed Polish-speaking Catholic landowners and nobles far more heavily than their German-speaking Protestant counterparts and discriminated against them in various other ways. The Western Prussian cities had to pay higher taxes while, at the same time, they lost most of their political clout.

At the same time, Frederick II, inspired to an extent by Voltaire, consciously turned away from his enlightened civilizatory historiography and instead judged every aspect of life with regard to the Hohenzollerns' expansion of power. He thus became the first in a long line of historians who placed the political history of the state before everything else. Even when, from the 1950s onwards, a social history of Prussia began to emerge in West German historiography, much of that social history was primarily concerned with explaining the peculiar nature of the Prussian state. Hence, the state-centredness of Prussian history has never really been overcome and remains one of the key shortcomings of today's historical writings on the subject.

In his *Memoirs*, Frederick II heavily criticized the acquisition of the Prussian crown in 1701, which he regarded as rather unnecessary for the well-being of the Prussian state. It had more to do, he argued, with the vanity of Frederick I, who appears as the antithesis to Frederick William I. While the former is accused of wasting the state's resources on an expensive court life and on various aspects of representation, the latter's sobriety, sternness and prudence are portrayed as the very model of a Prussian king. This set the tone for many of the subsequent interpretations until Carl Hinrichs (1900–1962) pointed out that the first Frederick's understanding of power was completely different from that of his successors and hence had to be judged differently.[3] While Frederick I was still attempting to emulate the absolutism of Louis XIV, the coming to power of Frederick William in 1713 represented a fundamental caesura in the nature of absolutist rule in Prussia. There is a broad consensus in Prussian historiography after Leopold von Ranke (1795–1886) and Johann Gustav Droysen (1808–1884) that Frederick William should be viewed as the founder of modern Prussia because it was under his reign that the military, financial and administrative systems were all totally transformed. In an influential attempt to explain this transformation of Prussia in the first half of the eighteenth century, Gerhard Oestreich (1910–1978) introduced the concept of 'social disciplining' (*Sozialdisziplinierung*).[4] In his view, the social stability and political power of Prussia, surrounded by potentially hostile neighbours, rested on an increasingly internalized system of norms and values which stood at the heart of Frederick William's reform project. This undertaking cannot be adequately understood without reference to the king's religious beliefs. In particular, as Hinrichs never tired of pointing out, Frederick William's state was the embodiment of the Protestant ethics of hard work, rational organization and sober efficiency. Protestantism had significantly influenced many eighteenth-century North-Western European states such as Holland, Sweden, England and Russia (under Peter the Great), but nowhere was that influence more penetrating than in Prussia.

Many historical accounts distinguish between the rigorous Protestant absolutism of Frederick William and the 'enlightened absolutism' of his successor Frederick II. For much of the nineteenth- and twentieth-century historiography of Prussia, Frederician Prussia was the epicentre of what constituted Prussian history. In the Seven Years' War (1756–63), Frederick II challenged the delicate balance of power between the European powers and laid the foundations for the rise of Brandenburg-Prussia to great-power status, which then occurred in the first half of the nineteenth century. Yet while many nineteenth-century historians stressed the national mission of

---

3 Carl Hinrichs, *Preußen als historisches Problem. Gesammelte Abhandlungen* (Berlin, 1964).
4 Gerhard Oestreich, 'Strukturprobleme des europäischen Absolutismus', in Gerhard Oestreich, *Geist und Gestalt des frühmodernen Staates. Ausgewählte Aufsätze* (Berlin, 1969), especially pp. 191ff.

Frederick and drew a straight line between the Seven Years' War and the Wars of Unification fought by Prussia between 1864 and 1871, it needs to be emphasized that Frederick II was not concerned with German interests but only with the interests of the Prussian state and its ruling house. The history of Prussia under Frederick II cannot be understood by applying categories of the later nation-state. Eighteenth-century Prussianism was state-oriented; nineteenth-century Prussianism was nation-oriented. In his writings, Frederick had constituted the notion of a specifically Prussian idea of the state (which was harsh, achievement-oriented, tolerant, just and based on the ethics of duty and obedience), yet this state theory was different from nineteenth-century German nationalism (although, in many respects, it did become part of German nationalism).

Some historians, including Friedrich Meinecke (1862–1954), have argued that one should distinguish between Frederick II's ruthless Machiavellian foreign policy and his more enlightened domestic policies which culminated in the imposition of the rule of law and a general programme of 'reform from above'. However, both Frederick's domestic and foreign policies can ultimately be traced to the overriding concern for the Prussian state interest. His 'enlightened absolutism' was not concerned with applying abstract philosophical principles of the Enlightenment. Rather, it initiated a reform programme which aimed at optimizing the state's resources for the good of the state. Those who espoused the principles of an 'enlightened absolutism', such as the Prussian senior civil servant (*Geheimer Oberfinanzrat*) August Heinrich Borgstede (1757–1824), studied history so as to better comprehend the nature of the Prussian state. Such understanding was perceived as the crucial precondition for reforming the state in a sensible manner. Much has been made of the allegedly progressive nature of subsequent Prussian 'reforms from above' which, according to several historians, prevented a revolution in Prussia along French lines. By contrast, it has been pointed out more recently that Frederick II's organization of the state and the army in particular already had a number of structural weaknesses which ultimately contributed to the defeat of the Prussian state in 1806–7. As far as Frederick II's 'enlightened absolutism' is concerned, an interesting and as yet unanswered question was posed by Karl Otmar von Aretin (*1923) who suggested that 'enlightened absolutism' was largely a phenomenon of the economically backward states of central, Eastern and South-Eastern Europe.[5] Here much more comparative research would be needed.

Not all historians of Prussia in the eighteenth century were concerned with the state of Brandenburg-Prussia or the House of Hohenzollern. In

---

5   K. O. von Aretin (ed.), *Der aufgeklärte Absolutismus* (Cologne, 1974), p. 23.

eighteenth-century Royal Prussia, for example, the estates and burghers overwhelmingly resented the Hohenzollerns and were loyal subjects of the Polish crown. Seventeenth-century historians such as Christoph Hartknoch (1644–1687) hailed the Polish crown as the saviour of the democratic republican constitution of the Prussian people. In the eighteenth century, historians such as Gottfried Lengnich (1689–1744) were less enthused about the Polish crown because the latter had begun to encroach on Prussian freedoms in an attempt to centralize the essentially multicultural state by way of more uniform laws. Yet Lengnich took great care not to equate Prussia with the Hohenzollern dynasty, and he never spoke of any kind of 'German identity'. All of this had to wait for the apologists of Prussia-Germany in the nineteenth century who denounced 'Polish political anarchy' and 'magnate oligarchy'. Right up to the time of Chancellor Helmut Schmidt, the notion of a 'Polish economy' (*polnische Wirtschaft*) became a byword in German for chaos and incompetence. By contrast, Frederick II's part in removing Poland from the map of Europe for more than one hundred years had a significant impact on Polish perceptions of Prussia. From the late nineteenth century right through to Communist Poland and the most recent past, Polish historiography remained characterized by anti-Prussianism just as West German historiography continued to be dominated by pro-Prussian and anti-Polish views well into the 1960s. Only recently have historians from both Poland and Germany begun to destroy the ill-founded myths about the decline of Western Prussia under Polish rule and the equally fatal misconception of a flourishing Western Prussia under the efficiency of Hohenzollern absolutism.[6]

Before the University of Berlin was opened in 1810, Prussian history was taught primarily at the Universities of Frankfurt-an-der-Oder and Halle. In 1800, student numbers were minuscule: the University of Frankfurt-an-der-Oder had a total of 220 students and 19 professors, three of them historians. Most of the state-appointed professors propagated a specifically Prussian patriotism, which came to the fore in the 1790s in reaction to the threat of the French revolutionary 'virus' spreading to other parts of Europe. As history began to emerge only in the course of the eighteenth century as a modern academic discipline, much historical writing on Prussia was done by non-professional historians. Archivists, librarians, civil servants and lawyers like Friedrich William August Bratring (1772–1829), Siegfried William Wohlbrück (1762–1834) or Leopold Krug (1770–1843) were prominent writers of history. Non-professional historians continued to be important for

---

6   Of key importance here is Hans-Jürgen Bömelburg, *Zwischen polnischer Ständegesellschaft und preußischem Obrigkeitsstaat. Vom königlichen Preußen zu Westpreußen 1756–1806* (Munich, 1995).

the public image of Prussian history later on. One has only to think of Theodor Fontane's *Wanderungen durch die Mark Brandenburg*, of his histories of the Wars of Unification, of Gustav Freytag's *Soll und Haben*, or of Adolf Streckfuß's *500 Jahre Berliner Geschichte. Vom Fischerdorf zur Weltstadt* (first published in 1864, but which has since appeared in several editions) to recognize that public historical consciousness about Prussia was not shaped by professional historians alone. However, in the nineteenth century, as the discipline of history was becoming the leading discipline in the humanities, professional historians were increasingly formulating an exclusive right to the correct – that is, 'scientific' – interpretation of the past.

# Prussian historiography in the early nineteenth century

In the first half of the nineteenth century, Georg Wilhelm von Raumer's (1800–1856) economic, social and cartographic studies and then, especially, Ranke's *Neun Bücher preußischer Geschichte* (1847, republished in a revised and extended version as *Zwölf Bücher preußischer Geschichte*, 1874) were important milestones for historical research on Prussia. The foundation of the 'Association for the History of the Mark Brandenburg' in 1837 also developed into an influential forum for *Landes-* and *Provinzialgeschichte*. The Association published the journal *Märkische Forschungen*, which was replaced in 1888 by the *Forschungen zur Brandenburgischen und Preußischen Geschichte*. Furthermore, Adolph Friedrich Riedel (1809–1872) edited major documents of Brandenburg history in his 41-volume *Codex Diplomaticus Brandenburgensis* (1838–69). Historical studies continued to be encouraged by King Frederick William IV, whose close relationship to Ranke is well known.

The academization of historical writing meant the more rigorous application of methodological ground rules and the emergence of a 'scientific' (*wissenschaftlich*) ethos. The historist paradigm[7] led to a genetic and evolutionist idea of historical development: everything became explicable and

---

7  I suggest the replacement of the more common term 'historicism' by 'historism' to avoid terminological confusion. On the one hand, 'historicism' describes a notion, criticized and rejected by Karl Popper (1902–1994), that history develops towards a particular end according to predetermined laws. On the other hand, it refers to a concept, prominent among nineteenth-century German historians, which understands all political order within its own historical context. Hence, I propose to use the term 'historicism' only for Popper's concept and to introduce the term 'historism' for the German *Historismus* (in contrast to the German *Historizismus*).

understandable from its historical roots. As far as Prussian history was concerned, Ranke, often dubbed 'the father of historism', described Prussia as a 'newcomer' to the established European states and located its history firmly within the broader European picture. Much influenced by both Romanticism and Lutheran religion, Ranke came to adore the Prussian state. In particular, he praised a reforming Prussia that he identified with a self-consciously liberal civil service.

It is precisely this self-confident civil service which has often been credited with initiating the reforms from above which transformed much of the Prussian state and society in the decade between 1806 and 1817. The reforms laid the foundations for both the rapid industrialization of Prussia in the nineteenth century and the rise to great-power status between 1815 and 1866. The military reforms initiated by Scharnhorst and others have been held up as exemplary by decades of historians. Yet they have praised the reforms for very different reasons. Many nineteenth-century nationalist historians stressed that the army now became imbued for the first time with a truly national spirit. The army was celebrated as the 'school of the nation' (*Schule der Nation*). This line of reasoning became problematic at the end of the Second World War with the implication of the German army in genocide and mass murder. However, this did not prevent a renaissance of the theme in the context of West German remilitarization in the 1950s. It was now stressed that the Prussian reformers aimed at linking military reform to social reform. A true 'citizens' army' which would overcome the old militarism and help to defend Germany and Europe from the 'Soviet threat' could once again claim Scharnhorst as its ancestral founding father.

Even after 1945, nationalist historians such as Gerhard Ritter (1888–1967) attempted an ambitious apology of the Prussian-German army tradition in his *Staatskunst und Kriegshandwerk*, the first volume of which was published in 1954. However, in the debate following this book, more and more historians such as Ludwig Dehio (1888–1963) and Hans Herzfeld (1892–1982) criticized Ritter for restricting the problem of Prussian-German militarism to an issue of foreign policy. Instead they began to ask questions about the consequences of militarism on the domestic constitution of Prussia. In a groundbreaking dissertation, Otto Büsch examined this question in detail and argued that the militarization of Prussia in the eighteenth century had important repercussions for the social, economic and political outlook of Prussia.[8] A number of historians at the *Militärgeschichtliches Forschungsamt* in Freiburg increasingly came to write military history as part

---

8   Otto Büsch, *Militärsystem und Sozialleben im alten Preußen 1713–1807. Die Anfänge der sozialen Militarisierung der preußisch-deutschen Gesellschaft* (Berlin, 1962).

and parcel of the social and political history of Prussia-Germany.[9] The breakthrough to a political social history in West Germany in the 1960s focused attention on the analysis of processes and structures rather than the narratives about personalities and events.

For decades, the military as well as other reforms, in the areas of agriculture, administration, finance, bureaucracy, education and the constitution, were primarily regarded as a direct expression of the 'spirit of the Enlightenment' (*Geist der Aufklärung*) which aimed to put the Prussian state on a new foundation. The reformers, it was argued, wanted to strengthen the civic culture of Prussia by contributing to a greater participation of Prussia's middle-class citizens in the affairs of the state. From the 1960s onwards, historians began to argue that in fact pretty much the reverse had happened: the bourgeoisie was tied even closer to the state. One of the key protagonists of this historiographic change, Hans-Ulrich Wehler (*1931), now began to describe the Prussian reforms as 'defensive modernisation'.[10] Prussia, Wehler argued, was modernized from above in response to the threat posed by the French revolution to the traditional feudal elites. The latter defended their own position by reforming the state with the help of an efficient civil service so as to prevent a revolution. In some cases already, the 'enlightened absolutism' of Frederick II was perceived as anticipating the bourgeois transformation of European feudal societies in the late eighteenth and early nineteenth centuries. Hence the new social history combined methodological innovation with a more critical look at Prussia-Germany's traditions. The 'Bielefeld school' relied heavily on modernization theory in its attempt to understand Prussian-German history, and its political ambitions were closely tied to the Social Democratic Party of the late 1960s, intent on stabilizing and nurturing a 'Western-style' parliamentary democracy in West Germany. Ever since, there has been a vigorous debate as to the extent of the feudalization of the bourgeoisie in Prussia-Germany or the embourgeoisement of the feudal elites. The massive research project initiated by Jürgen Kocka (*1941) and Wehler at the University of Bielefeld in the 1980s seems to have at the very least relativized many of the initial assumptions about the feudalization of the bourgeoisie, especially with regard to the Prussian-German middle classes (*Bürgertum*).

---

9  Militärgeschichtliches Forschungsamt (ed.), *Handbuch zur deutschen Militärgeschichte 1648–1939* (Frankfurt-on-Main, 1964).

10  Hans-Ulrich Wehler, *Deutsche Gesellschaftsgeschichte*, vol. 1: 1700–1815 (Munich, 1987), pp. 347–548. Probably the most influential study pointing to the central role of the Prussian civil service in modernizing the Prussian state so as to avert a revolution was Reinhart Koselleck, *Preußen zwischen Reform und Revolution. Allgemeines Landrecht, Verwaltung und soziale Bewegung von 1791 bis 1848* (Stuttgart, 1967).

In the early nineteenth century, the 'objective' Ranke was also a prime example of such links between the writing of history and contemporary political ambitions. Between 1832 and 1836, Ranke edited the *Historisch-Politische Zeitschrift*, where his main aim was to defend both the historical record and, contemporary politics of his Prussian paymasters. Later, he even became official historiographer of Prussia. Quite early on, Hans Prutz (1843–1929) argued that Ranke's *Prussian History* of 1847 should be viewed 'less as a work of history and more as a historical-political manifesto aimed at defending the Old Prussian state and society as well as Prussian absolutism against the progress of Liberalism'.[11] Two main messages pervade Ranke's works on Prussian history. First, he believed the individual was subordinate to the will of the state. The states which had developed historically were, according to Ranke, sanctioned by God's will. Hence, service to the state was service to God. Secondly, he argued that Prussia did not have to go down the French path of revolution if it was strong enough to modernize and renew its political and social structures from within. If his loyalty to Prussia is beyond doubt, Ranke retained considerable scepticism about a united Germany. At the same time, however, he maintained that without Prussia, Germany would have had no effective state to represent its interests. Hence, his writings left the reader in little doubt: if a united German nation-state was on the cards, then Prussia would have to be at its core.

## The 'German vocation' of Prussia and the 'Hohenzollern legend'

For many nineteenth-century Prussian historians, Ranke's reasoning did not go far enough. Prussia, they argued, had a 'German mission' and Prussian history had a clear direction: the unification of Germany. In the first half of the nineteenth century, the Prussian historians attempted to combine their aim of a more liberal Prussia with their vision of a Germany united by the might of Prussia. Such an attempted reconciliation of national liberalism and the Prussian state manifestly failed in the revolution of 1848 in which Prussian historians played such a prominent role as 'revolutionaries' and deputies in the Frankfurt parliament. Thereafter, most Prussian historians, with notable exceptions such as Johann Gottfried Gervinus (1805–1871) and Theodor Mommsen (1817–1903), increasingly abandoned their liberal

---

11   Hans Prutz, *Preußische Geschichte* (Stuttgart, 1900), i, p. 4.

positions (or merely paid lip-service to them) and supported the illiberal yet powerful Prussia. Prussian constitutionalism allowed them to cling to the idea that, in the long run, it would be possible to unite the Prussian traditions with their liberal aspirations. They subsequently became fervent supporters of Bismarck's unification of Germany from above. Prussia was frequently compared with the role that Sparta and Macedonia had played in ancient Greek history. The Macedonians had united the Greek poleis and led them to victory over the mighty Persian empire. The Prussian ethos, with its sobriety, discipline and commitment to duty and obedience, was seen as a modern-day parallel to Sparta.

Among the most prominent and influential Prussians were Droysen, Heinrich von Sybel (1817–1895), Heinrich von Treitschke (1834–1896) and Gustav Schmoller (1838–1917). Droysen's 'History of Prussian Politics' (*Geschichte der preußischen Politik* in 14 volumes, published between 1855 and 1886) spelt out the Prussian telos most clearly and at greatest length. There was a straight line from the Teutonic Knights, who had brought 'superior German culture' to the East, to the creation of a strong military state under Frederick William, and to the establishment of a 'modern' and efficient state bureaucracy under Frederick II and the Prussian reformers of the early nineteenth century. From there, it was but a short step towards portraying the unification of Germany in 1871 as 'a historical necessity'.

Within Prussianism, the so-called 'wars of liberation' were now interpreted very widely as the first unsuccessful movement for a united Germany, which supposedly set the spark to the flames of the national movement across the German lands. The alleged 'awakening' of national sentiment in the early nineteenth century went hand in hand with an interpretation of the Prussian reform movement which saw the reformers essentially as national liberals attempting to initiate a reformist and evolutionary development which would lead to a compromise between bourgeois ambitions and the monarchic principle. Sybel, who said of himself 'I am four-sevenths professor and three-sevenths politician', spent much of his life in pursuit of an alliance of right-wing Liberals and Bismarckian Conservatives which, he argued, would defend the constitutional nation-state against its alleged enemies, such as Catholics, Left Liberals and Socialists. As a historian, he used the *Historische Zeitschrift* and the Historical Commission, both of which he helped to found, to propagate the idea of the historical necessity of the German nation-state as it had been created in 1871. And his own historical texts, most notably *Die Begründung des Deutschen Reiches durch William I* ('The Foundation of the German Reich by Wilhelm I', published in several volumes between 1889 and 1894), represented 'official' history writing *par excellence*: not only had it been Prussia's vocation to unify Germany, Prussia also appeared innocent in all three Wars of Unification, and the intra-Prussian as well as the intra-German controversies were all played down. An apology for Bismarck was combined with the most violent attacks on democrats and the tradition of 1848. The people, let alone the working classes, did not make as much as a single appearance in these volumes.

After his appointment to a Berlin professorship in 1859 (where he stayed until his death in 1884), Droysen became very much the centre of historical studies on Prussia. And it was another Berlin professor who in many ways succeeded Droysen as the doyen of Prussianism in Germany – Heinrich von Treitschke. Treitschke's historical writings were based on the Social-Darwinist belief that the nation-states were locked in a battle for the survival of the fittest. Racial overtones intermingled with Anglophobe, anti-socialist and anti-democratic sentiments to make Treitschke the most effective apologist of Prussia in the Wilhelmine period. He lent strong support to the Prussian Germanization policies in Poland and made anti-Semitism respectable in the centre of German society. His *Deutsche Geschichte* contains all the elements of Prussian myth-building which were to influence German historiography until 1947 and beyond. Take, for example, the question of the origins of Prussia. It was Treitschke who began talking about *das Ordensland Preußen*, thereby indicating that he saw the origins of Prussia in the Teutonic Order. Most eighteenth-century historians had been critical of the Order and instead sided with the old Prussians who had been forcibly Christianized by the Order. Treitschke's anti-Polish tendencies, however, led him to praise the Germanization policies of the Order and to recommend them with regard to the Polish-speaking population in Prussia. The Order became a means to legitimate the imperialist aims of the day and the emerging idea of gaining living space (*Lebensraum*) in the east. In more general terms, the Order was perceived as having adhered to certain values, such as sobriety, duty, precision and clarity of purpose, which allegedly fed into 'typical' Prussian values.

Next to Droysen and Treitschke, Schmoller was arguably the most important protagonist of the 'Hohenzollern legend' (*Hohenzollernlegende*), which consisted of two important myths: first, the national mission of the Hohenzollern to create a unified German nation and, second, the idea of a line of social, progressive and reforming kings who stood above class and through their politics alleviated class conflict. The latter was Schmoller's answer to the pressing social question which increasingly came to the fore in the last decades of the nineteenth century. According to Schmoller, the responsibility of the present Prussian king and German emperor lay with keeping up the tradition of social policies initiated by his predecessors. The state, in Schmoller's view, had a responsibility to look after the well-being of all classes in society and to ensure that no specific group or class interest dominated decision-making within the state. His groundbreaking studies on

the history of Prussia's administration were full of admiration for the reforms of Frederick William I who, largely through his modernization
of the civil service, transformed the Prussian state into one of the most
combative and efficient in the eighteenth century. The repercussions of
Schmoller's Hohenzollern apology can still be widely traced in post-Second
World War West German historiography – even in the work of Karl
Buchheim (1889–1982), who was more critical of Prussia than many of
his colleagues.[12] Schmoller founded the *Acta Borussica* in 1888, a massive
edition of sources which was the basis of many administrative and economic studies on Prussia until today. He revived the Association for the
History of the Mark Brandenburg, and for many years his Berlin professorship acted as one of the most important centres for Prussian studies. Many
younger historians, who had heard Schmoller lecture in Berlin, reported
how impressed they had been by his style and ways of approaching historical problems, especially by his emphasis on the importance of economic
history.

## The critics of Prussianism

While Prussianism dominated the production of historical texts at nineteenth-
century German universities, it was challenged by a number of formidable opponents. Theodor Mommsen (1817–1903) stood for a left-liberal
tradition which remained critical of Prussia's illiberalism and militarism.
Up to 1879, Mommsen belonged to those Liberals who had pinned their
hopes on a reforming and liberalizing Prussia. Yet, when Bismarck turned
to the Conservatives for support, Mommsen became more and more disillusioned with Prussian-German politics. In November 1879, Treitschke
justified the anti-Semitic movement and declared the 'Jewish question' an
important national problem for Germany in a famous article.[13] Mommsen,
who had been Treitschke's colleague and friend at the University of Berlin,
intervened and headed a campaign against anti-Semitism. Brave as it was,
Mommsen's intervention could not prevent the merging of nationalism and
anti-Semitism in the public consciousness of wider sections of the German

---

12  See Karl Buchheim, *Militarismus und ziviler Geist* (Munich, 1964), p. 21, where he talks
    about the Prussian state as 'the creation of the will of a few important rulers'.
13  The most important contributions to the ensuing debate, known as the Berlin anti-
    Semitism controversy, including Treitschke's original article which was first published in
    the 'Preussische Jahrbuecher' of 1879, are collected in Walter Boehlich (ed.), *Der Berliner
    Antisemitismusstreit* (Frankfurt-on-Main, 1965).

middle classes.[14] Confronted with illiberal and authoritarian politics at home and a megalomaniac imperialism abroad, Mommsen became increasingly depressed towards the end of his long life. He began to abhor the 'Germanic servility' of his countrymen, ridiculed the Pan-Germans as 'our national fools' and, in his political testament, even pleaded for a historic alliance of Left Liberalism with Social Democracy.

The Social Democrats were indeed the strongest political force not to be taken in by the predominant Prussianism of the Droysens, Sybels and Treitschkes. The small number of Social Democratic historians were banned from all academic institutions in Imperial Germany. Yet, this did not prevent them from trying to counter the many myths about Prussian history propagated by more mainstream 'scientific' German historians. Already in the 1860s, Karl Marx (1818–1883) himself had vigorously contested any notions that Prussian and German interests were one and the same. The Prussian state, he argued, depended on the continued non-existence of Poland and the benevolence of Tsarist autocracy in Russia. For Marx, the world had 'never produced anything more lousy than Prussia'. His condemnation of Prussia was, however, mixed with admiration for Prussia's modernity. Marxists agreed, for example, on the centrality of the Prussian reforms, yet, unlike the Prussian historians, they stressed that the prime motive for the reforms was to serve the interests of a developing capitalist economy in both agriculture and industry. Economics were more important than politics, and the ultimate aim of the reformers was to accommodate the economic interests of both aristocracy and bourgeoisie. The main arbiter between the interests was the bureaucracy, which emerged as the driving force behind the Prussian reforms. The reforms themselves laid the foundations for the development of Prussia from an 'agrarian industrial state' to an 'industrial agrarian state' in the first half of the nineteenth century.

Marxist admiration for Prussia's modernity stood next to the more explicit Prussianism of that other main intellectual founding father of German Social Democracy – Ferdinand Lasalle (1825–1864). He looked upon Prussia as Germany's Piedmont. Just as Piedmont was unifying Italy, Lasalle argued in his pamphlet 'The Italian War and the Task of Prussia', published in May 1859, so Prussia's military power would achieve national unity in Germany. However, as far as Lasalle was concerned, national unity and democracy were just two sides of the same coin. Democracy was interior self-determination of the people; the nation was exterior self-determination of the people. Lasalle looked favourably on a war between Prussia and

---

14  Christhard Hoffmann, 'Geschichte und Ideologie: Der Berliner Antisemitismusstreit 1879/81', in Wolfgang Benz and Werner Bergmann (eds), *Vorurteil und Völkermord. Entwicklungslinien des Antisemitismus* (Freiburg, 1997), pp. 219–51.

Austria-Hungary, for this was the only solution to the Austro-Prussian dualism which had prevented the formation of a German nation-state. Like the Prussian historians, he called on Prussia to bring about a unified German nation-state, yet, unlike most Prussians, he wanted to make that nation into a democracy.

In the 1890s and 1900s, Franz Mehring (1846–1919) continued to criticize both Prussia's aggressive foreign policy and the oppressive and illiberal domestic politics which gave privileges to the militaristic Junkers while disadvantaging workers and peasants. He castigated much of the historiography of Prussia for completely ignoring its long history of military despotism and the emergence of a class state.[15] In his *Lessing-Legende*, Mehring reminded his audience that eighteenth-century classical literature was part and parcel of the emancipatory struggle of the bourgeoisie against Prussian despotism, and he distinguished between the 'real' Lessing and his Prussianized legend. In his *German History* he wrote: 'The Prussian state has become great by permanently betraying Emperor and Reich and by exploiting and maltreating its working classes.'[16] In this history, the part of the villain was played by the Prussian aristocracy, that is, the Junkers. Prussia itself was described as a 'republic of Junkers' (*Junkerrepublik*). The Hohenzollerns, and in particular Frederick II, were portrayed as 'the most obedient servant of the Junkers' (*der gehorsamste Junkerknecht*), ultimately unable to break their political and economic power. The exploitation of the workers and peasants especially, made a mockery of the notion of the Hohenzollerns as social monarchs (*soziales Königtum*). When Mehring dealt with the Prussian army, he highlighted the brutal drill, the common maltreatment and savage punishment of soldiers and the high suicide rate among their ranks. Prussian mercantilism, Mehring argued, was not very successful and the alleged thrift of the Prussian monarchs was juxtaposed with an account of the wastefulness and unnecessary expense of Prussian court life. Apart from Mehring, it was notably his fellow Social Democrat, Max Maurenbrecher (1876–1930), who tried to demystify the Hohenzollern legend created by Schmoller and Prussian historiography in general.[17]

Unlikely allies of socialist historians in the fight against Prussianism were Catholic historians such as Friedrich Emanuel von Hurter (1787–1865),

---

15 Franz Mehring, *Lessing-Legende. Zur Geschichte und zur Kritik des preussischen Despotismus und der klassischen Literatur* (Berlin, 1893), which was written with the explicit aim to clear up the 'patriotic bric-à-brac (*Trödel*) of Sybel, Treitschke and similar historians'. See also Franz Mehring, *Deutsche Geschichte vom Ausgange des Mittelalters*, 2 vols (Berlin, 1910–11).

16 Mehring, *Deutsche Geschichte*, p. 57.

17 Max Maurenbrecher, *Die Hohenzollernlegende. Kulturbilder aus der preußischen Geschichte vom 12. bis zum 20. Jahrhundert*, 2 vols (Berlin, 1905).

Konstantin Ritter von Höfler (1811–1897), Johannes Janssen (1829–1891), Julius Ficker (1826–1902), Martin Spahn (1875–1945) and Ignaz Döllinger (1799–1890). South German historians in particular repeatedly raised their voices against a reform of the school curricula along Prussian lines. The Catholic *Historisch-Politische Blätter*, founded in the 1860s, and later the *Historisches Jahrbuch*, founded in 1880, were journals in which the Prussian myths were viewed with a great deal of scepticism. Catholics felt largely excluded by the Protestant definition of Germanness inherent in Prussian historiography. Yet Catholics were not necessarily less nationalist than the Prussians. Attachments to a 'greater German' (*großdeutsch*) notion of the nation remained strong among Catholic historians until 1945. Overall, Catholic historians of Prussia were few and far between. Meinecke's dictum that a Catholic history professor was a monstrosity certainly rang true in the ears of most of his Protestant colleagues in Imperial Germany and the Weimar Republic.

Some, like Ono Klopp (1822–1903), were effectively pushed out of German academic life by the Protestant Prussian mainstream. Klopp had described Prussia as an aggressive, expansionist and destructive power. 'Fridericianism', according to Klopp, was the underlying principle of the whole of Prussian history. Frederick II invented it and personified it more than any of the subsequent kings of Prussia. Klopp summarized the main characteristics of 'Fridericianism' thus:

> In its foreign policy it is the desire to conquer which finds its limits not in any moral values but in what is militarily feasible. In its domestic policy it is the principle of militaristic absolutism, i.e. the constant preparation of the state for expansionist wars. In both areas it tends to cloud its real aims and pretends to have others more suitable to gain popularity among those who look at things only superficially.[18]

'Fridericianism' was described as a kind of illness right at the very heart of Prussia which would continue to haunt the stability of the European peace and bode ill for a Germany unified under Prussian auspices. With such views, Klopp never secured an academic post in Germany and had to go into 'exile' in Austria, where one tended to look much more favourably on his particular brand of anti-Prussianism. The most distinguished of twentieth-century Catholic historians, Franz Schnabel (1887–1966), also was critical of Prussia: his history of Germany in the nineteenth century can be described in more than one sense as a counter-project to Treitschke's

---

18  Onno Klopp, *Der König Friedrich II von Preußen und die deutsche Nation*, 2nd rev. edn (Schaffhausen, 1867), p. 541.

history. He put more emphasis on the European context of German development and attached far more importance to non-Prussian sources and developments. Yet, even in the 1920s, he remained very much on the margins of the historical profession. Overall, although there were critics of Prussianism in the nineteenth and early twentieth centuries, the university-based, academic 'historiography' was remarkably successful in closing ranks against anyone challenging the Prussian orthodoxy. Mainstream German historiography in the second half of the nineteenth and the first half of the twentieth century adapted and to a certain extent modified the Prussianism of Droysen and Sybel, but its main parameters were never seriously questioned.

# PART ONE

# Politics, religion and society

CHAPTER TWO

# Frederick William I and the beginnings of Prussian absolutism, 1713–1740

### RODNEY GOTHELF

When Frederick William I ascended the throne in February 1713, he launched a fresh series of governmental reforms designed to establish and expand Berlin's authority throughout the widely scattered territories comprising the Brandenburg-Prussian state. Under previous Hohenzollern rulers, the dispersed territorial elites had successfully opposed almost all attempts by a ruler to impose his will on their province, and especially anything approaching a unified administration overseeing all the dynasty's possessions.

The traditional historical view has argued that Frederick William I established his authority throughout his lands quickly, smoothly and completely. However, more recent studies present a more complex and ambiguous picture of the establishment of absolutism in the Hohenzollern territories. This chapter will examine the factors complicating and sometimes impeding Frederick William I's efforts to establish his authority throughout Brandenburg-Prussia.

## Frederick William I as king

Overcoming the vast geographical separation and the power of local elites were crucial factors in Brandenburg-Prussia's emergence as a great power during the latter half of the eighteenth century. Frederick William I was partially able to do this by asserting his personal authority, often after long periods (in some cases, decades and even centuries) of poor control and management over state affairs, such as commerce and trade, infrastructure, defence, agricultural production, education, health and safety, and monetary affairs.

During the first half of the eighteenth century, the Prussian government remained highly personal in nature. Its effectiveness depended upon the king playing a central role in the day-to-day conduct of administration. Frederick William I ruled his territories from his own suite of offices within the royal residence, the so-called *Kabinett*. He read and annotated innumerable reports in his fractured and ungrammatical German, drew up numerous instructions and involved himself in every aspect of government. Not even apparently minor issues escaped his attention. During the winter of 1729, for example, officials in the administrative auditors' office (*Oberrechenkammer*), a central financial agency in Berlin, requested an additional allowance of firewood so they would not have to borrow against the following year's allocation in order to fuel the five heating ovens in their offices. Frederick William I responded that rather than burn more firewood, the officials should and must get along with their allocation and 'should make gentle fires'.[1] The king took the same obsessive interest in administrative minutiae at all levels of government. The personality and attributes of the king were crucial in determining the nature of the government over which he presided. Although Frederick William I had close personal advisers (many of whom had been influential while he was crown prince), none became as all-powerful as those under previous Hohenzollerns.

Frederick William I is perhaps the least understood Hohenzollern ruler during Brandenburg-Prussia's formative centuries, essentially because of his puzzling and contradictory behaviour.[2] Historians often cite anecdotal evidence revealing the king's uncontrollable outbursts of rage, which sometimes lasted days at a time, and his obsessive-compulsive behaviour towards family, friends and subjects alike. The king's behaviour may partly be attributable to a combination of the so-called 'royal malady' porphyria, or nephritic colic, and gout.[3] One of the best-known portraits of Frederick William I (Antoine Pesne's 1733 painting) shows him with his much-feared lacquered cane. It was more than a portrait prop and one he did not hesitate to use as

1 *Immediatbericht des General-Directoriums*, 26 February 1729, in *Acta Borussica Behördenorganisation. Denkmäler der Preußischen Staatsverwaltung im 18. Jahrhundert* (Berlin, 1892–1980) (reprinted 1986/87) 4:2, p. 440 (hereafter designated as ABB). I would like to thank the Department of History at the University of Notre Dame, Indiana. Their help with my appointment as a Visiting Scholar during the 1998–9 academic year assisted me greatly in completing this chapter. I am also deeply grateful to Hamish M. Scott for reading and providing valuable comments on the final draft of this chapter.

2 See the annotated bibliography for a brief description of the studies dealing with Frederick William I and his unusual personality.

3 Ida Macalpine, Richard Hunter and C. Rimington, 'Porphyria in the Royal Houses of Stuart, Hanover, and Prussia: A Follow-up Study of George III's Illness', in *Porphyria – A Royal Malady: Articles Published in or Commissioned by the British Medical Journal* (London, 1968), p. 49. On porphyria, see Abe Goldberg, 'The Porphyrias', ibid., pp. 66–8.

a motivational tool on unsuspecting officials.[4] This violent, cruel behaviour was a curious contrast to his profound religious beliefs that lent his character a puzzling quality.[5] Moreover, from his writings, one may easily get the impression that the king lacked basic intelligence; he not only wrote illegibly, but apparently could not construct a grammatically correct sentence in French, let alone German. This does not mean that Frederick William I was unintelligent or that he lacked the desire to increase education among his subjects. Writing skills were a requirement the king demanded of a would-be administrator and something in which he personally took a decisive interest with regard to a candidate's appointment.

The king lived a considerably less elegant lifestyle than not only his predecessor and father, Frederick III/I (1688–1713), as is often noted, but also his son and successor, Frederick the Great (1740–86). Under Frederick III/I, the Hohenzollern monarchy had acquired not merely a royal title, but a large-scale court and the representational culture to match, modelled on Louis XIV's Versailles. Frederick William I's first action upon his accession was to impose stringent economies, reducing sharply the number of court personnel and dismissing many from their posts. The salaries of those who remained were cut by up to 75 per cent. Courtiers were not the only ones to lose their jobs or incomes, for even the royal stables were reduced in size and the salaries reduced by at least one-half. The royal court was a shadow of its former self between 1713 and 1740, as the king concentrated scarce resources upon building up the army and developing the administrative structure which supported it.

Frederick William I underwent an apprenticeship in kingship while still crown prince. He was introduced to the day-to-day operation of government at age thirteen when, in 1701, he began to attend meetings of the high-level advisory body, the so-called Privy Council (*Geheime Rat*), and he became a

---

4    For anecdotes on this subject, see Ernest Lavisse, *The Youth of Frederick the Great*, trans. Mary Bushnell Coleman (Chicago, 1892), pp. 114–15; Ludwig Reiners, *Frederick the Great: An Informal Biography*, trans. Lawrence P. R. Wilson (London, 1960), pp. 36–52; Thomas Carlyle, *History of Friedrich II. of Prussia Called Frederick the Great*, 4 vols (London, 1873), i, p. 290.

5    The Hohenzollerns in the eighteenth century were Calvinist, as the family had been since it officially converted in 1613. Accordingly, Frederick William I believed that every action he took would be judged by God. This was as true for his personal conduct as much as it was for his devotion to the people over whom he ruled and for whom he was responsible. The success and happiness of his subjects were considered by him to be indications of his own success in the eyes of God: a God, Frederick William I believed, who judged him not only for his public actions, but also for his personal beliefs and conduct. Therefore, he struggled to be an example which his subjects would follow lest he lose the approval of his God. This was certainly the attitude which underlay many of the king's reforms and added to his personal style of rule.

formal and regular participant a year later. Here he saw at first hand the deficiencies of central administration and its inability to operate effectively at the provincial and local levels. In 1703, he began to take part in meetings of the influential Privy War Council (*Geheime Kriegsrat*), an agency established by his grandfather, the Great Elector, which oversaw all the military treasuries as well as all matters concerning supply and administration for the army. He also gained his first experience of military command at the age of thirteen when he was given his own company of cadets and made responsible for virtually every aspect of its operation. He eventually led his company into combat during the battle of Malplaquet (in the Netherlands) in the autumn of 1709 during the War of the Spanish Succession (1702–13/14), an experience which he later described as the greatest day of his life. His active involvement in high-level day-to-day government was to prove valuable to him in the administrative, financial, technical and tactical aspects of managing and controlling the military. He was introduced to financial management when he received the austere palace of Wüsterhausen, located south-east of Berlin, as a Christmas gift in 1698 when he was only nine years old. This obliged him to manage personally his household budgets, maintenance, and a staff which were all necessary to its smooth operation. While a young prince, therefore, he had gained considerable experience of high-level domestic and foreign policy, finance, central administration, management of the army, and his household. His early experience of these areas exerted a lasting influence on his goals after he became king.

It was the final years of his period as crown prince which best defined his role and involvement in government administration. Between 1709 and 1711, East Prussia experienced a major crisis with a plague epidemic and the onset of famine.[6] More than a third of the kingdom's inhabitants died as a consequence. Eighty per cent of these deaths were in the eastern region, which directly affected the government in Berlin since this was the area where the crown's workers (so-called royal domain peasants) and production suffered most of all. A significant source of the crown's income was affected. The officials in Berlin had been of little assistance in the crisis and within East Prussia there was a complete breakdown in virtually all aspects of government and the economy. The resulting reports demonstrated that

6   The best account can be found in Wilhelm Sahm, *Geschichte der Pest in Ostpreussen* (Leipzig, 1905). In addition, see Fritz Terveen, *Gesamtstaat und Retablissement: Der Wiederaufbau des Nördlichen Ostpreussen unter Friedrich Wilhelm I, 1714–1740* (Göttingen, 1954), and August Skalweit, 'Die ostpreussische Domänenverwaltung unter Friedrich Wilhelm I und das Retablissement Litauens', in Gustav Schmoller and Max Sering (eds), *Staats- und Sozialwissenschaftlichen Forschungen* (Leipzig, 1906), pp. 1–357.

much of the blame for the aftermath of the crisis rested with officials in Berlin. As a result, Frederick William I, as crown prince, became leader of an opposition party (*Kronprinzpartei*) at court which assured the fall of corrupt officials as the shortcomings of government within East Prussia and Berlin were admitted. In effect, this was an indictment by the crown prince against not only the central administration, but also his own father, his policies and advisers.

The future Frederick William I, therefore, was more than a passive spectator within his father's court. He had an important impact on his father's administration when, in late 1710 and early 1711, the crown prince acted to curb some of the problems in government. His experience of corrupt favourites taking control of large areas of administration was seen by the young Frederick William as an abdication of kingship. He subsequently noted as much in his instructions to his youthful successor, the future Frederick the Great, explaining that a ruler must take personal control over finances and the army, which he believed his father had failed to do adequately. Such direct and personal rule would not only contribute to order and obedience among the troops, according to Frederick William I, but would also secure respect from other states and 'make you a wise and honourable ruler'.[7] When Frederick William I came to the throne in 1713, however, the person of the king was the only link holding the widely separated territories of Brandenburg-Prussia together. A great many problems had to be overcome before it could become a more cohesive state.

## Some obstacles to the development of Hohenzollern absolutism

One of the major hindrances weighing in favour of the traditional elite and against Frederick William I's reform effort in any single territory was the fact that the king had so many separate territories, each with its own established authorities.

For Frederick William I, as for his predecessors, there was no single territory over which he ruled. Indeed, this was an important restriction upon and obstacle to Hohenzollern state-building throughout the eighteenth century. This territorial disunity remained a significant deterrent to the

---

7  Richard Dietrich (ed.), *Die politischen Testamente der Hohenzollern* (Cologne and Vienna, 1986), p. 223.

emergence of Prussian absolutism well beyond 1740. The Hohenzollerns ruled over a 'composite state' of the kind that was normal in sixteenth-century Europe. Until about 1700, many states were primarily monarchies comprising separate territories which were not necessarily geographically contiguous like those of England and Wales, Piedmont and Savoy, or Poland and Lithuania. Another state's territory, or a sea, often fragmented countries, such as those autonomous areas of the Habsburg monarchy in Spain, Italy and the Netherlands or, indeed, England and Ireland. This geographic situation had changed in the rest of Europe by the time Frederick William I came to the throne, but not in Brandenburg-Prussia.[8]

The extraordinary geographical diffusion of Brandenburg-Prussia's territories cannot be understated, and proved the most fundamental obstacle for Frederick William I to overcome. By the first half of the eighteenth century, other monarchs were usually able to point to a single and coherent body of territory on a map over which they were sovereign. As late as 1713, Brandenburg-Prussia, however, comprised roughly two dozen distinct and geographically separate parcels of territory which stretched from the River Rhine in the west of Germany to the Memel far to the east and covered essentially three blocks of territory with a combined population of approximately 1.5 million people. In the west, there were the principal Rhineland territories: Cleves, Mark and Ravensburg (gained in 1619). The second block was the Electorate of Brandenburg, the core territory of the monarchy, which lay astride the rivers Oder and Elbe. The Hohenzollerns had been in the southern portion of Brandenburg, the Mark, since the early fifteenth century. This was precisely the area that emerged as the heartland of Hohenzollern power and was expanded by the addition of Eastern Pomerania, Magdeburg and Halberstadt in 1648. At the conclusion of Brandenburg-Prussia's involvement in the Northern War in 1721, Frederick William I gained the territory of Vorpommern (including Stettin, which meant Brandenburg now had an important outlet to the Baltic) up to the Peene River for a cost of two million thaler. Brandenburg was no longer landlocked. The third block of territory was the Kingdom of East Prussia (over which the Hohenzollerns gained sovereignty in 1618) far to the east, separated by several hundred miles of Polish territory. Some impression of the distances involved is conveyed by the fact that Königsberg, the leading city of East Prussia, is today Kaliningrad, which lies near the Baltic Sea in the Russian enclave of the former Soviet Union. By comparison, the

---

8   See, for example, J. H. Elliott, 'A Europe of Composite Monarchies', *Past and Present* 137 (1992), 48–71 and H. G. Koenigsberger, '*Dominium Regale* or *Dominium Politicum et Regale*: Monarchies and Parliaments in Early Modern Europe', in H. G. Koenigsberger (ed.), *Politicians and Virtuosi* (London, 1986), pp. 1–25.

Brandenburg-Prussian town of Cleves, west of the Rhine and north-west of Cologne, was over 800 miles from Königsberg, literally on the other side of Europe.

What made the vast distances between the territories and the capital, Berlin, particularly complex and potentially troublesome, especially at a time of slow and unreliable communications, was that each block of territory had its own system of government, representative institutions, political traditions, legal system, local elite, coinage, weights and measures, dialects and even language. There were, for example, twenty-five different measurements for a pound weight, and two hundred different measurements for a bushel volume throughout the Hohenzollern lands.[9] This severely impeded the extent and expansion of Hohenzollern authority. The complex and, ofttimes, confusing array of customs and standards limited interterritorial communication and commerce as well as restricting the ability of the king to introduce reforms throughout his territories. Moreover, a message sent from Berlin to Königsberg in East Prussia normally took, in favourable weather conditions, about seven days during Frederick William I's reign. A reply took another week to be received, limiting Berlin's ability to react quickly and restricting the degree of control which the Hohenzollern ruler could exert.

Another crucial point which should always be remembered was that the Hohenzollern ruled over each territory with a different title, along with a separate administration and legal system. In Brandenburg, he ruled as Elector of the Holy Roman Empire. In East Prussia, he was addressed as king 'in' Prussia and not as elector.[10] The Hohenzollerns held separate princely titles for several territories, including the Orange lands, Halberstadt, Minden, East Frisia and Mörs, among others. Frederick William I was Duke of Magdeburg (gained in 1680), Count of Ruppin and Count of the Mark in Brandenburg as well as Ravensburg – again, each title was separate for each territory. Numerous other examples could be given. It further highlights the discontinuity among the numerous provinces which comprised the Hohenzollern monarchy and the problems Frederick William I faced when dealing with each territory. Each of the separate territories was a distinct unit and operated as such. The simple dynastic union provided by the personality and person of the Hohenzollern ruler was the only form of unity between the three blocks of territory.

---

9 Edgar Melton, 'The Prussian Junkers, 1600–1786', in H. M. Scott (ed.), *The European Nobilities in the Seventeenth and Eighteenth Centuries*, 2 vols (New York, 1995), ii, p. 72.

10 Frederick William I's father, Frederick I, was the first king in Prussia and recognized by other rulers under the condition that he was not entitled to use the title king 'of' Prussia but rather king 'in' Prussia.

On 13 August 1713, shortly after his accession, Frederick William I issued his famous Patent declaring the inalienability and indivisibility of royal lands. This was essentially a declaration of intent, unifying on paper all the Hohenzollern territories and announcing his intention to treat them as one. The achievement of real consolidation and unification would have to wait for further reforms under another Hohenzollern ruler after 1740, but this declaration had the effect of preventing the royal domain from being sold or given away by future monarchs and also from being annexed unofficially by the nobility.

Another obstacle to the consolidation of Hohenzollern rule was the resistance of the territorial elites to centralizing initiatives. The transition from producing paper initiatives to tangible reform of territorial authorities proved troublesome for the king throughout his reign. The established nobilities, and the much less numerous urban elites, were all-powerful within the borders of their particular territory and maintained a strong hold on provincial administration and commerce. The *Indigenatsrecht*, or 'right of the native born', stipulated that only natives, usually noblemen, of the province could hold office in the government of that territory. It is the best example of the type of privilege to which East Prussians were accustomed and in which Hohenzollern government acquiesced. This was the foundation of the continuing degree of East Prussian independence and self-government: it was a formidable obstacle against any extension of Berlin's control. Native noblemen could be guaranteed to resist any centralizing initiatives, and to uphold the traditional privileges of their own territory. Native East Prussians, for example, were the only ones permitted to serve in the Königsberg *Regierung*, the highest authority in urban and rural East Prussian government throughout Frederick William I's reign. In addition, the *Zünfte* or guilds of Königsberg held exclusive control over trade and commerce and are another example of where the *Indigenatsrecht* privilege was applied.[11] The East Prussian Estates regarded this privilege in 1657 as 'the whole country's but, above all, the indigenous nobility's greatest benefices'.[12]

The elite's local power was concentrated in the territorial governing bodies, the Estates, which comprised the nobility, urban elite and, in some cases, the clergy. These groups assembled together in the Estates were often the principal opponents of Hohenzollern absolutist policies well into the eighteenth century. Yet, negotiations with each territory separately also meant the Hohenzollerns could maintain divisions among them and keep them

---

11  Hugo Rachel, 'Handel und Handelsrecht von Königsberg', *Forschungen zur Brandenburgische und Preußische Geschichte* 22 (1909), 113. See also Carsten, *Origins of Prussia*, p. 203.

12  Cited in Hans Rosenberg, *Bureaucracy, Aristocracy, Autocracy: the Prussian Experience, 1660–1815* (rev. edn Boston, 1966), p. 53.

from coalescing into a unified group which could potentially confront the ruler. Indeed, the Hohenzollern monarchs were able to maintain and even promote the existing divisions between the territorial elites through their policies as well. By granting privileges and concessions, the Hohenzollerns ensured that the elites would co-operate with the government instead of with each other. The ruler bargained and negotiated, and in this way did something to reduce the power of the territorial elites. Frederick William I's reign, for example, saw a measurable but limited increase in Hohenzollern authority over certain territorial elites, namely, in Brandenburg and to a lesser extent Prussia and the western territories.

The king tried other approaches to bargaining with the Junkers as well. Like his father, Frederick William I continued royal support of Pietism, which came to underpin many of the economic, religious and educational policy reforms introduced after 1713.[13] Pietism was also seen by Frederick William I as a way to try to counterbalance the power of the Lutheran-dominated Estates, which controlled significant blocks of Hohenzollern territory. This is a consideration that is critical to explaining Frederick William I's support of the Pietist endeavours. As was noted earlier, there were significant concentrations of Lutherans spread throughout the Hohenzollern territories. In Brandenburg, for example, the famous Brandenburg *Recess* of 1653 confirmed that the nobility possessed the so-called *Patronenrecht*, the right of the provincial nobility to select and appoint religious leaders in the church. When this is combined with their dominant role within the Estates and their ability to direct the outcome of its meetings, it can be seen that the Junkers, in effect, controlled the affairs of Brandenburg. The effective monopoly of the provincial nobility over selection for religious as well as administrative positions provided a particularly formidable barrier that the king would need to overcome should he wish to increase his authority over provincial affairs. The Pietists were one group who allied with Frederick William I in order to make inroads into provincial society. This was an additional reason why the king worked to implement Pietist projects, particularly in education, which would spread to other territories, gain support and, he hoped, provide a bridgehead against the established territorial elites. The challenge for Frederick William I was considerable and was never completely met during his reign, often owing to the resistance waged by Lutheran leaders and nobles against the Pietists and the king.[14]

---

13  Pietism in this chapter is mentioned to show its role in the building of Hohenzollern absolutism. A more complete study of Pietism can be found in the chapter in this volume by Christopher Clark, pp. 68–88.

14  In addition to Melton, see Mary Fulbrook, *Piety and Politics: Religion and the Rise of Absolutism in England, Württemberg, and Prussia* (Cambridge, 1983), pp. 93–8 and 153–73.

# Restructuring the central agencies of the state

The large extent to which Brandenburg-Prussia was financially dependent upon foreign subsidies was a feature of Brandenburg-Prussian foreign policy that Frederick William I encountered both in council meetings after 1713 and on the battlefield. During the War of Spanish Succession (1702–13/14), when Crown Prince Frederick William fought with his company in Flanders, he experienced at first hand the consequences of Brandenburg-Prussia's dependence upon foreign subsidies and its diplomatic results. This was just one further shortcoming the crown prince saw with his father's regime. One anecdote recounts how the crown prince was taunted by officers from other countries with comments about Brandenburg-Prussia's continued reliance upon a foreign paymaster, and promised in response that, when he became king, Brandenburg-Prussia would support an army of thirty thousand soldiers without subsidies. In the event, he came close to tripling his alleged target: by his death in 1740, Prussia maintained an army over 81,000 strong entirely on her own resources.

The issue of foreign subsidies was one of personal importance about which Frederick William I wrote in his instructions for his successor in 1722. He noted that if a king wanted to have the devotion and loyalty of his troops, then that monarch must not only march and fight alongside his men, but his policies should not be driven by the lure of money (that is, subsidies or war reparations), but rather by the desire for new land and people. Many of the considerable territories of the Hohenzollern monarchy were sparsely populated and, therefore, economically under-exploited. There was a need to secure its economic base and thereby provide more resources to make Brandenburg-Prussia a self-sustaining military power.[15] This aim of economic independence or self-sufficiency, or 'autarky' as it was designated, was, he believed, the only secure foundation for the diplomatic freedom of action he craved. Many of the king's internal preoccupations were also linked to foreign concerns. Efficient revenue collection for the military, for example, was of critical importance if dependence upon foreign subsidies was to be removed and autarky established.

Frederick William I was to be successful in this aim. At his death in May 1740, he left his successor, Frederick II (the Great), a cash reserve of some eight million thalers that were stored in barrels in the vaults of the royal residence at Potsdam. The king did not want to leave the same financial difficulties to his successor as he had inherited from his own father, Frederick I. He was also careful to encourage his successor as early as 1722 to maintain

---

15 Dietrich, *Die politischen Testamente der Hohenzollern*, p. 238.

a 'well-larded treasury' by adding at least 500,000 thalers to it each year. Brandenburg-Prussia would maintain not only a formidable army with substantial financial reserves, but would also strive for freedom of diplomatic action, and he told his successor, 'You can wield great respect in the world and converse with the other [Great] Powers.'[16]

Some of these improvements may be attributed to the establishment of the General Directory (*General-Ober-Finanz-Kriegs-und-Domänen-Direktorium*) in 1723. Its establishment was the central initiative in a series of administrative reforms during the early eighteenth century that aimed to expand the ruler's authority throughout the Hohenzollern territories. There is little doubt that Frederick William I improved the operation of government at the central level by uniting military and financial administration.

Before the General Directory was set up in 1722–23, most governmental institutions in the Hohenzollern monarchy dealt with the affairs of a single territory. There were separate administrations for Brandenburg, East Prussia, the Rhineland territories, and the other Hohenzollern enclaves. Only two central administrative agencies with a remit covering all the dynasty's possessions existed in Brandenburg-Prussia. Both were concerned with revenue collection: the General Finance Directory (*Generalfinanzdirektorium*) oversaw the extensive royal domains, and attended to agrarian matters and the collection of taxation; the General War Commissariat (*Generalkriegskommissariat*) provided essential administration for the army and the fiscal revenue upon which it depended throughout the various Hohenzollern territories.

As the two agencies found their responsibilities frequently overlapped, competition between the two to extract the limited means available from the same sources intensified. Inevitably, the divergent aims of the two bodies clashed. Frederick William I sought to resolve this conflict when, in 1722–3, he merged the General War Commissariat and the General Finance Directory to form the General Directory, simultaneously bringing the county and tax councillors in the provinces under the authority of the newly established War-and-Domain Chambers (*Kriegs- und Domänenkammern*). Prussia's king wanted a central authority to oversee military and financial matters as well as other more general 'police' functions throughout the various territories. The General Directory was seen as the strong unifying institution through which these areas could be administered more effectively.

The most important administrative agencies within central government, including the General Directory, were organized on a collegial basis. These offices were not headed by a single responsible minister at the apex of a single administrative unit, in the way familiar in modern government.

---

16   Ibid., p. 233.

Brandenburg-Prussia had no principal head for a specific area of administration at this period. Instead, several individuals were collectively responsible for the administration of a department that often covered several areas, primarily geographical but also of government business. For instance, it was not until 1728 that Frederick William I established a single body to conduct diplomacy and advise him on foreign affairs.[17] There was a slow evolution towards single-function departments headed by one official with clearly defined objectives and hierarchies, but the idea was still in its infancy in 1740. With collegial government, therefore, a number of individuals were responsible for wide areas of government and reported to the king; there was not simply one minister in charge of one area of policy with a support staff devoted full-time to that administrative function. With this form of government organization at the very heart of Hohenzollern authority, a sense of collective responsibility among the college members quickly became established.[18]

The idea of collective responsibility was a feature of administration under the *Ancien Régime*, and was used in France with more success. It was not peculiar to the government of the Hohenzollerns, although it was increasingly employed by Frederick William I and may be directly traced to his own experiences while crown prince and to his father's managerial style of reliance upon single individuals. Under Frederick I, this was apparent throughout the government – from the king's continued use of first ministers to departmental heads to the central administrative officials in the territories. Although the collegial style of government was not unique to the Hohenzollerns, in Brandenburg-Prussia it appears to have been flawed through a lack of oversight of lesser officials, which resulted in governmental venality and breakdown. It was, however, to be characteristic of Frederick William I's administration at all levels.

Although the collegial style of government encouraged a search for consensus among college members and a sense of *esprit de corps*, it also frequently fostered conflict among officials throughout the administration. Jurisdictional conflicts continued unabated, though this was something which the establishment of the General Directory was intended to end. In fact, however, as a result of the General Directory, new conflicts arose between Berlin, the provincial governments and urban and local authorities.

The new conflicts added a new dimension to the traditional jurisdictional disputes between civilian and military authorities. Who, for example, should

---

17  Peter Baumgart, 'Zur Gründungsgeschichte des Auswärtigen Amtes in Preußen, 1713–1728', *Jahrbuch für die Geschichte Mittel und Ostdeutschlands* 7 (1958), 229–48.

18  See, for example, Reinhold Dorwart, *The Administrative Reforms of Frederick William I of Prussia* (Cambridge, MA, 1953), p. 222, fn. 7.

decide clashes over the location of ultimate authority – Berlin or the government of that particular province? New questions arose relating to the legality of one authority taking control of a particular type of business. Which authority would judge tax offenders? What positions were open to non-natives whom Frederick William I was against? Who should appoint local officials? There were even jurisdictional disputes about jurisdictional disputes. After the establishment of the General Directory, duplication and ill-defined distinctions of responsibilities continued to exist between individuals and separate institutions of government, which were not resolved even by Frederick William I's death in 1740. With such strong resentments and controversies over who should govern and how government should function simmering into the 1730s, it is evident that Hohenzollern authority still was far from absolute by the final decade of Frederick William I's reign.

## The expansion of the army

The administrative restructuring of the state allowed for the development of another important centralizing agency, the army, which reached a higher level of success than most other areas of reform. When Frederick William I became king in 1713, the army consisted of approximately 40,000 soldiers. At his death, it contained more than 80,000. This doubling is apparent from Table 2.1.[19] The disappearance of soldiers in the pay of Holland after 1713 was a direct result of Frederick William I's determination to reduce

Table 2.1   Growth of the Brandenburg-Prussian army, 1713–40

| Military branch | February 1713 | June 1715 | June 1731 | June 1739 |
|---|---|---|---|---|
| Infantry | 21,746 | 35,134 | 48,967 | 52,391 |
| Garrison and free guard companies | 4,841 | – | 3,650 | 4,720 |
| Cavalry | 7,737 | 9,914 | 15,876 | 17,842 |
| Artillery | 527 | 505 | 1,208 | 1,208 |
| Military engineers | – | – | 41 | 41 |
| In the pay of Holland | 5,096 | – | – | – |
| New garrison troops | – | – | 6,804 | 4,832 |
| Total | 39,947 | 45,553 | 76,546 | 81,034 |

19   Curt Jany, *Geschichte der Königlich-preußischen Armee bis zum Jahre 1807* (Berlin), i, p. 660.

the number of troops maintained by foreign subsidies; most other categories were significantly increased. Furthermore, the cost to the state of the support of such a large army (relative to its overall population) was extraordinarily high in proportion to overall state income and approached three-quarters of Brandenburg-Prussia's peacetime annual revenue.

Frederick William I conventionally has been considered the father of the Prussian army. Its creation, however, did not come about overnight. Indeed, several significant reforms were begun by Frederick William I's grand-father, the Great Elector, during the 1650s, while further innovations were undertaken by Frederick William I's father, Frederick III/I, when the size of the Brandenburg-Prussian army increased notably after the turn of the eighteenth century. Prussia's first king contributed significant numbers of his military forces to the support of the Holy Roman Emperor during the War of the Spanish Succession (1701–13/14) and the contemporaneous Great Northern War (1700–21). Most significantly, by 1713, there was a regular standing army that was controlled increasingly by Berlin. This standing army, however, was not fully under the direct and immediate control of the king and continued, throughout the reign of Frederick William I and into the reign of his successor, to comprise smaller territorial armies that were officered by the local territorial elite, with men from that locality dominating the rank-and-file. The armies of the Hohenzollerns were in-creasingly organized, administered, financed and officered through cen-tral government agencies and the king himself.

Besides his reforms of military training, staffing and administration, Frederick William I also developed an all-encompassing governmental administration that brought the army in close contact with traditionally non-militarized areas of government, for example, financial and tax affairs. To a certain extent, the king developed these administrative practices in innovative ways, which helped further direct state support for the army. Important reforms included mandatory payments from administrators into the king's personal treasuries that went to support the armed forces; the use of army officers in civil as well as military departments; an increasingly complex system of exemptions from military service in exchange for pay-ment to the crown; the use of company commanders, and invalid and retired soldiers in administration; cadet military academies for the sons of nobles and officers, which provided a natural feeder system to the military; and state monopolies, which prevented imports of crucial war *matériel*. One significant example of such a monopoly was wool, which went into the making of uniforms. Finally, there was the celebrated reform of recruitment in 1733, the so-called canton system of recruitment.

Brandenburg-Prussia's armaments industry was concentrated near Berlin in the Mittelmark. Frederick William I took measures throughout his reign to eliminate as far as possible the need to import raw materials necessary for armament production and even prohibited manufacturers from purchasing raw materials from outside the Hohenzollern territories. There were two primary reasons for this. First, the king was attempting to strengthen his own raw material production, which would help the self-sufficiency of Brandenburg-Prussia. Secondly, and as a corollary, he was attempting to stop money (in the form of gold and silver coins) from leaving his territories, which almost every European ruler attempted to do in the eighteenth century. Yet, as this was a period when the cost of raw materials was rising, more money was leaving the country than was entering, a situation in contradiction to the basic dictates of the mercantilist theory that guided Hohenzollern economic policies.[20]

Frederick William I claimed that he was his own finance minister and commander-in-chief – arguably the two most important dimensions of eighteenth-century domestic government – in early 1722 when the king noted the following as part of his instructions to his successor:

> Your finances must be managed by yourself and alone and the command of the army ordered by yourself and alone and the two matters arranged alone; then you shall have authority in the army through command and the love of your officers and civil servants because you alone have control of the purse, and you shall be respected and admired by the entire world by you being such a wise and honourable ruler. May Almighty God help you. Amen.[21]

Just as the king was deeply involved in broader issues of military planning and finances, so too was he involved at the level of the individual. The king took critical steps early in his reign that he hoped would alleviate related issues of a lack of career paths for lesser nobles, integration of the nobility into the state rather than simply their territory, and officer recruitment and training for young noblemen. Through his instructions of 1714 and 1717, the king formalized military instruction and established cadet academies.

In early eighteenth-century Prussia, military careers were difficult for members of the lesser nobility, largely because of the expense involved. This situation was improved during the reign of Frederick William I by the establishment of noble cadet academies that permitted the impoverished lesser nobles to send their sons to the cadet corps and thus secure a military

---

career for them. This reform was not universally popular among the lesser nobility, however: in several territories, there was disquiet and even resistance to the new initiative.[22]

Once cadets graduated from a cadet academy, the young officers' commissions, which were available on an increased scale because of the expansion of the army, were distributed by the king. In this way, crown and dynasty, and a territory's nobility gradually became linked and, to some extent, mutually dependent. The desire to maintain a position of military authority with its own accompanying social status grew slowly among the Junkers. The king wore the same uniform as captains and lieutenants, exclusively so after 1725.[23] There was both the personal association with Frederick William I by his appointment of the officers as well as a professional association through the identical outward appearance. Aside from generals, no officer was distinguishable by means of the uniform he wore from another with respect to rank and this created a kind of social equality with the king.

The nobility was a closed elite, which followed the king's professional example of duty. Nevertheless, the Junkers were slow to abandon their traditional suspicion of links with the wider Hohenzollern state. The speed at which Frederick William I was able to introduce and implement this change varied significantly across his territories, since officers and soldiers often served in their own provinces, thus impeding integration. In some territories, there was resistance to some of the king's most important reforms as late as 1740.[24] In that year, for example, an official (who was probably exaggerating) noted that several Junkers within the kingdom of East Prussia were ready to revolt.[25] It is clear, however, that despite such resistance, the Junkers were integrated into the army during the king's reign. The new military system clearly evolved in direct relation to Prussia's society and economy, and indeed became the institution which integrated these into a coherent whole.[26]

Practical problems impeded the implementation of the king's reforms. One example was that Frederick William I was able to establish a list of

---

22  ABB, 5:2, p. 776. The editors of the *Acta Borussica* have noted that in 1718, 1727 and 1738 there were similar examples of disquiet. See also Büsch, *Militärsystem und Sozialleben im alten Preussen, 1713–1807*, p. 82. Cf. F. L. Carsten, *Geschichte der preußischen Junker* (Frankfurt, 1988), pp. 44–5.

23  Neugebauer, *Die Hohenzollern*, p. 224.

24  See, for example, Jany, *Geschichte der Königlich-preußischen Armee*, i, p. 427.

25  ABB, 5:2, p. 776; Büsch, *Militärsystem und Sozialleben*, p. 82.

26  Ibid., p. 84. It should be noted as well that Büsch provides a familiar discussion demonstrating the Hohenzollern rulers' belief that the nobility were the natural leaders and officers in the military ranks. See pp. 89–93.

all noblemen in East Prussia on a regular basis only in 1738, when the members of the kingdom's elite were recorded in his *Vassallen Tabellen*. Reform of the military was an extended process, as was noted earlier, since the obligation of service in the officer corps was only slowly accepted. The elites particularly resented the mandatory enrolment of younger sons of the nobility into the recently established cadet academies. This did not amount to refusal of state service (*Staatsdienst*) as such, but the rejection of compulsory attendance at the academies with the corresponding inability to gain permission for foreign travel or study.[27] The kind of links between territorial elites and local administration that were to be found later in the eighteenth century were certainly not evident before 1723.

The advance of the territorial elites into the army and the parallel extension of Junker authority over their peasants were to be the next stages in the evolution of the East Elbian nobility. This was established by Otto Büsch, who noted that 'the military system as a social system became an expression of the political circumstances between king and nobility'.[28] The evolution, however, was to prove an extended one, which was still in progress throughout the reign of Frederick William I and matured into a coherent system only under Frederick the Great. It was crucially advanced by a reform introduced by Frederick William I, the canton *Reglement* finalized in 1733.

This *Reglement* was the final piece in the social, administrative and military edifice established by Frederick William I. Prior to 1733, there was less incentive for the nobility to accept the military just as there was significant resistance to monarchical authority. The canton system, the final piece in the celebrated alliance between crown and Junkers, was an additional incentive to nobles and especially younger sons who secured employment and some income. It raised the status and authority of the local nobleman even further and placed the responsibility for recruitment solely in the hands of the local estate Junker. In short, the canton system made possible the maintenance of a powerful native standing army on Prussia's scanty resources, which produced a more secure means by which the king was able to raise, maintain and train an increasing peasant-based army, while at the same time recruiting, maintaining and training an officer corps made up exclusively of the nobility.

Throughout the evolution towards the canton system of recruitment, the Hohenzollern armies were based on irregular recruitment and largely consisted of a mix of mercenary forces with Prussian subjects who were often forced into military service. In particular, this was the case for peasant

---

27  Carsten, *Geschichte der preußischen Junker*, p. 44.
28  Büsch, *Militärsystem und Sozialleben*, p. 79.

farm labourers, although the canton system was based on the number of fireplace hearths and varied considerably between provinces. East Prussia, for example, had a total of 64,720 fireplaces. The number of men in the various territorial military units also varied quite significantly. For example, in Brandenburg, the average infantry regiment contained about 5,000 men, while in both Pomerania and Magdeburg-Halberstadt, an average-sized infantry regiment was 5,900 men.[29] The recruitment of soldiers had, from the reign of the Great Elector until the early eighteenth century, been left to both royal officials loyal to Berlin and local territorial elites. Since the officials loyal to Berlin often did not have the manpower to recruit in the local and distant districts, this was left to local officials.

Before 1733, however, the arrangement between regimental commander and the king's officials could be considered positive for both sides. The king relinquished some authority at the local level and over certain commercial interests. He strengthened the bond between crown and Junkers, who found a potentially lucrative way to escape their often impoverished circumstances. Finally, his increased control over the military was assured. His troops were required to have two years of basic training and to return for exercises at least once a year. The common soldier's furlough was reformed significantly in 1733. Before this, a commander would routinely furlough a group of soldiers, thereby saving on their pay. This meant in practice that the troops would be sent back to being peasant labourers, sometimes even to the estate of their regimental commander or, once back on the estate, the Junker landlord. Common soldiers in effect became a commodity. Not only were men coerced into military service against their will, but it was also common for 'captains, or higher officers in their capacity as company commanders, [to discharge] men for money, [to sell] them to other companies or regiments for money, [to exchange] them with other troops, or [to give] them away as a matter of courtesy'.[30] Frederick III/I forbade this practice, but his initiative was unsuccessful and it appears to have continued throughout Frederick William I's reign and survived into that of Frederick the Great, as there were edicts forbidding it in 1743 and 1748, though its incidence appears to have declined after 1740.

Appointment procedures within the administration were extended and sometimes complicated by the necessity of paying the requisite levy to the king in support of his private military ventures, above all the regiment of tall grenadiers. There was almost always a payment to the king's *Rekrutenkasse*

---

29  Curt Jany, 'Die Kantonverfassung des altpreußische Heeres', in Otto Büsch and Wolfgang Neugebauer (eds), *Moderne Preußische Geschichte 1648–1945*, 3 vols (Berlin, 1981), ii, p. 784.
30  Ibid., p. 48.

(recruitment treasury).[31] This was established by Frederick William I, probably not before 1716. Payments into the *Rekrutenkasse* were compulsory not only for local government officials, but for the full spectrum of established officials of every territory during this period. Payments were regular and uniform across Brandenburg-Prussia; most importantly, they had to be made before a candidate was confirmed in his post. This was as true for the lowest-level tax collector as it was for the highest-level member of the General Directory – everyone had to pay into the king's private treasury.

The contribution to the recruiting treasury was essentially a tax for potential office-holders. The candidate's retention of the payment receipt was critical to the confirmation process as well. The receipt acted as the new official's authorization, which was shown for the formal appointment document to be issued. This letter, too, required a fee to be paid, as there was a customary stamp tax attached to the letter. The income from this *Stempelsteuer* was also put towards military purposes by the king. Both of these treasuries and the income generated in this way were under the jurisdiction of the *General Kriegskommissariat*, the central military administration that attempted to supervise military revenue from taxation, the military treasury, and equipment and supplies for support of the army. It was taken over by the General Directory after 1723.

This was not venal office of the kind that existed elsewhere in Europe and, above all, in France. It was rather a leading example of Frederick William I's fiscal opportunism, levying a tax upon a captive force of would-be administrators, and his ubiquitous search for revenue to support his military establishment. This system also suggests the anticipated income of officials, which was potentially considerable. Although salaries were not always paid, administrators received income in the form of fees and perquisites from most offices.

The *Rekrutenkasse* embodied the king's highly distinctive personal goals in two principal ways. First, it demonstrated Frederick William I's obsessive preoccupation with the recruitment of soldiers and with upholding the army's primacy within the Brandenburg-Prussian state. In particular, he was determined to secure funding for his private regiment of 'giants', a corps of grenadiers, all of whom were taller than six feet four inches, which was paid for from the *Rekrutenkasse*. Secondly, contributions made to the *Rekrutenkasse* were almost always the only way for individuals to secure an office or administrative duty, short of actual ownership, and the payment followed the actual appointment, which was made in the usual way. Payments to the *Rekrutenkasse* were thus the way appointments and promotions were finalized.

---

31  ABB, iii, pp. 429–30; Dorwart, *The Administrative Reforms of Frederick William I of Prussia*, p. 156.

The issue of tax collection became particularly acute in the early years of Frederick William I's reign. The urban excise tax and the rural *Kontribution* (a name which recalled its military origins) were the two traditional taxes which supported the monarchy. The completely different approaches to taxation – the one a tax on consumption, the other a tax on production – underline the division between urban and rural communities. Frederick William I placed particular emphasis upon efforts to make the collection of taxation more efficient. This was the corollary of his promotion of the end of any reliance upon foreign subsidies. There was an essential linkage between efficient tax revenue collection, the expansion of the army, and foreign subsidies.[32]

# Conclusion

The early years of Frederick William I's reign have traditionally been seen as a period in which Hohenzollern government first acquired a clear hierarchical division of duties. Although this may have happened to some degree at the central and highest level, primarily through the mechanism of various administrative departments after the establishment of the General Directory in 1723, duplication and ill-defined distinctions of responsibilities existed between individuals and separate institutions of government throughout Frederick William I's reign. This was not simply a legacy from Frederick III/I. The king was forced to draft and send hundreds of orders and reissue many over and over in an attempt to force the territorial governments to comply. Frederick William I worked hard to reduce the power of the territorial elite and their control over provincial agencies. However, traditional institutional structures maintained a role in essential administration, even in areas where the king had recognized the competence of other authorities. In particular, the Junkers maintained their status through their dominance over government. This, in turn, enabled them to collect taxation. It should be mentioned, however, that this was reduced through the king's increased control over the royal domain lands, and many of the revenues collected for the military were increasingly collected by the agencies and officials of the *Kriegs- und Domänenkammern*. As significant as this may have been, the simple facts remain that the territorial nobilities continued to possess primary authority over justice, local administration, important military matters, as well as religious questions in many regions. They did not begin

---

32  For example, see the Instruction for the General Directory in ABB, iii, pp. 591–2, 595.

to lose their authority as a group until the 1750s when further significant judicial and district administrative reforms were introduced by Frederick the Great.

It is remarkable not only that the Hohenzollern dynastic link between the scattered territories survived as long as it did, but that it was actually cultivated by the king. Frederick William I's rule did not go unquestioned and certainly was not absolute. He was able, however, to strengthen the hold he and his government and administration held over the assortment of territories, in conjunction with an army based in Brandenburg's capital, Berlin, which emerged as the nucleus of Hohenzollern authority. By the end of Frederick William I's reign in 1740, Brandenburg-Prussia was not yet a European 'Great Power', but it had become a leading Baltic power, as well as a German force. Overcoming such strong geographic and political hurdles is what, more than anything else, made Brandenburg-Prussia's early modern development unique in Europe. Inside Brandenburg-Prussia, however, Frederick William I's rule was always resisted by the territorial elites and was never absolute.

# CHAPTER THREE

# Piety, politics and society:
# Pietism in eighteenth-century Prussia

## CHRISTOPHER CLARK

Pietism emerged in the late seventeenth century as a movement for reform within Lutheran Protestantism. It was one of that broad palette of seventeenth-century European religious movements that challenged the authority of ecclesiastical establishments by calling for a more intense, committed and practical form of Christian observance than was usual within the established church structures. Pietism's influence was felt in most of the Protestant regions of German Europe, but it took a highly distinctive form in Brandenburg-Prussia. In most of the areas where it took root, the movement was greeted with distrust by both church and lay authorities; Pietist activists were attacked, prosecuted, dismissed from academic and pastoral offices and expelled from their towns or territories. In Brandenburg-Prussia, by contrast, for reasons that are discussed below, the Pietists were 'co-opted' by the electoral administration and the movement came to enjoy the patronage of one of the most prestigious Protestant dynastic houses; in the decades that followed, the Prussian cities of Halle, Berlin and Königsberg became the nerve-centres of a Pietist network that extended across much of the kingdom. With the support of the Brandenburg government under Elector/King Frederick III/I and King Frederick William I, the Pietists acquired a foothold within the universities, the civil service and the pastorate that enabled them to exert a sustained influence over the organizational life of the state.

In this chapter, we address the following questions: why was the Pietist movement supported by the Brandenburg administration? How did the gradually thickening 'alliance' between the Pietists and the secular authorities affect the character of the movement? And what impact did the movement have on the institutions and ethos of the Prussian state? Was Pietism implicated in the emergence of specifically 'Prussian' habits and values?

The chapter will conclude with some reflections upon the longer-term impact of Pietism on Prussian religious life.

# Philipp Jakob Spener and the origins of the Pietist movement

On 21 March 1691, Philipp Jakob Spener, Head Chaplain to the Saxon court in Dresden, was invited by the Elector of Brandenburg to take up a senior church post in Berlin. To some contemporaries, this must have appeared a surprising appointment. After all, Spener was well known as the leading figure in a movement for religious reform that had triggered unrest within the Lutheran territorial churches of the German states. He had been criticized by the Orthodox Lutheran establishment since the publication of his *Pia Desideria* (1675), an essay lamenting the deficiencies of contemporary religious life and proposing measures by which they might be remedied. Among the most problematic of these, in Orthodox eyes, was Spener's call for the foundation of groups for bible-reading and pious discussion (*collegia pietatis*), in which Christians would acquaint themselves more closely with Scripture than was possible within the framework of regular church attendance. Spener's own *collegium pietatis*, founded in 1670 when he was a senior church official in Frankfurt, had found widespread emulation in Lutheran communities. These 'conventicles' were viewed by many senior Orthodox officials as posing a threat to the centrality of liturgical ritual and the moral authority of the ordained pastorate.

By 1690, the Spenerite reformers – dubbed 'Pietists' by their detractors – were coming under increasing pressure from the Orthodox authorities. In the summer of 1689 at the University of Leipzig, August Hermann Francke, a graduate student in theology and a follower of Spener, flouted academic regulations, encouraged the formation of conventicles under student supervision, and denounced the traditional theological curriculum, prompting some students to burn their textbooks and lecture notes.[1] The academic authorities soon found themselves faced with a formidable 'student movement', and the Saxon government intervened in March 1690 to prohibit all conventicles and to stipulate that 'Pietist' students – it was in the course

---

1   M. Brecht, 'Philipp Jakob Spener, Sein Programm und dessen Auswirkungen', in M. Brecht (ed.), *Geschichte des Pietismus*, vol. 1, *Der Pietismus vom 17. bis zum frühen 18. Jahrhundert* (Göttingen, 1993), pp. 278–389 (here pp. 333–8); H. Leube, 'Die Geschichte der pietistischen Bewegung in Leipzig', in H. Leube, *Orthodoxie und Pietismus. Gesammelte Studien* (Bielefeld, 1975), pp. 153–267.

of this conflict that the term entered general usage – be excluded from admission to clerical office. Francke was driven out of the university.

In Hamburg, the conflict that broke out between the Orthodox establishment and Pietist sympathizers within the city's clergy was so intense that there was public unrest and fighting in the streets; the intervention of Imperial troops was required to restore order.[2] In Hessen-Darmstadt and Gießen, the Pietists managed to establish themselves, but only in the face of continuing resistance from the Lutheran establishment. Wherever recognizable Pietist groups emerged in specific localities, the situation remained unstable, not only because of the opposition of the Orthodox, but also because of the pressure from radical and separatist elements that threatened to hijack the reforming movement for their own ends. In many places, the new conventicles fell under the influence of radical critics of Lutheran orthodoxy who ultimately severed themselves entirely from the established churches.[3]

Spener himself had never intended the conventicles to function as vehicles for separatism.[4] He stressed that religious meetings must always take place under clerical supervision and should be disbanded if they incurred the disapproval of the church authorities.[5] But there was little he could do to impose his own agenda upon the growing Pietist movement, or to arrest the polarization of religious allegiances in areas where conflict had broken out between the Orthodox authorities and dissenting elements. In Dresden, where Spener had occupied the position of Senior Court Chaplain since 1686, the escalating conflict with the Orthodox – exacerbated by the reformer's uncompromising rigour in matters of public morality – soured relations with his employer, Elector Johann Georg. In March 1691, the Elector asked his Privy Councillors to 'have Spener quit his post without further ado, since we do not want to see nor hear this man any more'.[6]

Fortunately for Spener, an escape route presented itself in the form of an offer from Frederick III, Elector of Brandenburg, who wished to appoint him to a senior ecclesiastical and pastoral post in Berlin. Spener's appointment was followed by the recruitment of beleaguered Pietists from various

---

2 K. Deppermann, *Der hallesche Pietismus und der preußische Staat unter Friedrich III (I)* (Göttingen, 1961), pp. 49–50; Brecht, 'Philipp Jakob Spener', pp. 344–51.

3 J. Wallmann, 'Das Collegium Pietatis', in M. Greschat (ed.), *Zur neueren Pietismusforschung* (Darmstadt, 1977), pp. 167–223; Brecht, 'Philipp Jakob Spener', pp. 316–19.

4 P. J. Spener, *Theologische Bedencken* (Halle, 1715), Third Part (vol. 5), p. 293.

5 P. J. Spener, *Letzte Theologische Bedencken* (Halle, 1711), Third Part, pp. 296–7, 428, 439–40, 678; citations are from the reprint in D. Blaufuß and P. Schicketanz, *Philip Jakob Speners Schriften* (Hildesheim, Zurich, New York, 1987), vol. 15/2.

6 Cited in T. Kervorkian, 'Piety Confronts Politics: Philipp Jakob Spener in Dresden 1686–1691', *German History* 16 (1998), 145–64.

German territories to clerical and academic posts in Brandenburg-Prussia. Thanks to a network of influential connections, Spener was able to play a central role in the selection and placement of key activists. One of these was August Hermann Francke, who, having left Leipzig, had been forced only one year later to leave a subsequent post as deacon in Erfurt. In 1692, he was appointed to a vicarage in Glaucha, a satellite town of Halle, and professor of Oriental languages at the new University of Halle. His former Erfurt colleague, Joachim Justus Breithaupt, who had fallen from favour for defending Francke against the Orthodox, became the university's first professor of theology in 1691. A further veteran of the Leipzig quarrels, Paul Anton, was also appointed to a professorship. At the same time, Spener gathered and instructed a new generation of Pietist leaders in a new Collegium that met twice-weekly in Berlin.[7] This deliberate state sponsorship of the movement was at variance with the policies adopted in most other territories and it represented an important turning-point in the history of the Pietist movement. Why did it happen?

## The alliance between Pietism and the monarchy

The 'adoption' of the Pietist movement by Elector Frederick III and his chief officials must first of all be set in the context of the peculiar historical situation of the Brandenburg monarchy. Since the conversion in 1613 of Elector Johann Sigismund from Lutheranism to the (Calvinist) Reformed Church, the Brandenburg court had been part of a Reformed minority among a predominantly orthodox Lutheran population. This meant that tolerance – at least of another Protestant confession – was 'objectively' built into the practice of government in Brandenburg-Prussia.[8] An official policy of tolerance, however, did not guarantee the frictionless coexistence of the two Protestant confessions. The Calvinist monarchs used a largely Calvinist bureaucracy to manage the Electorate's affairs. The confessional divide between court and country meant that the tensions between the monarchical executive and provincial authorities that we associate with the development of continental absolutism had a religious flavour. The seventeenth-century monarchs of Brandenburg-Prussia attempted to deal with the confessional issue in a variety of ways. In the 1650s, the government tried suppressing

---

7 R. L. Gawthrop, *Pietism and the Making of Eighteenth-Century Prussia* (Cambridge, 1993), p. 122.
8 G. Heinrich, 'Religionstoleranz in Brandenburg-Preußen. Idee und Wirklichkeit', in M. Schlenke (ed.), *Preußen. Politik, Kultur, Gesellschaft* (Reinbek, 1986), pp. 83–102 (here p. 83).

dogmatic polemic, but with little effect. In the 1660s, the Great Elector inaugurated a campaign of aggressive 'Calvinization' designed to pave the way for a union of the two confessions. This policy failed and was abandoned, but it left a legacy of heightened mistrust between the Lutheran provincial nobilities and the Electoral administration.

In this context, it is easy to see how Philipp Jakob Spener's outspoken condemnation of interconfessional disputation in the reformist essay *Pia Desideria* must have endeared him to the Calvinist court of Brandenburg-Prussia. The fourth of Spener's six proposals for the betterment of contemporary religious life was that measures should be taken to limit theological and interconfessional polemics on the grounds that these were of little spiritual value; those who engaged in them tended to draw on profane reasoning rather than on the word of God and were more concerned with their own reputations than with establishing the truth. It was 'the holy love of God', rather than arguments, that anchored the truth in each individual; exchanges with those whose beliefs differed from one's own should therefore be undertaken in a pastoral, not a polemical, spirit.[9] In Spener's writings, dogmatic issues were marginalized by an overwhelming concern for the practical, experiential dimension of faith and observance. Christians were urged to practise 'spiritual priesthood' in their own lives by tending actively to the well-being of their fellows, observing, edifying and 'converting' them.[10] 'If we awaken in our Christians an ardent love, for each other in the first instance and thereafter for all mankind . . . then we have achieved virtually everything we desire.'[11]

Spener always remained respectful of the established Protestant churches and their liturgical and doctrinal traditions, and he was never a supporter of unionist projects.[12] Nevertheless, it was possible to see in his writings – as in the individualized, experience-oriented devotional culture of the Pietist movement as a whole – the outlines of a confessionally impartial Christianity that transcended the boundaries between Reformed and Lutheran Protestantism. By playing down the significance of dogma and the sacraments, and by emphasizing the indivisibility of the apostolic true church, Pietism prepared the 'inner basis' for the Prussian monarchy's supreme episcopacy over the Protestant confessions.[13]

---

9 P. J. Spener, *Pia Desideria: Oder hertzliches Verlangen nach gottgefälliger Besserung der wahren evangelischen Kirchen*, 2nd edn (Frankfurt-am-Main, 1680). Citations are from the reprint in E. Beyreuther (ed.), *Speners Schriften*, vol. I (Hildesheim, 1979), pp. 123–308 (here pp. 267–71).

10 Spener, *Pia Desideria*, pp. 250–2.

11 Spener, *Pia Desideria*, p. 257.

12 Brecht, 'Philipp Jakob Spener', p. 352.

13 Deppermann, *Der hallesche Pietismus*, p. 172.

In Halle, as elsewhere in Prussia, the appointment of Pietists to key positions gave rise to a rapidly escalating controversy with the local Orthodox clergy, to which Francke, who had not mellowed greatly since his days as a student activist in Leipzig, contributed in his usual spirited fashion. As the attacks increased in ferocity, the Pietists called upon their supporters in court and government circles. In 1692, the government ordered, at Spener's request, that a lay commission look into the matter and resolve the dispute. The result was an official finding in favour of the Pietists, ordering that they were no longer to be denounced as heretics. An announcement was to be made from the pulpits of Brandenburg-Prussia to the effect that Pietist 'teachings' regarding rebirth, illumination, self-denial and inwardness were not to be viewed as mere 'enthusiasm' or as wanton innovations, but should be acknowledged by all as 'divine truth'.[14] A series of royal orders issued at intervals during the 1690s prohibited pastors from using the pulpit to speak out against the Pietists.[15]

There were good reasons why Elector Frederick III should have chosen to furnish the Pietist movement with a secure base in the city of Halle. The Duchy of Magdeburg, within which the city was situated, had only recently become a Hohenzollern territory (in 1680) and was a stronghold of Lutheran orthodoxy, where the aristocracy had traditionally ruled without hindrance from the nominal sovereign, the absentee archbishop of Magdeburg. Until 1680, Reformed Protestants were forbidden to own land in the duchy and possessed no civil rights. The government in Berlin was determined to make no concessions to the obstreperous Lutheran oligarchy in the region. The take-over was followed by a period of tense confrontation between the government in Berlin and the local aristocracy. Against the wishes of the Lutherans, a Reformed-church chancellor was installed to administer the duchy. Taxes were raised at a drastic rate. In this context, the significance of state support for the local Pietist movement becomes clear. The Pietists were to be established in this province as agents of the government's confessional policy, to assist in the administration and cultural integration of an ultra-Lutheran province. The keystone of the government's cultural policy in the region was the foundation of the University of Halle in 1691 as the leading university of the Hohenzollern lands. With Pietists and distinguished secular thinkers in key administrative and academic positions, the University of Halle provided an irenicist antidote to the combative Lutheranism of the province. As a training institute for future pastors and church officials, it also provided the government with a

---

14   Deppermann, *Der hallesche Pietismus*, p. 74.
15   Brecht, 'Philipp Jakob Spener', p. 354.

politically and confessionally congenial domestic alternative to the ultra-orthodoxy of the Saxon theological faculties.

In addition to supplying the monarchy with means to enhance its confessional and cultural authority, the Pietists became deeply involved in the management of social problems and the provision of social services. They were implicated in efforts to set charitable provision upon an institutionally coherent foundation and thus emancipate it from its former dependence upon the fluctuating generosity of individual donors. Spener had long believed that poverty and its concomitant evils – idleness, beggary and crime – could and should be eliminated from Christian society by judicious reforms involving the forced or voluntary participation of the indigent in work programmes. In 1670, he had taken up the question of municipal responsibility for the poor in a memorandum addressed to the Frankfurt Ministry for Church Affairs. This document was widely reproduced and circulated in the German cities; the orphanage-workhouse established, on Spener's recommendations, to provide employment and religious instruction for mendicants, served as the model for a wave of similar foundations elsewhere.[16]

In this respect, as in his conciliatory confessional outlook, Spener found himself in tune with the aspirations and policies of the Brandenburg state; indeed, it is reasonable to assume that his reputation as a planner and organizer in the sphere of social provision played an important role in the decision to call him to Berlin. Shortly after his arrival, Spener was requested by the Elector to submit a memorandum outlining measures by which the current 'plague of beggars' – a consequence of the town's exceptionally rapid growth – could be brought under control. Spener recommended the suppression and policing of beggary and the centralization of charitable provision for persons requiring temporary or permanent care, arguing that the necessary funds should be raised through a combination of church poor-boxes, donations and state finance. The consequence of this campaign was a general prohibition of beggary, the creation of a permanent Poor Commission and the establishment of the Friedrich-Hospital for the Sick, the Elderly and Orphans (1702).[17]

In Halle, likewise, efforts were afoot to mount a co-ordinated attack on poverty and indigence. In 1695, shortly after his arrival in Halle, August Hermann Francke opened a poor-school financed by charity. As attendance grew, so did the income from pious donations. Soon Francke was able to admit orphans to the school, offering them accommodation and

---

16  K. Aland, 'Der Pietismus und die soziale Frage', in K. Aland (ed.), *Pietismus und moderne Welt* (Witten, 1974), pp. 99–137 (here p. 101).
17  Brecht, 'Philipp Jakob Spener', p. 290; Deppermann, *Der hallesche Pietismus*, pp. 58–61.

maintenance as well as free tuition in an atmosphere of engaged piety. Productive work formed the basis of the daily routine within the Orphanage. Emphasis was placed on practical and useful tasks, and the 'orphans' (many of whom were, in fact, the children of poor families) were regularly taken to visit the workshops of artisans, so that they might form a clear idea of their prospective professions. Between 1696 and 1699, Francke established the foundations for a 'knitting manufactory' (*Strickmanufaktur*), which would provide manual work for the orphans, while raising income for the independent maintenance of the complex. With the completion of new premises in 1701, the Orphanage began the systematic production of knitted hose for sale at the Leipzig autumn fair. Even after the attempt to raise income through child labour was abandoned as impracticable, skilled manual crafts remained a crucial component of the Orphanage's pedagogical programme.[18] It was this striking combination of education, productiveness through labour, and social provision that aroused the interest and admiration of contemporaries. Even when the original foundation had diversified into numerous distinct pedagogical and commercial institutions, it continued to be known as 'the Orphanage'.

Although Francke had originally directed his efforts towards the poor and orphaned, the reputation of the new school was such that it soon began to attract fee-paying children from families resident in Halle. The donations flowed in unabated and by 1698 Francke was able to begin construction of the broad and graceful stone building that today still dominates the Franckeplatz in central Halle. New fee-paying schools were founded to accommodate children from specific social and occupational backgrounds. The *Pädagogium*, founded in 1695, specialized in the education of children whose parents – many of whom were of noble estate – could afford the most costly education and care. The 'Latin School' founded two years later offered instruction in the 'foundations of learning' (*fundamentis studiorum*); the curriculum included Latin, Greek, Hebrew, history, geography, geometry, music and botany, all of which were taught by specialist teachers, a significant departure from contemporary educational practice. From 1699, children selected for their intellectual ability from among the pupils of the Poor School (later renamed the 'German School') were allocated subsidized places in the Latin School. The institution of 'free tables' (*Freitische*), whereby poor or temporarily impoverished students received free food and lodging in return for various services, helped to shield the educational environment from the impact of economic fluctuations in the locality; as one study has shown, poor harvests and hard winters tended to

---

18   E. Beyreuther, *Geschichte des Pietismus* (Stuttgart, 1978), p. 155.

be followed by a sharp rise in the number of pupils enjoying such subsidized places.[19]

Francke generated an impressive volume of printed publicity in support of his establishments, in which evangelical sermonizing blended seamlessly with appeals to the generosity of readers. Of these, the most widely known and influential were the *Footsteps of the still living and reigning benevolent and true GOD / for the shaming of unbelief and the strengthening of faith / Through a complete account of the Orphanage, Poor-Schools and other Care for the Poor at Glaucha in Halle*, published from 1701 in numerous new editions and reprintings.[20] With their exalted rhetoric and air of unshakeable self-confidence, these publications, distributed along a network of Pietist sympathizers spanning the breadth of Europe, conveyed a sense of the breathtaking ambition behind the Halle institutes. Halle Pietist publications interspersed reports on the good works and expansion of the Halle foundations with news of the flow of donations and material recycled from correspondence. Through this innovative formula, Francke and his followers aimed to stimulate a sense of immediacy and involvement among those who supported the work of the Halle foundations. The educational institutions were financed in part by pious donations, but Francke's intention was that the entire complex should ultimately be autonomous and self-funding; it should be a 'City of God', self-sustaining and complete, an emblem of the capacity of faithful labour to achieve a comprehensive transformation of society.[21]

In order to achieve a degree of self-sufficiency in practice, Francke encouraged the development of commercial operations within the Orphanage. The most financially important of these were the publishing house (with its own printing press) and the pharmacy. The sale of books from the Orphanage press at the Leipzig autumn fair began in 1699, on the basis of a privilege granted in the previous year. The volume of business expanded quickly and, by 1702, Francke was in a position to open a branch store for Orphanage books in Berlin; further branches opened in Leipzig and Frankfurt-am-Main. Close collaboration with faculty staff at the University of Halle meant that the Orphanage press was able to offer a catalogue of titles combining works of religious interest and secular treatises of high quality. By 1717, the house catalogue listed 200 titles by 70 authors. Between 1717

---

19  W. Oschlies, *Die Arbeits- und Berufspädagogik August Hermann Franckes (1663–1727). Schule und Leben im Menschenbild des Hauptvertreters des halleschen Pietismus* (Witten, 1969), p. 20.

20  On the *Fußstapffen* and other programmatic texts by Francke, see M. Brecht, 'August Hermann Francke und der Hallesche Pietismus', in M. Brecht (ed.), *Geschichte des Pietismus*, vol. 2, *Der Pietismus vom siebzehnten bis zum frühen achtzehnten Jahrhundert* (Göttingen, 1993), pp. 440–540 (here p. 475).

21  C. Hinrichs, 'Die universalen Zielsetzungen des Halleschen Pietismus', in C. Hinrichs, *Preußentum und Pietismus*, pp. 1–125 (here pp. 29–47).

and 1723, it printed and sold no fewer than 35,000 tracts containing sermons by Francke – a formidable commercial and publicistic achievement. Even more lucrative was the trade in pharmaceuticals by mail order (from 1702) through an extended and sophisticated system of commissioned agents. With annual profits of around 15,000 thalers in the 1720s, the *Medikamentenexpedition* was to become the most substantial single contributor to the Orphanage coffers. Further income accrued from brewing, newspaper and trading operations run from within the Halle complex. By 1710, the original Orphanage building had become the edifice of a large self-contained compound of commercial and pedagogical establishments stretching southwards into the vacant land away from the centre of the city.

Success on this scale would have been unthinkable without the concerted support of the government in Berlin and its servants in the province. Francke and his Pietist collaborators encountered the usual hostility and resistance from the Lutheran establishment in the city. Frequent interventions from above were required to counter the obstruction and protests of the Lutheran local officialdom. Printers in the province complained, with some justice, that the Orphanage's printing privilege diverged from normal contemporary practice by permitting the combined operation of a publishing and a printing business, and that this constituted an unfair trading advantage that would undermine the prosperity of guild printers in the region, but their protests – like those of the apothecaries, the brewers and other local guildsmen – met with official indifference. The Elector personally contributed 100,000 blocks of stone and 30,000 tiles free of charge towards the construction of the new Orphanage building in 1698–1701.[22]

Francke was acutely aware of the movement's dependence on the sponsorship of its powerful friends and he was as assiduous as Spener in cultivating court and government contacts, a task to which he brought all the charisma and intense sincerity that had moved his student audiences at the University of Leipzig. After a visit by Francke to Berlin in 1711 – during which the monarch is supposed to have responded to a report on Francke's achievements with the words: 'the man must be helped in every way' – the Orphanage was granted a privilege that placed it directly under the authority of the crown. Further privileges followed, securing income from a variety of official sources.

Relations with the Elector (crowned Frederick I in 1701) cooled towards the end of the reign, but the accession of Frederick William I, whom Francke had cultivated as crown prince, inaugurated an era of deeper co-operation, during which Pietism became, in the words of Carl Hinrichs, the 'state

---

22   Brecht, 'August Hermann Francke', pp. 478, 485.

religion' of Brandenburg-Prussia.[23] The crux of the new relationship was the close spiritual affinity between Francke and the new monarch, and the latter's strong sense of personal allegiance to the Pietist project in Halle. As Richard Gawthrop, an American scholar of the movement, has shown, Francke was not, strictly speaking, a 'Spenerite' Pietist, but an awakened Christian whose encounter with doubt, unbelief, rebirth and conversion predated his period under Spener's tutelage. Francke's untiring dynamism in the pursuit of his projects was thus not merely an attempt to realize the aims propagated in *Pia Desideria* and other programmatic texts, but a personal campaign to sustain the ever-endangered 'experience of faith' and to evade the despair and fear of meaninglessness that had tormented him before his conversion. The consequence was a dynamic, restless spirituality quite distinct from Spener's and an appetite for 'constant work and limitless sacrifice', characteristics that were reflected in the extraordinary colonizing energy of Halle Pietism. There were close analogies here with Frederick William I who, at the age of twenty, after the death of his first son, had gone through a 'conversion' experience that introduced an intensely personal dimension to his faith. The Elector's reborn spirituality furnished the basis for a commitment to the Pietist project that went beyond considerations of political utility.[24]

After a visit to Halle in 1713, Frederick William assured Francke that he could be relied upon for support in the event of any further conflict with the orthodox Lutherans of the municipal administration.[25] And indeed, as the Halle *Anstalten* continued to expand, they continued to enjoy official protection. As the collaboration between the monarchy and Pietist movement deepened, Pietists were increasingly implicated in projects designed to create a more homogeneous and centralized Prussian state. They played a central role in the planning and construction of a new educational system in Brandenburg-Prussia. The establishment of Halle-style educational foundations, which had begun under Frederick III/I, continued under his successor, who used Halle-trained Pietists to run the new military orphanage at Potsdam and the new *Kadettenhaus* in Berlin. In 1717, when the king issued legislation for compulsory schooling in Brandenburg-Prussia, 2,000 schools were planned (not all of which were actually built) on the Halle model.[26] By

23  C. Hinrichs, *Friedrich Wilhelm I., König in Preußen: Eine Biographie* (Hamburg, 1943), p. 597.

24  Gawthrop, *Pietism*, pp. 137–49, 211, 213 and *passim*; by contrast, Mary Fulbrook, *Piety and Politics: Religion and the Rise of Absolutism in England, Württemberg and Prussia* (Cambridge, 1983), pp. 164–7, stresses the utilitarian dimension of the relationship. See also W. Stolze, 'Friedrich Wilhelm I. und der Pietismus', *Jahrbuch für Brandenburgische Kirchengeschichte* 5 (1908), 172–205; K. Wolff, 'Ist der Glaube Friedrich Wilhelms I. von A. H. Francke beeinflusst?', *Jahrbuch für Brandenburgische Kirchengeschichte* 33 (1938), 70–102.

25  Deppermann, *Der hallesche Pietismus*, p. 168.

26  H. J. Schoeps, *Preußen. Geschichte eines Staates* (Berlin, 1968), p. 47; Gawthrop, *Pietism*, p. 255.

the late 1720s, training for at least two semesters at the Pietist-dominated University of Halle (for four semesters from 1729 onwards) had become a prerequisite for state service in Brandenburg-Prussia.[27] After 1730, the education, not only of civil servants and clergymen, but also of the greater part of the Prussian officer corps, took place in schools based on the Halle model and run by Pietists.[28]

The most important conduit for the propagation of Pietist values within the Prussian military was the network of field chaplains.[29] In 1718, Frederick William I separated the administration of the military church from that of the Orthodox-controlled civilian church and appointed a Halle graduate, Lampertus Gedike, as its director. Gedike acquired new powers over the appointment and supervision of army chaplains and used them energetically in favour of Halle candidates. Of all the army chaplains appointed to East Prussian posts between 1714 and 1736, for example, over one-half were former theology students from Halle.[30] The movement's influence on attitudes within the military was further reinforced by the fact that the education of cadets, war orphans destined for army service and the children of serving soldiers fell increasingly into Pietist hands.

How far-reaching were the effects of this impressive record? Although it is difficult to isolate the impact of the Pietists within the training structure from the effects of other changes in organization and administration of the military under Frederick William I (such as the introduction of the cantonal system of recruitment in 1727), it would appear that the ideals and attitudes propagated by the movement and sponsored by the sovereign as supreme warlord did leave their mark on the corporate ethos of the Prussian army. It is at least plausible to assume that the relatively low rates of desertion – by western European standards – among the Prussian common soldiery during the three Silesian wars reflected the heightened discipline and morale instilled by Pietist chaplains and instructors.[31] Among the officer corps, where the Pietist movement had a number of influential friends, it is likely that the Pietists, with their moral rigorism and sacralized sense of vocation, helped to discredit an older image of the officer as a swashbuckling, rakish gambler and to establish in its place a code of officerly conduct based on sobriety,

---

27 Fulbrook, *Piety and Politics*, p. 168. This requirement was extended to include the University of Königsberg in 1736.

28 M. Scharfe, *Die Religion des Volkes. Kleine Kultur- und Sozialgeschichte des Pietismus* (Gütersloh, 1980), p. 103; Beyreuther, *Geschichte des Pietismus*, pp. 338–9; Gawthrop, *Pietism*, pp. 215–46.

29 C. Hinrichs, 'Pietismus und Militarismus im alten Preußen', in Hinrichs, *Preußentum und Pietismus*, pp. 126–73 (here p. 155).

30 Gawthrop, *Pietism*, p. 226; Hinrichs, 'Pietismus und Militarismus', pp. 163–4.

31 For an argument along these lines, see Gawthrop, *Pietism*, p. 228.

self-discipline and serious dutifulness that came to be recognized as characteristically 'Prussian'.[32] With its at once worldly and sacralized concept of vocation, its focus on public needs and its emphasis on self-denial, Franckean Pietism may also have contributed to the emergence of a new 'ethic of profession' that helped to shape the distinctive identity and corporate ethos of the Prussian civil servant.[33]

Whereas Francke's distinctive mode of charitable provision was not widely emulated in Prussia or the German states – Spener's Frankfurt orphanage was far more influential[34] – the innovations in schooling introduced by Francke and his successors had a transformative impact on pedagogical practice in Prussia. The close alliance between the Halle Pietists and the monarch contributed to the emergence of schooling as a 'discrete object of state action'.[35] It was the Pietists who introduced professional training and standardized certification procedures for teachers and general-issue elementary textbooks for pupils. The Orphanage schools also created a new kind of learning environment characterized by the close psychological observation of pupils, an emphasis on self-discipline and an acute awareness of time (Francke installed hourglasses in every classroom). The day was sharply subdivided into periods of co-ordinated study in a range of subjects and periods of 'free time'; in this respect, the Halle regime anticipated the polarization of work and leisure characteristic of modern industrial society. Under these conditions, the classroom became the sealed-off, purpose-dedicated space we associate with modern schooling.

The transformation of schooling in Prussia along these lines was, of course, incomplete when Frederick William I died in 1740 and the movement lost its powerful sponsor. But the Halle model remained influential; in the 1740s and 1750s, the educationist Johann Hecker, a former teacher at the *Pädagogium* who had been trained at Francke's Teachers' College in Halle, founded a network of 'pauper schools' in Berlin catering to the neglected and potentially delinquent offspring of the town's numerous soldiers. In order to ensure an adequate supply of properly trained and motivated teachers, Hecker established a teachers' college (*Seminarium selectum praeceptorum*) on the Franckean model; he was one of several graduates of the Halle

---

32   Ibid., pp. 236–7.

33   See A. J. La Vopa, *Grace, Talent, and Merit. Poor Students, Clerical Careers and Professional Ideology in Eighteenth-Century Germany* (Cambridge, 1988), pp. 137–64, 386–8.

34   U. Sträter, 'Pietismus und Sozialtätigkeit. Zur Frage nach der Wirkungsgeschichte des "Waisenhauses" in Halle und des Frankfurter Armen-, Waisen- und Arbeitshauses', *Pietismus und Neuzeit* 8 (1982), 201–30.

35   For an outline of the legacy of Pietist innovations in the area of schooling, on which this account is based, see J. Van Horn Melton, *Absolutism and the Eighteenth-Century Origins of Compulsory Schooling in Prussia and Austria* (Cambridge, 1988), pp. 23–50.

College to set up such institutes in Prussian cities. He also founded the first *Realschule* in Berlin; the first to offer children of the middle and lower middle classes tuition in a range of vocational subjects, rather than the Latin-based, humanistic curriculum of the traditional secondary school. It was Hecker who popularized the practice of teaching pupils of like ability collectively, so as to maximize the efficiency of the teaching process; in an age which saw the beginnings of modern mass education, this was a crucial and lasting innovation.

As well as contributing to the standardization of education and public service, the Pietists directed their attention to the integration of the ethnic minorities in the Brandenburg monarchy. Pietist clergymen became involved in initiatives aimed at the education and re-Christianization of Lithuanians and Masurians in East Prussia. In 1717, when the Pietist Heinrich Lysius became Inspector of Schools and Churches for East Prussia, he called for the specialized training of clergymen for missionary and teaching work among the non-German-speaking communities in the East Prussian dioceses. As a result, after some initial disagreements, Lithuanian and Polish seminaries were established at the University of Königsberg.[36] By 1756, a senior consistorial official could observe that the campaign to provide Lithuanians with adequate religious and secular instruction had succeeded in integrating the 'stubborn old Lithuanian' into civil society to the extent that he was now able to fulfil his 'duties to the authorities'. This, he concluded, was 'a fine reward for the costs and efforts expended'.[37] The Pietists also provided support in the integration of some 20,000 Lutherans who entered Prussia as refugees from the Archbishopric of Salzburg in 1731–32, most of whom were sent by Frederick William I to live as farmers in the depopulated region of Prussian Lithuania. Pietists accompanied the 'Salzburgers' on their trek through Prussia, organized publicistic and financial support, supplied the new arrivals with devotional texts printed at the Orphanage and provided their communities in the east with pastors.[38]

A further area of evangelizing activity was the Pietist mission to the Jews. From 1728, there existed an *Institutum Judaicum* in the city of Halle, under the management of the Pietist theologian Johann Heinrich Callenberg, which ran a well-organized mission – the first of its kind – to the Jews of

---

36 F. Terveen, *Gesamtstaat und Retablissement. Der Wiederaufbau des nördlichen Ostpreussens unter Friedrich Wilhelm I* (Göttingen, 1954), pp. 86–92; on Frederick William I's concern for the evangelization of the Lithuanians, see Hinrichs, *Preußentum und Pietismus*, p. 174.

37 Cited in Fulbrook, *Piety and Politics*, p. 173.

38 M. Brecht, 'Der Hallische Pietismus in der Mitte des 18. Jahrhunderts – seine Ausstrahlung und sein Niedergang', in M. Brecht and K. Deppermann (eds), *Der Pietismus im achtzehnten Jahrhundert* (Göttingen, 1995), pp. 319–57 (here p. 323).

German-speaking Europe. Closely intertwined with the Orphanage complex, the *Institutum* was sustained by the eschatological hope for a prophesied mass conversion of Jewry articulated in the writings of Spener. In practice, however, its missionary efforts were focused largely on the conversion and occupational retraining of impoverished itinerants known as 'beggar Jews' (*Betteljuden*) whose numbers were on the increase in early eighteenth-century Germany.[39] The mission to the Jews thus embodied a characteristically Pietist blend of social awareness and evangelizing zeal. In their missionary endeavours, as in the other spheres of their activity, the Pietists earned official approval by contributing to the tasks of religious, social and cultural integration that faced the administration of the Brandenburg-Prussian state, helping to bring about the 'domestication', as one historian has called it, of 'wild elements'.[40]

By the 1720s and 1730s, Pietism had become respectable. As often happens in such cases, it had changed in the process. It had begun as a highly controversial movement with a precarious foothold within the established Lutheran churches. As Pietism gathered new adherents during the 1690s and into the new century, it continued to be burdened by a reputation for fanatical enthusiasm (*Schwärmertum*). There were still signs in the late 1690s that Spener was having difficulty containing the zeal of some of the more conscientious Pietist adherents.[41] By the 1730s, however, the moderate wing of the movement enjoyed unchallenged dominance, thanks to the groundwork laid by Spener and the tireless work of Francke and his Halle collaborators in channelling the surplus spiritual energies of Lutheran nonconformism into a range of institutional projects. A variety of radical Pietisms, some of them overtly separatist, continued to flourish in the German states, but the Prussian variant had shed its extremist fringe and become an orthodoxy in its own right. Infused with confidence, the second generation of Pietists used their dominant positions within key institutions to silence or remove opponents, much as the Lutheran Orthodox had done in an earlier era.

This position of unchallenged dominance could not be sustained in the longer term. It was undermined both by changes within the movement and by transformations in the political and intellectual environment. By the mid-1730s, the most influential and talented members of the founding generation of Halle theologians – Francke (1727), Paul Anton (1730) and

---

39  On the Pietist mission to the Jews see C. M. Clark, *The Politics of Conversion. Missionary Protestantism and the Jews in Prussia 1728–1941* (Oxford, 1995), pp. 9–82.

40  Scharfe, *Die Religion des Volkes*, p. 148.

41  See H. Obst, *Der Berliner Beichtstuhlstreit* (Witten, 1972); Gawthrop, *Pietism*, pp. 124–5; Fulbrook, *Piety and Politics*, pp. 160–2.

Joachim Justus Breithaupt (1732) – were dead; the successor generation did not produce theologians of comparable quality or public profile. The movement was further weakened by a division that opened up in the 1730s over an initiative launched by Frederick William I to eliminate the 'Catholic' elements in Lutheran ceremonial. The Halle Pietists had traditionally respected the distinctive historical cultures of the established confessions and were opposed to the Elector's high-handed tampering with the Lutheran liturgy. In this they found themselves at one, ironically enough, with the leadership of the Lutheran church, a fact that did much to repair the damage done by decades of feuding. But others within the Pietist establishment supported the king in his policy and contributed enthusiastically to its framing and implementation.[42]

The allegiance to the state that had won the movement such prominence thus threatened to divide it, and there were signs that the traditional Pietist tolerance of confessional difference was being supplanted, from within the movement itself, by an enlightened appetite for liturgical uniformity. These problems were compounded by the fact that the policy of favouring Pietists for civil service and pastoral posts encouraged the ambitious to employ adaptive mimicry in the service of their careers. For some, the temptation to manufacture narratives of conversion to a truer and more heart-felt faith was irresistible. This phenomenon – a consequence of the movement's success – was to leave the term 'Pietist' enduringly tainted with the connotation of religious imposture.[43]

After 1740, Pietism quickly declined in the theological faculties of the universities and among the clerical population of Brandenburg-Prussia. This was in part the result of a withdrawal of royal support from the Pietists. Frederick the Great was personally antipathetic to the 'Protestant Jesuits' who had enjoyed his father's protection, and consistently favoured enlightened candidates for posts in the faculties and the church administration, with the consequence that Berlin became a renowned centre of the Protestant Enlightenment.[44] The University of Halle, once the bastion of the movement, became a leading centre of rationalism, and was to remain so well into the following century. There was a gradual fall in the number of persons attending the Orphanage complex in Halle, and a corresponding decline in the circle of donors willing to support its activities. All this was reflected in the waning fortunes of the *Institutum Judaicum*, the Pietist mission

---

42  Gawthrop, *Pietism*, pp. 275–6.
43  On the association with hypocrisy see J. Wallmann, 'Was ist der Pietismus?', *Pietismus und Neuzeit* 20 (1994), 11–27 (here pp. 11–12).
44  Brecht, 'Der Hallische Pietismus', p. 342.

to the Jews, whose final annual report, published in 1790, opened with the observation that 'if we compare the earlier days of our institute with the present, then the two are as body and shadow [. . .]'.[45]

# The impact of the Pietist movement on Prussian society and institutions

How far-reaching was the impact of the Pietist movement on Prussian society and institutions? We have seen that the movement served the interests of the Brandenburg monarchy in a number of ways, relativizing the authority of the Lutheran Orthodox establishment, heightening discipline within the army and civil service, assisting in the incorporation of marginal social groups, and making a vital contribution to the education and training of officials in state service. The positive contribution rendered by the Pietists to the consolidation of absolutism in Brandenburg-Prussia offers a striking contrast with the political neutrality of the contemporaneous Pietist movement in Württemburg and the subversive impact of Puritanism in England.[46] Indeed, the American scholar Richard L. Gawthrop has even argued that the Pietists played a crucial role in enabling the Brandenburg state under Frederick William I to '[break] through the limits that had prevented any German territorial princedom from acquiring sufficient military and financial strength to challenge the post-1648 supremacy of the Habsburgs within the Empire'. The pre-1713 Hohenzollern state, Gawthrop suggests, showed little sign of its later power and prominence. The disastrous famine of 1708 revealed the corruption and weakness of the administration. The gap between the dynasty and the indigenous Junker elite was greater than in many comparable German territories. Moreover, the massive in-flow of subsidies, which had helped to consolidate the military and to swell the coffers of the elector-king, was on the point of drying up after the collapse of the Swedes at Poltava and the final defeat of Louis XIV in 1713. Against this backdrop it is clear, Gawthrop argues, that the remarkable expansion of state power under Frederick William I was not due to a 'continuation or intensification' of the state-building strategies of his predecessors. What was needed was not more state coercion or heavier taxation, but a 'powerful spiritual or ideological impulse' capable of energizing the administration,

---

45  J. J. Beyer, *Auszüge aus den Berichten des reisenden Mitarbeiters beym jüdischen Institut*, vol. 8 (Halle, 1790), p. 2.
46  This comparison is made in Fulbrook, *Piety and Politics*.

raising productivity and breaking the deadlock between the monarch and the indigenous elites. This impulse was provided by the co-option of the voluntarist energies released by the Pietist movement into a monarchical project founded on 'the ideology of state Pietism'.[47]

This is an important and thought-provoking argument, which offers a welcome rejoinder to those narratives that depict modernization as the outcome of an impersonal, structural, military or economic necessity. Some qualifications are none the less in order. Although the analogies between the monarch's intense Calvinist spirituality and Francke's 'Promethean' activism are clear enough, they do not in themselves support the claim that the far-reaching reforms introduced by Frederick William after 1713 were motivated by a desire to transform the state in the image of the Halle institutions. Nor is it clear that the monarch ever pledged allegiance to an ideology that could be called 'state Pietism'. There is a danger here of imposing a retrospective coherence upon a variety of disparate impulses. Moreover, there were limits to Halle's capacity to people Prussia with Pietist educators and officials; their presence in many regions and spheres of administration was minimal. Lastly, the étatization of Halle Pietism implied not only an increase in prestige but also a dispersal and dilution of its ideological and spiritual substance, as the connection between the growing ranks of alumni and the 'original' Pietism of the Halle type became ever more indirect. For all their self-sure, exalted rhetoric, the Pietists of Francke's generation were well aware of the danger that Pietism would be Prussianized long before Prussia became 'pietized'. In any case, one need not subscribe to every aspect of Gawthrop's thesis to accept his larger claim that Pietism made a significant contribution to the consolidation of absolutist govern-ance and the internal homogenization of Brandenburg-Prussia.

The broader social and cultural impact of the movement remains difficult to assess, the more so as Pietist movements in the German states were highly disparate and localized, and the boundaries between different vari-ants within and beyond the borders of the kingdom of Prussia are difficult to draw with any precision. But it is plausible to assume that Pietism, with its preference for restraint and understatement and its disdain for courtly luxury and wastefulness, contributed to the emergence of a self-consciously bourgeois – or *bürgerlich* – style of dress and comportment in the Protestant regions. There are also clear affinities between the introspective flavour of the Pietist spiritual biography – of which Francke's own narrative of his conversion became a widely known archetype – and the secular 'autobio-graphy' that was emerging in the mid-to-late eighteenth century as a literary

---

47   Gawthrop, *Pietism*, chs 1–3, pp. 211, 213, 222, 232.

genre.[48] For the Protestant German states as a whole and Prussia in particular, moreover, it has long been accepted that Pietism, notwithstanding its anti-rationalist animus, helped to prepare the ground for the Enlightenment. An authoritative study of the philosopher Christian Thomasius, often seen as an early exponent of enlightenment, went so far as to state that 'Pietism and enlightenment were not merely in parallel, they were inwardly at one'.[49] The movement's optimism and its future-oriented focus bore an affinity with the enlightened idea of progress, just as the Franckean preoccupation with education as a means of shaping personality 'gave rise to that comprehensive pedagogization of human existence that was an essential characteristic of the Enlightenment'.[50] And recent studies of developments in the physical sciences at the University of Halle have highlighted the ways in which the 'field of force' between Pietism and Enlightenment shaped the assumptions guiding scientific enquiry.[51] The emphasis on ethics over dogma and the commitment to tolerance in dealing with confessional differences likewise prefigured the fashions of the later eighteenth century – witness Kant's conception of morality as the highest sphere of rationally accessible truth, and his tendency to subordinate religious to moral intuitions.

It is in the nature of such arguments that they rarely progress beyond the identification of analogies and complementarities. It is surely significant, however, that some of the most influential Prussian exponents of enlightened and romantic philosophy were reared within a Pietist milieu. Johann Georg Hammann, for example, was educated at the Kneiphof school in Königsberg, a stronghold of moderate Pietism, and subsequently attended the city's university, where he came under the influence of the Pietist-inspired philosophy professor Martin Knutzen, and the introspective and ascetic quality of the Pietist outlook can be traced in his writings. Hammann even underwent a conversion experience of sorts, brought on by a period of close bible-reading and penitential self-observation.[52] The influence of Württemberg Pietism can be discerned in the writings of G. W. F. Hegel, who came to exercise a profound influence on the development of philosophy

---

48  R. van Dülmen, *Kultur und Alltag in der frühen Neuzeit*, vol. 3, *Religion, Magie, Aufklärung 16.18. Jahrhundert* (Munich, 1994), pp. 132–4.

49  See e.g. W. Bienert, *Der Anbruch der christlichen deutschen Neuzeit dargestellt an Wissenschaft und Glauben des Christian Thomasius* (Halle, 1934), p. 151.

50  M. Schmidt, 'Der Pietismus und das moderne Denken', in K. Aland (ed.), *Pietismus und Moderne Welt* (Witten, 1974), pp. 9–74 (here pp. 21, 27, 53–61).

51  See e.g. J. Geyer-Kordesch, 'Die Medizin im Spannungsfeld zwischen Aufklärung und Pietismus: Das unbequeme Werk Georg Ernst Stahls und dessen kulturelle Bedeutung', in N. Hinske (ed.), *Halle, Aufklärung und Pietismus* (Heidelberg, 1989), pp. 255–74.

52  W. M. Alexander, *Johann Georg Hamann. Philosophy and Faith* (The Hague, 1966), esp. pp. 2–3; I. Berlin, *The Magus of the North. Johann Georg Hamann and the Origins of Modern Irrationalism*, ed. H. Hardy (London, 1993), pp. 5–6, 13–14, 91.

and political thought at the University of Berlin; Hegel's conception of teleology as a process of self-realization was underpinned by a Christian theology of history with recognizably Pietist features.[53] Karl Philipp Moritz and Friedrich Schleiermacher were likewise influenced by the language and arguments of Pietism.

And what of the movement's longer-term impact on Prussian religious life? We have seen that the Pietist hegemony in the theological faculties and the church administration was swiftly dismantled after 1740. Rationalist theologians and pastors swept into the commanding posts, and the penitential style of sermon favoured by the Pietists made way for the didactic practical lectures satirized in Lenz's *Der Landprediger*. But there is reason to suppose that at least some of the distinctive features of Prussian Pietism were quietly absorbed into the fabric of popular devotional culture and thereby rendered 'natural' and uncontroversial.[54] In 1775, Friedrich Nicolai, the publishing impresario of the Berlin Enlightenment, observed in his novel *Sebaldus Nothanker* that the average Berliner 'could be described as Pietist rather than heterodox'.[55] Moreover, the Pietist movement's influence continued to be felt within discrete subcultures of Prussian Protestantism. Throughout the Frederician *Aufklärung*, Pietist devotional traditions were perpetuated in the dispersed communities of the Moravian Brethren, whose founder, Count Nikolaus Ludwig von Zinzendorf, had been a student at Francke's *Pädagogium* in Halle. Two Moravian communities (Bethlehemsgemeinde and Rixdorf) were established in Berlin during the 1750s. Pietist traditions also persisted in the households and conventicles of the *Stillen im Lande*, those 'quiet ones' who cultivated a religiosity diametrically opposed to the rationalist Christianity that prevailed in the churches and universities.

These were marginal groups, whose finely spun informal networks have left little trace on the kinds of records in which historians conventionally browse, and whose history remains anecdotal. It is clear, nevertheless, that these remnants of a Pietist tradition, however attenuated, helped to heighten the receptivity of certain individuals and social groups to religious revival in the opening decades of the following century. A good example is Johannes Jänicke (1748–1827), pastor at the Bethlehemskirche in Berlin, who had been educated at Hecker's *Realschule*. By the early 1810s, when Jänicke was in his sixties, his distinctively Pietist sermonizing and pastoral care

---

53  L. Dickey, *Hegel. Religion, Economics and the Politics of Spirit* (Cambridge, 1987), esp. pp. 149, 161.

54  P. Schicketanz, 'Pietismus in Berlin-Brandenburg. Versuch eines Forschungsberichtes', *Pietismus und Neuzeit* 13 (1987), 115–34 (here p. 121).

55  Cited in W. Wendland, 'Die praktische Wirksamkeit Berliner Geistlicher im Zeitalter der Aufklärung (1740–1806)', *Jahrbuch für Brandenburgische Kirchengeschichte* 9/10 (1913), 320–69; 11/12 (1914), 233–303 (here (1913), p. 326).

were once again in fashion and he found himself at the centre of a full-blown religious Awakening in which pious army officers and young men and women of distinguished noble lineage played a prominent part. The engaged Christians of this milieu read edifying texts from the Pietist canon, experienced traumatic 'conversions', often in each other's company, directed missions, and founded schools and charitable societies, characterized in many cases by a confidence in the imminence of 'better times'.[56] They were supported in these endeavours by a rapidly growing network of local associations patronized largely by pious artisans.

The orphanages established in the Rhineland by Count Adelberdt von der Recke-Volmerstein (1791–1878), which also catered for a time to the needs of impoverished converts from Judaism, signalled the revival of a providentialist activism with close affinities to Franckean Pietism. Like Francke, von der Recke had experienced an intense personal conversion (in 1812, under the influence of the mystical Pietist Jung-Stilling); like Francke, the count aimed to further 'the expansion of God's kingdom on Earth', expected his institutes to sustain themselves over the longer term from the inflow of pious donations, and was driven forward in his work by a chiliastic confidence that the work of the godly on Earth would hasten the advent of the end of days.[57] The relationship between the 'original' Pietism of the Spener–Francke decades and the multifaceted Awakening of the early nineteenth century is complex and indirect. The proliferation of evangelizing voluntarist organizations in the 1810s and 1820s was part of a supra-regional and international revival and owed as much to contemporary impulses from Switzerland and Britain as to the native traditions of German Protestantism. But the distinctive penitential flavour of Awakened religion, and the organized activism of many of its adherents, testify to the enduring impact of the ideals and organizational forms popularized by the Pietist movement in early eighteenth-century Prussia.

---

56  C. M. Clark, 'The politics of revival. Pietists, aristocrats and the state church in early nineteenth-century Prussia', in L. E. Jones and J. N. Retallack (eds), *Between Reform, Reaction and Resistance. Studies in the History of German Conservatism from 1789 to 1945* (Providence and Oxford, 1993), pp. 31–60 (here pp. 31–7).

57  On von der Recke see G. Viertel, *Anfänge der Rettungshausbewegung unter Adelberdt Graf von der Recke-Volmerstein (1791–1878). Eine Untersuchung zu Erweckungsbewegung und Diakonie* (Cologne, 1993), esp. chs 2, 3 and 4; E. Lindner, ' "Zum Heil Israels". Graf von der Recke Volmerstein and his Missionary Colony in Düsselthal 1822–1828', *Leo Baeck Institute Yearbook* 41 (1996), 143–60.

CHAPTER FOUR

# Prussia and the Enlightenment

## JOHAN VAN DER ZANDE

The Enlightenment has received ambiguous treatment in German scholarship. Generally speaking, Enlightenment concerns were long considered mundane compared to the thought of the towering figures of subsequent German literature and philosophy – Goethe, Schiller, Hegel and others. Moreover, enlightenment concerns were often considered to hold little value because of their association with French culture and the French Revolution to which many German historians were long ideologically opposed. Traditionally, historians have assumed – and, indeed, some still do – that the Enlightenment radiated out of Paris to other parts of Europe. Historical scholarship over the past few decades, however, has shifted the notion of the Enlightenment from a purely intellectual movement originating and based in France to a multifaceted Europe-wide intellectual and cultural movement. The French model of a bourgeois, anti-clerical and revolutionary programme is in the process of being replaced by that of a mosaic of national and even regional varieties in which the participation of other social groups, the continuous importance of religion, and more moderate political ideas are recognized. Historians now speak of conservative and religious forms of Enlightenment while continuing to insist that its adherents were everywhere intent on changing people's minds and manners, and on reforming the institutions of both the church and the state.[1] Accordingly, one has to take seriously the claim of many Prussians who, by the 1780s, thought of their country as a centre of Enlightenment (*Aufklärung*).

---

1   See, for example, Roy Porter and Nikulaus Teich (eds), *The Enlightenment in National Context* (New York, 1981). My thanks to Michael Curtin and Anne MacLachlan for critical remarks on earlier versions of this chapter.

Along with an awareness of the diversity of the Enlightenment has come a much greater appreciation of its socio-cultural forms. The Enlightenment was as much determined by dispensing and communicating knowledge in particular forms as by a specific stock of knowledge. Where people meet, they also fashion the ways in which they meet, and the Enlightenment saw these ways of life unfold in moral weeklies and journals, reading societies, Masonic lodges, coffee houses, personal correspondence, and through travel, all of which constituted enlightened sociability in Europe. A new view of the Enlightenment as a process of communication has emerged in which citizens fashioned a public sphere that set them apart from the state.[2] The analysis of this process requires the interaction of both intellectual and social history.

On the basis of these recent historiographical developments, the interpretation of the Enlightenment presented here emphasizes its complexity. It focuses on a number of Enlightenment thinkers who looked for a foundation of knowledge; the rise of Enlightenment anthropology (the 'science of man'), and the importance it had in shaping the public sphere in eighteenth-century Prussia; and on Enlightenment sociability – that is, the associations and institutions of the Enlightenment – and the emergence of the public sphere of critically enquiring citizens. This was probably the Enlightenment's most characteristic product. The chapter ends with a discussion on the debate which took place in the 1780s about the limits of the Enlightenment, before drawing some general conclusions.

# The social and political context of the Enlightenment

The Prussian Enlightenment occurred within a specific social and political context. Historians generally agree on the social background of those who adhered to the movement: they were a mixture of educated people from both the bourgeoisie and the nobility. There is more disagreement about the relationship between the Enlightenment and the rule of Frederick II. The king's writings and the admiration among both contemporaries and later commentators for his genius and accomplishments long fostered the mistaken belief that the Enlightenment itself ruled in Prussia.

The Enlightenment in Prussia-Germany is usually divided into two distinct periods with a turning-point occurring around 1760. The distinction

---

2  Hans Erich Bödeker, 'Aufklärung asl Kommunikationssprozeß', *Aufklärung* 2, Heft 2 (1987), 89–112. For an overview, see Ulrich Im Hof, *The Enlightenment*, trans. William E. Yuill (Oxford and Cambridge, MA, 1994).

between the two periods is founded on a change in intellectual attitudes that is closely related to changed social-intellectual circumstances. The early Enlightenment in Prussia, that is, before 1760, was based almost exclusively upon a single institution, the University of Halle. The late Enlightenment or the Enlightenment proper, which took place in the second half of the eighteenth century, was based upon a much larger public. It was also based in university towns such as Halle and Königsberg, but was increasingly located in other towns as well – in particular in the most populous city of the kingdom, Berlin. Although literacy rates did not change markedly, rapidly changing reading habits created a larger public. By 1750, the use of Latin was giving way to German even in scholarly fields such as philosophy and theology; theological and devotional books were giving way to books of a more secular character; and impressive folio volumes were being replaced by the more practical and less expensive octavo and quarto formats.[3] This process had, indeed, acquired such momentum that the Enlightenment was poised to become a relatively wide social movement. Berlin and Halle became important centres of the book trade. Even in Halle, this was the work of booksellers rather than the university, which until 1778 did not have a building for its library. Translations of French, and after 1770 increasingly also of British, authors made a wider German public familiar with western European ideas (one should be aware, however, of the translator's unintentional adaptations to German philosophical and cultural expectations and language).[4] Two-thirds of the total book production of approximately 175,000 titles in Germany in the eighteenth century occurred after 1750. Much of this vast new production consisted of light entertainment, but the blurring of the borderline between professional-academic literature and works for a larger educated public is indicative of the impact of Enlightenment ideas.

Socially, however, the Enlightenment, in Prussia as elsewhere, remained an elitist movement wedged between the king and his entourage and the populace at large. The vast majority of the lower classes almost never participated in the Enlightenment movement. Rather, they were at most the object of reform efforts from above (*Volksaufklärung*) aimed at encouraging efficient production on the land and in the craftsman's workshop, although there certainly was an enlightened element in the concern with, for example,

---

3  See Albert Ward, *Book Production, Fiction, and the German Reading Public, 1740–1800* (Oxford, 1974), esp. pp. 174–86 (Appendix I) with the figures of the book production at the Leipzig book fairs in 1740, 1770 and 1800 according to scholarly field.

4  For the importance of translations from the English see Bernhard Fabian, 'English books and their eighteenth-century German readers', in Paul J. Korshin (ed.), *The Widening Circle. Essays on the Circulation of Literature in Eighteenth-Century Europe* (Philadelphia, 1976), pp. 117–96.

the safety of the labourer in Prussian laws on mining. Economic rationalization, however, was not the same as the Enlightenment proper, which was concerned with individual moral self-improvement on the basis of the use of one's own reason.

Nor did the Prussian rulers have much to do with the Enlightenment. Contrary to a long-standing conviction, that is also true for the self-styled philosopher-king, Frederick II. Since the 1930s, historians frequently have used the unfortunate concept of 'enlightened absolutism' or 'enlightened despotism' to describe the reform policies of rulers like Frederick II in Prussia, Joseph II in the Habsburg lands, and Catherine II in Russia. But the impetus for their economic, administrative and judicial reforms was political – namely, to consolidate royal power and to turn their countries into strong states. In this pursuit, they not only continued the policies of their unenlightened predecessors, but were also guided by pre-Enlightenment ideas. The notions of the contractual basis of the state (as opposed to the divine right of kings), the ruler as servant of the state (as Frederick II famously claimed he was), and Cameralism, the state-oriented economic thought that emphasized the augmentation of revenue for the welfare of the state as the cornerstone of the economic order – all have their origins in the seventeenth century or earlier. Enlightened absolutism had nothing to do either with the Enlightenment as a moral enterprise or with the constitution of Enlightenment sociability. The term is a 'conceptual mistake of historiography', as the German historian Günter Birtsch rightly remarked.[5] It would be better to drop it altogether, or replace it with Birtsch's more accurate term, 'reform absolutism'.

Indeed, contemporaries and historians alike have interpreted Frederick II's rule as a 'monarchy of contrasts' marked by the stark discrepancy between absolutism and the Enlightenment.[6] Whatever the king's penchant for philosophy might have meant to him personally, he never let it interfere with what he saw as his principal task, the strengthening of the state under his personal control. There were occasional exceptions that confirmed the rule. At the beginning of his reign, for example, he abolished torture. As crown prince, he sharply criticized the political theory of Machiavelli's *The Prince* and, in doing so, earned the esteem of the renowned French Enlightenment thinker, Voltaire, who later spent several years as a guest at Frederick II's court. No sooner had Frederick ascended the throne, however, than he seized the rich province of Silesia from Austria on a flimsy legal

---

5   Günter Birtsch, 'Aufgeklärter Absolutismus oder Reformabsolutismus', *Aufklärung* 9 (1996), 101–9 (here p. 104). The term 'enlightened absolutism' was invented by the economic historian Wilhelm Roscher in 1847, but acquired currency only from the 1930s.

6   For example, Theodor Schieder, *Friedrich der Große: Ein Königtum der Widersprüche* (Frankfurt-am-Main, 1983).

pretext. Even his famed policy of religious toleration was primarily guided by pragmatic considerations of state, as it had been for his predecessors since their conversion to Calvinism in 1613. Since they ruled over a largely Lutheran population, religious toleration was an imperative. It recommended itself even more when the Great Elector, Frederick William (1640–88), as part of his population and mercantile politics, invited about 20,000 French Huguenots, most of them craftsmen, to settle on his lands after the revocation of the Edict of Nantes in 1685. Similarly, after Frederick II's annexations of Silesia (1740) and part of Poland (1772), it would have been politically foolish to antagonize the predominantly Catholic populations in these areas. Later, he forbade the introduction of an enlightened hymn book for use in the Lutheran church, not because he cared about it one way or another, but because of Orthodox opposition. One can draw the conclusion that Potsdam, like Versailles, was not a centre of Enlightenment even when one concedes that Frederick's own religious indifference facilitated both the rise of genuine enlightened toleration and an exceptionally free debate on religious matters during his long reign.

Understandably, the adherents of the Enlightenment were most grateful to Frederick II and mistakenly paid him tribute in the hope that he would yield to their cause. In particular, they had high expectations of the new Prussian civil law code that the high officials Chancellor Count von Carmer (1720–1801), Ernst Ferdinand Klein (1744–1810) and Carl Gottlieb Svarez (1746–1798) started preparing during his reign (but which was completed only well after his death in 1794). Like similar attempts in Bavaria and Austria, the goal of the new code was to rationalize the existing legal system. Its main purpose, however, was to subject all inhabitants, including the monarch, to the rule of law, although most of them would be excluded from participating in the lawmaking process. But Frederick II was reluctant in his support of the enlightened aspirations of his officials. He sometimes exempted himself from the law and intervened in judicial cases in the 'interest of the state'.

With both the ruler and the population at large mostly unaffected by the Enlightenment, its adherents were made up for the most part by the classes in between – the university educated (*Gebildeten*) among the nobility as well as the bourgeoisie. They were mostly officials in church and state, academics, Protestant pastors, and members of the bureaucracy and the liberal professions, such as lawyers, publishers and doctors. The church and the university produced most of them – that is to say, the *Gebildeten* were partly self-recruiting. Its adherents did not constitute a rank or class in themselves, but the emergence of this social stratum loosened the ties of corporate society with its judicially defined divisions between various orders, ranks and professions, within which it none the less remained.

A brief analysis of the approximately three hundred authors of the leading organ of the late Enlightenment in Germany, the influential *Berlinische Monatsschrift* (Berlin Monthly), shows that over eighty (27 per cent) came from the learned professions (professors and other educators); about sixty (20 per cent) were state officials; fifty (17 per cent) were clergymen, of whom twenty were high clerics and thirty pastors; and forty-five (15 per cent) belonged to the nobility. A similar picture can be drawn from the more than 430 contributors to the *Allgemeine Deutsche Bibliothek* (General German Book Review), except that they came from all over Germany, whereas a quarter of the authors of the *Berlinische Monatsschrift* lived in Berlin itself.[7] The relatively small numbers involved in Enlightenment culture are apparent from the fact that, even at its high point, the *Bibliothek* never exceeded more than 2,500 subscriptions for all of Germany. These figures clearly demonstrate the elite character of the Enlightenment movement, whether its adherents were noble or bourgeois.

The career of Friedrich Gedike (1754–1803) was typical for a man of the late Prussian Enlightenment. As a bright young man, he was endorsed by the respected high church official and Enlightenment author, Johann Joachim Spalding (1714–1804), for a position as teacher in one of the prestigious Berlin grammar schools. At the age of twenty-five, Gedike subsequently became its director. It was in that distinguished position that he published a number of works on school reform. Later, he became a member of the Prussian School Board and of the Upper Consistory, the state council that ruled the Lutheran Church in Prussia. In the 1780s, Gedike became co-editor of the *Berlinische Monatsschrift*.[8]

Like Gedike, many Enlightenment figures in Prussia were involved in directing government and church machinery at one level or another and were, therefore, economically dependent on the state. About half of the contributors to the *Berlinische Monatsschrift* were in state service. This meant that writing and publishing was never more than a sideline for them. It also meant that, with few exceptions, the basic attitude of the Prussian adherents of the Enlightenment was one of co-operation with, rather than opposition to, the state. For them, political liberty was an ultimate prospect dependent on the level of Enlightenment in society, not an immediate goal. Their first priority was freedom of thought and expression, that is, release from the guidance of others in the use of one's own understanding. They found support for their demand in Karl Abraham von Zedlitz (1731–1793), a

---

7   Horst Möller, *Vernunft und Kritik. Deutsche Aufklärung im 17. und 18. Jahrhundert* (Frankfurt-am-Main, 1986), p. 295.
8   Helga Eichler, 'Berliner Schriftsteller und Publizisten am Ende des 18. Jahrhunderts', *Jahrbuch für Volkskunde und Kulturgeschichte* 30 (1987), 19.

Silesian nobleman educated in Halle, who for the last third of Frederick's reign was Prussia's enlightened education minister and head of the Upper Consistory. His lenient censorship policy endeared him to the men of the Enlightenment, many of whom were his personal acquaintances. One of them, Erich Biester, the other co-editor of the *Berlinische Monatsschrift*, was his long-time secretary. However, the masterpiece of Zedlitz's tenure – his design of a school board independent from church supervision – was only effected after the death of Frederick II.

The demand for freedom of thought and expression in Prussia centred on religious matters. Indeed, the German Enlightenment in general focused on the problem of religion in society, and kept a middle course between what was perceived as superstition (*Aberglauben*) and what was perceived as unbelief (*Unglauben*). Enlightened theologians (*Neologen*) such as Spalding were, therefore, major players in the Enlightenment process, not because of some supposedly German penchant for the spiritual, but because of the memory of the religious wars of the previous century and the political fragmentation of the Holy Roman Empire. In important works written between the 1670s and the 1730s, Prussian theorists of natural law (in which rules of conduct were deducted from the common reason of humankind) such as Samuel Pufendorf, Christian Thomasius and Christian Wolff proclaimed freedom of conscience. That did not entail, however, the freedom to unreservedly advocate one's religious opinions; the fear was prevalent that the fragile political and religious equilibrium established by the Peace of Westphalia (1648) could be disturbed. The Peace of Westphalia contained the provision that territorial lords of the Empire had the right to decide the religion of their subjects. If the subjects' religion was not the same as their lords', the only legal recourse open to them was migration. Politics and religion were even more closely intertwined in the Lutheran territories. There the rulers, who were at one and the same time heads of their territorial churches, also dominated local religious affairs.

To emancipate oneself from these legal restrictions – or as Immanuel Kant ironically put it, from the 'guardians who have graciously taken up the oversight of humankind', in order 'to think for oneself' (*Selbstdenken*) – was precisely what supporters identified as the Enlightenment. Intellectual individualism – that is, 'to think for oneself' – implied the need to exchange one's thoughts with others, to openly express them in both speech and writing, including one's doubts and reservations. Some deplored the level of the ensuing debate, which, as already noted, was relatively free in Frederician Prussia. In an often-quoted letter written in 1769, the great playwright, Gotthold Ephraim Lessing (1729–1781), lamented that 'the freedom in Berlin to think and write amounts to nothing more than the freedom to produce as many inanities about religion as one likes'. He contrasted this freedom with the limits on political speech. If in Prussia one wanted to protest against despotism, one 'would soon learn which country was the most docile in Europe'.[9] Lessing's harsh judgement ignored, however, the political dimension of thinking for oneself about religion.

The tension between the political and religious dimensions that Lessing noticed is evident in Enlightenment endeavours to obtain a policy of free speech in Prussia. For example, E. F. Klein's essay on freedom of the press (dedicated to 'princes, ministers and writers') quoted extensively from Frederick's youthful writings. In doing so, Klein was reminding the king of his own tenets: 'So thought and so acted the great monarch, who has since become the model for princes and the object of admiration for all of Europe!' At the same time, Klein admitted the dangers of freedom of the press for the security of both state and religion by admonishing authors not to abuse it: 'Your writing is an arrow that you can no longer control once you have fired it.'[10] Klein's essay encapsulated mainstream enlightened thinking on the subject. It was not until the radical Saxon thinker and theologian, Carl Friedrich Bahrdt (1742–1792), who had found refuge in Prussia, that this moderate endeavour was transformed into a revolutionary claim. In 1787, with the threat of a more repressive regime under Frederick's successor, Frederick William II, Bahrdt published a substantial work (subtitled 'for rulers, censors and writers' in reference to Klein's essay) that declared freedom of the press, at least in matters of religion, to be an inalienable human right. No authority in state or church – and this is the revolutionary implication – could violate that right.[11] In short, if the Enlightenment did not significantly change the way in which Prussians were ruled, it did profoundly change the way in which the educated elite came to think about how they ought to be ruled.

## The two faces of the Enlightenment

As an intellectual-cultural movement, the Enlightenment is a very complex phenomenon, so complex that some historians have called it a way of life,

---

9  Lessing to Friedrich Nicolai, 25 August 1769, in Karl Lachmann (ed.), *Lessing's Sämtliche Schriften*, 23 vols (Leipzig, 1904), xvii, p. 298.
10  Ernst Ferdinand Klein, 'Ueber Denk- und Druckfreyheit. An Fürsten, Minister, und Schriftsteller', *Berlinische Monatsschrift* 3 (1784), 323, 329. An English translation can be found in James Schmidt (ed.), *What is Enlightenment? Eighteenth-Century Answers and Twentieth-Century Questions* (Berkeley, 1996), pp. 90, 93.
11  Carl Friedrich Bahrdt, *Über Preßfreiheit und deren Gränzen. Zur Beherzigung für Regenten, Censoren und Schriftsteller* (Züllichau, 1787). The most important sections in English translation are in Schmidt, *What is Enlightenment?*, pp. 97–113.

while others regard it as synonymous with the eighteenth century. Such all-inclusive views leave the Enlightenment without a face, so to speak. The interpretation offered in this section presents an Enlightenment with not one, but two faces – that is, philosophical Rationalism and the 'science of man'. Both were distinct responses to the intellectual problems posed by the almost continuous warfare of the seventeenth century. The first originated from the desire to establish a certain foundation of knowledge in the face of the contested truths claimed by the warring religious factions. The other, rarely discussed response involved the development of a 'science of man' – that is, a conception of virtuous people interacting peacefully in a harmonious society.

In the history of philosophy, modern Rationalism – the belief in the power of reason as opposed to religious faith or experience – is associated with the name of René Descartes (1596–1650). Pressed by the disaster of the religious wars to secure a ground for absolute knowledge, Descartes attempted to do so through the mathematization of science and the expulsion from scientific thought of all considerations based on (religious) value. In fact, however, science and religion were to remain intertwined for much of the eighteenth century and by 1750 philosophical Rationalism had lost most of its earlier appeal. In Germany, Christian Wolff (1679–1754), who taught at the Prussian University of Halle, was its last great representative. An impressive philosophical system-builder, Wolff's method was based on the mathematical model: he developed his system from one proposition to another, never proceeding if a preceding truth had not been firmly established. Thinking for oneself, Wolff believed, could be done only when clear and distinct concepts were available. In this way, he also proved the existence of God and the immortality of the soul. Wolffian rationalist philosophy dominated in the German Protestant universities between 1720 and 1760 before finally succumbing to another system.

In 1781, the philosopher Immanuel Kant (1724–1804), who taught at the East Prussian University of Königsberg, dealt a death-blow to Wolffian Rationalism when he published the *Critique of Pure Reason*, at the same time bringing about a revolution in philosophical thought. In this seminal work, Kant also demonstrated (as opposed to Wolff) that we cannot have rational, theoretical knowledge about God's existence or the immortality of the soul – these are subjects of faith only. This explanation had a great deal of appeal because it allowed people to keep religious faith, which they increasingly suspected could not be as easily proven as Wolff suggested, without it interfering with their otherwise scientific world-view. Kant's formulation of the 'categorical imperative' in his *Critique of Practical Reason* (1788) was also significant. According to Kant, duty is the unconditional source of our moral behaviour: a moral action is willed for its own sake, not because some good

– such as one's own happiness or social harmony – is expected from it. More than anything else, this notion of duty expressed for many later Prussian officials and scholars their distinctive self-understanding as a social class. But the doctrine is not a typical Enlightenment product and can be traced to a variety of other sources, notably the personal examples of Frederick William I and Frederick II and the way they conceived of the duties of kingship. Because of Kant's enormous influence, many historians have concluded that in his Critical philosophy Enlightenment philosophy exhausted itself. But this assumption ignores the other face of the Enlightenment.

The first traces of a 'science of man' are visible in Wolff's older contemporary, Christian Thomasius (1655–1728), who also taught in Halle. Generally known as the father of the German Enlightenment, Thomasius was interested in the knowledge of human behaviour rather than in building a solid foundation of all knowledge. For Thomasius, thinking for oneself meant primarily thinking about oneself in a social context. For this purpose, it was necessary to study human nature and to closely observe people as moral beings. The appropriate philosophical method of enquiry for this anthropological endeavour was Empiricism, which derives knowledge of the world from experience, rather than philosophical Rationalism. The role of reason was limited to that of common sense, or 'natural reason', as Thomasius called it. Reason was not, as it later became under Kant, a powerful tool within the limited range of science and philosophy, but was used as one tool alongside others, such as intuition, empathy and tact, to grasp the complex realities of human nature; it aimed at probability rather than certainty.

This anthropological dimension began to dominate Enlightenment philosophy in the second half of the eighteenth century. During this period, Enlightenment thinkers began to look at the human sciences, for which they developed increasingly sophisticated methods. This was particularly the case for the writing of history. By extending the field of observation of human actions to the past, more information became available about the wide range of possible human behaviour. The immense eighteenth-century interest in travel reports furnished Enlightenment thinkers with the observation of existing nations at different levels of civilization. The pursuit of their studies taught these thinkers that people are not autonomous, rational human beings, but producers as well as products of cultural and social values and processes.

This anthropological interest not only produced knowledge, but in the process also fashioned the public, whose members were described by that knowledge and who learned about themselves by absorbing it. Prior to 1720, the size of the reading public was still not much larger than it had been two hundred years before and most of their reading material consisted of either the Bible or devotional literature. Thomasius founded several journals in an attempt to reach out to a larger public. Moreover, a new genre was introduced into Germany from Britain – the so-called 'moral weeklies', short-lived but endlessly recycled publications that instructed their middle-class public in the problems of everyday life, and stressed the themes of rewarded virtue, appropriate manners and practical advice. The first such publication, *Der Patriot* (1724–6), appeared in Hamburg and boasted an astonishing five thousand subscribers. Moral weeklies also became popular in Prussia until the 1760s, when the whole genre started to decline. The great contribution of the moral weeklies to Enlightenment anthropology was that they pointed to the common humanity of all people, even when they remained divided along cultural-religious, social and political lines. The ideal of individual character represented in their pages was to be open and frank (*offenherzig*) with one's fellow human beings, or 'philanthropic' (*menschenfreundlich*).

This ideal was also forcefully presented in plays in which the heroic characters elevated the theatre to a true moral institution (*bürgerliches Theater*). By watching the characters on the stage, the audience learned to interpret their own behaviour. The true successor to the moral weeklies, however, was so-called 'popular philosophy' (*Popularphilosophie*), which catered to the educated public (*Gebildeten*) and considerably raised the level of philosophical reflection. Although found elsewhere in Germany, Prussia – and in particular Berlin – was a leading centre of popular philosophy. Most of those practising popular philosophy were men of letters who intentionally refrained from building philosophical systems and who barely touched on the philosophical problems concerned with the possibilities and limitations of the human understanding. Rather, they were interested in the study of man and, therefore, in subjects such as psychology, aesthetics, history and religion. In sharp contrast to Kant's moral doctrine, their primary concern was to understand moral action as the outcome of the complex situations of social reality and of insights into human nature illustrated by practical and historical experience. In short, the popular philosophers explored the moral and cultural formation of the citizen of the absolute state as much as that of abstract man. In some of their best writings, the notion of *Bildung* appeared – that is, education in the wide sense of cultivation of one's self. As a sociocultural concept, *Bildung* was to reach its peak in the nineteenth century, but without the emphasis on political and social conditions that was distinctive of popular philosophy.

The most prominent popular philosopher was Moses Mendelssohn (1729–1786), the son of a poor Jewish teacher and scribe. In the context of the more religiously oriented form of Enlightenment in Prussia, it is not surprising to find Mendelssohn both at the centre of Berlin intellectual life and participating in traditional Jewish scholarship. He played a major role in the Jewish Enlightenment (*Haskalah*) and in 1783 published *Jerusalem, or on Religious Power and Judaism*, in which he advocated political and religious toleration, as well as the separation of church and state, and civil equality for the Jews. This last point was also the subject of Christian Wilhelm Dohm's *On the Civil Improvement of the Jews*, a famous pamphlet written in 1781 for which Mendelssohn's life was a major inspiration. Mendelssohn's close friendship with Lessing was held up as a living example of toleration between enlightened Jews and Christians in Prussia. Indeed, Mendelssohn was the model for Nathan in Lessing's drama on toleration, *Nathan the Wise* (1779). In a sense, then, this friendship exemplified the outcome of the Enlightenment 'science of man' – that is, the realization that the individual is endowed with personal values that have to be respected by others, and that on this basis one could envisage social harmony.

# Enlightenment institutions and sociability in Prussia

Enlightenment society fashioned itself in the public institutions and private associations that emerged in the eighteenth century. The *Gebildeten* used these institutions and associations to fulfil their need to communicate, as well as to probe their ability to think for themselves. In the process, they created a public sphere that consisted of interacting private individuals who, although subject to the state as far as welfare policy and censorship were concerned, also tended to be independent from and potentially critical of the state. This is precisely where the historical importance of these associations lay. Enlightenment sociability slowly gave rise to modern urbane, polite, civil society, situated between the domain of official authority and the privacy of the family; Enlightenment ideas of toleration and 'public opinion' shaped its contents. Enlightenment thinkers tried hard to envision a uniform, critical public in a politically and socially fragmented Germany. To some extent, however, the public, ideally conceived as the totality of all critical readers, or alternatively as a linguistic unity, or even as a nascent German nation, remained itself very fragmented. According to the popular philosopher, Christian Garve (1742–1798), who was always sensitive to such issues, the concomitant notion of 'public opinion' – that is, the expressed consensus of many citizens through their own mature judgement – was still a recent phenomenon in Germany in the 1790s. Its full effects would be felt only in the next century.

The University of Halle, co-founded by Thomasius in 1694, was one of the first footholds of the Enlightenment in Prussia. Established with the goal of providing the future administrative elite, its curriculum focused on practical knowledge rather than on theological erudition, which was considered out of touch with everyday life. Free enquiry and teaching – if not directed against God or state – supplanted theological surveillance. The study of natural law and of experimental science was heavily favoured; German began to replace Latin as the language of instruction. With the expulsion of Wolff in 1723 at the instigation of the Pietists and the death of Thomasius in 1728, the university lost much of its lustre, although it continued to be a base of Enlightenment thought. Later in the eighteenth century, Johann Salomo Semler (1725–1791) developed a highly influential enlightened theology informed by a new historical methodology.

Another important Enlightenment institution was the Berlin Academy of Sciences. The Academy was originally founded in 1700 by the philosopher Gottfried Wilhelm Leibniz (1646–1715), and was supported by Sophie Charlotte, the wife and intellectual superior of Frederick I (reigned 1688–1713). Unfortunately, it had little chance to develop during the reign of the so-called 'soldier king', Frederick William I (1713–40). Only its reorganization by Frederick II after 1745 transformed the Berlin Academy into a truly enlightened institution. According to its statutes, it was meant to contribute to the greater welfare of the land. The Academy's division into four classes shows a wide concept of science: physics, mathematics, philosophy and philology; in the latter, history, German and Oriental languages were also cultivated. Frederick II had a preference for French-speaking or bilingual (French and German) members for his Academy. Indeed, French was the language for its formal proceedings until the 1790s. The Academy's long-standing secretary was the French-speaking Samuel Formey from the Huguenot colony in Berlin. Frederick refused German nominations such as Lessing and Mendelssohn, and local talent was admitted only by his successor, Frederick William II. This policy of exclusion shows Frederick's personal limitations, but, on the other hand, the use of French as the international language of the day facilitated the spread of the Academy's reputation abroad. It became a leading European institution in the fields of mathematics, physics, astronomy, chemistry and botany. Its enlightened potential was realized in particular by the famous prize contest it held on a regular basis. It should be stressed that not only European scholars of fame, but also many German scholars and *Gebildeten* submitted their French- or German-language answers to the prize contests.

Private forms of Enlightenment sociability, as opposed to the public institutions of university and Academy, developed later in the eighteenth century. Mendelssohn and Lessing, together with Friedrich Nicolai (1733–1811), started the development of private institutions in the late 1750s with an influential literary review journal, the *Briefe, die neueste Litteratur betreffend*

(Letters Concerning the Most Recent Literature). Nicolai then began his own review journal, the *Allgemeine Deutsche Bibliothek*, that for forty years was 'the torchlight of the nation'; it reached its peak in the late 1770s. In the early 1780s, its popularity was overtaken by the *Berlinische Monatsschrift*, edited by Erich Biester and Friedrich Gedike. In the 1790s, Garve helped to found the *Schlesische Provinzial-Blätter* (Silesian Provincial Journal), another highly influential journal that was published until the 1860s.

Although freemasonry, with its principles of brotherly love, charity and mutual aid, contributed to the process of sociability, its secrecy obviously ran counter to the ideals of enlightened public interaction. Also, the much-vaunted equality in the lodges did not square with their often strictly hierarchical organization. If secrecy meant only discretion, however, the lodges could meet the demand for sociability. The lodges could be carriers of enlightened thought, but that was not necessarily so. The highly secretive Masonic order of the Rosicrucians, for example, were firmly opposed to the Enlightenment, which they equated with a wholesale attack on Christianity itself. One of its members, Johann Christoph Woellner (1732–1800), became a high official in the reign of Frederick William II and in that capacity tried to stop the further development of the Enlightenment. There certainly was no automatic link between the Enlightenment and freemasonry, although assuming this link made it easier for later counter-revolutionaries to suspect both of having conspired to bring about the French Revolution.[12]

True enlightened sociability expressed itself differently. The Monday Club (founded in 1749), for example, with a limited membership of twenty-four, was the home of Berlin's intellectual aristocracy of authors, poets, scholars and high officials. In contrast to this club's goal of conviviality, the Wednesday Club of the 'Friends of the Enlightenment' (founded in 1783) was highly political. Its members included the popular philosophers Nicolai and Mendelssohn, and high officials in the Prussian administration such as Klein and Svarez. The secrecy of this club was deliberately designed to protect the freedom of the state officials that belonged to it to discuss political affairs outside their offices.

After the end of the Seven Years' War in 1763, coffee houses, reading societies, patriotic and economic societies emerged all over Prussia, not just in Berlin or Halle. In Germany, however, Prussia was far from being in the forefront of this development. By 1780, there were only twelve coffee houses in Berlin compared to over sixty in Vienna. Coffee had been introduced in Prussia a century before, but it remained a very costly drink despite being

---

12  Rudolf Vierhaus, 'Aufklärung und Freimaurerei in Deutschland', in Helmut Reinalter (ed.), *Freimaurer und Geheimbünde in 18. Jahrhundert in Mitteleuropa* (Frankfurt-am-Main, 1983), pp. 115–39.

adopted by the upper ranks of the middle classes by 1750 and by the lower classes slowly thereafter. In the 1750s, some hundred people frequented the 'Mathematical Coffee House' where, for a monthly fee, members from the Academy such as Leonhard Euler, grammar-school professors, and also men like Nicolai and Mendelssohn discussed matters of scientific interest. In the patriotic and economic societies, the most discussed topics were theology, social reform and economics. Some of these societies set prize essays and they sometimes implemented actual economic reforms on the local level.

Frequently, one form of society bred another: a Masonic lodge often was the origin of a reading society where one could collectively subscribe to domestic and foreign periodicals; some bigger coffee houses combined private club, reading-room and other functions. Most of these associations were socially exclusive because of the high fees or the prohibitive prices of the beverages. Moreover, women had no access to coffee houses until the very end of the century. By that time, a salon culture had blossomed in Berlin. Long familiar in France, salons were regularly held in private houses where guests would discuss the latest philosophical and scientific ideas as well as the arts. In Berlin, Nicolai hosted such a salon, but the most famous salon was led by a Jewish woman, Henriette Herz (1764–1847), the wife of the doctor and Enlightenment philosopher, Marcus Herz. Although all of these associations were highly diverse in character – ranging from the coffee house, where one could go without knowing whom one would meet, to the closed membership of the Masonic lodges and private clubs – these new social forms crossed the boundaries of traditional corporate society and fashioned the contours of modern, civil society.

## The debate in Prussia on the Enlightenment

In the 1780s, a widespread discussion began in Berlin about the nature and merits of the Enlightenment that soon engulfed all of Germany. Its numerous contributors showed an awareness of the complexities involved that has not always been appreciated by present-day critics of the Enlightenment.[13] Indeed, this late eighteenth-century discussion about the concept of the Enlightenment became a key issue of Enlightenment thought in Germany.

The question, 'What is Enlightenment?', was first posed by the Berlin theologian Johann Friedrich Zöllner (1753–1804) in the December 1783

---

13   Schmidt's *What is Enlightenment?*, which has opened up the debate to the English-speaking world for the first time, is subtitled, with only slight exaggeration, 'eighteenth-century answers and twentieth-century questions'.

issue of the *Berlinische Monatsschrift*. Zöllner was responding to the sugges-
tion in an earlier contribution to the same journal that the religious sanction
of marriage should be abolished and that purely civil marriage ceremonies
should be introduced. He feared that if this occurred the basic principles
of morality would be shaken, the value of religion diminished and, under
the cloak of *Aufklärung*, people's hearts and minds bewildered. 'What is
*Aufklärung?*' he asked and then continued, 'This question, which is almost
as important as "What is truth?" should indeed be answered before one
begins enlightening! But still I have nowhere found it answered.'[14]

Zöllner's question spawned a large-scale and wide-ranging discussion in
books and journals that went on for years and touched on such major issues
as the freedom of the press (should the lower classes be exposed to Enlightenment ideas?); the relationship between Enlightenment and religion
(Is, for instance, morality based in human nature or inextricably bound up
with church doctrine? How far should religious tolerance go?); and whether
the Enlightenment undermined political authority (Does the demand to
think for oneself extend to criticism of the ruler? Do citizens have a right to
resistance?). The answers to these and many other related questions were
as diverse and controversial as the questions themselves and unavoidably
played on the metaphorical use of the terms light and dark inherent in the
notion of enlightenment; some wished for as much light as possible, while
others warned that too much light could blind people. The debate acquired
further urgency because it was accompanied by repressive measures from
the new Prussian government after the death of Frederick II in 1786. Even
before the outbreak of revolution in France, the new government under
Woellner issued edicts on religion and censorship and began clamping down
on all-too-daring authors. After the execution of Louis XVI, Kant had to
comply with a royal order to stop writing on religious matters, which alarmed
the Orthodox, while Nicolai and Biester, the editors of the *Allgemeine Deutsche
Bibliothek* and the *Berlinische Monatsschrift*, found it expedient to have their
journals printed outside Prussia.

The most famous answer to Zöllner's question came from Kant and was
also published in the *Berlinische Monatsschrift*. In an often-quoted sentence,
Kant defined Enlightenment as 'mankind's exit from its self-incurred
immaturity'. Even more celebrated is his statement: '*Sapere aude!* Have the
courage to use your *own* understanding! is thus the motto of Enlightenment.'
Kant was referring, of course, to the long-standing tradition of thinking for
oneself as the criterion of an enlightened person. The motto 'dare to know'

---

14  Johann Friedrich Zöllner, 'Ist es rathsam, das Ehebündniß nicht ferner durch die Religion
    zu sanciren?', *Berlinische Monatsschrift* 2 (1783), 516.

(*sapere aude*) also had a long tradition. Originally formulated by the ancient Roman poet Horace, it was widely used in the eighteenth century. Kant emphasized that the Enlightenment was not an accomplished fact, but an ongoing process. By tying the present state of Enlightenment ('Do we live in an enlightened age?') to 'the century of Frederick', two years before the king's death, Kant indicated that he was aware of the dependence of this process on the political circumstances of the day.[15]

The celebrity of Kant's essay 'What is Enlightenment?' has obscured the fact, especially outside Germany, that it was part of a larger, widespread discussion. Zöllner had posed the question in the context of the debates of the Wednesday Club, closely associated with the *Berlinische Monatsschrift*. It published some of the papers that grew out of their discussions, such as those on the preparation for a new Prussian law code by Klein and Svarez, and Zöllner's essay on the expediency of civil marriages. Furthermore, Zöllner's question (What is Enlightenment?) immediately became the topic of another discussion in the club. It resulted in the publication of an essay by Mendelssohn in the *Berlinische Monatsschrift* in September 1784.

Mendelssohn's answer was at least as interesting as Kant's because it addressed the cultural dimensions of Enlightenment and clearly formulated its limits. 'Education (*Bildung*), culture and enlightenment', Mendelssohn declared, 'are modifications of social life.' Education, he explained, was composed of culture and enlightenment. Culture was more oriented toward practical matters and was attained through social intercourse and the arts, whereas enlightenment seemed to him more related to theoretical matters – knowledge and reflection about matters of human life. Mendelssohn continued to distinguish between people as human beings and people as citizens in society – that is, between the destiny of humans as human beings, who need only enlightenment, and that of humans as citizens who need both culture and enlightenment. Unfortunately, he noted, there were situations where these two qualities collided: 'Certain truths that are useful to humans, as human beings, can at times be harmful to them as citizens.' It could be, for instance, that some truths 'may not be disseminated without destroying prevailing religious and moral tenets'. In such cases, Mendelssohn was as adamant as Zöllner and his views on civic marriages; he did not want Enlightenment to proceed. 'Here philosophy lays its hand on its mouth! Here necessity may prescribe laws, or rather forge the fetters, that are applied to humankind, to force them down, and hold them under the yoke!' For Mendelssohn, the concerns of the citizen were more important than

---

15  Immanuel Kant, 'Beantwortung der Frage: Was ist Aufklärung?', *Berlinische Monatsschrift* 4 (1784), 481–95. English translation in Schmidt, *What is Enlightenment?*, pp. 58–64.

those of the human being, and even when this maxim was abused, 'the virtue-loving bearer of enlightenment will proceed with prudence and discretion and endure prejudice rather than drive away the truth that is so closely intertwined with it'.[16]

More than Kant, Mendelssohn realized that the process of Enlightenment took place in a social, public context. Kant argued from the perspective of the fundamental equality of all human beings; from his Jewish perspective, Mendelssohn had a better eye for the diversity of social and national developments to which the process of Enlightenment is and must be subjected. For Mendelssohn, an enlightened person recognized the limits of Enlightenment. This answer comes as no surprise when one considers the nature of the discussions which took place among the learned but practical members of the Wednesday Club. But both answers – from Kant and Mendelssohn – to Zöllner's question were products of the Prussian Enlightenment. One should not forget that a month before Kant's essay 'What is Enlightenment?' he published another entitled 'Idea of a Universal History from a Cosmopolitan Point of View', in which he integrated his individualist human being in a society that the individualist could not do without. For this antagonistic relationship between individual and society, Kant coined the memorable expression 'unsocial sociability' (*ungesellige Geselligkeit*).[17]

One result of the debate that took place during the 1780s and 1790s was the inflationary use of the term 'enlightenment'; each author played off his own 'true enlightenment' against the supposedly incorrect version of his opponents. Instead of leading to greater clarification, the debate led to more confusion, or at most, considering the nearly exclusive focus on Kant's essay until today, to a lopsided intellectual view of what enlightenment was. The challenge of Kant's Critical philosophy also attracted increasing attention, especially from a younger generation. Compared to this philosophical mountain whose dimensions would be explored with great cerebral satisfaction, all other Enlightenment philosophy seemed tame and superficial, or at best only preparatory to the Kantian pinnacle. Over time, the Prussian-German Enlightenment was reduced to the mere context of Kantian philosophy, at the cost of its many other intellectual and socio-cultural aspects.

In addition to this uneven outcome, the Prussian Enlightenment also showed more tangible results. One major legacy was the implementation of

---

16  Moses Mendelssohn, 'Über die Frage: Was heißt aufklären', *Berlinische Monatsschrift* 4 (1784), 193–200. English translation with minor alterations from Schmidt, *What is Enlightenment?*, pp. 53–7.

17  Kant, 'Idee zu einer allgemeinen Geschichte in weltbürgerlicher Absicht', *Berlinische Monatsschrift* 4 (1784), 392.

legal reform, even if only in mitigated form, with the proclamation of the new civil code of 1794 (*Allgemeines Landrecht für die Preußischen Staaten*) which remained in force until 1900. Its 'Preamble' declared the equality of all citizens before the law. Moreover, it guaranteed the independence of the judiciary from royal intervention, even though it also considerably restricted the judge's freedom to interpret the law. Other Enlightenment ideals were realized during the Prussian Reform Era with the establishment of Berlin University in 1810 as the high point of a general educational reform, and the emancipation of the Jews in 1812. Most importantly, however, the Enlightenment produced a growing literate public consisting of subjects who thought of themselves as personally endowed with social values and inalienable human rights that not even the state could violate. Their belief in Enlightenment notions of toleration and of intellectually and morally mature citizens has profoundly shaped modern society and, having survived even the darkest days of the twentieth century, continues to guide modern life.

# PART TWO

# The rural and urban environment

CHAPTER FIVE

# The transformation of the rural economy in East Elbian Prussia, 1750–1830

EDGAR MELTON

Around the middle of the eighteenth century, the agrarian economy in East Elbian Prussia, based on the market-oriented manorial system known as *Gutsherrschaft*, entered a long period of crisis culminating in reforms (1807–21) that dismantled the old agrarian order. Ironically, these reforms, while emancipating the peasantry from the most onerous obligations they had owed their noble landlords, also helped consolidate a new agrarian system in which the estate-owning nobility had far more economic power than they had enjoyed under the old system of *Gutsherrschaft*. The present chapter will try to account for this seeming paradox, while exploring the agrarian transformation in the five major East Elbian provinces: Brandenburg, Pomerania, the Neumark, East Prussia, and Silesia. Discussion will focus primarily on the system of *Gutsherrschaft*, the reasons for its crisis, and the agrarian reforms of the early nineteenth century. We will end with a brief overview of the new agrarian economy that consolidated itself in the period 1830–50.

## Prussian *Gutsherrschaft* around 1750

Despite regional and local variants in its practice and severity, *Gutsherrschaft* as an economic system had two basic characteristics.[1] It was, first of all, a

---

1 There is a huge literature on East Elbian *Gutsherrschaft*, for which the following works provide excellent starting-points: Heinrich Kaak, *Die Gutsherrschaft. Theoriegeschichtliche Untersuchungen zum Agrarwesen im ostelbischen Raum* (Berlin, 1991); Hartmut Harnisch, 'Probleme einer Periodisierung und regionaler Typisierung der Gutsherrschaft im mitteleuropäischen Raum', *Jahrbuch für Geschichte des Feudalismus* 9 (1985), 251–74; Christoph Schmidt, *Leibeigenschaft im Ostseeraum. Versuch einer Typologie* (Cologne, 1997).

market-oriented estate agriculture that provided the landed elite – both nobility and crown – with a major source of its income. The system's defining economic element, however, was its dependence on agricultural labour provided 'free' by the landowners' peasants, who were bound to their lords in varying degrees of unfreedom. In addition, noble landowners had the right (frequently exercised) to require the adolescent sons and daughters of their peasants to work for them as servants (at low fixed wages) for 3–5 years (*Gesindezwangsdienst*). It is also important to emphasize at this point that *Gutsherrschaft* was much more than an economic system; indeed, it embraced the totality of relations between the lord and his rural tenants. The latter not only owed the lord rents and dues, but were also subject to his legal jurisdiction and policing authority.

*Gutsherrschaft* first appeared in Prussia in the sixteenth century, and had consolidated itself by 1620. Recurrent demographic crises in the middle and late seventeenth century, combined with fundamental changes in the population structure, had, however, altered the system irrevocably, even if the changes did not become evident until much later. Here we will look at the social and economic organization of *Gutsherrschaft* in Prussia.

In the late eighteenth century, there were approximately 12,000 landed estates in East Elbian Prussia. Although most of these estates were organized on the basis of *Gutsherrschaft*, their size varied greatly. Robert Stein, author of a classic study on East Prussia, was able to determine the landholdings of most noble estate owners in that province around 1800, and divided them into three categories: petty (less than 500 acres), middling (500–2,500 acres) and large landowners (more than 2,500 acres). According to these criteria, 25 per cent of the estate owners were petty, 50 per cent belonged to the middling category, and another 25 per cent qualified as large landowners.[2] Based on less detailed evidence for the other East Elbian provinces, petty estate owners were apparently most numerous in Pomerania, middling estate owners dominated in Brandenburg, and Silesia had most of the great landowners.

Size was important, but for most estate owners, wealth and income depended primarily on the number of peasant and smallholding tenants, since this determined the total labour services and rents at the lord's disposal. Boitzenburg, the largest estate complex in Brandenburg, had 189 farmsteads in 1730, and Angerapp, one of the largest estate complexes in East Prussia, had 250 farmsteads in 1732.[3] Much more typical, however,

---

2 Robert Stein, *Die Umwandlung der Agrarverfassung Ostpreußens durch die Reform des neunzehnten Jahrhunderts*, 3 vols (Jena-Königsberg, 1918–34); vol. 1: *Die ländliche Verfassung Ostpreußens am Ende des achtzehnten Jahrhunderts* (Jena, 1918), p. 247.

3 Hartmut Harnisch, *Die Herrschaft Boitzenburg* (Weimar, 1968), p. 197; Karl Böhme, *Gutsherrlich-bäuerliche Verhältnisse in Ostpreußen während der Reformzeit von 1770 bis 1830* (Leipzig, 1902), p. 18.

was the estate belonging to Karl von Benekendorff in the Neumark, which had only 18 peasant farmsteads.[4]

What kind of labour services did the peasants provide their seigneurs? If the tenant were a 'full peasant', that is, he held a farmstead of at least one hide (40 acres), he normally owed labour services in the form of *Spanndienst*, which meant he had to send 1–2 workers (2–3 during the harvest) plus a team (*Gespann*) of oxen or horses (depending on the task). Sometimes a full peasant also had to provide additional labour services that did not require use of a draught team (*Handdienst*). Beyond these exactions, the full peasant also had to use his wagon and horses to transport a specified amount of the lord's grain or wood to market (*cartage*). In addition to the full peasants, however, most estates also had tenants with smaller holdings. The small-holders (sometimes known as cottagers) made up a diverse group that defies easy definition simply because it spanned a socio-economic spectrum that included semi-landless farm workers at the bottom, and peasants at the top. In some regions, a farmstead of 40 acres qualified as a smallholding, but most smallholders had considerably less, and many had only a few acres. They usually owed *Fußdienst* or *Handdienst*, which meant providing a worker (two during the harvest), but rarely ox or horse teams.

Because he supplied not only the labour, but also (in most cases) the teams required for ploughing, harrowing and harvesting, the full peasant occupied a key position within *Gutsherrschaft*. Nevertheless, the full peasant rarely had the time or the labour capacity to perform these services himself. A typical peasant farmstead of two hides (80 acres) had roughly 40 acres under cultivation at any one time, which was close to the maximum that a family could cultivate with its own labour. Given these demands on its labour, the peasant family did not personally perform labour services, but instead sent hired hands. This meant keeping at least two – and often more – hired workers, who usually lived and ate under the peasant's roof. These hired hands – and the extra horse or ox teams that the peasant also had to keep – were thus major expenses, but they were usually necessary, since they freed the peasant and his family for work on their own farmstead. The number of farm workers and extra teams the peasant had to maintain depended, of course, on the labour services he had to provide, and this varied greatly, according to a number of factors: conditions set by the estate owner, regional and local practices, and the legal status of the peasants. In most of Brandenburg and the Neumark, for example, a full peasant had to provide from two to five days per week of *Spanndienst*, while a smallholder might supply three or

---

4  *Berliner Beyträge zu Landwirtschaftswissenschaft*, 8 vols (Berlin, 1774–91), i, pp. 153–66. Hereafter cited as *Berliner Beyträge*.

more days per week of *Handdienst* and *Fußdienst*. There were, however, regions – Pomerania, the Uckermark (north-eastern Brandenburg) and the south-western part of East Prussia (*Oberland*) – where landlords demanded unlimited (*ungemessene*) labour services that in practice could reach 6–7 days per week.

Here, the peasant's legal status played an important role in determining his labour services. In East Elbian Prussia, the majority of peasants owned their lands outright, or held them as hereditary leaseholds (*Erbpächter*). In such cases, the owners could bequeath or sell their properties without seigneurial permission. Such peasant proprietors were most numerous in the German regions of Silesia (where they made up the vast majority of peasants and smallholders), but they were also numerous in western Brandenburg, the southern districts of the Neumark and parts of East Prussia.[5] Most peasants who owned their lands still had to provide labour services, however.

*Laßbauern*, or 'ordinary peasants', made up the second-largest legal category. Ordinary peasants did not own their lands outright, and even if (as was often the case) the ordinary peasant had hereditary tenure, he did not have full disposition over his farmstead and could not, for example, sell it without seigneurial permission. In practice, most ordinary peasants were probably able to pass on their farmsteads to one of their sons, but unless the peasant could prove hereditary tenure, the right to bequeath the farmstead depended on the will of the seigneur. The ordinary peasant could also enter into contracts, and was free to move, even against the Junker's will, once he had found a suitable tenant to take over his farmstead.

The group with the lowest legal status (and often the highest labour dues) was the serfs (*Leibeigene*), who were subject to unlimited labour services. Serfdom was generally confined to two regions, Pomerania and the neighbouring Uckermark (north-eastern Brandenburg), but also existed in the Polish regions of Upper Silesia, East Prussia and the Neumark. A serf could not of his own will leave his farmstead, nor could he sell it, although some serfs apparently had hereditary tenure. The most onerous aspect of serfdom, however, was the Junker's claim to unlimited labour services whenever and however the lord ordered, even daily, and with as many ox and horse teams as the lord had provided, all at his (the peasant's) own expense.[6]

At the same time, however, legal practices, drawing on the decisions and views of the Leiden-trained Pomeranian jurist David Mevius (1609–1670), may have exerted a levelling influence on the distinctions between serf and

---

5   George-Friedrich Knapp, *Die Bauernbefreiung und der Ursprung der Landarbeiter in den älteren Theilen Preußens*, 2 vols (Munich, 1927), i, pp. 202ff.

6   Karl von Benekendorff, *Oeconomia forensis oder kurzer Inbegriff derjenigen landwirtschaftlichen Wahrheiten, welchen allen, sowohl hohen als niedrigen Gerichts-Personen zu wissen nötig*, 8 vols (Berlin, 1775–84), i, p. 213. Cited hereafter as *Oeconomia forensis*.

ordinary peasant. In 1645, Mevius, a jurist and professor of law at the University of Greifswald, published a study of peasant servitude based on his own experiences judging legal disputes between lord and peasant in Pomerania. According to Mevius, an estate owner had no right to demand labour services that were out of line with local practices, or that were so heavy as to endanger the health or economic well-being of his peasants.[7] That Mevius's work regularly reappeared in new editions (the last edition appeared in 1773) suggests that it continued to provide Prussian jurists with basic precedents for judging disputes between peasants and their lords.

Another factor that helped to level differences between serfs and common peasants was the demographic crisis of the mid- and late seventeenth century, which had left thousands of farmsteads in Brandenburg-Prussia deserted, and forced noble landowners to offer favourable conditions (stipulated in written contracts) in order to induce prospective tenants to take over empty farms. If the tenant accepted a farmstead that the Junker had stocked with livestock and equipment at his own expense, he often had to agree to hereditary serfdom. In practice, however, some eighteenth-century landowners eschewed unlimited services from their serfs, probably because such demands, by provoking peasant flight, ran counter to their own interests.[8] At the same time, peasants with their own inventories could demand much better contracts, usually short-term leaseholds that clearly recognized their free status and carried limited labour services.[9]

In many regions of East Elbia, including West and East Prussia, Pomerania and the Uckermark, an increasing number of peasants held their farmsteads as leaseholds. There were two types of leaseholds – hereditary (*Erbpacht*) and term (*Zeitpacht*) – and under certain conditions (rising agricultural prices or rising demand for land), leaseholds could be advantageous to the seigneur because he could get higher rents. From the peasant's standpoint, the advantage lay in the contractual nature of the arrangement: the peasant negotiated a lease under terms he found acceptable, and even if (as was often the case) he agreed to some labour services, he retained his freedom and, once the lease expired, was free to leave or negotiate better terms. Once leaseholding took root, it seems to have spread, replacing more traditional arrangements, and term leases often developed into hereditary leaseholds.[10]

---

7 [David Mevius], *Ein kurtzes Bedencken über die Fragen so von dem Zustand, Abforderung und verwidertes Abfolge des Bauers-Leute, zu welchen jemand zuspruch zu haben vermeinet, bei jetzigen Zeiten* (Stettin, 1733), pp. 92–4.

8 Lieselott Enders, 'Bauern und Feudalherrschaft in der Uckermark im absolutischen Staat', *Jahrbuch für Geschichte des Feudalismus* 13 (1989), 270.

9 *Oeconomia forensis*, v, p. 234.

10 Stein, *Die ländliche Verfassung*, pp. 274–7.

In addition to the factors noted above, we should also remember that *Gutsherrschaft* was not a system of direct exploitation, as under Russian serfdom, where the peasant personally performed labour services for the seigneur. It was, rather, a system that Jan Peters has succinctly characterized as 'mediated exploitation', since it was not the peasant, but rather his hired hands who bore the physical burdens of labour services.[11] Most of the labour on which *Gutsherrschaft* depended was thus mediated through the peasant farmstead, which therefore stood between the estate owner and his labour force. Since this limited seigneurial control over the workforce, it was the neuralgic point in the entire system, and in the second half of the eighteenth century, it would force *Gutsherrschaft* into a crisis that could be resolved only by removing the peasant farmstead from its role in the system.

## Prussian *Gutsherrschaft* in crisis, 1750–1807

To locate the crisis of *Gutsherrschaft* in the second half of the eighteenth century may seem somewhat arbitrary, since the first signs of this crisis had already appeared in the late seventeenth and early eighteenth centuries, when landlords found it difficult to resettle their deserted farmsteads with tenants willing to bear the heavy labour services they demanded. The crisis did not, however, emerge in its fullest dimensions until the late eighteenth century, when the economic losses of the Seven Years' War, accompanied by high grain prices, brought the failings of *Gutsherrschaft* into much sharper relief. In the period 1763–1806, grain prices doubled, and Junker estate owners, hard-pressed for cash and eager to take advantage of the price upturn, pressed their peasants for more labour services. Their peasants reacted with various strategies of resistance that made the limits of the system clear, at least to many estate owners, and encouraged them to look for some solution to the problem.

In this section, we will view the crisis of *Gutsherrschaft* through the eyes of a perceptive and educated estate owner who experienced it first hand and tried to explain it to his fellow Junkers. One of the most prolific writers in late eighteenth-century Prussia – his published writings on Prussian agriculture and rural life include nineteen thick volumes – Karl von Benekendorff (1713–1783) nevertheless remains a neglected figure. Born into a noble

---

11  Jan Peters, 'Ostelbische Landarmut: Sozialökonomisches über landarme und landlose Agrarproduzenten im Spätfeudalismus', *Jahrbuch für Wirtschaftsgeschichte* 3 (1967), 285.

family with estates in the Neumark, Benekendorff studied at the University of Halle before entering Prussian civil service. As a protégé of Samuel von Cocceji, the Lord Chancellor, Benekendorff became president of the highest court in Silesia, *der höchste schlesische Gerichtshof*, where he proved an incisive and energetic jurist, streamlining legal procedures and cutting by half the number of unresolved cases. Unfortunately, his salary of 2,000 Reichsthalers seems not to have sufficed for his expenses, and he began dipping into state funds. Convicted of embezzlement in 1752, he spent seven years in prison and then returned to the Neumark, where he devoted himself to his estate and to publishing a deluge of works on East Elbian agriculture.

Benekendorff described in great detail the fundamental problems of Prussian *Gutsherrschaft*, and although it is not clear whether Benekendorff's writings had any influence at all on his fellow Junkers, or on the course of the agrarian reforms, the agrarian system that replaced *Gutsherrschaft* after the reforms embodied many of the changes for which he had argued fifty years earlier.

Benekendorff understood that the fundamental problem of *Gutsherrschaft* lay in the adversarial relationship between the estate owner and his peasants. The peasant was caught between two fundamental obligations: keeping his landlord satisfied, on the one hand, and maintaining his farm, on the other. The estate owner, however, was also trapped as long as he depended on the workers provided by his peasants, since pushing the peasants for more or better work had the effect of further poisoning the lord/peasant relationship. According to Benekendorff, a typical peasant with two hides (85 acres) could generally provide only 2–3 days per week of labour services without damaging his own household economy. Yet, as Benekendorff frequently pointed out, many landlords routinely undermined their peasants' economic well-being by demanding more. In the regions dominated by serfdom (mainly Pomerania and the Uckermark), where labour services were in theory unlimited, landlords were especially guilty of imposing ruinous labour services on their peasants. In Pomerania, Benekendorff had himself seen estates where the peasants had to provide daily labour services that included a draught team and 2–3 workers, in addition to working their own farms. There, despite large farmsteads with fertile soil, the peasants were usually impoverished, and often had to ask their seigneurs for help.[12]

According to Benekendorff, labour services were also a problem on estates where the peasants owed only moderate labour dues. The peasant was the worker's employer, providing him with room, board and livelihood,

---

12  *Oeconomia forensis*, v, pp. 52, 486, 493–506.

and the worker's loyalty was to him and not to the lord. Thus, when the farmhand had to divide his activities between the Junker's manor and his employer's farmstead, he naturally devoted most of his energy to the latter. As Benekendorff pointed out, every landowner knew how poorly the fields were ploughed by labour services, especially with hard soil, and attempts to supervise were in vain, since effective supervision would require one overseer for every peasant: 'As soon as the ploughman sees the lord or his overseer approaching from a distance, he tightens up the plough. The lord, or his steward, thus finds nothing to criticize, since the ploughman is ploughing the furrows in their presence. But as soon as they have turned their backs, he loosens the plough, which manages only to scrape the soil, rather than ploughing it thoroughly . . . So skilful is he at disguising his shoddy ploughing, that a superficial inspection cannot reveal it.'[13]

Confronted with shoddy labour services, the seigneur could, of course, punish the negligent worker, but Benekendorff cautioned against incarceration, and especially against excessive corporal punishment. Once, while visiting a friend's estate, he had shuddered with horror watching an overseer beat a peasant's hired hand mercilessly for some minor infraction. This, noted Benekendorff, was wanton brutality; several smart blows with a whip would have sufficed. But force also had its limits, and Benekendorff held that 'the constant punishment of disobedient subjects is one of the worst evils committed by landowners', especially since the bitterness and anger arising from constant conflicts with 'malicious and recalcitrant villagers' poisoned the seigneur's existence and even shortened his life.[14]

The peasants, moreover, had strategies that were often effective counters to labour service demands they found excessive or arbitrary. When, in 1723, a Prussian official named Christian Busse leased the crown estate Quilitz-Friedland in the Neumark, the peasants were providing labour dues of only two days per week, but Busse, on the basis of manorial documents, argued that the peasants were liable to unlimited labour services and demanded three, rather than two days per week. The peasants reacted with comic but effective responses, sending as workers military conscripts from a local detachment, whose military status exempted them from taking orders from the seigneur. In addition, when forced to cart hay and manure, the peasants drove their wagons recklessly, thus spilling out most of the contents before they reached their destination. Required to work the manorial fields, the peasants retaliated by sending weak draught teams and defective implements. The peasants might also send adolescent workers

---

13 *Berliner Beyträge*, i, p. 149.
14 *Oeconomia forensis*, v, pp. 34, 55.

who lacked experience or physical strength, or they even hired lazy or incompetent workers, since they could get them at the lowest possible wages.[15] Nevertheless, noted Benekendorff, the landowner who demanded daily labour services could hardly expect the peasant to send good workers. The peasant with daily labour services knew that his hired hands would be working almost exclusively for the Junker, and not on his own farmstead, and therefore hired the cheapest workers, not caring that they were incompetent and lazy, since it was the Junker's economy and not the peasant's that would suffer.[16]

Such conflicts could, at worst, provoke a lawsuit that might then trigger a rash of lawsuits on neighbouring estates. According to Benekendorff, many rural communities would have never thought of going to law against their seigneur if they hadn't been encouraged by the example of a neighbouring community that had won a case against its estate owner.[17] Benekendorff, who as a jurist had heard many cases in Silesia, also reminded his readers that peasant litigants could easily shock judges by their impoverished appearance, thus predisposing them to rule against the seigneur. In any case, he continued, most judges knew very little about the rural economy, and often simply assumed that a decision for the peasants was less damaging to the interests of the state than a decision for the landlord.[18]

Benekendorff may have exaggerated the readiness of courts to decide against estate owners, but there is no doubt that peasant resistance to labour services became increasingly widespread in the second half of the eighteenth century. Faced with this, jurists tried to avoid one-sided decisions, and instead sought to restore harmony through compromise decisions that provided some satisfaction to both sides and were thus acceptable to both parties. This policy, sensible though it was, may have dampened conflicts, but since it could not eliminate the basis of the problem (labour services), the conflicts and lawsuits continued.

In 1784, reacting to 'frequent complaints and quarrels between lords and peasants over labour services', Frederick the Great ordered the administration in East Prussia to establish *Urbarien* (1784). In these *Urbarien* (agreements

---

15   Heinrich Kaak, 'Vermittelte, selbstätige und maternale Herrschaft. Formen gutsherrlicher Durchsetzung, Behauptung und Gestaltung in Quilitz-Friedland (Lebus-Oberbarnim) im 18. Jahrhundert', in Jan Peters (ed.), *Konflikt und Kontrolle in Gutsherrschaftsgesellschaften* (Göttingen, 1995), pp. 66ff.

16   *Oeconomia forensis*, v, pp. 34–62.

17   Karl von Benekendorff, *Grab der Chikane worinn: Daß häufige Prozesse das größeste Übel eines Staats sind, gezeiget die wahren Quellen woraus sie ursprünglich enstehen . . .*, 3 vols (Berlin, 1781–85), i, p. 692.

18   *Oeconomia forensis*, v, p. 469.

between the lord and his peasants over mutual obligations), 'everything should be written out so clearly that both parties know exactly what is required of them . . . and therefore no further lawsuits or disagreements can take place between them'.[19] Frederick's initiative foundered on the resistance of the East Prussian nobility, but *Urbarien* were in any case an inadequate solution to the problem, since the mutual obligations between a lord and his peasants were simply too complex to regulate. Lord–peasant relations were, as Benekendorff put it, a Gordian knot that could be cut, but never untied. Again, however, this was only a part of the larger problem, and thus, as Benekendorff wrote, 'as long as our entire rural economy rests merely on compulsory labour dues, it [will remain] sick and puny'.[20]

## Resolving the crisis of *Gutsherrschaft*

Benekendorff believed that the estate owner could overcome the crisis only by shifting to wage labourers employed directly by the estate owner and thus completely under his control. As early as the sixteenth century, Prussian seigneurs had used hired labourers to supplement the workers provided by their peasants, since the labour services of the latter had rarely covered the total labour needs of the estate. These hired labourers were sometimes landless agricultural proletarians, but were often smallholders, since they received, as part of their wages, a small plot of land (1–2 acres), seed corn, and the right to graze a cow on manorial lands. By the mid-eighteenth century, landless and semi-landless farm workers may have accounted for two thirds of the rural population.

Benekendorff knew very well that estate owners were already using their own hired labourers, but, he argued, they weren't using enough of them, and they weren't employing them in the most advantageous manner. Benekendorff took as his model the Silesian *Dreschgärtner*, who combined characteristics of both the landless farm worker and the smallholder. Like the smallholder, the *Dreschgärtner* had land (normally less than two acres), a cow, and usually kept a maidservant. Like the smallholder, he and his wife had to work on the seigneur's estate (often daily), but for this work they received wages in cash or kind (including firewood, grazing rights, etc.). Most of the income earned by the *Dreschgärtner* and his wife came from

---

19  Stein, *Die ländliche Verfassung*, p. 354.
20  *Berliner Beyträge*, ii, p. 165.

harvesting and threshing. They received a tenth of the seigneurial grain they harvested, plus a share of what they threshed (every fifteenth bushel). This, combined with income from their plot of land (often sown with flax), and the wages they received, was more than enough for their subsistence needs.[21]

According to Benekendorff, the advantage of the Silesian system was that it rested less on compulsion than on the worker's self-interest. Thus, while the landowner who depended on labour services had to entrust his agriculture to workers who had no vested interest in it, the Silesian *Dreschgärtner* shared in the profits and losses of his seigneur, thus encouraging him to work as hard and conscientiously as possible.[22] Benekendorff had adapted the Silesian system on his own estate in the Neumark, abolishing labour services and replacing them with rent in kind, and working his estate entirely with wage labourers who presumably received wages and incentives similar to the Silesian *Dreschgärtner*. Benekendorff had also decreased his arable land by nearly half, leasing the rest out. By thus intensifying his cultivation, and switching entirely to (more productive) wage labour, Benekendorff claimed to have increased his yearly income from 1,500 to 2,400 thalers.[23]

In emulating the Silesian system, Benekendorff was being wise after the event, since many estate owners had already grasped the fundamental solution to the problem of *Gutsherrschaft*: a wage labour force directly dependent on the seigneur.[24] In East Prussia, where many eighteenth-century estates were worked with hired labour, the seigneurial alcohol monopoly, relatively limited in Brandenburg, may have played a determining role. The monopoly was especially lucrative on the large, populous estates in East Prussia, where estate owners might require their subjects to buy their beer and brandy from them at double the price to be found in the local towns. Moreover, a bushel of barley, brewed on the estate and then sold there, might bring the

---

21   For a detailed description of the Silesian *Dreschgärtner*, Johann Ziekursch, *Hundert Jahre schlesischer Agrargeschichte von Hubertusburger Frieden bis zum Abschluß der Bauernbefreiung* (Breslau, 1915), pp. 89–92.

22   [Karl von Benekendorff], *Vergleichung der märkischen und pommerschen Landwirtschaftsarten mit der schlesischen von einem unparteischen Wirtschaftsfreunde welcher beides in Schlesien und der Mark Güter besessen* (Halle, 1786), pp. 122–8. More than a century later, in 1892, Max Weber would make many of the same observations concerning the threshers working on East Elbian estates. See Max Weber, *Die Lage der Landarbeiter im Ostelbischen Deutschland*, in M. Weber, *Gesamtausgabe* (Tübingen, 1985–), Section I, vol. 3/1, pp. 71–128.

23   *Berliner Beyträge*, i, pp. 153ff.

24   [H. A. von Borcke], *H. A. Grafen von Borcke Beschreibung der stargordischen Wirtschaft in Hinterpommern nebst G. M. L. von Wedells Vorlesung in der patriotischen Gesellschaft zu Breslau . . .* (Berlin, 1783), pp. 21ff.

seigneur a profit 300 per cent higher than shipping the grain to a market and selling it there.[25] The large East Prussian estate of Reichertswalde, belonging to the Dohna family, exemplifies the advantages gained from a seigneurial economy based on cash rents and the alcohol monopoly. In the early eighteenth century, the estate had 95 peasant farmsteads and more than 17,000 acres of land. The owner, Christoph Friedrich von Dohna, freed his peasants from much of their labour services in exchange for high cash rents. The peasants continued to provide some labour services for the relatively small seigneurial demesne (roughly 1,600 acres) but much of the work was done by wage labourers hired directly by the estate. The estate also purchased additional grain (presumably barley) from the peasants. In 1710, cash rents, together with the sale of beer and spirits, accounted for 80 per cent of Dohna's estate revenues.[26] Even seigneurs with estates close to Königsberg, the largest grain market in East Prussia, might earn more from their alcohol monopoly than from the direct sale of grain.[27]

This does not, of course, explain why many other estate owners continued to rely on labour services, instead of commuting them to yearly rents, and thus completely dismantling *Gutsherrschaft* on their estates. The most plausible answer is that, while some estate owners had already shifted entirely to wage labour, most were not ready to take the risk of doing away completely with the labour services their peasants provided. At the same time, however, most estate owners had increased their manorial wage labour force, while decreasing their peasants' labour services in favour of cash rents. Thus, for example, in the East Prussian district of Brandenburg, 42 per cent of the seigneurial peasants were providing moderate or heavy labour services (at least 60 days per year) in 1750. By the 1780s, however, only 22 per cent were providing more than 60 days per year.[28] One finds a similar pattern in some districts of Brandenburg.[29] In short, Prussian estate owners were far less dependent on their peasants' labour services by 1800 than in 1750, and this contributed greatly to the success of the agrarian reforms.

25  *Oeconomia forensis*, i, pp. 43ff.
26  Heide Wunde, 'Aspekte des Gutsherrschaft im Herzogtum und Königreich Preußen im 17. und zu Beginn des 18. Jahrhunderts. Das Beispiel Dohna', in Jan Peters (ed.), *Gutsherrschaftsgesellschaften im europäischen Vergleich* (Berlin, 1997), pp. 228ff.
27  Marion Gräfin Dönhoff, *Enstehung und Bewirtschaftung eines ostdeutschen Großbetriebes. Die Friedrichsteiner Güter von der Ordenzeit bis zur Bauernbefreiung* (Königsberg, 1936), pp. 48ff.
28  Freidrich-Wilhelm Henning, *Dienste und Abgaben der Bauern im 18. Jahrhundert* (Stuttgart 1969), p. 115.
29  Lieselott Enders, 'Individuum und Gesellschaft. Bäuerliche Aktionsräume in der frühneuzeitlichen Mark Brandenburg', in Jan Peters (ed.), *Gesellschaft als soziales Modell. Vergleichende Betrachtungen zur Funktionsweise frühneuzeitlichen Agrargesellschaften* (Historische Zeitschrift 18), pp. 170–1.

# The agrarian reforms, 1807–21

According to traditional periodization, the Prussian reform era began in 1807, but reform legislation had already begun as early as 1763, when Frederick the Great initiated a series of agrarian reforms on crown domains. Although there were crown peasants in all the East Elbian provinces, they were most numerous in East Prussia, where they accounted for 55 per cent of all peasants, and in Brandenburg, where they made up a third of the peasant population. In Silesia and Pomerania, they accounted for less than 10 per cent. Since the early eighteenth century, most of the crown domains had been leased to private farmers from non-noble backgrounds (*Domänenpächter*), who, like noble estate owners, organized their leased domains as *Gutsherrschaften* based in large part on labour services provided by the crown peasants. Thus, while labour services on crown domains in some regions (East Prussia) were relatively mild, general conditions of crown peasants do not seem to have differed qualitatively from those of seigneurial peasants. From 1763 to 1808, however, a series of decrees established hereditary tenure for crown peasants, permitted them to redeem their labour dues through cash payments, and, finally, made it possible for them to become free owners of their farmsteads. Again, these reforms affected only the crown peasants, and the redemption dues placed a crushing burden on many households. Nevertheless, by 1807, the abolition of labour services on crown domains was well under way, with only half of the crown peasants still providing such services.

The reforms that began in 1807 were a response to Napoleon's military defeat of Prussia in 1806. The political collapse that followed had brought to power a ministry led by Baron Karl vom-und-zum Stein (1757–1831), a Westphalian nobleman long in Prussian service. The political crisis gave Stein and his supporters the chance to initiate a reform programme, and while Stein's reform ministry ended in 1808, his successor, Karl August von Hardenberg (1750–1822), furthered the programme, which included freeing the Prussian peasants from seigneurial rents and dues, and securing for them full ownership of their farms.

Legislation began with the October Edict of 1807, which proclaimed that 'after St Martin's Day (11 November) 1810, there will be only free people, as is already the case on the royal domains in all the provinces'. The Edict thus managed to be simultaneously precise and vague. How would the rural population be freed from the rents and dues they owed their seigneurs? Would they receive the lands they held before the reform? Would seigneurs receive compensation for the loss of their feudal rents and obligations? If so, how much compensation and in what form? How would seigneurial lands be disentangled and separated from peasant lands, and how would common lands be divided? The subsequent agrarian legislation (especially 1811, 1816 and 1821) addressed these and other problems.

The reform legislation dealt with two basic groups of peasants and small-holders: those who owned their lands outright and those who did not (serfs, ordinary peasants, term leaseholders). As already noted, most (75–80 per cent) of the peasants and smallholders actually owned their own lands outright, and for this fortunate majority, the terms of the reform (laid out in the Dissolution Ordinance of 1821) were very favourable. Indeed, since the peasants and smallholders in this group already owned their lands, they needed only to apply for 'dissolution' of the rents and dues they owed their seigneurs. Once the peasant applied for dissolution, a cash value was assigned to the rents and labour services he owed, and the peasant could choose to pay this in cash or land (most apparently paid in cash). Initially, only the peasants and the larger smallholders were eligible for dissolution, which excluded a very large group, the Silesian *Dreschgärtner*, most of whom owned only a few acres. This exclusion, however, led to numerous conflicts, and in 1845 the Silesian *Dreschgärtner* also became eligible for dissolution.

The agrarian reforms were far less favourable for the peasants and small-holders (20–25 per cent of the total) who did not own their own lands outright. This group included those who neither owned their own lands, nor had any rights to inherit them (for example, non-hereditary lease-holders); it also included, however, peasants and smallholders who, though they did not own their lands outright, nevertheless enjoyed some sort of hereditary tenure. According to the terms laid out in the Regulation Edict of September 1811 (later amended by the Declaration of 29 May 1816), peasants and smallholders in this group received ownership of their lands, but for this they had to pay their seigneurs a heavy compensation in land or its cash equivalent. The peasant or smallholder who decided to pay in land then had to cede as much as half of his land to his seigneur. He also had to pay the seigneur a sum for the dissolution of rents and labour services he owed. Again, however, this disadvantaged group of peasants and smallholders was a distinct minority and, thanks to the recent (and truly pioneering) work of Hartmut Harnisch, we now know that the reform was quite favourable for the majority of peasants, as well as for many smallholders.[30]

The agrarian reforms required more than fifty years, although most of the reforms had been completed by 1848. In 1800, there were approximately

---

30   Harnisch, *Kapitalistische Agrarreform und industrielle Revolution* (Weimar, 1984), especially pp. 66–101.

400,000 peasant and smallholder households in East Elbian Prussia; by 1848, 90 per cent (360,000) of them had gone through the reforms. Of this number, 20 per cent (70,000 households) had not owned their lands outright and had paid a very high price for their land and freedom. The other 80 per cent (290,000 households) had already owned their lands outright, however, and had simply paid the required sum to dissolve the obligations they owed their seigneurs.

## Results of the reforms

Although the terms of the reforms were quite favourable for the majority of the peasants and larger smallholders, the major beneficiary was the estate-owning nobility, which retained a number of its privileges, including police and legal jurisdiction over the local rural population. More important, the estate owners received more than a million acres of land from their former tenants as compensation, including 85 per cent of all common lands. Estate owners also acquired another 1.5 million acres from the peasants through annexations and buy-outs. Another result of the reforms, the separation of seigneurial holdings from peasant lands, made it much easier for estate owners to replace the old three-field crop rotation with more advanced cropping systems. This did not happen at once, but the separation made it possible.

Despite these gains, many noble landowners foundered in the decades after reform. Most of the Junkers had entered the nineteenth century with their estates heavily mortgaged, and some could not weather the losses incurred during the Napoleonic wars and the agrarian crisis of 1817–26, when grain prices fell drastically. As a result, a third of the landed estates in Pomerania, and half of those in East Prussia, changed hands between 1806 and 1829, mostly because of their owners' bankruptcy. The reforms had, moreover, removed any social restrictions on ownership of landed property, and the estates of bankrupt nobles often passed into bourgeois hands. We should not necessarily assume, however, that these changes marked a decline of the Prussian nobility. A recent study of the landholding patterns of 83 Junker families from the late eighteenth through the early twentieth centuries shows that the agrarian reforms brought the beginnings of a functional specialization within the nobility, a separation between those who had no interest in farming and those who became professional farmers. While the former increasingly sold their estates and devoted themselves entirely to military or bureaucratic careers, the latter accumulated increasing amounts of land. In short, fewer Junkers retained their ties to the land, but those who stayed on the land, did so on a larger and more successful scale.[31] Moreover, for those who weathered the credit and agrarian crises, there was generally smoother sailing after 1827. True, estates were much more expensive to operate, since they now depended entirely on wage labour, but the evidence suggests that estates also yielded increasing incomes after 1830, if only because grain prices were higher and estate owners now had more land. Much greater profits would come after 1850 and were linked with fundamental infrastructural improvements that included improved cropping systems, higher-per-acre labour inputs and the introduction of rail transport.

The agrarian crisis also hit part of the peasantry and smallholders very hard. Those who had gone into debt to avoid ceding part of their lands were especially vulnerable, and some were forced to sell out. Those who had compensated their seigneurs with land, rather than cash, were generally better off, since their farmsteads, though now smaller, were not burdened by monetary obligations. Altogether, more than 10 per cent of peasant and smallholder farms disappeared as the result either of the agrarian reforms or of the agrarian crisis of the 1820s. At the same time, however, much new land was brought under cultivation, and new farmsteads were created, so that the number of new farms exceeded those lost. Many peasants, moreover, compensated for the loss of land by intensifying their agricultural operations, harvesting as much as before, even though their farmsteads were only half their previous size.

Throughout most of East Elbian Prussia, the conditions of farm workers seem to have changed little, at least on the surface. The farm worker remained a hybrid combination of smallholder and wage labourer, who still received much of his wages in kind. In East Prussia, a *Dreschgärtner* and his wife each worked full-time for their employer from ploughing through harvest, and part-time during the remaining months. For this they received a dwelling and garden plot, firewood, fodder, grazing rights, a food ration, and every tenth bushel of grain they threshed. In addition, they received cash wages that accounted for about 60 per cent of their total income.

Wages for farm workers varied considerably, but it is possible to discern some general patterns. Wages increased rapidly in the second decade of the nineteenth century, then fell in the 1820s, followed by a gradual increase of only 16 per cent during the period 1830–50.[32] We can follow this wage

---

31 See the fascinating article by Ilona Buchsteiner, 'Adel und Bodeneigentum – Wandlungen im 19. Jahrhundert', in Wolfgang Neugebauer and Ralf Pröve (eds), *Agrarische Verfassung und politische Struktur. Studien zur Gesellschaftsgeschichte Preußens 1700–1918* (Berlin, 1998), pp. 37–63.

32 Anna Neumann, *Die Bewegung der Löhne der ländlichen 'freien'; Arbeiter im Zusammenhang mit der gesamtwirtschaftlichen Entwicklung in Königreich Preußen vom Ausgang des 18. Jahrhunderts bis 1850* (Berlin, 1911), pp. 150, 189, 207.

trend in much greater detail on the well-documented estate of Kohlo, in the region between Brandenburg and Lower Silesia, where real wages (both in cash and in kind) grew by 15 per cent in the period 1826–40.

Wage statistics, useful as they are, tell us little, however, about the experience of being a farm worker, especially the more onerous aspects of the farm worker's life: the utter dependency on an employer's caprice, having to live always at his beck and call, and the unremitting physical demands of pre-industrial agriculture. These conditions may have weighed especially hard on female labourers, who also had to function as wives in patriarchal households. In any case, when a rail line was built in the 1850s linking Kohlo to Berlin, it was above all the young women who rushed to take advantage of the chances for employment in Berlin. As one contemporary wrote of Kohlo and its region:

> Once the railroad created better communications with Berlin, the city gradually drained off the supply of farm workers, especially women. What began as a trickle has become a terrible flood, creating a severe shortage of female [agricultural] workers. . . . [The landowners' offer] of better wages, better food and less work has not sufficed to stem the flow of girls to Berlin. The lure of the city has reached such proportions that a country girl now considers it humiliating to work on an estate as a milkmaid.[33]

## Conclusion

Summarizing the political accomplishments of the Prussian nobility in the early nineteenth century, Robert Berdahl writes that: 'In the years that separated the agrarian reforms from the revolution of 1848, the Prussian nobility established and consolidated the modern basis for the political power that it would exercise at least until the end of the Second Empire in 1918.'[34] A similar assessment applies to the economic power of the noble landowners. At the beginning of our period, around 1750, the Prussian agrarian economy was dominated by *Gutsherrschaft*, an estate agriculture that relied mainly on labour provided by its peasant farmsteads. By the late eighteenth century, the problems inherent in the system had reached crisis proportions, leading to escalating conflicts between lord and peasant, and undermining the estate owners' control over their labour force. By the 1830s, the landed

---

33  Hanns Seidler, *Die wirtschaftliche Entwicklung des Gutes Kohlo (Niederlausitz) seit 1825 mit besonderer Berücksichtigung der Arbeiter- und Lohnverhältnisse* (Leipzig, 1927), pp. 61, 109ff.

34  Robert Berdahl, *The Politics of the Prussian Nobility – The Development of a Conservative Ideology, 1770–1848* (Princeton, NJ, 1988), p. 374.

estate and the peasant farmstead were still there, but the connection between the two – the peasant's role as provider of labour to the landed estate – had been completely severed. In its place stood a growing population of wage labourers employed directly by the estate owner and dependent on his will and patronage.

This transformation left many individual estate owners behind, but as a ruling elite, the landed nobility emerged greatly strengthened from this period of crisis and reform. The Junkers' success lay partly in their ability to adapt to new social conditions in the late eighteenth century. Faced with their peasants' increasing resistance to labour services, many estate owners hired their own wage labourers, thus taking a major step toward abolishing *Gutsherrschaft* well before the reform era began. Indeed, as early as the 1760s, one Pomeranian seigneur had discovered the potential advantages of such workers when he wrote that: 'The farm worker and his family . . . should be supplied with nothing except a dwelling, a small vegetable garden, and the right to graze one or two cattle . . . because, in order to have inexpensive and industrious workers, everything must be done to keep them in the greatest possible dependence.'[35]

The primary reason for the Junkers' success, however, lay in the structure of Prussian *Gutsherrschaft*, which, as we have seen, was a peculiar hybrid that combined elements of 'feudal' lordship with free wage labour. The peasant's obligation to provide labour services to the seigneur rested on the latter's status as noble landowner, but most of the actual labourers appear to have been free workers living with their peasant employers – and working for them in exchange for wages in cash and kind. *Gutsherrschaft*, in short, already rested largely on wage labour, and its transformation did not require a radical transition from unfree to free labour (as was the case in Russia), but rather a change in the system through which agricultural labour was provided and paid for. The reforms that institutionalized this change were advantageous not only to estate owners, but to most (perhaps 80 per cent) of the peasants, who were able to dissolve their hated labour services under relatively favourable terms. This helps explain why, other than in parts of Upper Silesia (where resistance to labour services had frequently escalated into rural revolts in the late eighteenth and early nineteenth centuries), the agrarian transformation was generally a peaceable process. The crisis of *Gutsherrschaft* was real enough, but it was never serious enough to threaten the existence of the old social order.

---

35  Cited in Edgar Melton, 'The Decline of Prussian *Gutsherrschaft* and the Rise of the Junker as Rural Patron, 1750–1806', *German History* 12 (1994), 348.

CHAPTER SIX

# The development of the Prussian town, 1720–1815

KARIN FRIEDRICH

A ruler, intent on increasing his own glory, will try to . . . hamper the development of the flourishing cities in their own provincial assemblies through the voices of the jealous nobility and the minor towns; also the lords, courtiers and soldiers are fond of [the ruler], as they depend on him, and want to be fed by the hard-labouring inhabitants; hence it seems that they accumulate their power merely for their own benefit and to the disadvantage of the common good. And it seems that the rulers want to diminish all cities and impoverish the population, to prevent them from hindering their designs, and to make them obey to all their commands . . . *a furore Monarcharum libera nos Domine* [from the fury of monarchs liberate us, Lord].[1]

The traditional picture of Prussia, both of the Brandenburg territories and of the provinces farther east, is characterized by a dynastic and noble-dominated society, whose cities – with the exception of the court centres of Berlin and Potsdam – started to flourish only with the arrival of large-scale industrialization. As a result, most textbooks and general syntheses of Prussian history have avoided treating the development of towns and urban society prior to the mid-nineteenth century as separate themes. Even publications accompanying the much-celebrated exhibition on Prussia in 1981 in Berlin, which consciously targeted social, economic and cultural topics, treated urban society only marginally.[2] An exception to the rule is the work

1 Pieter de la Court, *Anweisungen der Heilsamen Politischen Gründe und Maximen der Republiken Holland und West-Friesland* (Rotterdam, 1671), pp. 36–7. I would like to thank Professor Jürgen Schlumbohm and the Max-Planck-Institut für Geschichte in Göttingen for their generous research grant and the support I enjoyed during my stay in July 1998.
2 Manfred Schlenke (ed.), *Preußen. Politik, Kultur, Gesellschaft*, 2 vols (Hamburg, 1986).

of Francis Carsten, who looked more closely at the mechanisms which so apparently diminished the role of the early modern urban elites in Brandenburg-Prussia in as early as the fifteenth century, attributing their fate to the domineering role of the nobility rather than Hohenzollern absolutist designs.[3] In the quest for explanations for the alleged German 'Sonderweg', Otto Büsch went further. In his study of eighteenth-century Prussia, which focused exclusively on the nobility and the peasantry, he blamed the militarization of Prussian social life for the creation of an anti-bourgeois, anti-liberal value system, which prevented the development of civic consciousness and a modern idea of citizenship.[4] Both these approaches were perpetuated in most Anglo-Saxon historical works on Brandenburg-Prussia, which tend to focus exclusively on the role of the nobility and agrarian society,[5] neglecting not only the analysis of urban political and social life in the Hohenzollern territories, but also the great diversity of their historically formed local and regional conditions.

It is only in recent years that German historiography has revived a tradition of urban and regional history (*Landesgeschichte*), which was discredited after 1945 by the Nazis' unhealthy interest in a racially motivated 'ethnology', or had fallen into the hands of patriotic amateurs.[6] In the former GDR, local social history had continued to produce case-studies of Brandenburg, Pomeranian and Silesian towns and regions, albeit with a Marxist agenda, which showed little interest in urban elites. The abolition of ideological constraints in 1990, however, brought out the best of this East German tradition and resulted in the production of a series of valuable local studies of all social groups.[7] Yet they have barely been noticed by Anglo-Saxon writers on Prussia, who continue to concentrate on the history of the Hohenzollern dynasty, in particular its political history and foreign politics.[8] Moreover, with a few exceptions, the territories which from 1466

3  Francis L. Carsten, *The Origins of Prussia* (Oxford, 1954), pp. 136–48.
4  Otto Büsch, *Military System and Social Life in Old Regime Prussia, 1713–1807* (Humanities Press, 1997), introduction.
5  Most influential, Hans Rosenberg, *Bureaucracy, Aristocracy and Autocracy. The Prussian Experience, 1660–1815* (Harvard University Press, 1966), and more recently, Robert M. Berdahl, *The Politics of the Prussian Nobility. The Development of a Conservative Ideology, 1770–1848* (Princeton University Press, 1988); also Francis Carsten, *A History of the Prussian Junkers* (Aldershot, 1989).
6  For a critique see Jörg Hackmann, *Ostpreußen und Westpreußen in deutscher und polnischer Sicht. Landeshistorie als beziehungsgeschichtliches Problem* (Wiesbaden, 1996).
7  For a good survey of both older and recent literature on Brandenburg towns, see Brigitte Meier, 'Die "Sieben Schönheiten" der frühneuzeitlichen Städte', in Ralf Pröve and Bernd Kölling (eds), *Leben und Arbeiten auf: märkischem Sand: Wege in die Gesellschaftsgeschichte Brandenburgs, 1700–1914* (Bielefeld, 1999), pp. 220–42.
8  Typical for the focus on political history in works in English, see Dennis E. Showalter, *The Wars of Frederick the Great* (London, 1996) and Brendan Simms, *The Impact of Napoleon: Prussian High Politics, Foreign Policy and the Crisis of the Executive, 1797–1806* (Cambridge, 1997).

to 1772–93 were part of the Polish crown, particularly Royal or Polish Prussia and Warmia, continue to be ignored by western historians.[9]

Until recently, if urban society in eighteenth-century Prussia was mentioned at all, it was either as an object of 'modernization' by the enlightened, centralized bureaucratic Hohenzollern state, or as the victim of over-zealous 'absolutist' monarchs, impatient with 'backward' attitudes associated with urban self-government and urban defence against exploitative taxation and military occupation.[10] In the case of Polish Prussia, the echo of Frederician propaganda, distorted statistics and a one-sided view of the allegedly oppressive economic policies of the hostile Polish nobility, especially towards the once-thriving Hanseatic cities of Danzig, Elbing and Thorn, still dominate German historical works, and Polish research remains generally unmentioned.[11]

Recent debates about Prussian history have centred around the definition and the effects of 'modernization', especially during the late Enlightenment and the reform period in the early nineteenth century. Was it governmental effort, often ill-adapted to local conditions and guided by mercantilist dogma, which triggered industrial and urban growth and social betterment? Or was it grass-roots initiative, the remnants of self-government, and of corporate and communal ideals, which – if not disrupted by governmental policies – made the transition to the modern state and a decentralized, autonomous and civic-spirited citizenry? Was, as Rolf Straubel asked, 'the traditional urban citizenry around 1800 really an undynamic social group, merely focused on defending their traditional immunities, and did changes merely emanate from the "new bourgeoisie"

---

9   The exceptions in German are Michael G. Müller, *Zweite Reformation und Städtische Autonomie im Königlichen Preußen. Danzig, Elbing und Thorn in der Epoche der Konfessionalisierung (1557–1660)* (Berlin, 1998) and Hans-Jürgen Bömelburg, *Zwischen polnischer Ständegesellschaft und preußischem Obrigkeitsstaat. Vom königlichen Preußen zu Westpreußen 1756–1806* (Munich, 1995), and in English [Karin Friedrich], *The Other Prussia. Royal Prussia, Poland and Liberty, 1569–1772* (Cambridge, 2000); all three contain extensive bibliographies, including works in Polish.

10   The former perspective has mainly been associated with Gustav Schmoller, 'Das Städtewesen unter Friedrich Wilhelm I', *Zeitschrift für Preußische Geschichte und Landeskunde* 11 (1874), 513–82, and his follower Walther Hubatsch, 'Ziele und Maßnahmen landesherrlicher Politik im Absolutismus gegenüber den Städten aus der Sicht des Verwaltungshistorikers', in Volker Press (ed.), *Städtewesen und Merkantilismus in Mitteleuropa* (Cologne/Vienna, 1983), pp. 31–44. The latter view was inspired by Hugo Preuß, *Entwicklungsgeschichte der deutschen Städteverfassung* (Leipzig, 1906; repr. Aalen, 1965).

11   Typical of such attitudes is the recently published *Handbuch der Geschichte Ost- und Westpreußens*, 3 vols (Lüneburg, 1996). For a major and well-researched revision of this approach, see Bömelburg, 'Die königlich preußische bzw. westpreußische Landesgeschichte in der Frühen Neuzeit. Streitschrift', *Nordost-Archiv*, Neue Folge VI, Heft 2 (1997), pp. 607–28, and Karin Friedrich, 'Facing Both Ways: New Works on Prussia and Polish–Prussian Relations', *German History* 15 (1997), 256–67.

[of royal officials]?'[12] Prussian urban history needs to deconstruct the stereotypical image of smooth absolutist state-building on the one hand, and on the other the paradigm of a 'backward', self-interested, defensive and stubborn burgher-society, naturally opposed to the intrusive central-ized state. What is needed is a closer look at the strategies townspeople developed for policies of mutual benefit and changing alliances between cities, nobles and state authorities.

## The end of the Teutonic Knights' state and the towns of Royal (Polish) Prussia

From the fifteenth century, the political and economic opportunities of cities in Brandenburg and in the territories of the former Teutonic Order differed greatly. In Brandenburg, the Electors had long curbed urban autonomy and interfered in election rights, built fortresses, restricted or banned participation in Hanseatic assemblies and regularly intervened in urban juridical procedures. In sharp contrast, the towns and cities on the Baltic coast formed the core of the resistance against the Teutonic Knights in 1454, when they rejected the Order's rule in favour of the Polish monarchy. They played a major role in the provincial diet, the bicameral Prussian *Landesrat*, composed of a noble and a city chamber, which negotiated strong constitutional privileges and immunities with the king of Poland. In 1466, after thirteen years of devastating warfare, Prussia was split into two parts, one remaining in union with the Polish crown, under the name of Royal Prussia (later Polish Prussia), comprising the richest and politically most powerful Prussian cities of Danzig, Thorn and Elbing, whereas the eastern territories, including the three cities of Königsberg, remained under the rule of the Teutonic Order.

When in 1525 the last Grand Master of the Order, Albrecht of Hohenzollern, adopted Lutheranism, he secularized the Teutonic state and declared himself duke in Prussia (and a vassal of the Polish king). Königsberg, like the rest of Ducal Prussia, was not part of the Holy Roman Empire and became the Hohenzollerns' most important commercial centre. Yet, until the first partition of Poland in 1772, East Prussian cities remained in the economic shadow of their Polish Prussian counterparts, except during periods of war in the Polish-Lithuanian Commonwealth, particularly the Second

---

12   Rolf Straubel, *Frankfurt (Oder) und Potsdam am Ende des Alten Reiches. Studien zur städtischen Wirtschafts- und Sozialstruktur* (Potsdam, 1995), p. 8.

Northern War (1655–60) and the Great Northern War (1700–21), when Danzig's exports suffered greatly, and the province was successively devastated by Swedish, Polish, Russian and Brandenburg troops. During the sixteenth and seventeenth centuries, the Prussian burghers developed a strong identity as Prussian citizens of Poland-Lithuania, loyal to the Polish crown and Commonwealth, proud of their right to participate in their provincial diet, to take part in the election of the Polish kings, to maintain their own law code (Kulm law) and their own urban and provincial courts and to mint their own money. The king of Poland confirmed their exemption from certain tariffs, and the privilege to have only natives appointed to offices, as well as the right to elect or co-opt their own magistracies, judges and aldermen of the three 'orders' which formed the city government, including representatives from the citizenry.

Although the position of the Royal Prussian towns weakened – through the closer parliamentary union first of the provincial nobility with the Polish parliament in 1569, and then particularly of the smaller towns that were expelled from the lower chamber of the provincial diet in 1662 – the three large cities, above all Danzig, without doubt profited from their incorporation into Poland. Long-standing trade relations with the Netherlands, England, Sweden, German Hanseatic towns, Russia and the Livonian ports, made Danzig a powerful and rich trading centre, which depended on close economic co-operation with the Polish and Lithuanian nobility and its grain transports down the Vistula river.[13] Detailed research has shown that even the network of smaller Polish Prussian towns contributed considerably to the economic success of the province through local markets and regional exchange, and that the traditional picture of urban decay in Polish Prussia – perpetuated by both German and Polish historians[14] – needs urgent correction. The exaggeration of population figures for the Prussian towns in the fifteenth and sixteenth centuries is matched only by the underestimation of population growth, particularly in the suburbs around towns and cities in the eighteenth century, where urban life and trade flourished in a less regulated manner than in the guild-dominated town centres within the old walls.[15] The relentless propaganda of Hohenzollern officials, keen on sending back to Berlin exaggerated reports of the 'disastrous' conditions recorded in

---

13   Artur Attman, *The Russian and Polish Markets in International Trade, 1500–1600* (Gothenburg, 1973).

14   Typically, Maria Bogucka and Henryk Samsonowicz, *Dzieje miast i mieszczaństwa w Polsce przedrozbiorowej* (Wrocław, 1986), and on the German side, Walther Hubatsch, *Friedrich der Große und die preußische Verwaltung* (Cologne/Berlin, 1973).

15   See the frequently overlooked, but invaluable research results of William Dwight van Horn, 'Suburban Development, Rural Exchange and the Manorial Economy in Royal Prussia, 1570–1700' (Ph.D., Columbia University, 1987), pp. 42, 48–54, and *passim*.

the newly annexed Polish Prussian territories in 1772 and 1793, ignored the fact that it was the imposition of Frederick II's *cordon sanitaire* in 1770 that had wrecked the province's economy. The Prussian king erected a militarily controlled barrier on the pretext of containing the threat of a cattle plague epidemic, cutting Danzig and Thorn off from their vital communication lines with their hinterlands and shipping links with foreign ports. Moreover, since the 1760s, hostile tariff policies and the deliberate flooding of the cities with counterfeit coin from the Prussian monarchy had ruined the economy of most towns in the area and triggered a steady exodus of the most prosperous burgher families to the Holy Roman Empire or Poland. Thus Hohenzollern financial and military intervention put an end to Poland-Lithuania's most flourishing cities, which, after the restoration of peace in 1721, had begun a slow but steady recovery, so that by the 1740s and 1750s, for a short time, Danzig was once again the most significant grain-exporting port in the Baltic.[16]

Population figures also indicate that Polish Prussian towns and cities on average were larger than those of East Prussia (a kingdom from 1701), or Pomerania, or Brandenburg. Dozens of smaller towns in Polish Prussia, such as Marienburg (Malbork), Graudenz (Grudziądz), Konitz (Chojnice) and Kulm (Chełmno) contained around 2,000 inhabitants. Polish numbers, which are meant to emphasize the decline of the urban milieu in eighteenth-century Poland-Lithuania, still suggest that up to 30 per cent of the population in Royal Prussia lived in towns. Danzig's population in the second half of the eighteenth century reached 50,000 (not counting the sprawling suburbs with a further 35,000–40,000), while Thorn and Elbing reached 10,000–12,000, excluding the suburbs.[17] Although these cities had refused to join the Polish Diet (*Sejm*) along with the Royal Prussian senators and envoys from the lower Prussian chamber in 1569, all three cities kept resident envoys in Warsaw. They tried to influence political debates in favour of urban and commercial interests by lobbying – and often also bribing – the king, influential noble envoys and members of the Polish senate, frequently with success. Despite repeatedly protesting its autonomy, Danzig, as the most powerful of the Polish Prussian cities, not only contributed large sums towards the maintenance of the Polish army, but during

---

16 Bömelburg, *Zwischen polnischer Ständegesellschaft*, pp. 376–98; Jörg Hoensch, 'Der Streit um den polnischen Generalzoll, 1764–66. Zur Rolle Preußens und Rußlands beim Scheitern der Finanzreform Stanisław Augusts', *Jahrbücher für Geschichte Osteuropas* 18 (1970), 355–88; Gerard Labuda *et al.* (eds), *Historia Pomorza*, vol. II/2: 1657–1815 (Poznań, 1984), pp. 90–1; Edmund Cieślak, 'La situation politique et économique de Gdańsk dans la seconde moîtié du XVIIIe siècle', *Acta Poloniae Historica* 44 (1981), 77–94.

17 Bogucka and Samsonowicz, *Dzieje miast*, pp. 369, 381–2; Bömelburg, *Zwischen polnischer Ständegesellschaft*, p. 115.

the Northern Wars defended its allegiance to the Polish crown against the Swedes, the Russians and in particular Brandenburg more staunchly than many leading members of the Polish and Lithuanian nobility.[18]

Almost all Polish Prussian towns and cities were royal cities, with the exception of five episcopal towns in Warmia and one private town, owned by the Weiher family in the palatinate of Pomerania. The vitality and confidence of the smaller Polish Prussian towns, even after their expulsion from the provincial diet, is demonstrated by the alliance they founded in 1683 (renewed in 1702 and 1738), to press their demands and fight off economic competition from local noble landlords and royal office-holders (*starostas*), to pool information and to lobby the three major cities, Danzig, Elbing and Thorn, to represent urban interests and to finance legal cases against nobles encroaching on their liberties. As late as 1767–8, the small towns of Polish Prussia sent embassies to the *Sejm* in Warsaw to present their grievances. Although the results were modest, these initiatives are a sign of the strong identification of the Polish Prussian burghers with free citizenship and their desire to maintain a political voice of their own.

# Brandenburg-Prussian towns and Hohenzollern rule

In contrast, the poorer soil conditions in Brandenburg and its less densely populated and urbanized provinces of Kurmark, Altmark, Neumark and Uckermark meant that Brandenburg's cities were neither a significant political partner for the nobility, nor a match for Hohenzollern designs to use them as a source of steady income and as places to station garrisons to protect the extensive borders of their territories. From the 1660s, excise taxes were levelled not only on beer, but on a great variety of goods, thus favouring rural and noble brewing and crafts, which were tax-exempt; the office of *commissarius loci* (*Steuerrat*) was introduced to control and eventually curb the local magistrates' few remaining powers, to oversee the collection and administration of the excise, and to head the local *policey*, including fire ordinances, building regulations, the settlement of foreigners and the control of receipts and bookkeeping by the town treasurer. In comparison with Königsberg's commercial importance and its infrastructure, the Brandenburg capital, Berlin, looked like a poor country cousin, although population figures started to pick up under the rule of Prussia's first king, Frederick I, whose

---

18  Edmund Cieślak, *History of Gdańsk* (Gdańsk, 1995), pp. 212–17.

pride in expanding his court in Berlin led to a busy schedule for craftsmen and artists.[19] In eighteenth-century East Prussia, no other town reached the size of Königsberg: very few towns exceeded 2,000, and the majority numbered below 1,500.[20]

The wider reforms introduced under Frederick William I also had a direct impact on the town constitutions and the burghers' relationship to the state. The newly formed canton system and the merger of the Finance Directory and the War Commissariat into one central bureaucracy, the General Directory (*General-Direktorium*), in 1722–23, had a centralizing effect on towns subject to the king (*Immediatstädte*), and increasingly also interfered with the internal affairs of towns leased to or owned by the nobility (*Mediatstädte*). Despite being given the epithet 'the Soldier King', Frederick William I conducted his urban policies in a mercantilist spirit. Rather than putting an emphasis on fortification, as the Great Elector had done, he encouraged trade and manufacturing activities, expecting to gain from tariffs and taxes for the state treasury.[21] Frederick William's attempts to implement central government control and introduce the excise in the towns of all Hohenzollern territories, from Cleves and Mark in the west to Memel on the Lithuanian border, met varying degrees of resistance. Critics pointed out that the excise had a detrimental effect on cities: merchants avoided excise towns whenever they could, while smuggling flourished. Moreover, the excise hit the poor hardest and seriously undermined local markets and exchange. None of these complaints won the king's ear. Instead, the 'Rathäusliche Reglement', introduced in 1714, enforced tighter budgeting control of urban treasuries by royal officials, disempowered magistrates, and imposed 'police chiefs' usually unfamiliar with local conditions and needs.[22] Soon no new houses could be built, no new burghers admitted, no urban properties leased, no taxes passed or abolished, no legal procedures

---

19  In 1700, Königsberg's population was 40,000–45,000; by 1730, Berlin's population reached 58,000, but over 14,000 belonged to the military garrison. The economic upturn of Berlin and Potsdam was interrupted, however, by Frederick William I's rejection of luxury production and his attempts to force manufacturers into producing utilitarian goods and army supplies, especially cloth for uniforms. Wolfgang Neugebauer, 'Staatsverwaltung, Manufaktur und Garnison. Die polyfunktionale Residenzlandschaft von Berlin-Potsdam-Wusterhausen zur Zeit Friedrich Wilhelms I.', *Forschungen zur Brandenburgischen und Preußischen Geschichte*, Neue Folge 7, 2 (1997), 233–57 (here pp. 239, 244).

20  *Historia Pomorza* II/2, p. 399; *Handbuch der Geschichte Ost- und Westpreußens*, vol. II/2, p. 65.

21  Gerd Heinrich, 'Staatsaufsicht und Stadtfreiheit in Brandenburg-Preußen unter dem Absolutismus (1660–1806)', in Wilhelm Rausch (ed.), *Die Städte Mitteleuropas im 17. und 18. Jahrhundert* (Linz/Donau, 1981), p. 156.

22  G. Schmoller, 'Das Städtewesen unter Friedrich Wilhelm I.', pp. 520–36. Frederick William's political testament stresses the need to send state officials to provinces they did not know to prevent 'fraternization'; C. A. Macartney, *The Habsburg and Hohenzollern Dynasties in the Seventeenth and Eighteenth Centuries* (New York, 1970), p. 316.

initiated, and no salaries increased without the consent of the royal tax collector (*Steuerrat*).

Research into the effects of Hohenzollern mercantilism and centralization policies has triggered a lively debate about their benefits for the modernization and expansion of urban centres in Brandenburg-Prussia in the eighteenth century, especially after 1740. Gerd Heinrich's approach, which stresses royal intentions of boosting urban industry and trade pronounced in the Prussian kings' testaments and other official documents, is not convincing, as it fails to compare government propaganda with real results and local conditions. Heinrich repeatedly concentrates on the glorification of the alleged achievements of the Prussian monarchy, rather than economic evidence.[23] It is certainly true that substantial government subsidies were poured into Berlin, which resulted in an impressive increase in production and population figures. Even in the capital, however, the subjection of the magistracies to the control of the War-and-Domain Chamber (*Kurmärkische Kriegs- und Domänenkammer*) – a central governmental organ to administer rural demesnes, and poorly acquainted with the needs of cities – led to disorder and corruption through the sale of offices to poorly qualified officials. Further legislation under Frederick II in 1746 deprived the magistrates of all control over the urban police, subjected all transfers of urban property to royal authorization, and strangled local financial investment and commercial initiative. Representatives of the citizenry, the so-called *Stadtverordnete*, were little more than assistants to the police director, with supervisory functions. In 1766, the General Directory took control of Berlin's budget, initiating a struggle behind the scenes between the king, the *Kurmärkische Kammer* and the Directory for influence over the capital's affairs. By 1770, the city council also lost control over the right to nominate or elect urban judges, and jurisdiction over anything but civil cases involving sums up to 1,000 thalers. It was only with the reforms of 1808 that the state handed back some powers to the magistracies, leading to a more harmonious and balanced approach to what Berthold Grzywatz has called 'true communal government'.[24] This assessment, with its happy ending, has been contested by Evamaria Engel, who applies Peter Blickle's criteria of communalism – the self-government, collegial organization, participation of the citizenry and a sense of civic duties and the common good Blickle observed

---

23  Gerd Heinrich, 'Der preußische Spätmerkantilismus und die Manufakturstädte in den mittleren und östlichen Staatsprovinzen (1740–1806)', in Press (ed.), *Städtewesen und Merkantilismus*, pp. 301–23.

24  Berthold Grzywatz, 'Residenziale Kommunaladministration im Zeitalter des Absolutismus. Die Konstituierung staatlich-städtischer Integration am Besipiel Berlins', *Zeitschrift für Geschichtswissenschaft* 5 (1998), pp. 406–31 (here pp. 411, 414–15, 428–30).

in the towns of south-west Germany[25] – to the towns of Brandenburg. Engel concludes that the lack of economic power and the provinciality of Brandenburg towns, and the complete incorporation of Berlin into the state apparatus under Frederick II, prevented the emergence of communal values to which Blickle has attributed long-term effects of modernization and democratization.[26]

Case-studies from towns such as Potsdam and Frankfurt-an-der-Oder, and even more so from Silesia and Pomerania, indeed paint a negative picture of the ability of towns under Hohenzollern rule during the eighteenth century to preserve economic and political autonomy. Frederick II's declared wish to help cities improve their trade and manufacturing activities by 'preserving in the old provinces the freedom to elect their magistrates', and to intervene 'only when they abused these elections' to favour an internal oligarchy,[27] had little bearing on reality, particularly after the Seven Years' War (1756–63). Potsdam, which became an *Immediatstadt*, or royal town, only in 1737, should have profited from the expansion of the Hohenzollern palace complex, and from the proximity of Berlin, which attracted trade and labour to the area around the capital. Yet it still needed massive investment by the state. In contrast to older assumptions that the stationing of soldiers invigorated local crafts and created a lively market, a more complex picture emerges from detailed social and economic research. From 1714, a large garrison was stationed permanently in Potsdam. Although the building industry experienced several profitable decades under Frederick II, building palaces for the court, as well as barracks, ammunition stores, manufactures and new homes (such as the 'Dutch quarter', purpose-built to accommodate soldiers within families), other crafts and trades were less favoured. From the 1740s, the military population, which included soldiers' families, constituted 30–35 per cent of the population; by 1801, 18,000 civilians lived alongside a garrison of 9,000.[28] Most complaints to the city council, which was entirely appointed by state officials and under royal control, concerned soldiers illegally engaging in trade and undercutting

---

25   Peter Blickle, 'Kommunalismus. Begriffsbildung in heuristischer Absicht', *Historische Zeitschrift* 13 (1991), 5–38.

26   Evamaria Engel, 'Die Stadtgemeinde im Brandenburgischen Gebiet', *Historische Zeitschrift* 13 (1991), 333–58.

27   Heinrich, 'Staatsaufsicht und Stadtfreiheit', p. 157.

28   Straubel, *Potsdam und Frankfurt/Oder*, p. 95. In comparison, in Berlin in 1786, the civilian population of 113,763 faced 33,625 military personnel, while smaller Brandenburg towns, such as Insterburg or Spandau, housed between 32 and 35 per cent military. In the Kurmark, in 1787, the average of garrison population per town was 19.5 per cent; Klaus Schwieger, 'Das Bürgertum in Preußen vor der französischen Revolution' (Ph.D., Christian-Albrechts-University, 1971), pp. 117–18.

local guild prices, particularly in the brewing and distilling business. Of 74 beer-sellers in Potsdam and its suburbs in 1796, 22 were members of the army or veterans who had received concessions, and who were all bound to the condition to own or lease property in the city.

In the long term, it is true, life with the garrison did create a symbiotic relationship between the military and the civilian population, involving money-lending, mutual trade and the exchange of houses and property. Whenever the troops left the town, however, to engage in war, or when the state treasury decided to curb its investment in the city and the garrison, the urban economy suffered heavy losses and disturbed the artificially sustained local market. Even Gustav Schmoller, who was one of the most vociferous partisans of the Hohenzollern drive to centralization, had to admit that the massive military presence in towns such as Potsdam created a 'state within a state' of officers, haughtily demanding control over urban civil jurisdiction and an unprecedented level of requisitioning of civilian resources, including forced recruitment. Repeated legislation after 1752 against arbitrary military jurisdiction over civilians and illegal military orders compelling burghers to serve in the guards, show that the coexistence of the garrison and town spheres was far from harmonious. Not infrequently, royal *Steuerräte* openly took the side of the civilian population against military excesses. In 1782, in the Silesian city of Glogau, for example, Frederick II punished the *Steuerrat* with imprisonment in the fortress after he supported the town authorities against illegal recruitment measures by the local garrison commander.[29] The militarization of civic society thus led to an arbitrary and little-regulated domination of garrison cities by the army, fostering an atmosphere of passivity among the burgher population and the magistracies.[30]

Traditionally a town based on crafts, Frankfurt-an-der-Oder (another *Immediatstadt*) found it harder than heavily subsidized Potsdam to recover from the Seven Years' War (1756–63). The decline of its textile industry in the second half of the century triggered an exodus of artisans, for which demand created by the students and professors attached to the university could not compensate. By 1803, there were nineteen manufactures in Potsdam, compared with only five in Frankfurt. The unemployed often served as recruits drafted through the canton system. Despite the close involvement of the *Kriegs- und Domänenkammer*, the Frankfurt city council maintained a

29  Schwieger, 'Bürgertum in Preußen', pp. 133–7.
30  Schmoller, 'Das Städtewesen', pp. 566–77; also Brigitte Meier, 'Städtische Verwaltungsorgane in den Brandenburgischen Klein- und Mittelstädten des 18. Jahrhunderts', in Wilfried Ehbrecht (ed.), *Verwaltung und Politik in den Städten Mitteleuropas. Beiträge zu Verfassungsnorm und Verfassungswirklichkeit in altständischer Zeit* (Cologne/Vienna/ Weimar, 1994), pp. 177–81 (here p. 177).

greater degree of self-government until the 1790s, when tensions between the magistrates and the citizenry provided the king with the opportunity to intervene. Yet even the local *Steuerrat* often spoke up in the city's favour, rejecting some of the more dogmatic mercantilist policies of Frederick II and his successor, and defending the city's guild system, which in contrast to more deregulated urban economies, such as that of Berlin, was vital to the survival of Frankfurt's trades. The fact that guild structures and the presence of so-called *Ackerbürger* (burghers with an extra income from agricultural activities) were so persistent in Frankfurt, however, was not necessarily a sign of 'backwardness', but evidence for the great variety of economic and social structures even within one province or region. In fact, some of Frankfurt's richest burghers owned vineyards and land, and thus counted as *Ackerbürger*, whereas the poor soil around Potsdam prevented its population from benefiting from additional agricultural income.[31] Although Frankfurt had to accommodate a much smaller garrison population than Potsdam, and a large part of the population was exempt from the canton regulations through the pursuit of their crafts and trades, the urban authorities tried very hard to secure a general ordinance for exemption from recruitment for the whole city. When new recruiting areas were added to the Prussian state through the annexation of the Polish territories in 1793, Frankfurt still did not gain its exemption, but at least was elevated from an infantry to an artillery canton in 1795. This gave those burgher sons who had to serve the chance to advance into the officer ranks, whereas the infantry reserved all higher ranks to the nobility. Belonging to the artillery canton boosted burgher pride in being distinct from the lower classes and peasantry. It did not last: Frankfurt reverted to an infantry canton in 1799, due to the restructuring of canton boundaries.[32]

The official goal of stronger government *dirigisme* over the Brandenburg towns was the abolition of 'abuse' and 'corruption' among the old urban oligarchic elites. Liselotte Enders, in her work on the territorial and private towns of the Uckermark, has shown, however, that despite the appointment of officials and the substitution of the former citizen-representation by officially nominated deputies (*Stadtverordnete*), corruption continued unabated. The disappearance of corporate bodies of self-government from within the citizenry upset the balance between government and governed within the cities, turning burghers into subjects, without any means of resisting the

---

31  Straubel, *Potsdam und Frankfurt/Oder*, pp. 22, 134–6, 170 ff.
32  Martin Winter, 'Preußisches Kantonsystem und städtische Gesellschaft. Frankfurt an der Oder im ausgehenden 18. Jahrhundert', in Ralf Pröve and Bernd Kölling (eds), *Leben und Arbeiten auf märkischem Sand: Wege in die Gesellschaftsgeschichte Brandenburgs, 1700–1914* (Bielefeld, 1999), pp. 243–65 (here p. 257).

official exercise of power and its corruption.[33] Yet the border towns of the Uckermark demonstrate the limits of government measures: the 1728 ordinance prohibiting the collection of money for legal procedures against corrupt magistrates by the citizenry proved unenforceable. One instrument aimed at eradicating such abuses was the professionalization of state-appointed judges who from 1735 had to pass state examinations.

It was not only royal towns which resisted increasing state intervention. Protest also came from the nobility who saw their power over their leased or privately owned towns (*Mediatstädte*) curbed and their urban subjects doubly administered and burdened, by the *Steuerrat* as well as their own *Domänenkammer*. The councillors of most private towns were poorly paid employees who had to supplement their income through the cattle trade or other agrarian activities. Hence, contemporary officials frequently categorized the smallest and most rural of these towns as large villages and part of the countryside, while historians have studied them as part of noble and agrarian structures rather than urban history.[34] Yet despite Frederick William I's appeal to his successor to increase the number of towns, especially in Prussian Lithuania,[35] several small towns in Brandenburg were deprived of their urban constitutions and absorbed into the royal domains as so-called *Amtsstädte*. Moreover, the reforms of 1722–3 extended control by the nobility over the councils in private towns where offices – often sold to the highest bidder – rarely attracted enterprising burghers, owing to the lack of influence attached to council duties. Only where noblemen took the initiative to compete with neighbouring towns – private or royal – and invested in their own urban properties, could a *Mediatstadt* avoid the story of decline and agrarianization so typical of the majority of private towns. In such towns, the *Ackerbürger* usually were in the highest income brackets, frequently employing servants and labourers themselves, or functioning as creditors for the local landlord. Against the odds, burghers in such towns also developed or maintained their urban identity in clear distinction to the rural subjects in the countryside. Such apparently minor differences were of

---

33  Liselotte Enders, *Die Uckermark. Geschichte einer kurmärkischen Landschaft vom 12. bis zum 18. Jahrhundert* (Weimar, 1992), p. 459. Brigitte Meier has demonstrated that local urban elites wasted no time in integrating state-appointed 'foreign' officials through marriage and property exchange; hence oligarchic practices continued among officials who 'went native'; B. Meier, 'Städtische Verwaltungsorgane', p. 179.

34  Klaus Vetter, *Zwischen Dorf und Stadt. Die Mediatstädte des kurmärkischen Kreises Lebus. Verfassung, Wirtschaft und Sozialstruktur im 17. und 18. Jahrhundert* (Weimar, 1996), p. 22; Frank Göse, 'Zwischen adliger Herrschaft und städtischer Freiheit. Zur Geschichte kurmärkischer adliger Mediatstädte in der Frühen Neuzeit', *Jahrbuch für Brandenburgische Landesgeschichte* 47 (1996), 55–85 (here p. 56).

35  Political Testament of 1722, in Macartney, *The Habsburg and Hohenzollern Dynasties*, p. 313.

great importance to the local population. It mattered a great deal to them whether they managed to preserve a few remnants of local jurisdiction within the city, or whether they depended on the town owner's manorial courts in every instance.

During the course of the eighteenth century, the royal bureaucracy increasingly established a foothold in noble private towns with the help of the excise system. Considering that 57 per cent of towns and almost a third of the urban population of Brandenburg (not counting Berlin) belonged to this category, the interest of state administrators in their economic and tax potential is understandable.[36] Complaints by royal towns that the rural population and even their own burghers preferred to buy their beer and other goods from privately owned towns, which were exempt from taxes on beer and spirits and thus could keep their prices low, had led to an extension of the excise to private towns in 1681 – with little initial success. The imposition of the excise therefore depended on the energetic intervention of local state officials who infringed upon older noble privileges, albeit in a highly unsystematic manner. By the end of the eighteenth century, however, both excise collection and recruitment on the basis of the canton system from private towns became the rule rather than the exception. Yet this did little towards improving the economic or legal status of the burghers of private towns. They still were drafted for labour services and did not possess burgher rights, despite being free men. In addition, the canton system called upon the majority of inhabitants from private towns, since their professions or status rarely qualified them for exemption from military service. Owing to their modest economic opportunities, they were also unable to benefit from state investment in industry and trade, which focused on large royal towns.

After the Seven Years' War, the economic pressures on small royal towns were compounded by the establishment of the *Régie* in 1766 (an office responsible for the indirect taxation system). Small cloth-makers and textile manufacturers suffered, as state monopolies favoured larger industrial enterprises, cutting out the *Verlagssystem* – a system of merchandise distribution through wholesale merchants who purchased from the producer. In Uckermark towns such as Templin, state monopolies wiped out the remaining local guilds, and trade moved across the border to Mecklenburg. Decades of Prussian bureaucratic government from above had not been able to eliminate the corruption and mismanagement of local elites, but had left the burghers with even fewer instruments for opposing such abuses.[37] In the 1790s, conflicts

---

36  Vetter, *Zwischen Dorf und Stadt*, p. 150.
37  Enders, *Die Uckermark*, pp. 614, 625–8.

between the citizenry and the appointed magistrates escalated. In 1796, for example, the burghers of Prenzlau no longer recognized their authorities and started to riot. From 1798, compromise and the gradual transfer of participatory rights to the citizenry in Brandenburg royal towns prepared the ground for the reforms of the early nineteenth century.

## The towns of Prussian Silesia

The military annexation of Silesia in 1740 (see Chapter 7) had opened up new sources of state income and provided Prussia with a rich agricultural and proto-industrial potential. As a result, royal policy was targeted at taking as much control of the cities as possible. In the 1741 ordinances for the Lower Silesian towns, Frederick II declared their income 'chamber revenues . . . administered as his own revenues'. And in his 1752 testament, he explicitly excluded the Silesian cities from the privilege of electing their own magistracies.[38] The lack of trust in local urban government outside the Brandenburg heartlands is also reflected in the measures imposed on East Prussian cities (which Frederick refused to visit), in particular the once-rebellious Königsberg, which from 1724 had been deprived of election rights, necessitating the royal confirmation of every single councillor co-opted by the current council. From 1783, no paid office in the city could be filled without the consent of the Prussian chamber in the General Directory. Similarly, from 1760, the magistrates of the Silesian capital Breslau were not even appointed by the king, but by the *Kriegs- und Domänenkammer*, the office usually engaged in the administration of the countryside. The fact that Breslau had been a flourishing urban centre with a large merchant population and considerable civic pride was not taken into account: from 1760 to 1793, there was not a single merchant representative on the state-appointed council.[39]

In his classic work on Frederician policies in Silesia, Johannes Ziekursch concluded that the annexation by Prussia did not bring Silesia any advantages; in fact, Breslau's economy suffered badly from its rude separation from its traditional Austrian and Saxon trading connections. Soon after the Prussian take-over, Breslau had to surrender its ammunition and armaments, its salt and grain stores; taxation and contribution absorbed all

---

38 Schwieger, 'Das Bürgertum in Preußen', p. 382; Frederick II's 1752 testament, in Macartney, *The Habsburg and Hohenzollern Dynasties*, pp. 332–3.
39 Schwieger, 'Das Bürgertum in Preußen', pp. 391, 395.

excess income until 1786, when the financial regime was loosened. Its manufacturing industries, despite the increase of plants and production sites under the Prussian administration, did not generate more income in the early nineteenth century than they had in the first half of the eighteenth.[40] As in Brandenburg and in East Prussia, the mercantilist idea that production and thus the bulk of taxation should come from the towns, where both the urban and rural populations should purchase their goods, did not work. Although economic relations between town and countryside were never strictly divided, it was also true that many villages and domains provided for the needs of their population without having to rely on urban production and trade.[41]

The causes of urban decline in Silesia were manifold, but mostly originated in the advantage most craftsmen, brewers and artisans in the countryside enjoyed through lower taxes and prices over the heavily taxed towns, which, also in Silesia, were soon burdened with garrisons and additional competition from among trades and craftsmen protected by the army. As garrison towns were considered to profit from the military presence, they had to pay higher contributions (*servis* tax). Despite several attempts to reduce the number of craftsmen in the countryside, different market needs – e.g. more functional dress styles and hardier types of cloth for rural occupations – persuaded the authorities that some crafts had to be tolerated in the villages. Competition worsened when state officials introduced new settlers, usually Huguenots or other religious refugees, who further crowded the market.[42]

The *Régie* also devastated the Silesian brewing industry. Excise revenues from Tarnowitz, for example, fell from 782 thalers in 1781 to 587 in 1790. Now, even government ministers were alarmed by the impoverishment of the Silesian towns. In 1794, Count Hoym, the minister for Silesia, wrote in a memorandum: 'In this province, the . . . raised tariffs on beer, spirits and meat have caused the decline of the small, especially private towns, so that in some places, there is no brewery and no butcher left.'[43] Following the Russian example of Potemkin's villages, builders and carpenters had to pretend to work on houses during Frederick's visitations in the province,

---

40  J. Ziekursch, *Das Ergebnis der friderizianischen Städteverwaltung und die Städteordnung Steins am Beispiel Schlesiens* (Jena, 1908), pp. 12–20.

41  Walter Diamant, 'Studien zur Wirtschaftsgeschichte der Städte in Pommern, der Kur- und Neumark unter Friedrich dem Großen und seinen nächsten Nachfolgern bis 1806' (Ph.D., Friedrich-Wilhelms-University, 1913), p. 6.

42  Ibid., pp. 48, 51; around 1800, the number of workshops of several crafts in the countryside had overtaken urban provision. In Pomerania, for example, 272 blacksmiths in the towns competed with 683 in the countryside, 790 tailors in towns versus 1,049 tailors for the country, and 141 urban carpenters versus 174 rural ones (p. 48).

43  Ziekursch, *Das Ergebnis der friderizianischen Städteverwaltung*, p. 42.

while in reality, building-stock declined owing to the widespread poverty of the population.[44] A widening gap between an articulate and educated urban stratum from which officials and magistrates were recruited, and the increasingly impoverished masses polarized urban society not only in Silesia. Reports circulated about 'miserable mud houses' without tiled roofs and a generally rural character accentuated by 'dung-hills near the streets' in the Silesian capital at the end of the eighteenth century.[45] Sixty years of Prussian government, which had completely excluded the citizenry from the conduct of urban affairs, badly prepared the city for the industrialization of the nineteenth century.

## The annexation of the Polish Prussian cities

It is worthwhile to compare this reality with the propaganda spread by Prussian officials and Frederick II's own reports about the allegedly miserable state of the cities annexed from Poland. Frederick's openly expressed contempt towards the Poles, whom he called 'cowards and arrogant – in a word, the last nation of Europe', is well documented.[46] Prusso-German historiography has perpetuated this picture over the centuries, yet few German historians even today point out the malicious distortions which dominated Frederick's views of the old Commonwealth and its history. Without taking into account the king's image of Poland, an analysis of his policies and the propaganda he disseminated about the state of the Polish Prussian cities remains difficult. The travel reports by ministers, such as Voß or Stein in the early 1780s, which reveal the combined effects of the *cordon sanitaire*, hostile tariff policies and the civil war raging in Poland-Lithuania, talk about misery and serfdom and 'German burghers' who suffered from 'oppression'

---

44 Gerhard Günzel, *Österreichische und preußische Städteverwaltung in Schlesien während der Zeit von 1648–1809 dargestellt am Beispiel der Stadt Striegau* (Breslau, 1911), pp. 77–8. Frederick's travel reports from Silesia admit that many small towns looked run-down and miserable, but blame it on their 'originally Slavonic habit' of house construction or on the neglect by the noble owners of these towns; Ernst Pfeiffer, *Die Revuereisen Friedrichs des Grossen besonders die Schlesischen nach 1763 und der Zustand Schlesien von 1763–86* (Berlin, 1904; repr. Vaduz/Lübeck, 1965), pp. 138–41.

45 Ziekursch, quoting from travel reports of 1781 and 1802, pp. 46–7. In 1786, Prussian government statistics recorded that in the Silesian town of Schweidnitz, from among 489 houses, only 82 were brick buildings, while the remaining houses were made of wood or clay. The urban population of Silesia decreased from 22 per cent in 1756 to 17 per cent in 1807 (p. 61).

46 Bömelburg, *Zwischen polnischer Ständegesellschaft*, pp. 205–12; also Stanisław Salmonowicz, 'Friedrich der Große und Polen', *Acta Poloniae Historica* 46 (1982), 73–95.

145

by a morally corrupted Polish nobility.[47] A closer look reveals a more complex picture. Reports by local Prussian officials sent to the province to record the property and state of affairs in several small, mainly Polish-speaking towns, such as Mewe and Stargardt, in the former Polish Prussian palatinate of Pomerania, mention 'well-built houses, well located for trade due to their vicinity of the Vistula river . . . where the inhabitants had suffered from the recent unrest which reduced their trade'. Kept in a very neutral, matter-of-fact tone, the visiting officials also reported from Stargardt that the city was 'quite well built, and has several well-to-do inhabitants and [is] well suited to receive a cavalry garrison. The college of magistrates consists entirely of craftsmen, and two judges. Its secretary, Grim, is very talented and able, and accompanies [the visitors] on their further travels.'[48] Further research into the economic development of small towns in Polish Prussia has shown that during the decades before the first partition (1772), local markets actually expanded.

Moreover, Frederician policies were based on the erroneous assumption of a uniform social and economic 'Polish' model. Yet, in contrast to many other provinces in Poland-Lithuania, the majority of Polish Prussian peasants in the eighteenth century lived under a tenant system based on rent contracts, instead of serfdom, with a close symbiotic relationship between market towns and countryside. When from 1806 the reforms of Stein and Hardenberg introduced the emancipation of serfs in all Prussian territories, these decrees had practically no meaning in the West Prussian countryside, since the state serfdom widespread in East Prussia, Silesia or Brandenburg bore no resemblance to the traditional status of personal freedom of Polish Prussian tenant farmers.[49] Under Polish rule, towns and cities in the palatinate of Pomerania had seen a population increase, especially in the suburbs, of around 36 per cent, and the beginning of a profitable textile trade, which hardly speaks of stagnation or decline. Hence, the introduction of steep excise rates in the towns and the particularly heavy contribution of 33.5 per cent for Polish Prussian peasants after the Prussian take-over, was a blow to the local economy.[50] Most of the money disappeared into the

---

47  For example in Robert Schmidt, *Städtewesen und Bürgertum in Neuostpreußen. Ein Beitrag zur Geschichte der bei den letzten Teilungen Polens von Preußen erworbenen Gebiete* (Königsberg, 1913), pp. 16–17.

48  'Besitzergreifungsprotokolle v[om] J[ahre] 1772', *Zeitschrift des Historischen Vereins für Marienwerder* 7 (1883), 88–106 (here pp. 90, 99).

49  Bömelburg, *Zwischen polnischer Ständegesellschaft*, pp. 410–11.

50  As a clearly discriminatory measure, Protestants were taxed lower than Catholics. Ludwig Boas, 'Friedrich des Großen Maßnahmen zur Hebung der wirtschaftlichen Lage Westpreußens', *Jahrbuch der Historischen Gesellschaft für den Netzedistrikt zu Bromberg* 3 (1891), 34–64 (here p. 36).

central state treasury and the army funds without being reinvested into the province.

In contrast to Silesia, which received its own ministry, the administration of Polish Prussia was merged with the government of East Prussia, under the president of East and West Prussia in the General Directory, Johann Friedrich von Domhardt (d. 1781). His task was to implement Prussia's hostile policies against the city of Danzig, which, like Thorn, had remained under the Polish crown from the first to the second partition in 1793 with the help of Russian guarantees. Domhardt's aim was 'to humiliate the city . . . which was a thorn in the flesh of the Prussian monarchy', including the unrealistic project of forced recruitment of all subjects born in the Danzig territories and the 'conscious destruction of the prosperity of Danzig's merchant community'.[51] Despite the Prussian monarchy's enlightened image, the Polish Prussian patriciate knew only too well that their self-government and prosperity were threatened by a Prussian take-over. In 1772, Christian Klossmann, the *Bürgermeister* of Thorn, attacked the *despotismo berolinensi*: 'God protect us from this neighbour. . . . I'd rather live under the Poles on 6 Huben of land than under the Prussians on 18 [Huben]: insufferable servitude'. And in Danzig, Johanna Schopenhauer, whose family left the city in 1793, reacted to the news of the first partition: 'The Prussian came overnight . . . like a vampire into our doomed fatherland . . . our desperation had turned into wild anger and hatred against everything Prussian, motivated by the decision to defend the last ray of this sun of freedom that was left to us to fight for it with our lives and property.'[52]

Danzig's armed resistance against the Prussian occupation in 1793 had no effect. The exodus of many merchant families and continued economic decline took their toll: all urban and provincial constitutions based on the participation and representation of the noble and burgher estates were abolished, citizens were turned into subjects, paying to keep 100,000 men in arms. The open contempt and the harsh policies against Danzig and Thorn, which had continued under Frederick William II, not only caused resistance against Prussian rule in the West Prussian territories, but also stirred the conscience of several contemporary civil servants and officials.[53] Mistakes and errors were admitted, albeit quietly. Mainly under the moderating influence of Leopold von Schroetter, and then under Count Karl von

---

51   Erich Joachim, *Johann Friedrich von Domhardt. Ein Beitrag zur Geschichte Ost- und Westpreußens mit Friedrich dem Großen* (Berlin, 1899), pp. 122–3, 126.

52   Johanna Schopenhauer, *Jugendleben und Wanderbilder*, ed. W. Cosack (Danzig, 1884), p. 42.

53   For example, Baumann, *De l'administration Prussienne dans les ci-devant provinces Polonaises. Essai pour servir au développement des causes . . . Avis aux nouvelles autorités établies sur ces provinces* (n.p., 1808).

Hoym, the harsh methods of creating complete uniformity with the rest of the Prussian territories were alleviated during the annexation of 'South Prussia' (Poznań and the rest of Great Poland and parts of Mazovia) in 1793 and of 'New East Prussia' (the rest of Mazovia, including Warsaw, and territories farther east, extending to the Lithuanian border) in 1795–6.

As a concession to the Polish nobility, local representatives, appointed by the government from among the nobility, acquired administrative tasks, although provincial estate assemblies were abolished. In South Prussia, minister Karl August von Struensee succeeded in keeping the cities exempt from excise regulations, although Schroetter failed to convince the Prussian king of the benefits of a unified land and town tax. Frederick William II even actively discouraged the development of towns in the annexed territories, and several smaller towns saw their urban status taken away from them, with profit for the nobility. The first attempts at reform, in 1802, did little to lighten the burdens of the towns in the former Polish provinces, but even expanded noble control over town markets and introduced the excise in three-quarters of South and New East Prussian towns, despite the warning by several ministers that it would hurt the local markets.

To speak of an 'urban Renaissance', as Wolfgang Neugebauer has done, not only ignores the scope of self-government and the economic success which the autonomy of the West Prussian cities enjoyed before 1772–93, but overestimates the role which 'magistrates' appointed or elected by state officials were allowed to play in the Prussian monarchy.[54] Although Neugebauer is right to warn against a simplistic picture of an all-powerful and uniform 'absolutism', the fact that such cities as Memel or Tilsit in East Prussia were allowed to elect their judges from among (state-appointed) town officials, was hardly a sign that representative government by politically active and responsible citizens was officially encouraged. It is true that the citizenry of Danzig, after losing their Third Order representing guild masters and merchants in the urban government in 1793, fought hard and successfully for the retention of some degree of citizen participation and preserved the election of 24 deputies, mainly from the merchant class.[55] Compared to the former autonomy under the Polish crown, however, the extension of the system of *Steuerrat* and the subjection of the West Prussian cities to the Prussian chamber of the General Directory had broken the former political power of the patriciate. It was only as a result of the crisis of

---

54  Wolfgang Neugebauer, *Politischer Wandel im Osten. Ost- und Westpreußen von den alten Ständen zum Konstitutionalismus* (Stuttgart, 1992), pp. 126–52.

55  Erich Hoffmann, 'Die Instruction für die Danziger Stadtverordneten vom 9. August 1805', *Mitteilungen des Westpreußischen Geschichtsvereins* 34 (1935), 15–22 (here p. 15); Cieślak, *History of Gdańsk*, pp. 297–8.

the Napoleonic occupation, which declared Danzig a free city under French control (1807–13), and the weakness of the Prussian state in the aftermath of the defeats at Jena and Auerstedt, that voices which had argued for more active pro-urban policies were finally heard.

# The impact of the urban reform work: the *Städteordnung* of 1808

The urban reform regulations (*Städteordnung*) of 19 November 1808 bestowed upon local government the dual functions of an urban and a state instrument. These reforms concluded a long process of integrating into the state the great variety of individual provincial and local powers. The *Städteordnung* addressed, however, the imbalance which the notoriously inflexible and restrictive ordinances of the eighteenth century had imposed on the Prussian cities: it handed over to local magistrates the appointment of officials, control over the treasury and bookkeeping, trade and industry, transport and licensing, whereas the representative body of urban deputies (*Stadtverordnete*) were charged with communal administration, the police and the judiciary.[56] The goal was to form a united 'community' of urban citizens, no longer divided by corporate privileges and bodies, such as the guilds, although the reforms allowed for the survival of a few categories of inhabitants with limited burgher rights.

The response was mixed. Census voting rights ensured that the circle of people allowed to elect the deputies was kept small. In Potsdam, for example, of 13,758 burghers, only 971 had the right to vote.[57] Some towns, which had been deprived of their elected councils and any form of self-government decades or even a century before, could not cope. Several Silesian towns and cities asked to be exempt from the reforms, eager to ensure the survival of their guild structures, which were economically unable to face a deregulated market. On the other hand, the towns of West Prussia felt that the reforms did little to restore the degree of autonomy they had once enjoyed, and the more industrialized cities on the Rhine, which had never faced a strong nobility, thought the reforms anachronistic.[58] Hence,

---

56  Harad Schinkel, 'Polizei und Stadtverfassung im frühen 19. Jahrhundert. Eine historisch-kritische Interpretation der preußischen Städteordnung von 1808', *Der Staat. Zeitschrift für Staatslehre, öffentliches Recht und Verfassungsgeschichte* 3 (1964), 315–34 (here p. 332).

57  Ingo Materna and W. Ribbe (eds), *Brandenburgische Geschichte* (Berlin, 1995), p. 403; see also Paul Nolte, *Staatsbildung als Gesellschaftsreform. Politische Reformen in Preußen und den süddeutschen Staaten, 1800–1820* (Frankfurt-am-Main, 1990), pp. 56–62.

58  Nolte, *Staatsbildung*, pp. 59–62.

historians who have emphasized the radical nature of the Prussian reforms, on the one hand underestimate the survival of an autonomous burgher spirit, opposed to centralized state policies, especially in the territories annexed from Poland; on the other hand, they denounce too categorically the 'immaturity' and 'backwardness' of Prussia's guild-based urban societies and their alleged economic and political inertia. In 1815, after a century of reforms aimed at unifying the Prussian provinces – old, new and annexed – the picture still survives of a heterogeneous conglomerate of local and regional traditions, which generations of state officials had in vain tried to suppress. The reforms, though a new example of central initiative, implicitly acknowledged that the 'absolute' nature of Prussian monarchy had been a myth all along, and that the great regional diversity of Prussia's towns and the vitality of the burgher classes continued to be a force to be reckoned with.

# PART THREE

# The state and the army

# CHAPTER SEVEN

# Prussia's emergence as a European great power, 1740–1763

H. M. SCOTT

## The sinews of Prussian power

Prussia's dramatic and unexpected emergence as a leading European state was the most important development in her eighteenth-century history. It can be dated precisely to its middle decades. In 1740, at Frederick William I's death, Brandenburg-Prussia was – in Frederick the Great's precise formulation – a kingdom in name, but an electorate in fact.[1] This expressed the Hohenzollern monarchy's relative insignificance when its most celebrated eighteenth-century ruler came to the throne. Prussia played an important political role only within the Holy Roman Empire and northern Europe. When her subjects in the Kingdom of Prussia are included, she was the most populous German territory after the Habsburg Monarchy and since 1697 had been head of the *corpus evangelicorum*, the Protestant party within the Holy Roman Empire. Within the Empire, her rise was striking. It was the first time one of the electorates had secured political equality with – and, by 1763, a degree of ascendancy over – the House of Habsburg, with its large territorial power-base, comprising the family's Hereditary Lands (Austria and Bohemia), together with the Kingdom of Hungary. The Habsburgs also filled the post of Emperor which – except briefly in 1740–45 – was hereditary in the family from the mid-fifteenth century until the first decade of the nineteenth.

Brandenburg-Prussia was one of the larger electorates – Saxony, Bavaria and Hanover were the others – which were sufficiently powerful to be seen as more than German states. On the European stage, however, she was a

---

1  Frederick II, *Histoire de mon temps* (Leipzig, 1879 edn), iv, pp. 213–14. I am very grateful to Professor Derek Beales and Dr Derek McKay for their helpful comments on an earlier version of this chapter.

third- or, at best, second-rank power in 1740. Twenty-three years later, the situation was very different. Frederick the Great returned from the Seven Years' War of 1756–63 having resisted a seemingly overwhelming coalition headed by Austria, France and Russia, avoided the territorial losses which had appeared inevitable, and in the process established his kingdom as a leading continental power. It was now one of the five great powers, which individually and collectively dominated the European states-system, a transformation which could not have been predicted when Frederick the Great ascended the throne.[2]

Prussia's rise filled a quarter-century during which there was an important clarification in the way Europe's rulers and statesmen assessed political strength.[3] In the mid-eighteenth century, the established, traditional and very generalized indicators – geographical size, apparent wealth, military power, political success – were given more precision through calculations which measured a state's population, its economic resources and the effectiveness with which these could be mobilized, the size of its army and, where appropriate, its navy. These measures were then used to assess a state's relative power and the policy it was likely to pursue. By these yardsticks, eighteenth-century Prussia was never really a great power: it always lacked the demographic and economic resources to compete with the established leading states. In 1740 her population was around 2.25 million; by 1786, and largely due to the important territorial acquisitions Frederick had made, it had climbed to some 5.8 million. The population density was particularly low by European and even German standards. All the other continental great powers were far stronger demographically. France at mid-century was still Europe's most populous state, with around 25 million inhabitants. Russia, which simultaneously joined the continental elite during the Seven Years' War, had some 23 million subjects at Catherine II's accession in 1762, while in that same year the central lands of the Habsburg Monarchy had around 14 million. Even the fifth member of the family of great powers, the island kingdom of Britain (excluding Ireland), had between six and seven million inhabitants during the Seven Years' War.

---

2   The best overall survey of Prussia's impact upon Europe is to be found in the standard life-and-times by Reinhold Koser, *Geschichte Friedrichs des Grossen*, 3 vols (6th–7th eds, Berlin, 1925). Among more recent discussions, that by Theodor Schieder, *Friedrich der Grosse: ein Königtum der Widersprüche* (Frankfurt-am-Main, 1983), pp. 127–224, is particularly noteworthy.

3   See Harm Klueting, *Die Lehre von der Macht der Staaten: das aussenpolitische Machtproblem in der 'politischen Wissenschaft' und in der praktischen Politik im 18. Jahrhundert* (Berlin, 1986), for the general development. This approach can be found in Frederick the Great's Political Testaments of 1752 and 1768 (see *Die politischen Testamente der Hohenzollern*, ed. Richard Dietrich [Berlin, 1986]) and in the noted work by the Prussian official Jacob von Bielfeld, *Institutions politiques*, 2 vols (The Hague, 1760).

Prussia was also poorly endowed with economic resources. With the exception of the Westphalian territories – Cleves, Mark and Ravensberg – with their mixed and relatively prosperous agrarian economies and higher level of urbanization, the Hohenzollern lands were poor and backward, and contained little rural industry. Mostly subsistence agriculture, with small surpluses, prevailed throughout the central provinces of Brandenburg and Pomerania. Contemporaries styled Brandenburg 'the sandbox of the Holy Roman Empire', so wretched was its soil. The Kingdom of East Prussia, separated until 1772 from the Hohenzollern heartlands by several hundred miles of Polish territory, was little – if any – better, with equally poor soil and an inhospitable climate. Its commercial economy also provided an unpromising basis for great-power status. Grain and grain-based products were exported from East Prussia and, to a lesser extent, from the monarchy's heartlands. But commercial activity was at a low ebb, and largely driven by the demands of the Prussian state, while poor internal communications meant that its territories were bypassed by the major continental trade routes. The urban sector was similarly underdeveloped, at least by western European and even western German standards.

The very list of the widely scattered territories ruled by the Hohenzollerns in 1740 highlights another major obstacle to Prussia's political rise. Her possessions were exposed and scattered across half the continent: from enclaves in Westphalia through the heartlands of Brandenburg, Pomerania and Magdeburg in central Germany, astride the rivers Elbe and Oder, to distant East Prussia. The resulting problems of self-defence, in the face of threats from hostile neighbours and during a period when the acquisition of territory was the principal aim of all foreign policy, were considerable: the eastern border of East Prussia lay some 750 miles distant from the westernmost possessions in the Rhineland, a particularly great distance in an era during which communications were slow and unreliable. As Voltaire remarked, Frederick was really 'King of the border strips'. All the great powers faced wide-ranging and dispersed political commitments, as a consequence of their territorial extent. What made Prussia's position unique was the very limited resources available to support such wide-ranging involvement.

Territorial dispersal, together with the very limited demographic and economic resources, were always serious obstacles to Prussia ever securely establishing herself as a great power. Yet Frederick also inherited considerable assets when he succeeded his father on 31 May 1740. Foremost among these was an army unusually large for a country of its size and population. Successive Hohenzollern rulers, aware of the vulnerability of their possessions, had built up a large military force for self-defence. Its creation had shaped domestic developments since the Great Elector's accession in 1640, and during Frederick William I's reign it ordinarily consumed around 70 per cent of the state's annual revenue in peacetime. At Frederick's accession, this force was some 80,000 strong, impressive on the barrack square, but untested in combat. With the exception of some operations in the Rhineland in 1734, during the War of the Polish Succession, it had not fired a shot in anger since the siege of Stralsund in 1715. The last important Hohenzollern victory had been gained as long ago as 1675, when the Great Elector won an unexpected success over the renowned Swedish army at Fehrbellin, though Prussian contingents had fought impressively in the Allied armies during the War of the Spanish Succession.

This powerful army was supported, and to a considerable degree made possible, by a system of conscription, which had taken its final shape in 1733. The famous cantonal system enabled a first-class army to be maintained on the scanty available resources and contributed significantly to Prussia's political emergence. An officer cadre was provided by the territorial nobility: under Frederick William I, the Junkers had come to dominate the military commands and, to a lesser extent, the civil administration. He also bequeathed to his son a war-chest (*Staatsschatz*) of eight million thalers in gold coin, wrapped up in sacks and stored in the basement of the royal palace in Berlin. Finally, Frederick inherited an admired and relatively efficient administrative system, the centrepiece of which was the General Directory, set up in 1723. Within the limitations of eighteenth-century government, this was relatively successful in extracting the men, money and agrarian produce needed to support the army and pay the other expenses of the Prussian state.

With the benefit of hindsight, it can be seen that the military and administrative foundations which had been laid by 1740, together with the degree of social integration achieved under Frederick William I, would provide a strong basis for Prussia's eighteenth-century career as a great power. But these advantages, in the estimation of most contemporaries, were insufficient to overcome the drawbacks, above all Prussia's territorial vulnerability and her basic poverty in people and economic resources. This was her Achilles' heel, and it preoccupied Frederick the Great throughout his reign. Eighteenth-century Prussia always lacked the resources required to establish herself securely as a great power. The achievement of her rulers, and especially of Frederick himself, was to make her a first-class state on a material base more appropriate to a country of the second or even third order. Even by the king's death in 1786 and after the important acquisitions of Silesia, East Friesland and West Prussia, the Hohenzollern monarchy remained only the thirteenth-largest European state in terms of population and the tenth in terms of its geographical extent, though its army ranked fourth (or even third) in size.

There was more to the status of a great power, however, than resources: these were only one factor in a complex equation. The eighteenth-century states-system was based upon a considerable degree of reciprocity. If established great powers treated a state as one of their number, then that country *ipso facto* became a member of Europe's political elite. It thus resembled a British gentlemen's club: election by the existing members was a precondition for admission. Prussia became a great power through her startling military and, to a lesser extent, political successes between 1740 and 1763, despite lacking the essential material base. Her eighteenth-century pre-eminence was thus founded upon sand. It was only after 1815 that the Hohenzollerns gained the resources to support the leading European role to which they aspired and which they would play after the middle of the nineteenth century. The territorial settlement established by the Congress of Vienna enormously enhanced Prussia's demographic and economic power, and endowed her with a much stronger strategic position, after the loss of most of the eastern provinces gained by the three partitions of Poland-Lithuania during the eighteenth century and their replacement by substantial and wealthy territories in western Germany.

Mid-eighteenth-century Prussia had one additional advantage that proved decisive. This was the personality of her remarkable king, Frederick II (widely known as 'the Great' from the end of the Seven Years' War onwards, if not actually earlier). Political leadership was always important and sometimes decisive within the competitive states-system of eighteenth-century Europe, and never more so than where Prussia was concerned. Resources and external recognition were vital in the creation of a great power. But there was another essential quality, which existed at a conceptual and philosophical level. To become a member of Europe's political elite, a state – or, rather, its ruler and the monarch's advisers – had to think and act like a great power.

In Prussia's case, the crucial moment in this transition was Frederick the Great's accession at the end of May 1740. His predecessor had accepted Prussia's secondary political role, pursuing essentially limited objectives – such as the established Hohenzollern dynastic claims to the western German enclaves of Jülich and Berg (which were located next to the dynasty's Rhineland possession of Cleves). Frederick William I had always operated within a relatively narrow and prescribed political framework and had usually been content to follow the lead of the Emperor, Charles VI. The contrast after his son's accession was striking and significant. From his earliest days upon the Hohenzollern throne – indeed, from his days as crown prince – Frederick the Great thought and acted like the ruler of a first-class power, and within a quarter-century he had secured this status for Prussia. Believing that the political *status quo* was not an option and that territorial expansion was essential to overcome Prussian poverty and strategic vulnerability, the young king pursued the expansionist aims which he believed to be the logical conclusion of his father's impressive domestic achievements. His political vision was far wider than that of his predecessors, encompassing the whole European diplomatic chessboard. This was apparent in an immediate enlargement of Hohenzollern aims – demonstrated in the invasion of Silesia at the very end of 1740, little more than six months after Frederick had ascended the throne – which transcended the purely dynastic and largely German objectives that had driven policy under Frederick William I. Central to this was Frederick's determination that his state would be politically independent, rather than – as under his own father – subject to outside influences in the conduct of its foreign policy.

Prussia's eighteenth-century trajectory as a great power is inextricably bound up with the career and reign of Frederick the Great. By his political vision, his military successes and his diplomatic skills, he made his kingdom into a first-class state, while all his life aware that Prussia lacked the resources to sustain this role and that it would prove to be transient. His decisive political leadership was the result of remarkable abilities and an ego to match.

It was facilitated by a silent revolution in Prussian government shortly after Frederick's accession, which gave the new king complete control of Berlin's diplomacy. Until 1740, day-to-day responsibility for Prussia's foreign policy had been exercised by the *Kabinettsministerium*, under the king's overall direction.[4] Set up in 1728, and known as the *Kabinettsministerium* after 1733, it was organized – like all Hohenzollern government – on a collegial basis. It embodied the assumption that two or more advisers should together discuss policy, meet diplomats, correspond with Prussia's own representatives in other capitals and conduct negotiations, all directly supervised by the king. In the early weeks of Frederick the Great's reign, these arrangements were altered. Confident in his own abilities and anxious to demonstrate them, and openly contemptuous of those who had served his father, whom he held responsible for Prussia's political subservience during that reign, Frederick took over complete and direct responsibility for Prussian foreign policy, which he retained until the very end of his life. The experienced officials in the *Kabinettsministerium* and especially the leading adviser,

---

4    There is a detailed, if rather ideologically coloured, study by Meta Kohnke, 'Das preussische Kabinettsministerium', *Jahrbuch für Geschichte der Feudalismus* 2 (1978), 313–56, which summarizes an unpublished thesis of the same title (Humboldt University, [East] Berlin, 1968). See also H. M. Scott, 'Prussia's royal foreign minister: Frederick the Great and the administration of Prussian diplomacy', in Robert Oresko *et al.* (eds), *Royal and Republican Sovereignty in early modern Europe: Essays in memory of Ragnhild Hatton* (Cambridge, 1997), pp. 500–26.

Heinrich von Podewils, found their status and responsibilities downgraded to that of mere secretaries. They were mostly excluded from the formulation of policy, at least towards the major states, and while they continued to hold audiences with foreign diplomats, these became largely formal in nature: their own ignorance of Prussian policy meant that there was nothing to discuss. Policy was instead drawn up and executed by the king himself, who conducted the bulk of correspondence with Prussia's own diplomats and also negotiated personally with foreign representatives in Berlin. Since – in addition to acting as his own foreign minister – Frederick was also commander-in-chief of the army, there was an unusual degree of coherence and unity in Prussian decision-making, in contrast to the divided counsels which prevailed in the capitals of rival powers. Rapid and incisive decision-making was to be one foundation of Prussia's political rise.

## Prussia's emergence, 1740–6

That emergence was inaugurated by the sudden and wholly unexpected invasion of Silesia in December 1740. This wealthy and strategically located Habsburg province, nominally part of the Kingdom of Bohemia, lay to the south and east of the principal Hohenzollern territory of Brandenburg. It was not an immediately obvious Prussian target.[5] When Frederick, as crown prince in the early 1730s, had mused about possible future annexations, it had not been mentioned. His list of potential territorial gains had comprised Polish Prussia, Swedish Pomerania, the neighbouring Duchy of Mecklenburg and Jülich-Berg. Berlin, however, had not always been unaware of the attraction of Silesia. Under the Great Elector, a plan had been drawn up to seize the province, not on the basis of any legal right, but simply as a political *coup*. This scheme was rediscovered in the Hohenzollern archives in 1731 and may have been known to Crown Prince Frederick, though this cannot be definitively established. Prussian claims to Silesia had not formed part of Berlin's policy under Frederick William I, though that ruler had been preoccupied with pursuing what he regarded as his dynastic rights. The long-established Hohenzollern claims to the province, or at least to parts of it, were duly paraded in 1740, but these were tendentious and at

---

5   It seems first to have been mentioned in Podewils's paper of 29 October 1740, drawn up as part of the conference between the king, Field-Marshal Schwerin and the foreign minister at Rheinsberg: *Politische Correspondenz Friedrichs des Grossen*, ed. J. G. Droysen *et al.*, 46 vols (Berlin, 1879–1939) [hereafter *Pol. Corr.*], i, p. 75.

best a smoke-screen for annexation. Dynastic rights, so crucial for Frederick William I, were less important to Frederick than power politics. Legal niceties influenced the new king far less than calculations rooted in assessments of political opportunity and advantage. The seizure of Silesia was a defining moment in Prussia's rise to great-power status: it revealed the new ideology of *raison d'état* that now drove Hohenzollern policies.

Frederick became a contemporary historian of considerable significance, with unique access to the archives (which he exploited) and a central role in the events he described. The king subsequently penned an account of the invasion, in his *History of My Own Times* (*Histoire de mon temps*), in which he explained how the decision to invade was carefully considered and based upon the favourable circumstances in 1740–1. Austria was paralysed and vulnerable after the unexpected death of Charles VI on 20 October 1740. The emperor's lack of a male heir had barred the Habsburg succession to the Holy Roman Empire, to which a woman could not be elected, and imperilled that to the Monarchy itself. The Pragmatic Sanction provided for the succession of his daughter, Maria Theresa, to the dynastic possessions that made up the Habsburg Monarchy, but she inherited an enfeebled and near-bankrupt polity. It had been defeated in two wars during the previous decade, the first over the Polish Succession (1733–5) and then against the Ottoman Empire (1737–9, fought in alliance with Russia), at the end of which Vienna had had to cede some of the territorial gains secured by the Peace of Passarowitz (1718). Austria's army was in a wretched condition, her treasury was empty, while the youthful and inexperienced Maria Theresa lacked generals and political advisers.

The international constellation was also portrayed in Frederick's narrative as being highly favourable to Prussia. Britain and Spain had been at war since 1739 and, though France was unofficially aiding her Bourbon cousin in Madrid, Frederick believed that she would assist him if he attacked her traditional enemy, Austria. Russia – which would always loom very large in Frederick's political calculations – was paralysed by the death of the Empress Anna in the same month as Charles VI. She was succeeded by a faction-riddled regency for the child-emperor Ivan VI, who would in turn be swept from the throne in 1741 and replaced by Elizabeth.

Frederick's analysis has been widely influential, underlining the extent to which the king has been his own historian. Yet, it was strongly tinged by hindsight. In the closing months of 1740, France's decisive support could not be relied upon, since Versailles' policies were shaped by the veteran minister Cardinal Fleury, who now sought peace with Austria and instead was preparing to confront Britain. The king's account also gives insufficient weight to the spontaneity and youthful adventure that lay behind the invasion. Prussia's ruler subsequently wrote of his 'rendezvous with fame', his desire to 'see his name in the gazettes', and his wish to in-augurate his reign with a striking political *coup*. His conduct at this time, and his correspondence for these months, reveal few suggestions of mature political calculation and much evidence of youthful bravado and rapid improvisation.[6]

Within eight days of Charles VI's death, Frederick had decided to invade. In view of the time taken for the news to reach Berlin, this means that the king decided to act very shortly after he received word of the emperor's death.[7] Both his chief diplomatic adviser, Podewils, and the leading military figure, Field-Marshal Kurt Christoph, Graf von Schwerin, urged caution and in effect advised against the enterprise. The episode highlighted the king's complete control of Prussia's policy. Podewils and Schwerin exempli-fied the older traditions, which had hitherto prevailed: the avoidance of risk, peace at almost any price, the pursuit of dynastic claims by tenacious diplomacy rather than a military *coup*, far less one with all the apparent risks of attacking a great power, albeit one with serious short-term problems. The decision to invade was Frederick's alone, and exemplified the new spirit which guided Prussia's policy. Opportunities were there to be seized, and Prussia's king judged that which presented itself in 1740 to be uniquely favourable. He may also have feared that Bavaria or Saxony might act if Prussia did not herself seize the political initiative.

The Habsburg Monarchy was, in fact, even more vulnerable than it appeared to be. Silesia contained fewer than 8,000 men, reflecting Vienna's confidence in Prussia's support for the Pragmatic Sanction.[8] Most of the Austrian army was still based in Hungary or Transylvania, in the after-math of the Turkish War. Frederick by contrast had built up his army since his own accession, and now had some 82,000 men under arms. On 16 December 1740, he led a force 27,000 strong across the frontier into Silesia, encountering minimal Austrian resistance. Though the severe Silesian winter and the state of the roads posed considerable problems for the invaders, the province was overrun within six weeks. By the end of January 1741, most of the territory (Upper and Lower Silesia, together with the County of Glatz) along with its capital, Breslau, was under Prussian control. An attempted Habsburg counter-attack in the spring was unsuccessful. In

---

6  *Pol. Corr.*, i, pp. 73–149, *passim*.
7  Indeed, on the very day that he heard of Charles VI's death, Prussia's ruler set aside 200,000 thalers to purchase foreign rye in the event of war, in itself an indication of how his mind was already working: W. O. Henderson, *Studies in the Economic Policy of Frederick the Great* (London, 1963), p. 9.
8  Precise figures for the size of the Austrian and Prussian armies are given by Peter H. Wilson, *German armies: war and German politics, 1648–1806* (London, 1998), pp. 247–8.

April 1741, the well-drilled Prussian infantry won a signal if decidedly fortuitous victory over the Austrians at Mollwitz. This battle was notable for the king's absence from the battlefield during its decisive phase, after the failure of an initial cavalry charge, which he had ordered. It was the first important Prussian victory since the Great Elector's reign, and its laurels belonged to the young king. The success, however, had been gained not by Frederick, but by the veteran commander Schwerin and the disciplined fire of the Prussian infantry, honed on the training ground under Frederick William I.

Mollwitz was primarily significant in a European context. During the final years of his life, Charles VI had secured widespread international support for the Pragmatic Sanction. Though several states were prepared to advance claims to parts of Maria Theresa's inheritance, none did so directly until Prussia's invasion revealed the extent of Austrian vulnerability. Only Bavaria, which had earlier rejected the Pragmatic Sanction, had challenged her accession. Frederick's initial victory, and his successful occupation of Silesia, encouraged the formation of a wide-ranging coalition directed against Austria. The League of Nymphenberg, an anti-Austrian alliance, which took shape during 1741, eventually contained Bavaria and Saxony (two middle-ranking German states with their own claims to parts of the Habsburg inheritance), the North Italian state of Savoy-Piedmont, Spain and, crucially, France, where a military faction at court headed by the marshal-duc de Belle-Isle overthrew Fleury's pacific policies and launched a war intended to destroy Habsburg power once and for all. French military intervention in 1741, rather than the earlier Prussian seizure of Silesia, was to prove crucial in bringing about Austria's military defeat.

The War of the Austrian Succession would not be concluded until October and November 1748, when the Peace of Aix-la-Chapelle was signed. Yet Prussia was actually at war for less than half this time: some three years out of a total of eight. German scholarship, acknowledging this, refers not to the 'War of the Austrian Succession', but to the 'First Silesian War' (1740–2) and the 'Second Silesian War' (1744–5). By spring 1742, Frederick's war-chest was all but exhausted, and in June he signed a unilateral peace with Maria Theresa (the Treaty of Breslau, confirmed by a second agreement at Berlin in the following month) by which Prussia withdrew from the war in return for guaranteed possession of Silesia. When this appeared to be threatened by an Austrian recovery in the middle phase of the war, the king re-entered the fighting in August 1744. Impressive victories over the Austrians at Hohenfriedberg (June 1745) and Soor (September), together with the decisive success won by the veteran Prussian commander, Prince Leopold of Anhalt, at Kesseldorf (December), enabled the king to conclude another unilateral settlement with Vienna. By the Peace of Dresden (December 1745), Frederick withdrew from the struggle for the final time in return for a further guarantee of Silesia. The eventual peace settlement at Aix-la-Chapelle confirmed Prussian possession, and provided an international guarantee that the king valued greatly. The Hohenzollern monarchy's enhanced international status was evident in the way in which both her present ally France and her would-be ally Britain competed for the honour of inserting this clause into the final settlement.

Frederick gained Silesia by exploiting the wider continental struggle and allowing other states to bear the brunt of the fighting against Austria. Convinced of Prussia's strategic vulnerability and believing that scarce resources forced him to fight what he termed 'lively and short wars' – his father's war-chest had been seriously depleted after only two campaigns – the king pursued an opportunistic and single-minded strategy that gained him a new province and considerably enhanced international standing, at the price of a well-deserved and enduring reputation for faithlessness where international agreements were concerned. The three occasions on which he had deserted the anti-Austrian coalition – first in October 1741 by the truce of Kleinschnellendorf disguised by a sham siege, then by the unilateral settlements of Breslau–Berlin and Dresden – were not forgotten by his partners, especially France, and would come back to haunt him in the years ahead. Prussia's armies had won some significant victories, though there had been reverses as well: the retreat from Bohemia in the final months of 1744 had been close to a disaster. Prussia's army, however, had gained considerably in reputation. Neighbouring states, such as Hanover (whose elector was also king of Great Britain) and Saxony (whose ruling family were also kings of Poland-Lithuania until 1763), were alarmed by the new potential of the Prussian military state. The extent to which its revenues and resources were devoted to the single objective of supporting a formidable army, now approaching 150,000 strong, caused particular anxiety among other continental states. There is no doubt that Prussia's striking gain, which was extremely unusual in the eighteenth century because it had involved seizing territory from an established great power rather than a second-rank or declining state, increased her political standing. Other chancelleries were far more aware of Prussian power than a decade before, and were anxious to understand how such a poor and seemingly vulnerable state could support such a formidable army. They therefore collected and analysed all the information they could about the Hohenzollern monarchy and its remarkable ruler.

It is important, however, not to exaggerate what Frederick had accomplished by 1748. He had gained territory and prestige for his state, and renown for himself, but he had not made Prussia a great power.[9] That would not be accomplished until the Seven Years' War had been fought and drawn. Silesia was a considerable addition, particularly for the impoverished Hohenzollern monarchy. Though economic motives had not played any part in the invasion, the new province's importance to Prussia came to be primarily commercial. In 1739 – the last year of Habsburg rule – it had paid one-quarter of the direct taxation collected by Vienna from the so-called Hereditary Lands, which testified to its prosperity and economic importance. Populous and with a strong agrarian economy, it brought the king one million new subjects, including a substantial Protestant minority who welcomed the Prussians as liberators. The Oder, which ran through Silesia and then Brandenburg on its way to the Baltic, was now a potentially important commercial artery. The thriving Silesian linen industry was crucial to Prussia's backward economy while, with state support, woollen production would develop impressively. The new province's economic importance was evident in the fact that, within a decade, it was providing no less than 45 per cent of Prussia's total exports. It thus brought what the Hohenzollern monarchy had hitherto lacked: a manufacturing region. In the longer perspective, its abundant mineral resources would provide one basis for a significant nineteenth-century Industrial Revolution.

At the time, however, it posed problems for the government in Berlin. The new province had to be integrated into the Prussian administrative system and this proved to be a difficult and protracted process, while fortifications had to be improved to make it more defensible. Its acquisition increased the already extended borders that had to be defended, while the wedge it drove between Saxony and Poland-Lithuania, united in a personal union under the Wettins, strengthened that dynasty's enmity towards Prussia. Above all, Austria was unreconciled to its loss, which compromised Habsburg security and military strategy. Prussian possession of Silesia meant that the invasion route from its foothills across the Bohemian plain to the very gates of Vienna lay open, with only Moravia as a defensive barrier behind which Austrian forces could organize. From his Silesian redoubt, Frederick could and did invade Bohemia at will, and this proved to be significant during the Seven Years' War. Silesia's strategic and material benefits, however, were less important than its symbolic importance for both Prussia and Austria. By securing the province, Prussia signalled to her neighbours and to the leading European states that she was a rising political force, was now knocking on the door of the great powers and might soon enter their ranks.

---

9 Prussia's continuing political inferiority within an international system dominated by Britain, France and (perhaps) Austria, is apparent from the King's analysis in the Political Testament of 1752: *Die politischen Testamente*, ed. Dietrich, p. 344 and *passim*.

# Consolidation, 1746–56

Frederick himself acknowledged the considerable, but still incomplete, progress his state had made on the European stage. He saw, more clearly than many foreign observers, the shortcomings of the Prussian army, upon which his international position ultimately depended. The period of peace which followed the end of the First Silesian War in June 1742 had seen determined efforts to put right the major weaknesses evident in the Prussian cavalry and to improve the infantry, and these were resumed after 1745. During the next decade, the Prussian army was significantly overhauled and considerably expanded under the king's personal supervision in a series of inspections, parades and manoeuvres. Simultaneously, administrative changes were made to strengthen Hohenzollern government and particularly its ability to exploit the new province of Silesia and to encourage the development of state industries. Their broader aim was to integrate the Prussian economy still further into the military state. Its success was apparent in the increasing proportion of royal income spent on the army. Under Frederick William I, this had been around 70 per cent. Between 1740 and 1756, it rose to 83 per cent and, during the Seven Years' War, it would reach 87 per cent.

This domestic consolidation was undertaken for purely defensive purposes. After 1745, and to some extent from as early as 1742, Prussian foreign policy was passive, being conservative and defensive in nature. This did not mean that the king had abandoned the desire for further territorial gains, if favourable opportunities presented themselves. East Friesland, and with it direct access to the North Sea, was secured in 1744, as part of a complex dynastic dispute. The king still had covetous eyes on Polish Prussia, the wide corridor of land which separated Brandenburg and East Pomerania from the distant Kingdom of Prussia. But he believed that any gains would probably have to be postponed until a future reign, because the annexation of Silesia had put all his neighbours on their guard and opportunities simply would not arise. The acquisition of the province, he wrote on one occasion, was like a book, the first publication of which was a great success, but all subsequent editions failed.[10] By this he meant that Prussia would have to re-establish trust among the other states before seeking further territorial gains. He was acutely aware of Prussia's strategic overextension and of the still-limited resources that would be available to resist an Austrian attempt to recover the province: he well understood that Vienna was unreconciled to its loss. He also recognized

---

10   Political Testament of 1752: *Die politischen Testamente*, ed. Dietrich, p. 346.

that Prussia remained a second-class power. It is striking that in his confidential survey of foreign policy, drawn up as part of the first Political Testament in 1752, he did not rank his own Hohenzollern monarchy among Europe's leading states. His analysis assumed that the international system was dominated by Britain and France, the only two unambiguous great powers, and that the next most powerful states were Austria and (in a different way) Russia.

Domestic consolidation, not further foreign adventure, was now the king's priority. Prussia's security was believed to depend upon the established alliance with France, which rested upon shared hostility towards the Austrian Habsburgs. He declared upon one occasion that the Duchy of Lorraine (from which Maria Theresa's husband, Francis Stephen, had been expelled in 1737 and which would eventually become part of the French monarchy) and Silesia were two sisters. France had married the younger and Prussia the elder, and this circumstance forced them to pursue the same policy.[11] Frederick's own conduct, however, had already weakened his ties with Versailles. During the War of the Austrian Succession, he had abandoned France on three separate occasions, by signing unilateral agreements with Vienna in defiance of his treaty obligations: in October 1741, June 1742 and December 1745. This had secured Silesia, but at the price of worsening relations with France, where his desertion was neither forgotten nor forgiven. In the short term, however, the War of the Austrian Succession had strengthened the Franco-Prussian axis. This was because Bavaria's decline, strikingly evident during the 1740s, had made Prussia the principal basis for France's policy within the Holy Roman Empire. Prussia's French alliance appeared secure as long as Versailles' foreign policy retained its established anti-Austrian orientation, and in 1748, at the end of the latest attempt to destroy Habsburg power, that seemed unlikely to change.[12] Prussia's essential problem was that her acquisition of Silesia had been made possible by the existing diplomatic constellation, but her own rise threatened and eventually destroyed those very patterns upon which she depended.

Before long, a new direction in Austrian foreign policy posed a challenge to the Prusso-French axis.[13] Its proponent was a Moravian nobleman, Wenzel

11 Political Testament of 1752: *Die politischen Testamente*, ed. Dietrich, p. 344.
12 For the king's confidence on this point, see Political Testament of 1752: *Die politischen Testamente*, ed. Dietrich, p. 346.
13 The classic, though occasionally somewhat determinist, account remains Max Braubach, *Versailles und Wien von Ludwig XIV. bis Kaunitz: die Vorstadien der diplomatischen Revolution im 18. Jahrhundert* (Bonn, 1952), pp. 360–456; for Kaunitz's early career, see Grete Klingenstein, *Der Aufstieg des Hauses Kaunitz: Studien zur Herkunft und Bildung des Staatskanzlers Wenzel Anton* (Göttingen, 1975), pp. 158–301. The recent study by Lothar Schilling, *Kaunitz und das Renversement des alliances: Studien zur aussenpolitischen Konzeption Wenzel Antons von Kaunitz* (Berlin, 1994), provides a thought-provoking examination of his approach to international relations at this period.

Anton von Kaunitz, who was one of a group of younger advisers who had emerged during the 1740s and came to prominence in 1749, during debates in Vienna about the future direction of Habsburg foreign policy. He appreciated that Prussia's rise within Germany between 1740 and 1745 had made Frederick the greatest enemy of Maria Theresa, and sought to realign Habsburg priorities to take account of this. The recovery of Silesia was seen as the principal Austrian objective, and important administrative and military reforms were already under way, in preparation for a future war. They were accompanied by a reorientation of Vienna's diplomacy, which now recognized Prussia and not France as its principal enemy. With Maria Theresa's decisive support, Kaunitz argued for and set out to create not merely a *rapprochement* with Versailles, but an actual alliance. Sent to France as ambassador (1750–2), he unsuccessfully pursued such a treaty: at this point, the established diplomatic patterns held firm. In 1753, Kaunitz was appointed Habsburg foreign minister (*Staatskanzler*) and, though for the moment his planned alliance with France made no obvious progress, Austria's eventual aim was clear.

By the second half of 1755, Prussia's international position was beginning to unravel, against a background of an undeclared Anglo-French war in North America, which was heightening tension within Europe and threatened to spread to the continent.[14] Frederick had always feared the potential power of Russia and the threat it presented to his own East Prussian kingdom. He knew that the Empress Elizabeth and her leading minister, the Chancellor Alexis P. Bestuzhev-Riumin, were anxious to weaken Prussian power, which was seen as a potential rival in the eastern Baltic and an obstacle to further Russian expansion westwards. Frederick was aware that a Russo-Austrian agreement signed in 1746, the so-called Treaty of the Two Empresses (renewing an alliance first concluded twenty years before), contained a secret clause which provided for the partition of the Hohenzollern monarchy. Yet, until the mid-1750s, Frederick believed that Russia's lack of a wealthy ally would protect him from attack. He calculated that St Petersburg's own poverty and backwardness was so great that only subsidies could propel the Russian military machine into action.[15] In September 1755, Europe's leading commercial state, Britain, concluded a subsidy convention (that of St Petersburg) putting Russian troops and ships at London's disposal as part of the British diplomatic effort to threaten Prussia (France's ally) and in this way protect George II's Hanoverian homeland should war spread to Europe. Though this convention was never ratified and so remained

---

14   Frederick's foreign policy in the critical months from mid-1755 until late August 1756 can be followed in *Pol. Corr.*, xi–xiii *passim*.

15   Political Testament of 1752: *Die politischen Testamente*, ed. Dietrich, pp. 334, 348.

stillborn, it set in motion a series of events which revolutionized European diplomacy and involved Frederick in the new war that he had long dreaded.

The king feared Russia and her threat to East Prussia. This, together with the apparent British–Russian axis, forced Frederick to act to strengthen his own security. In January 1756, building on some generalized British approaches, which had begun in the middle of the previous year, Prussia's king signed a remarkably vague agreement – far short of a treaty of defensive alliance – with Britain, the so-called Convention of Westminster. This provided for joint action to protect the peace of Germany, if the Anglo-French colonial war should lead to a French attack on Hanover. It was a further part of London's attempts to protect George II's Electorate through diplomatic agreements with continental powers. Though this proved a misjudgement on Frederick's part, by the winter of 1755–56, his options were rapidly narrowing and it was an understandable reaction to the Anglo-Russian agreement and Prussia's own deteriorating security position.

The Convention of Westminster had a decisive impact at the French court, where it was seen as Frederick's latest and most serious betrayal. This was especially serious as the Franco-Prussian alliance was about to lapse and needed to be renewed. Prussia's agreement with Britain ensured no new treaty would be signed. Instead, it breathed new life into the Austro-French negotiations, until then becalmed. Kaunitz's renewed offers of an alliance were accepted, and the resulting First Treaty of Versailles was formally signed on 1 May 1756. This conventional defensive alliance was the centrepiece of the famous 'Diplomatic Revolution' of that year, ending as it did a tradition of political rivalry and open warfare between the Austrian Habsburgs and the French monarchy that went back to the end of the fifteenth century. The Austro-French *rapprochement* was a particularly serious matter for Frederick, since it completed the encirclement of Prussia, which now stood isolated against three powerful enemies. The Hohenzollerns' principal foe, Austria, had alliances with France and Russia, and was preparing for a war that – Frederick believed – would be launched in spring 1757. Against this threatening background, the king seized the initiative and, on 29 August 1756, led his troops into neighbouring Saxony, thereby precipitating the continental Seven Years' War.

The invasion of Saxony, like that of Silesia fifteen years earlier, appeared to be a simple matter of aggression. That was the view of most contemporaries and has been the opinion of many later historians. To the charge of military aggression can be added that of diplomatic miscalculation. Austria's alliances with France and Russia were purely defensive in nature and required a Prussian attack to make them operative: as Kaunitz was well aware. If Austria had launched a war in spring 1757, the Habsburgs would have had Russia (which had mobilized for an attack on Prussia in spring

1756: one source of Frederick's anxieties at that time, until it was suspended), but not France on their side. French armies and subsidies, however, were crucial to Kaunitz's calculations. By invading Saxony, a member of whose ruling family was married to the French *dauphin* [heir apparent], Frederick ensured that Louis XV's monarchy would fight in the continental war and would commit her considerable resources to the defeat of Prussia. The king had always believed that his military superiority would enable him to win a war against Austria and Russia alone, but he now faced a conflict involving France as well.

The Prussian invasion of Saxony can be explained in less damaging terms. Frederick had wanted to avoid war, but once convinced it was inevitable, he set out to dictate its shape and nature. The decision to invade Saxony was, once again, his alone: only General Hans Karl von Winterfeldt, a rising star in the Prussian military establishment, among his advisers and immediate family supported the war. By mid-June 1756, the king was convinced that he would be attacked in the following spring, and might even have to face three armies simultaneously.[16] Determined that any war must be as short as possible to protect Prussia's limited resources, he concluded that he should seize the initiative. Frederick was also concerned about the frontier with Saxony, which was only fifty miles from his own capital, Berlin. He feared that the Electorate would be used as an advanced bridgehead for an attack.[17] Supplies could be moved rapidly down the River Elbe, which flowed through the Electorate before bisecting Hohenzollern territory. Prussia's king also seems to have believed that Saxony was, or would soon become, a member of the coalition that threatened him. In these circumstances, there was a strong military argument – and as war approached, military factors came to predominate over diplomatic considerations in Frederick's thinking – for a pre-emptive strike. In 1744–5, Prussian troops had violated the Electorate's territory, after its ruler had re-entered the war on Austria's side, in a dress rehearsal for their behaviour after 1756. In the event, Frederick's actions in the late summer and autumn of that year enjoyed apparent success. The Elector's army was surrounded and disbanded, and 18,000 soldiers were incorporated into Prussian regiments, though many subsequently deserted. The Saxon ruler was permitted to withdraw to his Polish kingdom, where he remained until the end of the Seven Years' War. His electoral territories were despoiled to support Prussia's struggle for survival: more than one-third of the entire cost of Prussia's Seven Years' War was to be raised from the occupied Electorate. Yet the

---

16  See the correspondence for these months in *Pol. Corr.*, xii.
17  Dennis E. Showalter, *The Wars of Frederick the Great* (London, 1996), p. 132.

invasion of Saxony, however successful and even prudent it may have seemed to its author, has helped to consolidate Frederick's historical reputation as a reckless aggressor who had twice thrust the continent into destructive and extended conflicts.

# Survival, 1756–63

The anti-Prussian coalition during the Seven Years' War consisted of two established great powers (France and Austria), Russia, which was about to join their ranks, the second-class state of Sweden, together with contingents of soldiers from the Holy Roman Empire. Though she sent an army 20,000 strong to Germany, the Swedish contribution was to prove negligible. Her military and financial weakness was exposed by the desultory campaigning undertaken from her base in Swedish Pomerania (the western half of Western Pomerania) between 1757 and 1762: at most, this tied up Prussian regiments that might otherwise have been committed to other fronts. The Swedish state was near-bankrupt, the army in Germany was starved of funds, and its noble commanders were reduced to depending upon their own private credit to avert starvation among their troops. Sweden's insignificant contribution to the war effort was periodically the target of Frederick's humour and derision. When, in 1762, her plenipotentiary arrived at the Prussian camp to sue for peace, the king at first feigned surprise: surely, he asked, their two countries were not at war? The soldiers from the – mainly Catholic – princes of the Holy Roman Empire made a more significant military contribution, especially during the early years of the struggle. They provided between 20,000 and 30,000 men each year to the coalition and, in so doing, highlighted the 'German civil war' dimension of the conflict, particularly in its early campaigns.

The main burden fell upon the three principal allies: Austria, France and Russia. Their military effort was hampered by political considerations. Kaunitz's alliance, so overwhelming on paper and in the resources upon which it could draw, proved to be less powerful in practice. This was in part due to the novelty of coalition warfare, still in its infancy: it would be a further half-century, in the final stages of the struggle against Napoleon, before a truly effective coalition was created by the allies, one that was capable, through diplomatic co-operation and the pursuit of an agreed strategy, of maximizing the military potential of the participants. A very different situation prevailed during the Seven Years' War. Military co-operation between Vienna, Versailles and St Petersburg was incomplete, and no co-ordinated strategy was pursued with the consistency needed to defeat Prussia. Such co-operation was handicapped by the existing political tensions, which divided the new allies and which were, in some degree, exacerbated by the reverses suffered during the war.

The fundamental problem was that the Diplomatic Revolution had brought together established enemies in a temporary partnership. This was particularly evident where Franco-Russian relations were concerned.[18] From the start of the eighteenth century, France had been aiming to shut Russia out of Europe by means of alliances with Sweden, Poland-Lithuania and the Ottoman Empire (the famous *barrière de l'est*). For centuries, the French monarchy had been the rival of Austria and had fought numerous wars against the Habsburgs of Madrid and Vienna. France's war-time co-operation with Russia was distant, and the two states broke apart amidst mutual acrimony in 1761. That with Austria was more enduring (nominally it survived until 1792) and harmonious, but still came under considerable strain, particularly as the anticipated defeat of Prussia did not materialize and French commitment to the struggle was reduced.[19] Austria, for her part, was suspicious and fearful of Russian power in the eastern half of the continent. A war fought to restore Vienna's traditional pre-eminence in Germany and Central Europe would be compromised if Prussian influence were simply replaced by Russian. This anxiety increased as the war progressed and Russia's forces assumed a greater share of the allied military effort. This was particularly significant after the great Prussian defeat at Kunersdorf in August 1759, when Frederick the Great was saved by Austria's unwillingness to co-operate militarily with the victorious Russian army, while Russia's commander did not see why his forces should bear the whole burden of the struggle.[20]

The three allies viewed the conflict in different ways, and this influenced their military operations.[21] The defeat of Prussia was a common goal, but how this was to be secured was another matter. Austria, predictably enough, viewed it simply as the Third Silesian War (as German-language historical scholarship styles it), a struggle to regain the lost province. It was to be pursued through the traditional eighteenth-century strategy of cautious advances conducted with due regard for lines of communication, a war of position, sieges and occasional battles, conducted with the aim of reconquering Silesia acre by acre. This approach was exemplified by the leading

---

18   There is a solid modern study by L. Jay Oliva, *Misalliance: a Study of French Policy in Russia during the Seven Years' War* (New York, 1964).

19   See most recently Eckhard Buddruss, *Die französische Deutschlandpolitik 1756–1789* (Mainz, 1995), esp. ch. 3.

20   There is a detailed study by D. E. Bangert, *Die russische-österreichische militärische Zusammenarbeit im Siebenjährigen Kriege in den Jahren 1758–59* (Boppard am Rhein, 1971).

21   For some stimulating reflections on the nature of the military struggle, see Johannes Kunisch, *Das Mirakel des Hauses Brandenburg* (Munich, 1978).

Habsburg commander for much of the war, the mediocre Field-Marshal Daun. St Petersburg's aim was the annexation of East Prussia, which could then be exchanged with Poland-Lithuania for the Duchy of Courland, strengthening Russia's western frontier and strategic position in the eastern Baltic. The isolated Kingdom of Prussia was occupied by Russian troops from January 1758 until the final stages of the war, reducing the incentive to pursue the total military defeat of Prussia, which would in any case have been difficult. Russia's war effort was handicapped by the logistical short-comings of her army, magnified by the problem of distance: though Poland-Lithuania – in the eighteenth century a Russian satellite – was used as a forward base, her slow-moving forces could appear only with some difficulty on Central European battlefields. From time to time, St Petersburg's military effort was hobbled by one political consideration. In September 1757, the Empress Elizabeth suffered a stroke, and her health declined thereafter. Her heir was the Grand Duke Peter (who would rule for six months in 1762 as Peter III), who was a renowned Prussophile. The danger that he might be about to ascend the throne periodically handicapped Russian military operations. No prudent commander could ignore the possible change of ruler in St Petersburg. Yet, despite these drawbacks, Russian troops bore the brunt of the allied war effort, particularly during the second half of the conflict.

This was due in considerable measure to France's reduced role in the war from 1759 onwards. French soldiers and French subsidies had been crucial to Kaunitz's planned strategy: in 1756, Louis XV's monarchy was still the leading continental state, though the conflict would reveal its decline. France was fighting not one war, but two: on the continent against Prussia, and on the high seas and in the colonies against Britain, the latest round in her eighteenth-century rivalry with that power. Even the abundant French re-sources – or at least such of them as could be mobilized for the war effort – were inadequate to support two simultaneous wars, as defeats mounted up in both struggles. On the continent, France wanted a swift victory over Prussia, in order to concentrate on the struggle with Britain. Her consider-able commitment to the 1757 campaign ended in disaster, as Frederick the Great's army won a startling victory at Rossbach (November 1757) over a Franco-Imperial army twice its size: a defeat that destroyed French military power and political credibility for a generation. In the winter of 1758–9, under the influence of a new foreign minister, the duc de Choiseul, France scaled down her commitments to the war in Europe and instead concen-trated resources against Britain. French troops operated only in Westphalia, seeking to occupy and perhaps make inroads into Frederick the Great's western flank, while the bulk of the fighting fell upon the Austrians and, increasingly, the Russians.

The shortcomings of Kaunitz's grand coalition contributed significantly to Prussia's survival. Eighteenth-century wars tended to produce marginal victories and limited political gains for one side or the other. Prussia's decisive acquisition of Silesia in the 1740s had been extremely unusual and, arguably, unique. The kind of comprehensive victory needed to prise the province from Frederick's hands was always improbable, and made more unlikely by the shortcomings evident in the allied war effort. Yet Frederick the Great's survival was due principally to his own considerable efforts and to the resilience and intrinsic strength of the Prussian military state, when compared to that of his enemies. It was particularly remarkable in view of the fact that Prussia was not merely encircled, but vastly outnumbered by her enemies. The Hohenzollern army during the Seven Years' War was about 150,000 strong. Austria alone fielded as many as 200,000, though this total was reduced in the final two years of the struggle.

Prussia's strategic position proved to be stronger than her enemies appreciated, and Frederick skilfully exploited this advantage. The dispersal of Hohenzollern possessions made her appear vulnerable, particularly to a coalition that encircled her, but by abandoning the Westphalian territories (from the very outset of the fighting) and effectively accepting that East Prussia could not be defended, the king was able to draw maximum benefit from his central position: the Seven Years' War was principally fought in Pomerania, Brandenburg, Silesia, Saxony and Bohemia. In this way, the disadvantages of encirclement and the lack of defensible frontiers were considerably reduced, and the benefits of a compact position for most of the struggle maximized. Adopting a strategy of interior lines, and striking first against one enemy and then another, Frederick was able to keep his enemies divided. During the Seven Years' War – after 1757, when his attempt to go on the offensive so nearly came to grief – the king pursued what the great German military historian Hans Delbrück rightly characterized as a 'strategy of exhaustion' (*Ermattungsstrategie*). Within what was fundamentally a defensive strategy, he carried out a series of sorties against each of his enemies and successfully prevented them from uniting and delivering the decisive blow that their far superior resources should have brought. In the event, Prussia sustained an extended war better than any of her enemies.

Frederick was able to do this because, for much of the war, his own vulnerable left flank was protected by a British-financed 'Army of Observation', commanded by Prince Ferdinand of Brunswick and containing German mercenaries and some British regulars. This was the most important benefit that Prussia derived from her wartime partnership with Britain, which rested upon a subsidy treaty first concluded in spring 1758 and renewed annually until 1761, but which dissolved, amidst considerable mutual acrimony, in the following winter.[22] Frederick also received an annual subsidy of £670,000 for four years, and this contributed almost one-fifth of the total costs of the war. Prussia may also have secured a measure of psychological support from her British connection, since it meant that she was not totally isolated. Yet the Prusso-British partnership was never more than a temporary wartime expedient, born of mutual isolation and characterized by strain and distrust. In retrospect, the surprising thing is not that the two states eventually split, but that they remained partners for so long. Britain saw Frederick as her continental ally against France, not against Austria or Russia (who were not formally London's enemies during the Seven Years' War), and this restricted her contribution to the Hohenzollern war effort. The Prusso-British axis was even less securely based than the alliances that fought against Frederick the Great.

Prussia's home front proved remarkably resilient, and more successful than those of her enemies in raising the money and the men needed to support the war effort. As the demographic cohort was exhausted, the cantonal system was placed under considerable strain, and in the final campaigns was producing recruits far inferior to the infantry who had contested the early battles. In recognition of the reduced military quality of the Prussian rank-and-file, the king relied more upon his artillery in the struggle's final years. However, Frederick was probably better provided with recruits, and with conscripts of a superior quality, throughout the war than his principal enemy, Austria, whose manpower problems were at times acute. Only the Russian army, drawing upon a much broader demographic base and a relatively efficient, if brutal, system of conscription, enjoyed a more plentiful supply of soldiers. In a similar way, the Hohenzollern administration – despite the salaries of its officials being paid in vouchers rather than cash for extended periods (1757–9; 1761–2) and sometimes suspended altogether – was better able than its Austrian or Russian counterparts to scrape together the *matériel*, soldiers and money needed to sustain the military effort. The Seven Years' War, at one level, simply demonstrated the relative superiority of the Prussian military state over the administrative and army systems of its principal enemies. This underpinned the success of Frederick's 'strategy of exhaustion'.

The king himself likened Prussia's survival to that of a trapeze artist, creeping towards safety along the high wire with the ever-present danger

---

22   There are impressive studies of the alliance by P. F. Doran, *Andrew Mitchell and Anglo-Prussian Diplomatic Relations during the Seven Years' War* (New York, 1986), and of its break-up by Karl W. Schweizer, *Frederick the Great, William Pitt, and Lord Bute: the Anglo-Prussian Alliance, 1756–1763* (New York, 1991).

that he would fall to his death.[23] This image captured the desperate straits to which Frederick, his army and his monarchy were frequently reduced. His own contribution was immense, not least in refusing to admit defeat in the most desperate circumstances, while the army fought bravely and sometimes heroically. Prussia and her king hung on for a draw, and in the process became a great power. That survival was secured principally on the battlefield and on campaign. The Seven Years' War established Frederick as the leading commander of his age, though his military record was far from perfect. In the fighting after 1756, Frederick lost as many battles as he won: seven or eight out of sixteen (depending on whether Zorndorf is seen as a Prussian defeat, a victory, or – most plausibly – simply as a bloody stalemate). Several of his victories were important to the eventual outcome. The striking victory at Rossbach (November 1757) and the even more impressive success at Leuthen (December 1757) retrieved a seemingly hopeless position. They enabled Prussia to surmount the first crisis of the conflict, created by the king's own miscalculation in going on the offensive in the first full campaign of the war. In 1760, victories at Liegnitz (August) and Torgau (November) effectively ended Austria's hopes of military victory over her bitter enemy.

In the end, Frederick was saved by the death of one of his most implacable foes, the Russian Empress Elizabeth, in January 1762. Her successor, Peter III, rushed to sign first an armistice and then a peace settlement with his hero Frederick the Great. Though the Emperor was in turn swept from the throne by his wife, who became ruler as Catherine II, Russia did not re-enter the war and Austria – after one final and indecisive campaign – was forced to accept peace in February 1763 at Hubertusburg. Russia's withdrawal in 1762, rather than Frederick's own survival after the shattering defeat at Kunersdorf in 1759, was the real 'miracle of the House of Brandenburg'. At the same time, however, it highlighted the ambiguity of Prussia's new-found pre-eminence by the closing stages of the Seven Years' War.

The nineteenth-century German historian, Leopold von Ranke, once defined a great power as a state that could survive an attack by two or more major states on its own resources and without outside aid. This definition was familiar to the eighteenth century. By that yardstick, Prussia was clearly a great power by 1763. She had survived an extended conflict with three major states and emerged without suffering any territorial losses: the Peace of Hubertusburg restored the territorial *status quo ante bellum*, an outcome that had seemed improbable – not least to Frederick himself – for most of

---

23  Schieder, *Friedrich der Grosse*, p. 191.

the war. The Seven Years' War had also seen the Russian state, with its immeasurably greater potential resources, join Europe's political elite, mainly through its impressive military performance. For the first time, Russia's soldiers had played an important role in a general European war, rather than simply in a conflict in the Baltic region or in the south against the declining Ottoman Empire, and had even defeated the impressive Prussian army, which was regarded as the continent's leading military force. Russia had gained no territory from the fighting, but her prestige was much enhanced and she emerged as the real winner in the European Seven Years' War. Catherine II's empire was very clearly a rival to Prussia for ascendancy in Northern and Eastern Europe, and potentially the dominant power throughout the eastern half of the continent.

Prussia's new position as a European great power was, from the first, flawed. It rested upon insufficient demographic and economic resources to support the obligations of its enhanced political stature, while its widely scattered territories made it more vulnerable than any other major state. To adapt Frederick's own description of his inheritance two decades before, Prussia was now a great power in name, but a second-class state in fact. Above all, its position was already being challenged by the other rising power of the mid-eighteenth century, Russia. The Prussian king's achievement had been to maximize the assets and minimize the limitations of his monarchy, thereby making himself accepted as a member of Europe's elite. The Hohenzollern monarchy's enhanced position was far from securely established. Even Frederick the Great could not conjure away the mighty rival that had emerged to challenge Prussia's new-found international power.

# CHAPTER EIGHT

# 1763–1786: the Second Reign of Frederick the Great?

## H. M. SCOTT

In March 1763, a month after the Peace of Hubertusburg was signed, Frederick returned to his capital, Berlin, which he had visited only once, and then very briefly, during the Seven Years' War.[1] The city's inhabitants prepared a reception for their saviour, to celebrate Prussia's survival against overwhelming odds. Frederick, however, ignored the ceremonial welcome, appearing only momentarily at a window. He shunned the cheering crowds in the streets and the courtiers in the palaces, and soon went instead to Potsdam, pausing in Berlin only to see some of his generals and a couple of favoured diplomats, and to greet his own estranged wife (whom he had not seen for seven years) with the immortal words: 'Madame has grown fatter'.[2] This episode inaugurated, and in a more fundamental sense than simple chronology, the 'Second Reign of Frederick the Great', which extended from the conclusion of the Seven Years' War until the king's death in August 1786.[3] These decades were shaped by different priorities and policy objectives and constitute a quite distinct period in Prussia's eighteenth-century history, though they have been far less studied than the dramatic first half of the king's reign.[4]

---

1  I am very grateful to Sabina Berkeley for her invaluable research assistance, and to Derek Beales, T. J. Hochstrasser, Derek McKay, Dennis E. Showalter and Peter Wilson for their helpful comments on a draft of this chapter. Constraints upon space have made it impossible for me to deal with their points as fully as I would wish.

2  See the description in Chester V. Easum, *Prince Henry of Prussia* (Madison, WI, 1970), pp. 226–37.

3  For the concept of a ruler's 'second reign' see John Guy, 'Introduction: the 1590s – the second reign of Elizabeth I?', in Guy (ed.), *The reign of Elizabeth I: court and culture in the last decade* (Cambridge, 1995), pp. 1–19.

4  The principal exception to this neglect is the important work by Ingrid Mittenzwei, *Preussen nach dem Siebenjährigen Krieg* ([East] Berlin, 1979). But it is striking that when Professor Mittenzwei came to survey the whole period in her brief biography, she devoted some two-thirds of her pages to the period up to 1763: *Friedrich II. von Preussen* ([East] Berlin, 1980).

# Bureaucratic absolutism or personal monarchy?

Eighteenth-century Prussia was always a strongly personal monarchy and not, as historians have often wrongly assumed, a protean bureaucracy. Frederick, in other words, ruled as well as reigned, and was always the focal point of government. The task of rebuilding and strengthening the Prussian state was one that the king was determined to shoulder himself. Prussia's ruler was an egoist who carried belief in his own superior abilities almost to the point of megalomania. Frederick delegated less and less after the Seven Years' War, and personally directed more and more of the key activities of Prussian government. As he wrote to the provincial chamber of Breslau in 1783: 'You have no right of initiative whatever. All matters must be reported to me directly.'[5] There was some decentralization and delegation during the second reign, in specialized fields as diverse as justice, education and mining, where Frederick could identify people he regarded as reliable administrators. But the general trend was that of increased centralization and rigid monarchical control.[6]

Whatever the situation in practice, the theory was quite clear: Frederick, alone and unaided, ruled Prussia and made all the important decisions, demanding unquestioning obedience. Military hierarchy and discipline were applied to the administration as well as to the army. The dominance of the nobility in its higher levels assisted the creation of a military ethos in civilian government. A leading administrator, the mining expert Friedrich Anton von Heinitz, significantly commented that Prussia's ruler 'believes that through experience he is strong enough to rule without advice and to follow the plan he has made, to remain true to it and through it to give [the state] order and strength'.[7] These activities automatically increased because of the need to restore the shattered fabric of the Prussian state after 1763, and this in turn led to a significant alteration in the nature of government. In import-ant respects, moreover, its personal nature was to be strengthened after the Seven Years' War, as the king shouldered more and more of the burdens of state. This had two closely related dimensions. The first is that Frederick now resided permanently at Potsdam; the second is his greater personal control over the entire governing machine.

---

5 Quoted by Walter L. Dorn, 'The Prussian Bureaucracy in the eighteenth century', *Political Science Quarterly* 46 (1931), 403–23, at p. 414.
6 See his comments in 1768: *Die politischen Testamente der Hohenzollern*, ed. Richard Dietrich (Cologne and Vienna, 1986), p. 612.
7 Quoted by Walther Hubatsch, *Frederick the Great: Absolutism and Administration* (Engl. trans.; London, 1975), p. 226.

Frederick's personality and attitudes stand at the heart of his second reign and did most to shape it. The king had worn himself out in the defence of his state, and contemporaries who had not seen Prussia's ruler for seven years were amazed by his physical decline on his return from the war. He had departed in 1756 as a reasonably vigorous man of 44; he returned as an exhausted, prematurely aged and increasingly cranky old despot of 51. Already known – behind his back – as 'Old Fritz', *der alte Fritz*, he had been broken in health and perhaps in spirit, too, by his exertions during Prussia's struggle for survival, as he never allowed anyone – above all himself – to forget. With a pronounced stoop and permanently clothed in an old and roughly patched blue army greatcoat, which was stained by the snuff which Frederick took ceaselessly and was replaced only every few years, the king's elderly appearance now presented a sharp contrast to the halcyon days before the Seven Years' War. It was an accurate guide to his declining health. Frederick's own constitution had never been especially robust and throughout his life he suffered periods of ill-health, which became more frequent and severe as the second reign progressed. By now, his teeth were falling out, his face was drawn and pale, his body increasingly emaciated. During the autumn of his life, Frederick suffered from ailments that included gout, piles, chest-pains, stomach cramps, fits of choking and bouts of fever.[8] He almost died in 1775, when his life was despaired of for many months.

The war years had taken a heavy toll of his immediate family and of his closest military collaborators. Among the latter, the fighting had seen the deaths in action of the senior commander, Schwerin, the rising star of Prussian military life, Winterfeldt, and the dependable Field-Marshal Jacob Keith. Within his own family, his mother and his beloved sister Wilhelmina had died, as had the heir to the childless king, his younger brother, the Prince of Prussia, Augustus William. He had been brutally banished from the army and from Frederick's presence after his military blunders and, by implication, his cowardice during the retreat from Bohemia in 1757, and he died in internal exile less than a year later. This highlighted the problem of the Hohenzollern succession, which now rested on the flabby shoulders of the king's nephew, the adolescent Frederick William. This was a particular concern in view of the increasingly personalized nature of the Hohenzollern monarchy, and throughout the second reign, the king brooded frequently on the situation that would arise when the fat, stupid, bovine crown prince (as he viewed his successor) ascended the throne.

The change in Frederick was more than merely physical. His greatest German biographer, Reinhold Koser, described him on his return from the

---

8  Hubatsch, *Frederick the Great*, p. 124.

Seven Years' War as being 'gloomy, cold and hard, like a sunless winter's day'.[9] Personal traits apparent during the first half of the reign became more pronounced after 1763. The loss of so many family members and collaborators intensified his isolation and contributed to the sombre tone of the second reign. The royal dinner parties at which favoured *literati* and military men were entertained at Potsdam soon became a pale shadow of the convivial gatherings before 1756 and, before long, were much reduced in scale. The king's solitude reflected the extent to which his overpowering sense of duty now dictated his whole life. It made him fiercely protective of his own time, and unwilling to squander it on anything he believed unnecessary. His day was structured with military precision and by an invariable timetable of work, with few opportunities for leisure. The king rose at daybreak and began with foreign affairs, going on to consider domestic and financial policy and concluding with reports from military inspectors. Royal decisions were dictated and then turned into written directives, and these were duly signed in the afternoon or early evening. This routine varied only when Frederick was ill, and it enabled a vast amount of business to be transacted.

The ageing Frederick grew more remote, misanthropic, caustic and capricious, and ruled increasingly by fear. Administrators and officials suffered the king's wounding sarcasm, and received much simple rudeness and open ridicule. His frank contempt for his subordinates rested upon a profoundly unattractive view of human nature. Frederick believed, as he wrote in his second Political Testament, that 'Human beings move if one drives them, and stop the moment one ceases to drive them forward'.[10] His constant theme throughout the second reign was that orders must not merely be issued; their execution must be supervised. The royal martinet reinforced precept with example, through tongue-lashings to summary dismissal and even legal prosecution.

Frederick believed that he was surrounded by the venal and the merely incompetent: he remarked to the provincial chamber of West Prussia that you could always hang a hundred officials with a clear conscience, since if you found one honest man among them, you would be fortunate.[11] This distrust took more tangible forms. Throughout Prussian government, there were powerful royal officials, known as fiscals (*Fiskale*), whose sole job was to

---

9   Quoted by Gerhard Ritter, *Frederick the Great* (Engl. trans.; London, 1968), p. 185. Koser's *Geschichte Friedrichs des Grossen* (3 vols; 6th–7th edition, Berlin, 1925: but largely completed by 1914) remains the standard political biography and contains the fullest available account of the period 1763–86.
10  Quoted by Hubatsch, *Frederick the Great*, p. 232.
11  Quoted by Dorn, 'Prussian Bureaucracy', p. 421.

report directly to the king on the honesty and diligence of their colleagues, from the lowest to the highest, and to handle the legal prosecution of any malefactors. An established feature of Prussian government before 1740, these men were to be particularly active after 1763, when their numbers were increased. Frederick also used the practice of asking two or three individuals to report directly to him on the same issue, as a way of checking up on his subordinates. Punishment tended to be swift and exemplary. When, in September 1766, the privy finance councillor, Erhard Ursinus, penned a critical report on Frederick's commercial policies, particularly state subsidies to the silk industry, he was shut up in Spandau for a year on a charge that was probably trumped-up.[12]

Prussia's army bore the brunt of the king's displeasure precisely because it occupied the central place in his policies. Officers were demoted and whole regiments lost seniority when their deportment in parades and man-oeuvres did not come up to scratch. Royal actions, in the military and other spheres, often appeared to rest on the whim of the moment. In the short term, the king's towering personality papered over the cracks that were appearing between the ruler and the army and administration upon which Prussia's great-power position ultimately depended. During his final decade, these divisions were increasingly apparent, and their legacies were one source of the problems facing the Prussian monarchy after 1786.

While eighteenth-century Prussia was clearly evolving towards a bureau-cratic state, the monarchy and government were in important respects more traditional and personal, and also more peripatetic, than has sometimes been appreciated.[13] The king commanded his armies in person and this meant that he was absent on campaign whenever Prussia was at war; he seems to have been in the field for more than a quarter of his entire reign. During peacetime, too, he was frequently on the move, conducting army reviews, carrying out manoeuvres with its regiments, or putting the civil administration through its paces. Inspection tours through the Prussian provinces were undertaken annually in May, June and August. After 1763, Frederick still maintained a punishing schedule of journeys and reviews, though the pace slackened during the 1770s and 1780s as he grew older and, eventually, infirm. These reviews were crucial to Frederick's system of government, enabling him to interview provincial officials and even ordinary subjects, examine local conditions and the work of provincial admin-istrations, and in this way make himself less dependent upon the written

---

12  For this episode see Mittenzwei, *Preussen*, pp. 39–51.
13  There are some interesting reflections in Eberhard Naujoks, 'Die Persönlichkeit Friedrichs des Grossen und die Struktur des preussischen Staates', *Historische Mitteilungen* 2 (1989), 17–37.

reports which flowed into his Potsdam study. He strongly recommended these journeys to his own successor as the essential way to control Prussia's officials.

The king's physical location was crucial within this strongly personalized system of government. After 1763, Frederick permanently withdrew to Potsdam, a garrison town (containing 8,000 soldiers) and also a significant manufacturing centre, some fifteen miles to the south-west of the capital. It was not merely the principal royal residence. After 1763, Potsdam came to be the main focus of Prussian government. During the second reign, the ageing ruler spent less and less time in his capital and cut himself off entirely from all except a handful of key subordinates, such as his brother Prince Henry (though his influence rose and fell), the foreign ministers Karl Wilhelm Finck von Finckenstein and Ewald Friedrich von Hertzberg, and favoured administrators like Ludwig Philipp von Hagen and Friedrich Anton von Heinitz. Even these men had no guaranteed role in the making of policy, which remained the king's sole responsibility. At Potsdam, Frederick focused all his diminishing energies on planning the reconstruction and future security of his exhausted kingdom. Apart from a handful of ceremonial occasions, usually with distinct political purposes, there were only two occasions each year when the king went to Berlin for more than a day or two at a time: for the festivities at Carnival (December–January) and for the public army manoeuvres in late May.

This growing and, before long, almost complete isolation was crucial for the changed nature of government. The king, its focal point, might be at Potsdam, but all the central administrative departments – Foreign Office (*Kabinettsministerium*), General Directory, Departments of Justice and Ecclesiastical Affairs, military agencies and so forth, together with the personnel who staffed them – were permanently located fifteen miles away in Berlin. His ministers, who until 1756 had been able to secure personal access to and decisions from the king, now found themselves beyond the iron curtain that surrounded Potsdam, reduced to receiving written instructions from the remote ruler. This physical separation was crucial for the more personalized monarchy which emerged after the Seven Years' War.

It built upon developments during the first half of Frederick's reign. From his accession, the king had reduced the role of the *Kabinettsministerium* in foreign policy and had himself handled not merely the most important negotiations, but much of the day-to-day correspondence with Prussian diplomats abroad.[14] In order to cope with the volume of paper generated

---

14   See H. M. Scott, 'Prussia's royal foreign minister', in Robert Oresko *et al.* (eds), *Royal and Republican Sovereignty in early modern Europe: Essays in memory of Ragnhild Hatton* (Cambridge, 1997), pp. 500–26.

by this direct royal control of foreign policy and by the ruler's role in government, the so-called *Kabinett* had grown quite significantly.[15] It was quite distinct from the *Kabinettsministerium* and, indeed, from all the formal structures of eighteenth-century Prussian administration. The *Kabinett* was really a team of secretaries, often of lowly and invariably non-noble birth – in contrast to Prussia's ministers, who were almost always noblemen – who were in direct and daily contact with the king.[16] The increased role and importance of these secretaries were apparent in their subsequent elevation to the rank of cabinet councillors. Unlike the various ministries, which remained in Berlin, members of the *Kabinett* always accompanied Frederick when he was travelling or campaigning; indeed, its head for much of the king's reign, August Friedrich Eichel, had suffered the indignity of being captured by the Austrians after the Prussian victory at Soor in 1745, though he was soon repatriated through the usual exchange of prisoners of war. The *Kabinett* provided essential copying services. Its members turned royal decisions into formal instructions to subordinates, the famous cabinet orders through which Prussia was governed more and more.

The *Kabinett*'s role had expanded notably during the Seven Years' War when the king had visited his capital only once. Before Frederick departed for the front at the beginning of the 1757 campaign, he had issued an order conferring an unusual degree of initiative upon the General Directory, making it solely responsible for raising money for the war. This initiative, and the administration's growing independence, has been seen as a crucial point in the relationship between ruler and civil service.[17] What has been less appreciated, though in the longer perspective it would be more significant, is the *Kabinett*'s enhanced role during the fighting.[18] Throughout the Seven Years' War, the centre of Prussian government continued to be where the king was. Aided only by Eichel and a handful of secretaries, Frederick personally handled all the details of troop movements and supply, maintaining a remarkably extensive correspondence and accomplishing what would later demand the attention of an entire general staff. The king also

---

15 There is a brief, authoritative introduction by Otto Hintze, which forms part of his magisterial survey of Prussian government: G. Schmoller *et al.* (eds), *Acta Borussica: Denkmäler der Preussischen Staatsverwaltung im 18. Jahrhundert – Die Behördenorganisation und die allgemeine Staatsverwaltung Preussens im 18. Jahrhundert*, 16 vols (Berlin, 1894–1982) [hereafter referred to as *ABB*], vi:i, pp. 59–66.

16 Hermann Hüffer, 'Die Beamten des ältern preussischen Kabinetts von 1713–1808', *Forschungen zur brandenburgischen und preussischen Geschichte* 5 (1892), 157–90, is informative on the personnel of the *Kabinett*.

17 H. C. Johnson, *Frederick the Great and his Officials* (New Haven, 1975), esp. ch. 6.

18 This is apparent from the documents printed in *ABB* vols ix–xii, *passim*. It is noted by Hubatsch, *Frederick the Great*, pp. 113–14.

devoted some attention to broader issues of government. This circumstance enhanced both the importance of the *Kabinett* and the personal standing of Eichel.

The Seven Years' War had created an even more executive style of monarchy than had prevailed before 1756, and this continued throughout the second reign at Potsdam, considerably strengthening the king's personal control of domestic government.[19] He alone united the diverse, overlapping and frequently confusing elements in Prussian administration. Only the king and the *Kabinett* could take a general view of the Prussian monarchy. This process and the resulting administrative reorganization were partly facilitated by demographic accident. The Seven Years' War saw the deaths of a number of prominent officials who had begun their careers – often in the General Directory – under Frederick William I and had remained influential throughout the first two decades of Frederick's own reign.[20] The king was then able to appoint younger, hand-picked top officials who helped reshape central government after 1763.

Prussia's king had always been critical of the General Directory, its slowness, and the collegial principle that it embodied and that provided opportunities for exactly those ministerial disagreements that he detested. Though – just like his father – he had become the President of the General Directory in 1748, the same year he issued an important new Instruction to guide its operations,[21] he became increasingly suspicious of this key body and, eventually, downgraded it. The arrival of the *Régie* in 1766 removed one principal function, collecting taxation,[22] while its decline was accelerated by the creation of more specialized ministries and by the way powerful individuals, such as Hagen and Schulenburg, acquired personal administrative fiefdoms during the second reign.

The practice of bypassing the nominally responsible central department was extended throughout domestic administration after the Seven Years' War. The *Kabinett* gradually replaced the General Directory, as more and more the king ruled directly from Potsdam through a team of secretaries, rather than through the relevant Berlin departments. The ministers heading the latter remained in Prussia's capital and saw the king only once a year, when they would report on their department's work and receive royal

---

19   The final volume of *ABB* contains a brief but suggestive survey by Peter Baumgart, 'Tendenzen der spätfriderizianischen Verwaltung im Spiegel der Acta Borussica', xvi:ii, pp. xxi–xxxvii.
20   These men are listed in Johnson, *Frederick the Great*, pp. 160–1.
21   This is notably detailed and is illuminating on the king's views on government: it is printed in *ABB*, vii, pp. 572–655.
22   See below, pp. 196–7.

approval for their next year's budget; at other times, written orders were sent from Potsdam. After 1775, even the annual personal interview was abolished; henceforth, the king would review two departmental heads at a time. However, leading officials might at any moment be summoned to defend their conduct in individual meetings with the king: these became much more common during the second reign.

The General Directory and the other departments in Berlin were also sidelined as the king corresponded directly with his provincial adminis-trators and army commanders. The cabinet orders, so characteristic of Frederick's government, originated in directives from his study, turned into formal instructions by secretaries from the *Kabinett*. After 1763, these were increasingly sent directly to officials in the provinces, rather than routed through the General Directory and then the responsible departments in Berlin.[23] The provincial administrators were, in turn, expected to reply directly to the king. Up to twelve cabinet orders a day were being issued during the king's later years.[24] The greater workload that this imposed led to a rise in the number of *Kabinett* secretaries and clerks: after 1768, when Eichel died, the total doubled from three to six. These men provided a small and highly flexible executive at the apex of the administrative pyramid, responsible only to the king. Simultaneously, the *Kabinett* was form-ally divided into three sections: foreign policy, domestic administration and military affairs.[25] This approximated to the totality of Prussian government, and underlined the crucial role of the parallel administration that had grown up in Potsdam.

In this way, the king's personal control of foreign policy and military affairs was extended during the second reign to all areas of Prussian govern-ment. To facilitate royal decision-making, the king insisted that the reports he received each day should be no longer than two pages. The vital role of the *Kabinett* secretaries was apparent in Frederick's recommendation – in his Personal Testament of January 1769 – to his successor that 'They have a good knowledge of affairs and they can, at the beginning of the reign, advise the king on many things of which they have knowledge and which are unknown even to Ministers'.[26]

---

23   This shift was becoming apparent by the early summer of 1763: in April and May, the majority of cabinet orders were being sent to the General Directory; by June and July, these were going mainly to provincial administrators and administrative bodies: see *ABB*, xiii *passim*.

24   Theodor Schieder, *Friedrich der Grosse: ein Königtum der Widersprüche* (Frankfurt-am-Main, 1983), p. 298.

25   On the reorganization in February 1768 after Eichel's death, see *ABB*, xiv, pp. 449–52.

26   Quoted by Hubatsch, *Frederick the Great*, p. 223.

# Aping the great powers?

Frederick's overriding aim after 1763 was to secure Prussia's position among the great powers: this determined both foreign and domestic policy throughout the second reign. The seizure and successful defence of Silesia had made Prussia a member of Europe's political elite, yet she clearly lacked the resources to sustain such a role. The king was uncomfortably aware of the narrow margin of Prussia's survival in the Seven Years' War and recognized that a further conflict might well destroy his state and his own life's work: henceforth, peace was his greatest priority. Where others were awed by the Hohenzollern monarchy's military strength and admired its remarkable ruler, Frederick saw only the scanty resources and strategic vulnerability, real obstacles to Prussia remaining a great power. The king's analysis was too pessimistic: his own state was probably stronger, and his rivals certainly weaker, than he believed. In particular, he overestimated Russian power, because of his serious reverses at the hands of the empress's troops. His new-found respect for Austria's military might, evident in his collecting detailed and up-to-date information on her army and finances, was also carried to exaggerated lengths.[27] Though the Habsburg army had performed much better during the Seven Years' War, it long remained inferior to that of Frederick. But the king's analysis, and the problems of resources and strategic vulnerability that underpinned it, shaped policy after 1763.

Frederick characteristically joked about Prussia's central problem. During his final decades, he remarked more than once that the Hohenzollern coat of arms should contain not a black eagle, but a monkey: all Prussia could do was ape the great powers.[28] The fundamental problems of exiguous resources, territorial dispersal and incomplete political integration evident during the period of political emergence, not merely remained, but had been starkly revealed during the Seven Years' War. The western enclaves had been occupied by the French and Austrians, and such loyalty as these territories possessed to the king in far-away Berlin had been attenuated, as older regional identities re-emerged.[29] Much more seriously, East Prussia had been governed by Russia after January 1758 and had been returned only in June 1762. Frederick chose to believe that the kingdom's political elite had collaborated with their Russian occupiers, and seldom visited the

---

27  See Geheimes Staatsarchiv Preussischer Kulturbesitz, Berlin-Dahlem, Rep. 96.46.F1, fos 18–23; cf. Rohd to Frederick II, 1 January 1768, Rep. 96.46.K.

28  For example, to Lucchesini in 1781: Schieder, *Friedrich der Grosse*, p. 259.

29  There is an excellent recent study of this by Horst Carl, *Okkupation und Regionalismus: die preussischen Westprovinzen im Siebenjährigen Krieg* (Mainz, 1993).

territory.[30] His capricious attitude, however, could not disguise the fault-lines within the Hohenzollern monarchy revealed by the conflict, when a permanent Russian take-over of East Prussia (then possibly exchanged with Poland for Courland) had seemed possible.

One of Frederick's earliest initiatives on returning from the Seven Years' War was the construction of the *Neues Palais* (New Palace) at the far end of the park at Potsdam. It was not completed until 1769, and was on a much larger scale than previous Hohenzollern palaces, consuming scarce funds needed for post-war reconstruction. It was a vast, architecturally resplendent palace where Frederick never lived permanently, though he had operas performed in its theatre: it became the principal royal residence only after his death. Its building at this time was a deliberate act of policy, meant to prop up Prussia's shaky great-power position. It was intended to impress political rivals, being used primarily to house the privileged foreign visitors permitted direct access to the king in his Potsdam redoubt.

Prussia's international position, however, was to be primarily defended by armed might and by the avoidance of war. The Seven Years' War had raised the reputation of the Prussian army and of its commander-in-chief to new heights, a model to be emulated by its rivals. Admiring foreigners made the pilgrimage to Berlin, hoping to see at first hand the famed blue-coated regiments and, if they were especially fortunate, to catch a glimpse of the Great Frederick, now one of the wonders of the modern world. The potential of this was quickly appreciated by Prussia's king, who welcomed foreign military experts and curious civilians to Berlin's annual May parades and exercises. His soldiers and their officers drilled with parade-ground efficiency, underlining to an admiring Europe the continuing strength of Hohenzollern military power. This, like the *Neues Palais*, was a form of propaganda for the benefit of Prussia's rivals. Its military significance was negligible: the important manoeuvres took place away from the capital and prying foreign eyes, often in Pomerania and Silesia and usually in the autumn.

Frederick believed that the Prussian military machine needed to be rebuilt, refined and perfected, and after 1763, he devoted considerable energy to this task.[31] The means was hierarchical control imposed by an increasingly demanding and arbitrary king, reinforced by strict and frequently harsh discipline and incessant drilling, as officers and men became mere cogs in a

---

30  In 1768, he wrote that its nobility had been 'more Russian than Prussian' during the Seven Years' War: *Die politischen Testamente*, ed. Dietrich, p. 588.

31  There are admirable introductions by Dennis Showalter, 'Hubertusburg to Auerstaedt: the Prussian Army in decline', *German History* 12 (1994), 286–307, and the same author's *The Wars of Frederick the Great* (London, 1995), ch. 7; cf. his chapter in this volume, pp. 220–36.

great military machine. The long-term consequences were deleterious, as became evident in Frederick's last campaign, the brief and strategically barren War of the Bavarian Succession (1778–9), a successful attempt to prevent Austria from annexing the Electorate. This demonstrated how initiative at all levels of command had been eroded by a decade and more of royal dictatorship exercised by a remote king: in sharp contrast to the close personal links that had done so much to maintain morale in the army during the first half of the reign. In the short term, however, the twin gods of drill and discipline maintained Prussia's forces at an impressive level of readiness.

The king's efforts to overhaul the army began at the top. Behind the well-known efforts to hound middle-class officers out of regiments to which they had been commissioned during the emergency of the Seven Years' War, lay not merely an established social preference, but a distinct military purpose. Frederick believed that only men of noble birth possessed the attributes essential to exercise command, and he set out to establish an overwhelmingly Junker officer corps.[32] These efforts were to be successful: at his death, there were only 22 commoners out of 689 majors and senior officers.[33] Simultaneously, determined efforts were made to improve the professional training received by young noblemen intent upon a military career. The *Académie des Nobles* set up in 1765, in which Frederick took a personal interest, had a curriculum intended to provide the best training for officers anywhere in Europe.

The composition of the rank-and-file was similarly subjected to royal scrutiny, though with fewer immediate results. During the second half of the Seven Years' War in particular, Frederick had been forced to rely more heavily upon native conscripts than he had wanted: the problem inherent in the much-admired cantonal system was that it could weaken the crucial agrarian base of Prussia's economy by diverting peasants into his regiments. The king's efforts to increase the proportion of non-Prussians in his forces were not completely successful, though they were aided by his army's high reputation after the war. By 1786, out of a total effective force of around 190,000 men (itself 40,000 more than in 1763), no less than 110,000 were recruited from outside the Hohenzollern lands, usually from other German territories.

Behind the extension of hierarchical control over Prussia's army lay a broader purpose. Frederick's experiences during the second half of the Seven Years' War had convinced him that Prussia's security demanded an enlarged army ready for immediate war: it was henceforth to be maintained

---

32   This was obviously linked to his efforts after 1763 to assist the nobility to rebuild the economic basis of their power: see below, pp. 195–6.

33   K. Demeter, *The German Officer Corps* (Engl. trans.; London, 1965), pp. 3ff.

as 'a front-loaded military deterrent'.[34] As the king wrote in his 1768 Political Testament, 'This state cannot maintain itself without a large army, [since] we are surrounded by enemies more powerful than ourselves against whom we may at any moment have to defend ourselves.'[35] The Prussian army must be able to intimidate its enemies and, if war broke out, to win early victories, thereby preventing a repetition of the kind of life-and-death struggle that the Seven Years' War had become. It was, therefore, kept in a higher state of military preparedness than the forces of his political rivals. To this end, military supplies were stockpiled, exactly as they were in Austria after 1763: by the eve of the War of the Bavarian Succession, Prussia's arsenals housed no less than 1,376 recast artillery pieces and a staggering 140,000 muskets, while the magazines contained grain to feed two armies 70,000-strong for two campaigns.[36] This impressive build-up was accomplished at the cost of severe economizing in the army's day-to-day functioning: at times, the cavalry was forced to graze its horses, rather than feed them, and to perform its exercises on foot. But it achieved Frederick's aim of raising military preparedness to a wholly new level. That objective was also evident in the determined and successful efforts to create an annual budgetary surplus and in the huge war-chest built up in the *Staatsschatz*. By the king's death, this was 51 million thalers, more than six times the figure in 1740 and twice that in 1756.[37]

Prussia's army was intended to support and reinforce a foreign policy with one overriding objective after the Seven Years' War: the preservation of peace. Frederick's achievement had been to make his state a first-class power on third-class resources, and he knew that any further fighting would imperil the very existence of the Prussian monarchy because of its relative weakness. This objective was initially facilitated by wider changes within the European diplomatic system. All the major continental states were exhausted after 1763, one reason for an extended period of peace: there was to be no general European war, involving more than two great powers, for a generation.[38] More important, however, was the political division of Europe into two largely separate spheres. This had been apparent during the Seven Years War, accelerated during the first decade of peace, and was firmly established by the mid-1770s. In the west, Britain was engaged in a maritime and colonial rivalry with her established eighteenth-century enemy

---

34  Showalter, 'Hubertusburg to Auerstaedt', p. 344.
35  Quoted by C. A. B. Behrens, *Society, Government and the Enlightenment: The Experiences of Eighteenth-Century France and Prussia* (London, 1985), p. 36.
36  Christopher Duffy, *The Army of Frederick the Great*, 2nd edn (New York, 1996), p. 311.
37  Hubatsch, *Frederick the Great*, pp. 138, 147; cf. above, p. 156, for the earlier totals.
38  Although, of course, every great power fought at least one war before 1783.

France, who was allied after 1761 to Spain, ruled by Louis XV's cousin. The two Bourbon powers hoped that the planned war of revenge upon Britain, launched in 1778–9 with their support for George III's rebellious North American colonists, would not extend to Europe. French policy since 1763 had aimed only to neutralize the continent during any future Anglo-Bourbon war, and France consequently played a much-reduced diplomatic role. This was apparent to Frederick, who was determined not to be dragged into any future conflict between the western powers and to avoid any alliance with them after the Seven Years' War.

This situation in western Europe allowed the three eastern powers to achieve dominance in the rest of the continent. Within this regional diplomatic system, Russia held the balance of power between Prussia and Austria. In 1763–4, Frederick was able skilfully to exploit Catherine II's need for foreign support when a vacancy on the elective Polish throne was created by Augustus III's death.[39] In the eighteenth century, Poland was a Russian satellite, and the empress wanted to perpetuate this control by having the Polish nobleman and her own former lover, Stanislas Poniatowski, elected as the next king. Frederick's political backing and the availability of his army to support Catherine's policy were important sources of this Russian success. The king's price was a Prusso-Russian treaty of defensive alliance, signed on 11 April 1764, to last for eight years in the first instance. Twice renewed – in 1769 and 1777 – the Russian alliance remained the basis of Frederick's diplomacy until the early 1780s. This alignment contributed in two crucial ways to Prussia's security. It neutralized his established enemy Austria, who could not, as Vienna knew, risk attacking when Prussia could call on Russian help. More importantly, however, the alliance also neutralized the threat of Russia, now feared more by Frederick than any other power, and removed any danger to East Prussia.

The Seven Years' War had created in Prussia's ruler an exaggerated and enduring fear of Russia.[40] This was rooted in his assessment of the potential

---

39   The most detailed survey of Frederick's later foreign policy is in Koser, *Geschichte Friedrichs des Grossen*, iii, pp. 270–332, 383–410 and 485–507; a recent comprehensive treatment is Frank Althoff, *Untersuchungen zum Gleichgewicht der Mächte in der Außenpolitik Friedrichs des Großen nach dem Siebenjährigen Krieg (1763–1786)* (Berlin, 1995). Wolfgang Stribrny, *Die Russlandpolitik Friedrichs des Grossen (1764–1786)* (Würzburg, 1966) is a workmanlike treatment of the crucial relationship with Russia. A brief survey is provided by H. M. Scott, 'Aping the Great Powers: Frederick the Great and the Defense of Prussia's International Position, 1763–86', *German History* 12 (1994), 286–307.

40   The king's changing attitude is discussed incisively by Schieder, *Friedrich der Grosse*, pp. 225–59; see also Walther Mediger, 'Friedrich der Grosse und Russland', in O. Hauser (ed.), *Friedrich der Grosse in seiner Zeit* (Cologne/Vienna, 1987), pp. 109–36. For his new-found fear of the Russian army after the Seven Years' War, see *Die politischen Testamente*, ed. Dietrich, p. 622.

power of Catherine II's empire, which – he told his brother Prince Henry in 1769 – 'was a terrible power which will make all Europe tremble'.[41] Though he seriously underestimated the size of Russia's population, which he believed was around nine million in 1768 when it was actually over 23 million, his fear of Catherine's state reflected his view of its potential and his appreciation of its strategic invulnerability: control over Poland meant it was difficult to attack during the eighteenth century. Above all, it reflected his serious reverses at Russia's hands. His defeats at Kay and Kunersdorf in Russia's *annus mirabilis* of 1759 had created a fear of her military power that the king carried to the grave and transformed his earlier contempt for her armies into respect and alarm. He feared less their commanders and striking power than their numerical strength and ability to win victories by accepting losses on a scale that no other army could tolerate, and certainly not Prussia with her limited demographic resources.

The Russian alliance of 1764 was probably Frederick's greatest political triumph. It united him during the later 1760s and 1770s to the power he feared most, gave him some degree of control over St Petersburg's foreign policy, and effectively neutralized his principal enemy, Austria. He devoted considerable time and care to strengthening this crucial alliance, particularly through an extensive and prolonged private correspondence with the Empress Catherine II, unsurpassed in its mutual insincerity and conducted, on his side at least, in a tone of unctuous flattery.[42] Yet, his Russian treaty was always less securely based than its longevity might suggest. It had been accompanied, and to a considerable extent made possible, by the rise of Nikita Panin, Catherine II's foreign minister during the first half of her reign and the principal architect of the celebrated 'Northern System'. This aimed to stabilize the regions on Russia's western borders through a wide-ranging series of alliances – with Prussia being the most important – and in this way facilitate a period of peace for much-needed domestic reform. This was attractive during the first decade of Catherine II's reign, when her own priorities were also internal. But increasingly the 'Northern System', and the Prussian alliance upon which it rested, was undermined by events.

Foremost was the unexpected outbreak of a Russo-Turkish war in autumn 1768. At first, this worked to Frederick's advantage, as he renewed his Russian alliance in 1769 and, more important, exploited the situation to secure the support of the other two eastern powers for a partition of Poland, implemented in 1772. By this, he annexed the future Hohenzollern province

---

41   Quoted by Christopher Duffy, *Russia's Military Way to the West: Origins and Nature of Russian Military Power 1700–1800* (London, 1981), p. 74.

42   This is printed in *Sbornik imperatorskogo russkogo istoricheskogo obshchestva*, 148 vols (St Petersburg, 1867–1916), vol. xx.

of West Prussia. It was a major acquisition, since it united the Hohenzollern heartlands of Brandenburg and Pomerania to the distant Kingdom of Prussia and created a solid wedge of Prussian territory stretching across central and north-eastern Germany: until then, it had been cut off from the core of the Hohenzollern state by several hundred miles of Polish territory. It came, however, at the price of a weakening of Prussia's fundamental alliance. Russia's victories over the sultan's armies and the resulting dramatic territorial gains to the north and east of the Black Sea in the Peace of Kutchuk-Kainardji in summer 1774, revealed the scale of Ottoman decline and awakened Russia's interest in further territorial expansion to the south. Simultaneously, Kaunitz was reassessing Habsburg foreign policy in the context of Catherine II's considerable gains, which Austria had aped on a smaller scale by seizing the fertile province of Bukovina from the prostrate Ottoman Empire in 1775. Kaunitz appreciated the attractions of a Russian alliance and further expansion in the Balkans for Vienna, especially since these could be a way of controlling the rising power of Russia. Links with St Petersburg were also essential if Silesia was ever to be reconquered, and this remained Vienna's aim, though there was no intention of attempting it while Frederick the Great was alive. During the later 1770s, Austria was moving hesitantly towards a *rapprochement* with St Petersburg, and this was accomplished – as his first important political act – by the Emperor Joseph II when he began his personal rule on the death of his mother, Maria Theresa, in November 1780.

In early summer 1781, Austria and Russia concluded a secret treaty.[43] This was quickly apparent to Frederick, who recognized as early as September that his cherished Russian alliance had been supplanted by the Russo-Austrian axis, which he himself had always regarded as more logical, directed as it could be against the Ottomans in south-east Europe and against himself in Germany.[44] The eclipse of Panin, architect of Russia's Prussian alliance, in the autumn of 1781, underlined that the king now faced the isolation that he had dreaded ever since the end of the Seven Years' War. Efforts to re-open links with France and even Britain during the 1770s had come to nothing, and Prussia was now forced to confront a powerful, if still secret, Austro-Russian alliance alone. This isolation was one important source of Frederick's anxieties during the 1780s, when the problems of sustaining Prussia's great-power position were starkly highlighted.

---

43   Isabel de Madariaga, 'The Secret Austro-Russian Treaty of 1781', *Slavonic and East European Review* 38 (1959–60), 114–45, is the standard account of its conclusion and the unusual form it took.

44   *Politische Correspondenz Friedrichs des Grossen*, J. G. Droysen *et al.* (eds) (46 vols; Berlin, 1879–1939), xxxxvi, pp. 153–5; 178.

His second reign itself ended with an ironic coda. In 1784–6, when Joseph II again sought to annex Bavaria, this time by an exchange involving the Southern Netherlands, Frederick placed himself at the head of a League of German Princes (*Fürstenbund*), which successfully resisted the emperor's aims. The ageing Prussian monarch who, almost half a century before, had risen to prominence by ignoring the structures of the Holy Roman Empire and had treated the emperor simply as a rival German ruler, ended his days as the patron of the same fossilized imperial structure he despised.

## Conquering new provinces in peacetime

Frederick described Prussia in 1763 as being 'like a man with many wounds who has lost so much blood that he is on the point of death'.[45] This graphic image conveyed the destructive impact of the Seven Years' War, especially upon the central and eastern provinces – Silesia, Brandenburg, Pomerania – which had borne most of the fighting. The ceaseless campaigning had disrupted agriculture and commerce. Farms lay abandoned, their peasants either dead, or refugees or permanent settlers in neighbouring territories: as many as 90,000 may have fled during the conflict. The war had also severely affected the region's trade and its few urban centres, depriving them of their life-blood of commerce, while individual towns had been bombarded and lay in ruins, above all Küstrin. Throughout the Hohenzollern monarchy, the demographic losses had been enormous. Pomerania lost some 70,000 inhabitants, one-fifth of its entire population; Silesia 45,000, the Neumark and the Kurmark together 114,000. Even those territories where the fighting had been less intense had suffered: East Prussia had 90,000 fewer inhabitants when the war ended, and the western provinces 65,000. Overall, it is estimated that about 400,000 Prussian subjects had died during the Seven Years' War, some 10 per cent of the population.

Demographic losses on this scale were an especially serious matter for a country so thinly populated and for a king who believed that a numerous and prosperous population was the very foundation of Prussian power.[46] One principal objective throughout the second reign was to make good these losses and to strengthen Prussia demographically. The *Rétablissement*, as the recovery measures are generally known, aimed not merely to repair

---

45 Quoted by Behrens, *Society, Government and the Enlightenment*, p. 81. On the aftermath of the Seven Years' War, see especially Mittenzwei, *Preussen*, ch. 1.
46 *Die politischen Testamente*, ed. Dietrich, p. 494.

the ravages of the war, but, more fundamentally, to create a stronger domestic base, to underpin Prussia's new great-power status.

This was mainly to be done by attracting immigrants, principally from other German territories. Potential colonists were lured by promises of land, cash bounties and tax exemption for a period of years, together with assurances about religious toleration. Prussian immigration offices searched ceaselessly both for potential agricultural colonists and for the more highly prized skilled craftsmen. Their efforts enjoyed considerable success: about 250,000 immigrants arrived in Prussia during Frederick's reign, the majority after 1763. These colonists were settled in the regions that had been particularly devastated by the fighting: Eastern Pomerania was resettled especially energetically and successfully. The new province of West Prussia, annexed from Poland in 1772, was deliberately colonized by settlers who were Protestant and German, in contrast to the Catholic and Polish natives: as many as 3,200 families arrived during the final third of Frederick's reign, as part of a deliberate attempt to change the character of the area.[47] These policies strengthened Prussia demographically, though the king's territorial annexations (Silesia, East Friesland and West Prussia) brought in far more new subjects. A combination of natural increase, immigration and the new provinces together raised the total population to 5.8 million by 1786. This was more than two and a half times the figure at the king's accession in 1740, but Prussia still had the smallest population among the five great powers.

These new inhabitants needed cultivable land upon which to settle. This was a further stimulus to reclamation schemes to increase the supply of land available for agriculture through draining Prussia's extensive marshlands. In 1753, Frederick had spoken of 'conquering a province in peacetime' (he had in mind the first phase of the particularly successful Oder reclamation scheme). This established policy was pursued during the second reign, with the draining of the Netze and the Warthe marshes, and the second phase of the Oder reclamation. All these schemes provided significant amounts of new land for cultivation: in Farther Pomerania, the arable land was increased by 10 per cent through such schemes during the 1760s and 1770s.

The monarchy's basic poverty had been highlighted by the Seven Years' War. Here, too, established policies came to be more systematically and extensively pursued during the second reign, and also to be brought under tighter central control.[48] Frederick's ultimate aim was autarky – which had guided Prussia's economic policies since Frederick William I's reign – to be achieved principally through protectionism and increased state control.

---

47  William W. Hagen, *Germans, Poles and Jews: the nationality conflict in the Prussian East, 1772–1914* (Chicago, IL, 1980), pp. 43–4.
48  Mittenzwei, *Preussen*, p. 134.

Efforts to improve internal communications were redoubled, mainly by building canals, such as the Bromberg canal, completed in 1776, which provided a link to the Vistula, and by making rivers more navigable: foremost among such schemes was the building of locks on the Ruhr in 1780. Road communications were relatively neglected, because Frederick feared they might be used by his enemies in wartime, and because he suspected transit trade could deprive him of revenue and undermine autarky: an illustration of his primitive but deeply held economic principles.

Though Prussia was overwhelmingly an agrarian economy and a rather poor one, the king's personal interest in this area was limited. He sponsored the setting up of model farms, and he encouraged efforts to import new techniques from the Dutch Republic and England to improve yields, alongside the publication of journals to disseminate such new ideas. More fundamental initiatives were not attempted. Though Frederick in his writings made much of his own opposition to serfdom, which he viewed as an affront to the doctrine of natural rights and an obstacle to economic modernization, he made only one half-hearted, unsuccessful attempt at reform. The key question of serf reform was broached immediately after the Seven Years' War, in the first instance for Pomerania. The immediate and entrenched opposition from the province's noble Estates convinced him that any amelioration in the peasantry's condition would undermine the social, economic and military foundations of the Prussian state, and this was unthinkable. Nothing effective was done for the overwhelming majority of serfs for another half-century.

Their treatment contrasted sharply with the considerable help given to the nobility in the central provinces to assist them to recover from the Seven Years' War. Frederick intended that the Junkers would continue to provide the backbone of the Hohenzollern state, serving primarily as officers in his expanded army and, to a lesser extent, in the upper levels of the administration, and he was alarmed at the nobility's weakened condition in 1763. Estates had been ruined and abandoned, families had become burdened by massive debts and by the loss of many adult males on the battlefields. To assist their economic recovery, and also to prevent noble estates (*Rittergüten*) from passing into the hands of the middle class, the king proclaimed a moratorium of five years on the repayment of all noble debts. He then sponsored the establishment of rural credit institutions, known as *Landschaften* and established initially for Silesia in 1769 and then for Brandenburg (1777) and Pomerania (1781); East Prussia, which Frederick believed had collaborated with its Russian occupiers, did not receive its *Landschaft* until two years after his death.

These institutions were to provide cheap and guaranteed credit for nobles restoring their estates and rebuilding their family finances. They could raise cash through mortgages of up to half or even (in some provinces) two-thirds of the value of their estates. This credit was less expensive than normal borrowing, because it was backed by the state and by a province's entire nobility. The *Landschaften* possessed one immense advantage: they protected the principle that only nobles should own noble land while securing funds from the middle class, who in turn received stable and guaranteed returns from their loans. The result was not quite what the king had originally intended, however. The Junkers, whose incomes were in any case rising because of the sharp increase in grain prices during the final third of the eighteenth century, used the cheap credit not to modernize their existing landholdings, but to buy new estates, which could in turn be mortgaged to finance further purchases. This launched a speculative inflation in land prices, although – in the longer perspective – it can be seen also to have strengthened the landed power-base of the East Elbian nobility during the next century.

Efforts were also made to build up Prussia's manufacturing sector through subsidies to individual entrepreneurs and through the establishment of a favourable, protectionist tariff regime.[49] In the depressed economic aftermath of the Seven Years' War, Frederick had been obliged to bail out and take over several manufacturing enterprises, and this set the pattern of increasing state involvement to generate much-needed income and to direct Prussia's economic development. Silk manufacturing was especially favoured by the king, being both supported by subsidies and protected by tariffs. Woollen and textile production were also encouraged, while Heinitz presided over an important expansion of mining and iron production. The state's growing role – and its ceaseless search for income – was also evident in a whole series of initiatives during the second reign: the setting up of the Berlin Bank (1765) and the Overseas Trading Company (1772), together with the establishment of monopolies for tobacco (1766) and for coffee (1781), and of a state lottery. These enhanced central control over important areas of the Prussian economy and generated much-needed income, though whether they assisted the country's longer-term economic development is more problematical.

One main preoccupation after 1763 was to increase tax income to fund the build-up of the army and the wide-ranging state activities such as land reclamation, settlement and manufacturing. This lay behind the celebrated experiment of the *Régie*, the most unpopular initiative of the second reign, but also the most successful, if judged in terms of the fiscal motives for its introduction. Against the background of declining fiscal revenues and an

---

49  Mittenzwei, *Preussen*, is important for the discussion which follows.

especially alarming fall in the Excise in the depressed post-war economic climate – in 1763, tax payments had had to be remitted in certain provinces – Frederick demanded an annual increase of two million thalers. When the General Directory replied that this was impossible – and in so doing further weakened its own declining position – Frederick put five French tax experts, headed by de la Haye de Launay, in charge of indirect taxation, though the actual collection was always undertaken by Prussian officials. The *Régie* was established in 1766 and remained responsible for the indirect taxation system (but not for the rates at which it was levied) for the rest of the king's life. Though it aroused considerable opposition and criticism, its success was evident in the sums raised for the royal coffers. These were also boosted by income from some of the other economic initiatives during the second reign. One calculation is that the monarchy's income by 1786 was three times the annual figure in 1740, a substantial increase even when inflation is taken into account.

These policies all involved an intensification of state control and, in many cases, more personal initiative or scrutiny by Prussia's king. The priorities of domestic policy after 1763 were all a response to the Seven Years' War and its manifold legacies, and they involved a modification, though not a complete rejection, of the enlightened absolutism that had done so much to shape Frederick's policies before 1756.[50] The humanitarian aims of the Enlightenment were still evident in some areas of policy. Religious toleration, for example, remained fundamental and was held out as an inducement to prospective immigrants. These decades also saw important progress, encouraged by the king, in the immense task of legal codification, efforts which would reach fruition less than a decade after his death when the celebrated *Allgemeine Landrecht* ('General Law Code for the Prussian Territories') was issued in 1794. The post-1763 period also saw significant initiatives in educational reform, as the king provided limited funds for schools and schoolmasters. The overriding priority in domestic policy, however, was always that of strengthening the base of Prussia's great-power position.

## The legacies of the second reign

Frederick's personal involvement was immense: his devotion to decision-making and to governing Prussia is clear. Yet, there was always a gap between his intentions and the reality of government, and during the king's

---

50   See Schieder, *Friedrich der Grosse*, pp. 284–307, for a persuasive argument that the king's
     policies were influenced by the Enlightenment.

final decades this became a gulf. The sheer detail of administration, particularly as its activities expanded rapidly, was always an insurmountable obstacle to Frederick's determination to govern personally and to practise what would now be described as micro-management. The volume of public business reached proportions quite beyond the capacity of a single person – even one as dedicated as Prussia's ruler – yet Frederick still held to the principle of absolute royal control. The myth of royal omnicompetence was sustained despite mounting evidence to the contrary. In the short term, this squeezed initiative or willingness to accept responsibility out of the Prussian system at all levels: no subordinate would risk the king's elemental disfavour. Both in the army and in the administration, Frederick discouraged subordinates from accepting responsibility and in this way carrying forward the work of strengthening and defending Prussia. There was very little autonomy outside the royal study.

The principal weapon against this rigid hierarchical control was concealment, increasingly deployed by officials at all levels of government. Administrators, fearful of Frederick's fury and harshness, omitted matters and, sometimes, distorted their reports to suit the royal whim of the moment. The structures of Prussian government were incapable of discharging the many tasks that they were expected to undertake. One of the clearest demonstrations was provided by developments in the new territory of West Prussia, annexed in 1772.[51] Frederick was very hostile to this area, which he was determined to treat harshly and to exploit in the wider interests of the Hohenzollern state. But these objectives seem to have been beyond the capacity of the new Prussian government, and during the following decades incorporating the new province caused considerable administrative difficulties. This exemplified the problems within government during the 'second reign'. During the old king's final decade, his orders began to be only partially obeyed and even ignored, as his officials grew weary of their oppressor and looked forward to a new reign. Frederick's bitter reaction when he realized this was predictable, and was a further step in the breakdown of royal control.[52]

In the longer perspective, these developments proved even more damaging to the Hohenzollern monarchy. As the second reign progressed and the ageing ruler found the burdens of government greater and greater, the administrative machine began to work less smoothly. It was dangerously dependent upon the fragile health of a ruler who was bound to grow old.

---

51  There is now a major study by Hans-Jürgen Bömelburg, *Zwischen Polnischer Ständegesellschaft und Preussischem Obrigkeitsstaat: vom Königlichen Preussen zu Westpreussen 1756–1806* (Munich, 1995).

52  Hubatsch, *Frederick the Great*, pp. 225–6.

Frederick's own physical decline led to a parallel deterioration in the efficiency of the state apparatus. During his extended and serious illness in 1775, the wheels of government did not stop turning, but they certainly slowed down.[53] Frederick's willpower was not in doubt, but his physical capacity to carry the burdens he had heaped upon himself was impaired. Much remains to be discovered about later Frederician government, particularly during the final decade of the king's life. But it seems inconceivable that detailed research will not reveal a state machine in decline, as its ageing head became less and less able to carry the massive administrative burden. The danger of such an over-centralized system of government was that when the monarchical engine was removed, the whole structure would seize up.

It was not simply a matter of political and administrative structures, crucial as these were. The policies pursued during the second reign, and the degree of integration between them, were potentially dangerous in themselves. In the short term, they could be justified – and were, by the king – as the inescapable price of defending Prussia's flawed position as a great power, the principal legacy of the Seven Years' War. But these priorities inhibited and may even have distorted social and economic evolution: witness the unexpected consequences of the *Landschaften*. Short-term imperatives could be pursued only by ignoring the future. Prussia's survival as a great power led to a long-term distortion of the kingdom's economic, social and institutional evolution.

The eventual impact upon the Prussian state was much more serious, though it took two decades to become fully evident.[54] Two parallel but rival systems of government now existed: one at Potsdam, one in Berlin. The advance of the *Kabinett* at the expense of the established agencies of government was to be a source of political tension and, ultimately, political collapse. Until 1786, the king's towering personality and remarkable abilities, together with his single-minded devotion to ruling Prussia, had ensured that the members of the *Kabinett* remained scribes and only occasionally unofficial advisers. Frederick's system of government, however, was always bound to be impermanent, since none of his immediate successors could match his ability, energy and devotion to ruling. Under the less forceful and less able Frederick William II (1786–97) and the notoriously indecisive Frederick William III (1797–1840), it was to be a very different story. During Frederick the Great's second reign, ministers had been marginalized and supplanted.

---

53  This is confirmed by the documents for that year printed in *ABB*, xvi:i.
54  These have recently been brilliantly explored by Brendan Simms, *The Impact of Napoleon: Prussian high politics, foreign policy and the crisis of the executive, 1797–1806* (Cambridge, 1997).

Though they recovered some authority after his death, there were severe limits to their power. The *Kabinett*'s expansion had led to the emergence of a skeleton administration at Potsdam, which replicated the official agencies of government in Berlin. The potential for confusion and conflict was obvious: here lies one major source of the crisis of the old Prussian state.

And this was to be the principal, if delayed, consequence of Frederick the Great's 'Second Reign'. After August 1786, there was to be a vacuum at the heart of Prussian government, which neither Frederick William II, nor Frederick William III, nor their ministers, could fill. It would principally be filled by the increasingly influential *Kabinett* secretaries, who became the real advisers to the king: 'ministers in secret', as their bitter political rival Karl August von Hardenberg once styled them.[55] Although the outward appearances of orderly administration continued, behind this façade an atavistic struggle for supremacy developed in the antechamber of power. A political system created by a remarkable and hard-working ruler grew increasingly strained as he grew older, and finally collapsed after his death. The removal of Old Fritz's towering presence was quickly followed by the dissolution of political authority, which came to be fought over by the favourites in the new king's immediate entourage and particularly in the *Kabinett*. This 'perverted system of government'[56] was a legacy of Frederick the Great's highly personalized monarchy, which had been strengthened during his second reign. It was to be an important source of the catastrophe of 1806, when Napoleon's shattering victory was followed by the collapse of Prussia's *Ancien Régime*.

---

55  Quoted by Otto Hintze, 'The origins of the modern ministerial system', in Felix Gilbert (ed.), *The Historical Essays of Otto Hintze* (New York, 1975), pp. 218–66, at p. 246.
56  The description is that of Otto Hintze: 'The origins of the modern ministerial system', p. 246, who went on to declare that 'it was notoriously responsible for the catastrophe of 1806'.

# CHAPTER NINE

# The Prussian military state, 1763–1806*

## HAGEN SCHULZE

Count Mirabeau, who was later to become one of the great figures of the French Revolution, a man who was rich and cultivated and the author of elegant and somewhat obscene social novels, felt as though he were on another planet when he was at the court of Frederick the Great. His deep admiration for the king brought him to Potsdam in 1786, but this did not prevent him from serving the French monarchy as a secret agent. He reported back to Versailles that the typical Prussian industry was the military system and that: 'The Prussian Monarchy is not a country that has an army, but an army that has a country, in which, as it were, it is just billeted.'

Whether Count Mirabeau actually said this or not is not really important, although it is worth noting that in his later publications the phrase is nowhere to be found.[1] But he could have said it and it was later repeated countless times as a standard quotation about Prussia, and later Germany, that was held right up to the present day. What struck the French count was a characteristic feature that remained a fundamental difference between Prussia and the other European states. One set of figures makes this difference quite clear – the expenditure on the army.

A characteristic of the absolutist state was the predominance of the court as reflected in state expenditure. In France, the share of the budget spent

---

* Translated from the German by Philip G. Dwyer.
1 The quotation appears among numerous German and French authors with anti-Prussian tendencies and is constantly attributed to Mirabeau. It was quoted for the first time by the military historian Georg Heinrich von Berenhorst, *Aus dem Nachlaß*, (ed.) E. von Bülow (Dessau, 1845), i, p. 187.

on the court in 1770 was almost 50 per cent; the army barely 20 per cent. In 1768, the court of Vienna spent 23 per cent of its income on itself and 48 per cent on the army – the relatively high expenditure on the army was, however, of short duration, was used for an urgent and necessary reform and was almost exclusively covered by raising loans. Of the entire expenditure of Bavaria in 1770, the court claimed 42 per cent compared with the army's 30 per cent. As for Prussia, in 1786, the year of Frederick the Great's death (in other words, in the middle of a long period of peace), the army took no less than 75 per cent of the overall household income. Of the 25 per cent that was left over, 5 per cent went to the war treasury, the administration received 7 per cent, a further 7 per cent went to agriculture and a total of 6 per cent was retained by the royal court.

That Prussia was a military state was obviously not the discovery of anti-Prussian thinkers. Even admirers of the Frederician state, like the Saxon officer who was present during a storm when Frederick inspected a parade one year before his death, saw this as Prussia's decisive characteristic. He wrote:

> Above all else, I wish that the martial spirit which prevails so totally [in Prussia] was in our army. . . . However, this martial spirit is not the work of one man – even if that man were the general of all generals – but the work of time, luck, weaponry and the sovereign. The sovereign must, if not in reality, at least appear to be a soldier, and must make this profession first in the state. For as long as it remains of secondary importance man cannot be happy and will strive after something that appears more honourable, profitable and better. The Duke of Brunswick thinks himself more of a Prussian lieutenant-general than a Duke. This and other such like things certainly contribute towards the martial spirit. A high opinion and solid confidence in oneself contributes a great deal, on the other hand, to victory. . . .
>
> This is the way it is in every aspect of the Prussian state. Wherever one looks, one sees other *Stände* [Estates] extend their hand to the soldier class to always bind themselves totally to that class.
>
> Everything indicates that Prussia is the foremost military state and that its inhabitants are just as happy, if not happier, than in other states. It was through the army that the monarchy came into being and as long as its feet remain firmly planted, as long as it has a king who is also a soldier, it will remain, in spite of its powerful neighbours, the first and foremost German monarchy.[2]

---

2 First Lieutenant von Warnsdorff, 'Über Friedrichs des Großen letzte Revue in Schlesien 1785', *Deutsche Revue* 31 (1906), 339ff.

# Prussia's geopolitical imperative

There are reasons for the overwhelming predominance of the army. Above all was Prussia's geographical position. From the end of the Middle Ages right up to the twentieth century, the development of the state has determined the fate of Europe. England, France, Spain, the Ottoman Empire, Russia, Sweden and later the Netherlands, as well as Denmark at times, were all on the periphery of Europe and had more or less natural frontiers, with both a geographical, political, economic and cultural centre. In the middle, on the other hand, was Europe's no-man's-land, with a host of larger or smaller territorial states and cities that lay between Maas and Memel, Etsch and Belt, in which, as a general rule, a German dialect was spoken, but which, incidentally, were dependent upon the religion of their respective sovereigns, while the emperor and the Reich appeared remote and removed from the reality of life.

There are a number of reasons why a modern great power did not develop in this geographical area during the same period as the rest of Europe. There was no natural centre and no natural borders. The country was open on all sides, while its geographical trade routes were hacked up by rivers and mountains. Certainly, in the period before the Reformation, during the reigns of Maximilian I (1493–1519) and Charles V (1519–56), there was an attempt to develop something like a united German state out of the transnational, or rather metaphysical, organization/construction of the 'Holy Roman Empire of the German Nation'. In the following period, however, German unity became the victim of the struggle between Reformation and Counter-Reformation. Whereas the war between denominations was decided one way or the other in every other European state, in Germany it remained undecided and became fossilized to a certain extent in the political/territorial principle of *cuius regio, eius religio,* covering a territorial fragmentation that corresponded to the religious divisions, with consequences that remain apparent in German political culture up to the present day.

This fragmentation was to remain the principle of the constitution of the Holy Roman Empire, an organization that did not represent a state, but rather a state of law: the essence of government, its organization and its power were largely passed on to the territories, imperial cities and self-governing knights. Their 'liberties' and sovereign rights were, since the end of the Thirty Years' War, guaranteed through an international treaty, the Peace of Westphalia (1648). As the international constitutional lawyer, Pufendorf, has pointed out, from that time on the imperial constitution, an 'irregular political body not unlike a monster', was regarded as part of international, European law. In other words, the organization, the rules

203

and the basis of the German Empire's domestic policy were of concern for all European powers.

This situation was no coincidence, but rather a logical outcome of the European order. The continent had been held in balance only through the amorphous nature of its centre, and a look at the map will show why. Whosoever possessed this area was master of all Europe, whether it was one of the peripheral European great powers or a power that had emerged from the centre. Every concentration of power in Germany worked like a revocation of the measures ensuring the European balance of power. The consequences were a regular formation of hostile coalitions, the success of which were all the more likely since a central European power had to maintain several sides at the same time and because it did not dispose of defensible borders.

For this reason, Germany's European neighbours regarded the 'liberties' of over 300 small German states as a guarantee of peace and the survival of the political balance of power. That is why the European states guaranteed the survival and independence of the minor princes and imperial cities and why each attempt by a great power to attack Germany invariably brought about rivalry on the central European scene. This explains why the Habsburg attempt to bring the imperial conglomerate into a more or less modern state under Vienna's direct control failed. In the period which followed, the Austrian Habsburgs increasingly turned towards East and South-East Europe and to Italy, and lost comparable influence in Central Europe. This was the beginning of Austria's long journey out of German history, which came to an end temporarily in 1866, and definitively in 1945.

Into this central European power vacuum entered an ascending Brandenburg-Prussia, which disturbed a sensitive balance of power. What emerged was a lasting, essentially artificial territorial construction that came into being through the Hohenzollerns' sheer will to govern and their enormous organizational talents: Brandenburg in central Germany, Cleves, Mark and Ravensberg on the lower Rhine, and Prussia (later called East Prussia) on the farthest north-eastern rim of the German-speaking area, which already lay outside the borders of the Holy Roman Empire. A unified national territory comparable to France, Bavaria and even the Hereditary Lands of Austria did not exist. There were several scattered national territories of this type in the region, but they usually survived the accidents and fortunes of war and dynastic succession to which they owed their existence for only a short time. Prussia was the exception because it found a successful answer to its problem.

That problem consisted of a seemingly insoluble paradox. Prussia's central European position demanded a policy which did not threaten any of its neighbours. At the same time, however, the state stood on the verge of

Table 9.1   Population of the European powers around 1700

| State | Population (millions) |
| --- | --- |
| Prussia | 3.1 |
| Poland | 6.0 |
| The Habsburg States | 8.8 |
| Britain | 9.3 |
| Spain/Portugal | 10.0 |
| Russia | 17.0 |
| France | 20.0 |

an existence that was exposed to every pressure exerted on its open borders. This situation led to two historically tried-and-tested solutions. Prussia had either, like the Empire as a whole, to open itself to political influence from its neighbours and allow them to affect and control its policies. This was the path chosen by the other great central European state, Poland. The result for the Polish state was the undermining of its sovereignty, domestic anarchy and, finally, its partition between its neighbours. Or, alternatively, Prussia had to organize and arm itself to such an extent that it was in a position to carry out and win any war, even against a coalition, on its scattered and unprotected borders. Unlike other European powers, which would have to reckon with contributions and territorial cessions in case of defeat, but whose core would always remain untouched, each conflict for Prussia was a matter of life and death. In addition, Brandenburg-Prussia was destitute, had practically no natural resources at its disposal and possessed a comparatively smaller population (see Table 9.1).

In comparison with the other European states, Prussia had 'a tenth [of the surface] and three-tenths of the population, but was the third or fourth European power in military terms'.[3] That is why the military sector predominated. That is why there was a bureaucratic organization of all walks of life, right down to the smallest detail, so that all forces could be mobilized. That is why the character traits of exertion, seriousness, lack of urbanity and joie de vivre, which became part of Prussian – later German – characteristics, made Prussia so unpopular among its European neighbours. All of these were prerequisites for the survival of Brandenburg-Prussia.

Over and above this, Prussia survived through a curious social and governmental organization that, in its formative stages, was at the same time a

---

3   Kurt Hintze, 'Die Bevölkerung Preußens im 17. und 18. Jahrhundert nach Quantität und Qualität', in Otto Büsch and Wolfgang Neugebauer (eds), Moderne Preußische Geschichte, 3 vols (Berlin, 1982), i, p. 305.

military system. As such, Prussia was in a unique position. Ever since the end of the Thirty Years' War, standing armies had been created everywhere in Europe, but essentially as a representation of continental power alongside palace architecture and court etiquette as an integral part of the Baroque apotheosis. Rulers of the period were, it is true, absolutist, but were anything but absolute. They simply ruled over royal capitals and the upper echelons of the administration. The public administration was still in corporate hands; the prince ruled indirectly or through mediation. Real princely freedom lay with the army, in the standing regiments that embodied not only the power and the glory of the prince, but above all his personal sovereignty, as seen from the outside and even more so from within.

While armies elsewhere in Europe were essentially nothing more than the expansion of the Royal Household, in Prussia, from the reign of Frederick William I (1713–40) on, it was understood that each subject was a social individual in all areas of life. Above all, military obligations left their mark on rural existence, and it has to be remembered that around 80 per cent of the population lived in the countryside. From 1733, the country was divided into levying districts, the so-called 'cantons'. Each canton served a regiment as the basis of compulsory recruitment. In ideal cases, the *Gutsbesitzer* (the owner of land) in each canton was also the captain of the company belonging to that regiment. In this manner, the rural *Gutsuntertanen* (the lord's peasants who were bound to the land and subject to forced labour) were allocated the dual role of soldier and farmer; hence the close reciprocal relationship between the manor and the company and between the canton and the regiment resulted in the perception by the rural population that the social and military systems were one. The establishment of the peasantry on the land, emancipation from military service and marriage were dependent upon the regiment. The methods of punishment were determined by reciprocal stimuli between the *Gutsherrschaft*[4] and the army. Beatings for soldiers in service, as for soldiers on leave, taught the peasantry blind obedience. The peasant was constantly aware of having to maintain a partly rural, partly military role through various obligations to service and through his uniform, of which at least one piece had to be taken home and constantly worn. This dual role completely determined the peasant's life.

In terms of numbers, the peasantry bore the brunt of the military burden of the state. The existence of the army, however, was dependent upon the noble *Gutsherren* (lords of estates) and their next of kin, who constituted a

---

4   There is no English equivalent. It is a term that describes the lord's political power, but which also refers to the considerable degree of authority the lord enjoyed over the person of the peasant. It covered areas such as marriage, the possibility of practising a trade or leaving the land, all of which required the noble lord's consent.

pool for the officer corps, just as much as on the support of the peasantry. At the same time, the peasant's socage service (*Frondienste*) appeared to be an indispensable basis for the existence of aristocratic officers. The relationship between *Gutsherrlichkeit* (the essence of noble land ownership) and an officer's character contributed to the unusually strong social position of the Junkers in the Prussian state during the eighteenth century and, indeed, right up to the twentieth.

# The position of the nobility

This position was not obvious. In western Europe at least, the struggle between the aristocracy and territorial sovereigns during the sixteenth and seventeenth centuries was decided largely in favour of the latter. The prototypical case of absolutism, that of France, shows the transition from a politically and economically uprooted to a domesticated court nobility. That is, the nobility lost little by little its corporate rights, but retained its social privileges. As the noble privileges of the landowners were lost and former noble property increasingly went to middle-class owners who had become rich through trade and manufacture, the nobility became drawn to the court. Noble incomes were no longer made up of fortunes based on agricultural property but on pensions and positions allocated by the king, not on the grounds of legal obligations or according to objective results, but rather out of the fullness of his absolute power and grace. The recipient was literally under the obligation of the king's favour or disfavour.

Prussia was different. The power of the Brandenburg margrave and elector was, in comparison to western European monarchies, still very young. It was only during the sixteenth century that they succeeded in achieving their territorial claims, often by violent means. But the total deprivation of power of the unruly landowning nobility proved to be impossible and the danger of a renewed disintegration of territorial sovereignty was ever present.

And so the Great Elector, Frederick William (1640–88), the first Prussian king, Frederick I (1688–1713 – Elector of Brandenburg until 1701, king thereafter), and the so-called 'soldier king', Frederick William I (1713–40) – during the last third of the seventeenth century and the first third of the eighteenth – reached a compromise between sovereign and Junker. Frederick William I could not quite carry through his plans, which were set out in a famous letter to the East Prussian *Stände* dated 13 January 1717. They had complained about the king's new taxes and had maintained that the country would be ruined. Frederick William I replied in his broken high-Prussian style, which was a mixture of German, Latin, French and Polish:

'The whole country will be ruined? That I don't believe, but I believe the Junkers' right to political opposition will be ruined. I will stabilize the princely sovereignty like a rock of bronze.'[5] And so the unruly Prussian nobility was taken in hand like nowhere else in Europe. It was almost as firmly tied to the land as the peasantry because the noble manor was in practice not for sale and because considerations of class made an occupation other than agriculture impossible. Furthermore, severe edicts forbade Junkers either to go abroad to study or to take service in a foreign army. A young noble had to expect almost compulsory admission into the royal cadet corps. As a result, everything boiled down to one honourable means of making a living offered by the king of Prussia as an alternative to agriculture – service in the officer corps – so that the noble 'knew no lord other than God and the king of Prussia'.[6]

In this manner, the Prussian nobility was tied to the crown, but this bond with the sovereign was almost exclusively based on personal loyalty between the king and the noble vassal. This is an important factor, since this exclusively personal trust relationship explains a great deal about the history of the Prussian/German officer corps, namely its behaviour after the November Revolution of 1919 and later, on another level, in the Hitler state. This bond was most clearly expressed in the oath that was sworn to the king, and not to the state or the legal system.

But the monarchy had to pay a price for the complete loyalty of the Prussian nobility. The officer corps became the domain of the nobility, something that it certainly had not been originally. Three generals of peasant stock shared the table of the Great Elector – Derfflinger, Lüdtke and Hennings – while in 1704, King Frederick I had explicitly assured middle-class officers of the guard that their promotions would be treated in the same manner as for the nobles. But in the penultimate year of Frederick William I's reign, in 1739, all 34 Prussian generals were noble and of the 211 staff officers only 11 were non-noble. Certainly, in times of war, the proportion of middle-class officers usually increased – possibly to stop gaps, possibly because in times of war ability was more important than birth. But hardly had peace returned than the officer corps assumed a feudal character. Of the 713 Prussian officers at the time of Frederick II's death,

---

5   'Tout le pays sera ruiné? Nihil Kredo, aber das Kredo, daß die Junkers ihre Autoritaet Nie pos volam wird runinirt werden. Ich stabilire die souveranité wie ein Rocher von Bronce.' Quoted in Friedrich Foerster, *Friedrich Wilhelm, König von Preußen*, i, p. 35. *Nie pozwalam* (I do not agree) was the formula with which the right of *liberum veto* was exercised in the Polish parliament.
6   Instructions from Frederick William I to his successor, January 1722, in G. Schmoller (ed.), *Acta Borussica: Behördenorganisation* (Berlin, 1893), iii, n. 249, p. 450.

only 22 were non-noble and these were to be found essentially among those branches where knowledge was more important than bravery and in which, for this very reason, little value was stored: the engineers, the sappers and the artillery. Finally, the *Allgemeines Landrecht* of 1794 defined the position of the nobility in a broader sense than the first Prussian constitution: 'The nobility, as the First Estate in the state, is principally responsible for the defence of the state as well as the support of its outward dignity and its internal constitution.'[7]

The privilege of the nobility over commissioned officers was not simply one of class, but also to a large degree an economic one, because from the company commander on, that is, from the captain on, the officer 'possessed' his unit in the fullest sense of the word. He received a fixed amount of money for the maintenance of the unit, to make use of as he saw fit; on top of that were further financial advantages in the form of rewards, gifts, sinecures, prebends, pensions, lucrative civil positions and even exemption from state taxes.

But the so-called 'company economy' was not the decisive factor. Much more crucial for the structure of the Prussian military state was the readiness of the monarchy to leave the core of its position of power with the agricultural nobility, namely, the landowners with their associated rights. Within the boundaries of the *Gutsbezirk* (district of the estate), the noble proprietor was virtually unlimited lord and master. The Prussian monarchs had also given the nobility economic, legal and political sovereignty over the peasants living on the *Gutbesitz* (estate). The *Gutbesitzer* (estate-owner) was vested with police powers and jurisdiction in the first instance in his district. As patron, he led the supervision of the church and school. Just as he was subject to the king, so, too, the peasant was subject to the *Gutsherr* (lord of the estate); sovereign power stopped on the borders of the *Gutsherrschaft*. Therein lay the political significance of the virtually unlimited sovereignty of the noble *Gutsherren* in the home, on the farm, in the village, in church and school: all state policies that were directed to the countryside were usually mediated through the power of the *Gutsherren*.

The power of the *Gutsherren* received further weight through the fact that more than half the country was subjected to private *Gutsherrschaft*. The authority of land was even further supported through regional constitutions, those self-administering corporate districts in which the noble exerted his political mediatory position between sovereign and the rural population. The *Landrat* (local official), as the lowest representative of the organ of state bureaucracy in the countryside, was the *Gutsherr* who, like the other *Gutsbesitzer* of the region from whose ranks he came, was elected by them and who

---

7   *Allgemeines Landrecht für die preußischen Staaten*, part 2, chapter 9, § 1.

suggested his appointment be confirmed by the king. The special position of the nobility in *Ancien Régime* Prussia was, as a result, not only socially and economically determined, but had a thoroughly political character because that special position rested upon the governance of the land and its inhabitants.

In the course of the systematic incorporation of the traditional Prussian landed aristocracy into the army's canton administration, the Junker class gained a position of ascendancy in the social structure of the old Prussian monarchy. The king, who was obliged to force his noble vassals to assume the position of officers in the army because of the conditions of the social structure of the old Prussian monarchy, was for the same reason obliged to protect and preserve the nobility as a class in its property and privileges. And so the military system as a social system became an expression of the political relationship between king and nobility whose fundamental significance was formulated in Frederick William I's Political Testament, written for reasons of state in 1722:

> My successor must consider this to be a policy and seek it out, that from all his provinces and especially Prussia . . . the nobility and counts who are employed in the army and the children who are pressed into the cadets . . . is a formidable thing for his service and the army and for the peace of his lands.[8]

The rural cantonist and the property-owning noble officer were inseparably tied to the military state. They were the two pillars of the Prussian monarchy that in the course of the second half of the eighteenth century became an additional characteristic of what was felt in the rest of Europe to be an exemplary civil administration (and this made up a decisive part of its famous efficiency). Like the beginnings of the officer corps, the upper echelons of the administration were to a large extent filled by nobles, usually officers who had resigned, while the middle and lower echelons of the public service, as well as public school teachers, were recruited essentially from non-commissioned officers who had finished their service. From 1725 on, in order to advertise the almost total homogeneity of the state and army in Prussia, the king constantly wore a uniform, which thereby became the 'king's dress'; the highest honour for a subject of the Prussian crown was to wear the king's dress.

After the Peace of Hubertusburg in 1763, small Brandenburg-Prussia, the 'sand pit of the Holy Roman Empire', became the fifth great power. Because of a strongly felt difference in quality and its ascendancy in the face

---

8  Cf. note 6.

of geography, numbers and probability, it remained disliked by the rest of Europe, even if it was feared and respected. Certainly, the long, slow separation of Brandenburg from the rest of the Empire contributed to its ascent, something that was encouraged by the lack of Imperial influence in north Germany and by its increasingly weak Polish and Swedish neighbours. The international situation in the eighteenth century – the struggle between England and France over the domination of the seas and the occupation of a large colonial empire, with the resultant constellation of European alliances – also made the rise of Prussia possible. Frederick's genius in the field, together with a suicidally obstinate will and fairy-tale luck, also has to be taken into account. But without the peculiar social system of this country, without the concentration of military power to which everything was subordinated, Prussia would not have been capable of such an upturn.

This was the Prussia from which a specific picture of German militarism was drawn, whose tradition shaped the history of Prussia-Germany right up to the twentieth century, and which in part was to shape essential areas. But it would be too easy to assume that this complex structure, 'Prussia', lived on in the social, political and economic conditions of Germany, as well as in the *mentalité* of the people and the political and military elite right up to the present day. The situation was considerably complicated by a new factor that pushed its way onto the scene towards the end of the eighteenth century and lent the drama a new direction: the French Revolution and its consequences.

## The French Revolution and its consequences

The social and political changes that occurred in France after 1789 also led to decisive changes in French military affairs, namely, the technical and tactical aspects, and also to a new relationship between the army on the one hand and the state and society on the other. We know today that the birth of the French revolutionary armies did not occur at the same time as the rights of man and bourgeois equality of 1789. The old French line army of the *Ancien Régime* continued to exist for many more years, almost as though the Revolution had not occurred. Only with the first defeats of the army against the anti-French coalition, concluded by the majority of the European states after the execution of Louis XVI in January 1793, were revolutionary measures called for in the military field. The French National Convention passed a law on 24 February 1793 declaring that all French citizens from the ages of 18 to 40 could serve under arms. Article 109 of the Constitution of 1793 declared with classical laconism: 'Tous les français sont soldats' – all Frenchmen are soldiers.

The political-military principle of the democratic state concept was expressed in this new phase of the Revolution that succeeded to power. Within the one and indivisible nation, the citizen and the soldier were identical, at least as an idea. The citizen was responsible for both civil and military duties; universal suffrage and universal and equal conscription were corresponding means to defend freedom and the motherland. The revolutionary idea of the *volonté générale* (the general will) entered into military affairs; the army was no longer the exclusive component of the executive, but rather a part of the bourgeois state. The change in the constitution brought about the law of 23 August 1793 on the general arming of the people – the *levée en masse*. The realization of the principle of arming the people in a functioning republican-oriented national army is inseparably linked with the name of Lazare Carnot, a former captain in the royal engineers, who at the beginning of the Revolution had already written a memorandum entitled 'Tout citoyen est né soldat' (Every citizen is born a soldier), and who at the time of direst need on 14 August 1793 entered the Committee of Public Safety and took over control of the military section. In compliance with Rousseau's dictum that 'each citizen should be a soldier through duty, none as a profession', he understood that in order to motivate conscripts he had to hammer home the realization that not only the success of the Revolution but the survival of the nation was dependent on them.

The voluntary nature of each individual in battle was a new and veritable revolutionary element in the nature of warfare and one of the foundations upon which the young generals of the new army bestowed security and decisiveness. There was a close relation between this and the changes that took place in French tactics. The French no longer needed to concentrate their troops in close formation on the battlefield through fear of mass desertion, which crippled the armies of absolutism and which prohibited independent manoeuvres of small units. The French *tirailleurs* no longer proceeded in closed line formation, but rather in loose formations, with individuals fighting, firing and taking cover and winning for the army a considerable tactical elasticity. Breaking down armies, which could manoeuvre only with great difficulty, into smaller units (divisions and brigades) increased its operative manoeuvrability. This led to a totally new type of warfare in Europe, the results of which are well known: the coalition armies were destroyed, and the French revolutionary armies advanced to the Rhine and beyond and defeated the much better-trained and disciplined troops of their absolutist opponents in a type of Blitzkrieg. The armies of the *Ancien Régime* found themselves in a difficult position against these ambassadors of freedom. One Prussian officer enviously thought that although the soldiers of the standing armies were not lacking in courage, they would always remain inferior 'because their souls did not drive their bodies in the same manner as those enflamed by enthusiasm'.[9] Moreover, such victories were deserved by decisive, daring and imaginative leaders like Lazare Hoche, Jean-Victor Moreau or Napoleon Bonaparte, who would hardly have been given a chance to get beyond a subordinate position in the old army. Sheer numbers also played a role: the numerical superiority of the revolutionary armies overwhelmed their opponents on the battlefield.

In retrospect, it would appear that the leaders of the Prussian state and army were blind to these developments. We know that the experiences of one war justify the defeats in the next. This is exactly what happened to Prussia. Both the Silesian War and the Seven Years' War were won against overwhelming superior might, as a result of which it was believed that Prussia possessed the best military-state administration in Europe. The consequences led to the paralysis of the military and political spheres while the social sphere was set into motion.

In the course of the second half of the eighteenth century – and this had decisive consequences for Prussian-German social history, over and above the political culture of the whole of the nineteenth century – a social class developed, which, for want of a better term, was called the 'educated bourgeoisie'. This class was made up of a very heterogeneous mixture of public servants, pastors, university and high school teachers, doctors and, to an extent, officers, all united by one thing: they exercised their offices and professions not because of the class to which they belonged but because of their educational, mostly academic, qualifications. The increasing requirements of the absolutist state for educated intelligence in the recruitment of higher public servants played a decisive part in the origins of this class. Prussia introduced a state exam for lawyers in 1755 and for all other higher government officials in 1770, and the state supplied the educational establishments for their education, which in number and quality surpassed most other European states.

The nobility in the king's service were also obliged to conform to bourgeois education standards when they wanted advancement in the administration. As a result of the *Allgemeines Landrecht* of 1794, the educated classes were explicitly privileged, enjoyed exemption from taxes and military service, and were subordinated to royal law courts. This enabled a mixed noble–bourgeois educated elite to develop outside the Estate system, which was much stronger than the professional bourgeoisie tied to the state and monarchy in France which facilitated education and careers.

---

9   K. F. von der Knesebeck, *Betrachtungen über den jetzigen Krieg und die Ursachen seiner falschen Beurteilung* (n.p., 1794), pp. 56f.

In this respect, Prussia was more modern than the otherwise exemplary *Ancien Régime* France. The discontent of the underprivileged and the socially neglected, which created a revolutionary bourgeoisie in France, found much less fertile soil in Prussia. Certainly, Prussia's administrative and educated bourgeoisie were imbued with the international ideas of the Enlightenment, which had its most important cultural centres in Germany in Berlin and Königsberg. Consequently, the contrast with the nobility as a corporate organization with legally documented prerogatives always remained a painful thorn, and the intolerance of the social and political order of the eighteenth century contradicted Kant's idea of 'mankind's exit from its self-incurred immaturity', a view commonly held by the reading and discussion-hungry bourgeoisie.

As a result, the French Revolution was without exception joyfully welcomed by the Prussian intelligentsia, but at the same time it was certain a similar occurrence would not be repeated in Prussia. The Prussian foreign minister, Count Hertzberg, could, with the approval of the educated Berlin public, categorically declare a few months after the outbreak of revolution in France that 'the Prussian government was not despotic',[10] and for the most part the middle classes shared the opinion of Adolphe von Knigge: 'I maintain that we have no reason to fear nor occasion to wish for a revolution in Germany.'[11] That the Prussian government was not despotic can be shown through the string of reforms before the Reform Era, from the General Legal Code (*Allgemeines Landrecht*) of 1794 to the abolition of hereditary subservience among the peasantry, and the beginnings of the tax and excise reform after the appointment of Baron vom Stein to the ministry of finance and the economy in 1804. The bonds between the state, the crown and the bourgeoisie were stronger than ever. But, in spite of that, the increasing rigidity and structural inflexibility of the Frederician state were painfully felt.

The army, in particular, had sat on the laurels of its previous successes. One of the reasons for the earlier Prussian military victories was the excellent manner in which the spirit of discipline reigned, which also aroused the admiration of Prussia's opponents. As a result, it was difficult to object to the civil service and the civilian population getting too much discipline. The art of warfare, as a few young critical officers at the end of the eighteenth century saw, had increasingly deteriorated and had become completely formalized through a mass of fixed rules that regulated exercises and left no room for initiative among commanders, and smothered any movement

---

10   Kurt von Raumer, 'Zur Beurteilung der preußischen Reform', *Geschichte in Wissenschaft und Unterricht* 18 (1967), 344.

11   A. von Knigge, *Joseph von Wurmbrand (1792)*, G. Steiner (ed.) (Frankfurt-am-Main, 1968), p. 11.

towards independent tactical imagination. During Frederick the Great's reign, the lower ranks of the army had already become demoralized because the troops were held together exclusively through force and discipline. On top of that, the canton system was being undermined because men were increasingly needed in agriculture and manufacturing, and the large gaps in army personnel were tending to be filled by foreigners who were often recruited against their will.

That this army was no match for the French citizen-soldier was perfectly well understood, but only by a few. Educated officers who lived in the intellectually enlightened world and who shared the philanthropic and practical views of the bourgeoisie were rare. Prussia's cadet schools, particularly the *Académie des Nobles* of the Berlin cadet corps, formed a small elite for service in the general staff, but the majority of officers remained ignorant and even held ignorance to be a military virtue. Book learning was long held to be an unnecessary and dangerous cause of civilian grumbling. 'It is not good to have a lot of educated generals,' thought a respected general at the end of the 1780s; 'the commander of the advanced guard, and perhaps one other, that is enough; the others are there to take the bait otherwise there are cabals.'[12] Kant's demand that 'mankind exit from its self-incurred immaturity', and that he have 'the courage to use his own understanding', hardly found any sympathy in the deliberately isolated milieu of the Prussian officer corps. The result was a divide between civilians and the military that was going to become typical of relations between the Prussian/German bourgeoisie and the officer corps. The army did not take part in the bourgeois age (with a few exceptions), and sought rather to maintain an unequivocal and pre-established world in which the bourgeois gave way before the noble officer. This was certainly not a belated realization – King Frederick William III gave the following Cabinet order in 1798:

> I must despair at how particularly young officers want to maintain their precedence over civilians. I want to show the prestige of the military there where it is essentially of advantage to it, namely on the battlefield where they are meant to protect their fellow citizens with life and limb. Moreover, a soldier should never, no matter what his class, subject the least of my subjects to a snub because it is they, not I, who support the army, their bread is the kingpin of the army that I command. . . .[13]

Also, one should not think that the education of the few enlightened officers was very far-reaching. Even the Hanoverian artillery officer, Gerhard von

---

12   Hermann von Boyen, *Denkwürdigkeiten und Erinnerungen 1771–1813* (Stuttgart, 1891), i, p. 201.
13   Johannes Scherr, *Deutsche Kultur- und Sittengeschichte* (Leipzig, 1882), p. 506.

Scharnhorst, who entered Prussian military service in 1801 and immediately founded a 'Learned Military Society', hardly learned how to read, write and calculate in his youth; his later memoirs carry the traces of a neglected education. He and other young officers – Berenhorst, Bülow, Knesebeck – used military writings to advocate a fundamental reform of the Prussian army. As early as 1795, Hermann von Boyen, later Field-Marshal and Minister of War, wrote in the monthly journal *Bellona* calling for the 'Liberty of the Back' (*Freiheit des Rückens*) – in other words, the abolition of corporal punishment – but with the characteristic reasoning that soldiers can transform themselves from 'exact functioning tactical machines and rigid automats' through more humane education methods and that the 'warrior, ennobled through the light of the Enlightenment, would carry out manoeuvres and linear tactics with all the more exactitude as a result of more humane treatment; the application of more humane methods would lead to this objective and would obviate the reasons for internal revolt'.[14] Even the biggest problem for the military high command, mass desertion, would fall off as a result. This was certainly not the spirit of the Revolution at work, but rather that of enlightened absolutism. But these officers were, nevertheless, accused of 'Jacobinism' and 'infatuation with the Revolution', and as a consequence of his publications, Boyen was downgraded on the active list. That the army of Frederick the Great had become a fossilized, immobile organization is no better illustrated than through the bitter advice given to his son by Scharnhorst in December 1805:

> You write that, in the midst of it all, you could not prevent yourself from fighting. This honours your courage and patriotism. But learn, my son, to overcome this virtue early on. It has always caused me, and especially at the moment, more grief than any other burden. Moreover, I do not wish that you ever become a soldier; it would be difficult for you to find contentment. You cannot serve the French and the other armies are for the most part in such a state that, in the future, little honour is to be had with them. Old age, weakness, idleness, ignorance and cowardice on the one hand, work and decisiveness on the other. . . .[15]

The army, it was becoming more clear, was no longer capable of learning and behaved according to a complex system of rules that no longer functioned. Closed systems of this nature break down sooner or later.

---

14  Friedrich Meinecke, *Das Leben des Generalfeldmarschalls Hermann von Boyen* (Stuttgart, 1896), i, p. 245.
15  Scharnhorst to his son William, Gotha, 19 December 1805, in Karl Linnebach (ed.), *Scharnhorsts Briefe* (Munich, 1914), i, pp. 265f.

The collapse was just as unexpected as it was spectacular. After a long period of diplomatic manoeuvring, Prussia suddenly declared war on France in 1806. Napoleon obviously wanted to provoke a clash by continually attacking Prussian territory and by a demonstrative lack of regard for Prussian interests. The Prussian military were completely convinced that they could reprimand the Corsican. The double battle of Jena-Auerstedt took place on 14 October 1806 after a number of encounters had already led to Prussian withdrawals.

The collapse of the Prussian army at Jena-Auerstedt was so complete that no other large battles followed. Napoleon advanced into Prussia almost without any opposition; at Magdeburg, the entire army gave itself up without a single shot being fired, as did most of the other Prussian forts with the exception of Kolberg, which held out for months under the command of the merchant Nettelbeck and the previously completely unknown Major von Gneisenau. After the army had proven its military incompetence, it seems as though it wanted to declare its moral bankruptcy, too. The Prussian king, who had been obliged to withdraw into the farthest reaches of north-east Prussia, and who had been left in the lurch by his Russian ally, finally had to sign the victor's Diktat at Tilsit on 9 July 1807. The territorial acquisitions of the Second and Third Partitions of Poland were taken away, as well as all regions west of the Elbe. The region between the Elbe and the Oder, including Berlin, was occupied by French troops, and Prussia had to pay an indemnity to France that well exceeded its ability. Almost overnight, Prussia had gone from a European power to a second-rate power, and its definitive disappearance from the map seemed probable. Prussia, which had become great through its army, had foundered also because of its army.

This unprecedented collapse was necessary in order to break the fossilized structure of the old Prussian military state. The superiority of French revolutionary ideas was, to paraphrase Karl Marx, convincingly demonstrated through its translation into material power in the truest sense of the word. Every analysis of the defeat and every attempt to draw conclusions from the 'resurrection' of Prussia must keep this in mind. And that is also what happened: the Prussian reformers, whether civilians like Hardenberg, Stein, Altenstein and Schön, or military men like Scharnhorst, Gneisenau, Boyen and Clausewitz, made the question of French superiority the starting-point of their reflections. However – and this had serious consequences for the development of the Prussian state – Napoleon, the heir to the ideas of 1789, was perceived as the conqueror and hated national enemy of Prussia. What was new, the impetus, the disruption, worked deeply after the defeat, but it came from without and was linked with the deepest humiliation Prussia had had to submit to in its history. The idea of the Revolution amongst Prussia's spiritually enclosed intellectual class had been accepted up to 1806 with a

certain approval. For the first time in German history, a discrepancy between the state and the people was a conscious possibility, and this discrepancy was ideologically underpinned. Expressions like liberty and equality,
which up till then were general philosophical terms, now held a very concrete political content around which intellectuals became divided. But the
spiritual impetus from France was discredited through Napoleon's invasion.
After Jena-Auerstedt, liberty and equality no longer meant, in the first
instance, bourgeois liberty from tyrannical despotism and equality of individual citizens in their social and political chances, but, rather, liberty from
foreign oppression and the equality of people and nations in a restored
Europe without French hegemony. The separation of Prussia from the
liberal-democratic currents of Western Europe was laid down here, and
with it the particular German relationship between the state and its armed
might.

In any event, the established forces of the Prussian state appeared un-
prepared for a stroke of misfortune such as Jena-Auerstedt and looked for
help to save what could be saved. The same situation was to occur again
in 1918: the old system of the old state could not hold out. Hardly anyone
mourned the death of military despotism. Even the pillar upon which the
system rested, the landowning nobility, was no longer united behind it. In
larger civilian circles, the voice of malicious joy predominated at the misfortune of the now-unemployed Junker-officer class. Only the fate of the royal
family, and above all of Queen Luise, honoured by the people, gave rise to
any feelings of sympathy. One felt, as Chief-secretary von Müller noted in
his journal on 7 October 1807, as though a weight had been lifted: 'The
Prussian system', wrote Müller, 'had won respect and admiration, but was
never supported by a true love and spiritual warmth among the people.'[16]

Thanks to its unique integration of state and army, *Ancien Régime* Prussia
had become a European great power. It was because of this rigid unity that
it collapsed in 1806. The unity of state and army seems unattractive and
foreign to today's observer, but perhaps the position of the army in the
social and political existence of *Ancien Régime* Prussia will help us understand
the position of the army in Third World countries. It is by no means an
exaggeration to say that the militarization of state and society in Asian,
African and South American countries is one of the few normal factors
that characterize almost all pre-industrial developing countries. As much as
these countries might differ, there appears to be a direct relation between
the heightened position of the military on the one hand, and the political

---

16   Friedrich von Müller, *Erinnerungen aus den Kriegszeiten von 1806 bis 1813* (Leipzig, 1911),
     p. 107.

independence and economic growth of Third World countries on the other. Militarization as a prerequisite of state self-assertion on the outside, consolidation within, the overcoming of regional particularisms, and the modernization of economic and administrative techniques – all of these traits can be found in a similar manner in the construction of state and society in pre-revolutionary Prussia, even though these traits were combined with the general political and social tendencies of Europe.

CHAPTER TEN

# Prussia's army: continuity and change, 1713–1830

DENNIS SHOWALTER

The history of the Prussian army between 1713 and 1830 is usually presented in terms of military achievement at the expense of social, economic and political development. Frederick William I creates a formidable war-fighting instrument at the price of organizing Prussian society for warmaking. His son establishes the Prussian army as the military arbiter of Europe while almost destroying the Prussian state. After 1763, four decades of over-confident stagnation culminate in the débâcle of 1806–7. A military reform movement creates from defeat's ashes a new model army, based on popular participation, that plays a key role in Napoleon's overthrow. After Waterloo, professional myopia and socio-political reaction turn back the clock to the days of *dirigisme* at the price of military effectiveness.[1]

This chapter approaches its subject from an alternative perspective by seeking to establish the synergies among army, state and society during Prussia's rise to great-power status from Frederick William I to Frederick William IV. Its first part concentrates on the factors of geography and diplomacy that shaped Prussia's state strategy and its military requirements. The second part analyses the nature of the army created as an instrument of that strategy – its function as a military instrument and its institutional role in a kingdom that rightly or wrongly became, during the period under consideration, a byword for militarization and a precursor of militarism.

---

1 The classic statements of this thesis are the Anglo-Saxon liberal formulation of Gordon A. Craig, *The Politics of the Prussian Army, 1640–1945* (Oxford/New York, 1956); and from a German conservative perspective, Gerhard Ritter, *Sword and Scepter*, vol. 1, *The Prussian Tradition, 1740–1890*, tr. Heinz Norden (Coral Gables, FL, 1969).

# Geography, diplomacy and Prussia's military requirements

Geography played a central role in Prussia's military development. Prussia's lack of territorial integrity was remarkable by seventeenth-century standards, and anomalous by those of the eighteenth and nineteenth centuries. Each of the kingdom's three segments was, moreover, significantly vulnerable in its own right. Cleves–Mark and Minden–Ravensburg, the original 'Prussian Westphalia', lay athwart one of the main strategic axes of early modern Europe, and Prussia found no permanent leverage in that region between 1713 and 1814. The Rhine and Ruhr territories acquired as part of the Vienna settlement were a Judas gift, intended to compel Prussia to support its neighbours against France. Brandenburg, too, was exposed on all sides, with nothing resembling defensible strategic frontiers. Nor would the terrain support a network of fortresses like those of northern France and the Low Countries, even if Prussia could have paid for one. Unilateral initiatives in the central region were undertaken at particularly high risk. Frederick the Great's seizure of Silesia in 1740 committed his state to a generation of wars that it barely survived. Karl von Hardenberg's effort to annex the entire Kingdom of Saxony in 1814 came close to replicating Frederick's results. As for East Prussia, a vulnerability masked for a half-century by Poland's decline and Russia's preoccupations was highlighted during the Seven Years' War, when a lengthy Russian occupation made significant strides in securing a transfer of loyalties in that exposed province. Successive acquisitions of Polish territory between 1772 and 1795 resulted in an 'overstretch' that Prussian policy-makers were by no means reluctant to modify at Vienna.[2] Even after 1815, Prussia remained burdened by another exposed frontier whose point defences, the fortresses of Königsberg, Thorn, Graudenz and Posen, absorbed a significant amount of the state's military budget in what was at best a passive deterrent.

Geography, in turn, facilitated a strategic culture of limitation: restricted aspirations for modest gains. Here the example of Prussia's eastern neighbours was instructive. Poland's delusions of diplomatic grandeur, unsupported by any systematic development of that state's military assets, had rendered her impotent by 1700. Sweden, by contrast, organized and conquered itself to exhaustion in a century, at the same time acquiring the kind of reputation

---

2  On this overlooked subject, see particularly William W. Hagen, 'The partitions of Poland and the crisis of the old regime in Prussia', *Central European History* 9 (1976), 115–28.

as a dangerous neighbour that Prussia, 'a mollusc without a shell', could even less afford. In the seventeenth century, Frederick William, the Great Elector, and his son and successor, King Frederick I, had increasingly based their security policies on an army efficient enough to be sufficiently attractive to great powers and grand coalitions that they would pay for its presence on their side and negotiate to keep it from their enemies. Frederick William I went a step further, rejecting foreign subsidies as a means of financing the army because of the accompanying sacrifice of political independence. In the context of that decision, the 40,000-man force he inherited was a dangerously awkward size. Too large to be overlooked, or treated merely as another German subsidy force, it was at the same time too small to be more than a makeweight in the game of power politics. The doubling of the army between 1715 and 1740 was accompanied by the systematic, comprehensive reorganization of the administration to support a military system designed to enable Prussia to set its own international agenda. It was accompanied as well by a broadly conciliatory diplomacy. Believing Prussia's interests best served by a stable international situation, Frederick William I took pains to alienate no one, consistently deferring to Austria in particular.

Frederick II's decision to use the army as something other than a passive deterrent reflected in good part the conviction that the *status quo* his father favoured was no longer viable. In particular, the complex network of treaties underpinning the Pragmatic Sanction – the right of Maria Theresa to succeed Charles VI on the throne of Austria – could not survive Charles's death. Austria was certain to be challenged on all its frontiers, perhaps dismembered, no matter what Prussia did or did not do. Frederick's only real choice was whether to be hammer or anvil, windshield or bug. The accuracy, legality and morality of Frederick's perceptions and decisions are less important for present purposes, however, than his commitment even in this context to creating a one-time *fait accompli*. The king's policy was based on the Prussian army's ability to overrun Silesia from a standing start, and then secure the province, perhaps by convincingly defeating the Austrians in the field, perhaps by deterring Austria from making more than a token fight before negotiating a permanent settlement.[3]

Instead, Prussia found itself facing eight years of war and preparation for war. Frederick remained consistently baffled by Austrian refusal to behave as a 'rational actor' by cutting its losses and coming to terms with the new *status quo*. But did that mean the concept of waging what Frederick called

---

3 Dennis Showalter, *The Wars of Frederick the Great* (London, 1995), pp. 28 *passim*.
M. S. Anderson, *The War of the Austrian Succession, 1740–1748* (London, 1995), is significantly less sympathetic to Frederick and his motives.

'short and lively' policy wars was wrong, or that it had been inadequately implemented? Between 1748 and 1756, Frederick continued to refine Prussia's army and infrastructure with the aim of creating a system that would be at the peak of its effectiveness on the outbreak of war. His intention was not to challenge the order of Europe, but to maintain Prussia's new position therein. In that context, he regarded the Seven Years' War as a product of his enemies' miscalculation of both Prussia's intentions and capacities. After 1763, instead of demobilizing, Prussia reorganized. When the final post-war shakedowns were completed, Frederick's army consisted of over 150,000 men, the central element of a foreign policy based on negotiation and deterrence. Its annual manoeuvres were developed into a showcase for the drill and discipline he regarded as external manifestations of the army's effectiveness. Also Frederick nurtured a 'cult of personality' that embraced his defeats as well as his victories to conclude that he was one of history's greatest generals. Anything encouraging belief in the risks of trying conclusions with Old Fritz and his faithful grenadiers was welcome in a state strategy assigning force the role of intimidation rather than implementation.

Frederick's foreign policy culminated in the 'Potato War' of 1778–9. Rather than being the fiasco described by misinterpreters of Clausewitz, this confrontation with Austria represented a war so limited it was scarcely a war, yet it resulted in a significant victory. Austria backed down from its intention of acquiring Bavaria by purchasing it from its new elector. No less significantly, from being the disturber of the Empire's and continent's peace, Frederick established himself as the primary defender of the sovereign rights established in 1648 by the Treaty of Westphalia and the international order confirmed at such cost during the Seven Years' War.

Frederick's successor, his nephew Frederick William II, was more loose cannon than rational actor. He sought glory and territory where it was to be found, probing his neighbours' boundaries with more energy than finesse. He was willing to take on diplomatic adventures without considering their financial implications. Yet, in practice, the new monarch continued to accept the virtues of a strategy of limited goals backed by credible force. The neatly executed suppression, at the request of Holland's Stadtholder, of the Dutch mini-revolt of 1787 was a classic example of an 'operation other than war' that demonstrated Prussia's capacity to maintain its interests across its immediate frontiers. The restoration of Stadtholder William was followed two years later by the deployment of no fewer than 145 battalions in Silesia and on the Saxon frontier in support of Prussia's claim to Polish territory as the price of neutrality in the war of Russia and Austria against the Ottoman Empire. An equally rapid mobilization against Russia in 1790 led Empress Catherine not only to reconsider her objections to Poland's further dismemberment, but to seek alliance with Prussia as an alternative to a possible Austro-Prussian connection.

These diplomatic successes were in good part the consequences of Prussia's potential rivals being engaged elsewhere. France, for example, was in no domestic position, financially or politically, to mobilize troops in 1787. Russia and Austria were too concerned with their respective ambitions and their mutual rivalries in south-eastern Europe to give Prussia a lesson in diplomatic manners. Prussia's achievements, however, owed much as well to a pragmatic matching of reach and grasp. Even between 1792 and 1795, Prussia was at pains to take no more than it willed of the war against revolutionary France. The determination of Frederick William II to continue participating in the anti-French coalition as his treasury emptied reflected his belief that maintaining treaty commitments was the other side of constant nibbling at the international system's fringes. It was an insurance policy against being outlawed, as Frederick II had been in 1757. The king's military and civil advisers, in contrast, concluded that sustaining the war was pointless in view of its high costs relative to the limited impact of both French armies and French ideology on Prussia's neo-Frederician system. Eventually, they convinced Frederick William to begin the negotiations that resulted in the Peace of Basle. That process, however, represented differences in approach to foreign policy, rather than a fundamental dispute over its defining principles.

Frederick William II's successor, Frederick William III, continued the pattern when he assumed the throne in 1797. Since the end of the Seven Years' War, Prussia had courted, sometimes at high prices, good relations with Russia. Nevertheless, the king and his counsellors refused to participate in the ramshackle Second Coalition that formed in 1798 despite Russian pressure, backed by British guarantees of subsidies and expressed in treaty terms offering Prussia virtual control of north Germany. Nor was the alliance tentatively proposed by France in May 1798 a more attractive strategic proposition. Here, too, Prussia remained cool, neither closing doors nor walking through them.

Prussia's behaviour was not entirely shaped by the factionalism and the indecision so often ascribed to government under Frederick William III. Underlying the debates and the infighting was an awareness that to choose sides confronted Prussia, positioned between contending powers, with the alternative risks of becoming either a glacis for one party or everybody's battlefield. What enabled the state to pursue its middle course for a decade was the army. For anti-French coalitions, actual and prospective, Prussian troops were increasingly seen as necessary in a successful continental war given the increasingly obvious shortcomings of the Russians, Austrians and

British. The problem lay in making a sufficiently attractive offer to bring Frederick William III to abandon the gambler's dream of winning without betting. From the perspective of the French Directory, and for a time Napoleon himself, Prussia was better conciliated than fought. Benevolent neutrality was rewarded in 1801 at the Peace of Lunéville by extensive territorial gains in northern Germany. These shifted the state's centre of gravity westward, towards the French sphere of influence. They also significantly improved Prussia's geographic cohesion – a fair exchange in the minds of Prussia's decision-makers.

The collapse of Prussia's state strategy in 1805–6 is often ascribed to the culpable short-sightedness of Frederick William III and his advisers in regard to French intentions, or to irreconcilable factionalism at decision-making levels. The flaw in each interpretation is solipsistic Prussocentrism. The focus of European politics during Napoleon's imperium lay in Paris, not Berlin. Napoleon's unfocused ambitions, combined with what seemed the limitless capacity of his army to sustain his pretensions, made diplomacy for the French emperor no more than the waging of war by other means. Appetite and power combined as well to escalate the stakes of those wars beyond anything a multipolar international system could sustain.

Prussia, with its alternate experience of military initiatives undertaken for particular, negotiable objectives, was unquestionably slow to recognize what amounted to a paradigm shift in French behaviour. Yet, even as understanding emerged, solid evidence suggested Prussia held a trump card in its army. When French troops overran the Electorate of Hanover in 1803, French diplomats suggested that Prussian patience would be well rewarded. In the event, Prussian troops occupied Hanover in October 1805, as the French withdrew expeditiously. This success only reinforced the confidence that led to Frederick William III's refusal to join the Third Coalition. The prospective adversaries seemed evenly enough matched to wear down each other, as they had regularly done since 1793. Even a French victory was likely to be achieved at a cost that would make Prussia's army an even greater makeweight in European affairs.

The actual results of the Austerlitz campaign left Prussia confronting an imperium that had suddenly abandoned any pretences of conciliation. The new conditions Napoleon proposed left Prussia in possession of Hanover only on French sufferance, and at the price of closing its ports to Britain. Frederick William accepted the terms in February 1806, but did not accept the reduction to client-state status they implied. Prussia mobilized in August and went to war in September – not unilaterally, but as a necessary gesture of good faith to an embryonic Fourth Coalition that would include Russia, Britain and Sweden. Just enough time remained in the normal campaigning season for one major battle. And even there, the Prussian army had to do no more than bloody Napoleon's nose, buying time for British guineas and Russian bayonets to bring to bear their respective influences. This was not an optimal situation, but neither did it seem obviously beyond the capacities of Prussia's military establishment. The war-hawks of 1806 included men of the calibre of Gerhard von Scharnhorst and Carl von Clausewitz, who initially did not see themselves as engaging in a forlorn hope. In fact, there were no obvious reasons to expect disaster before the campaign began – as long as the army performed up to reasonable expectations.[4]

Until the emperor's first abdication, it was Prussian statesmen and Prussian generals who stressed the importance of fighting the French wherever and whenever possible, leaving the consequences to take care of themselves. It was Prussian troops and officials who exploited the first occupation for plunder and vengeance. It was Prussian intransigence over the Saxon question that provided the first major concrete stumbling-block at the Congress of Vienna. This behaviour, however, is best understood as a consequence of Prussia's *de facto* loss of great-power status in 1806 – particularly, as will be shown later, the military aspects of that loss. After 1815, Prussia reasserted the place gained by Frederick the Great by playing a facilitator's role in the German Confederation, the Holy Alliance and the Concert of Europe. This conservative policy reflected the co-operative character of the international system. It reflected Prussia's perception of its own needs. And it reflected the changing nature of the relationship between army and society.[5]

# The nature of the army

The Prussian army, like most of its German counterparts, ended the seventeenth century as a force of 'true volunteers', Prussian subjects and foreigners who enlisted for every reason from hunger to a desire for change. Its exponential expansion under Frederick William I rapidly encountered a ceiling. The pool of potential volunteers was too small, and could not be increased by improved conditions of service that Prussia could not afford.

---

4 The military aspects of the above analysis are based heavily on Dennis E. Showalter, 'From Hubertusburg to Auerstaedt: the Prussian army in decline?', *German History* 12 (1994), 308–33. For the diplomatic context, cf. Philip Dwyer, 'The politics of Prussian neutrality, 1796–1806', ibid., 351–74; and Brendan Simms, *The Impact of Napoleon: Prussian High Politics and the Crisis of the Executive, 1797–1806* (Cambridge, 1997).

5 The best overview in a European context is Paul Schroeder, *The Transformation of European Politics, 1763–1848* (Oxford, 1994), pp. 445–711. L. J. Baack, *Christian Bernstoff and Prussia, 1818–1832* (New Brunswick, NJ, 1980), is solid for Prussian foreign policy in the Biedermeier era.

Prussian recruiting parties increasingly assumed the nature of press-gangs, to the point where some neighbouring states made recruiting for Prussian service a capital offence, like witchcraft and parricide. Frederick William responded by developing the canton system. In the form finalized in 1733, it divided the kingdom into recruiting districts based on 'hearths', or households, whose able-bodied men between 18 and 40 were registered for service. This, especially in peacetime, made selectivity possible to a degree unknown elsewhere in Europe. Frederick William's often-cited preference for tall soldiers was more than an idiosyncrasy driven by eccentricity. Linking size with fitness was a reasonable rule of thumb in an age when poor nutrition and hard labour broke men down early – and when regimental officers tended to be more concerned with the number of warm bodies in the ranks than their suitability for the field. Prussia's cantonists consistently impressed foreign observers as being big, well-proportioned young men, excellent raw material for a system that understood how to maximize their potential.[6]

Here, too, the Prussian army was successful. Its training methods were based on levels of individual instruction impossible to the mass armies of a later generation, with their large intakes and small cadres. A common practice was to put the recruit in the charge of a reliable old soldier who, for a share of whatever the recruit might possess or receive from home, provided basic instruction in dress and behaviour. The details of drill and uniform were left to the non-commissioned officers, but even they were instructed to deal patiently, if not always gently, with recruits who showed good will. It represents no whitewash of Prussian discipline to note that many of the more vivid horror stories were reported either by officers advocating a discipline based on mutual honour and mutual respect, or by men whose experiences in Prussian service were unhappy or unfortunate. As in any army, a disproportionate amount of punishment fell to a disproportionately small number: the dull-witted and the loud-mouthed, the sullen, the vicious, and those unfortunate enough to be made scapegoats by their superiors or their fellow-soldiers. Desertion, moreover, was the principal military crime, and cantonists usually had ties with home sufficiently strong to deter serious consideration of undertaking such a high-risk activity.

Nor was a soldier's life one of unrelieved misery in an alien environment. After his initial training, the cantonist spent as much as ten months of every

---

6   Still the best overview is Otto Büsch, *Military System and Social Life in Old-Regime Prussia*, tr. J. Gagliardo (Atlantic Highlands, NJ, 1997). Cf. as well Willerd Fann, 'Peacetime attrition in the army of Frederick William I', *Central European History* 11 (1978), 323–34; and 'Foreigners in the Prussian army, 1713–56: some statistical and interpretive problems', ibid., 23 (1990), 76–84.

year at home on furlough. With the regiment, a good part of his time was spent in civilian billets, outside the immediate supervision of his officers and sergeants, with corresponding opportunities to cultivate contacts and relationships that ranged from the romantic to the criminal. Soldiers off duty – cantonists or mercenaries – were left to their own devices to a degree inconceivable in British or American armed forces until recent years. They could dress much as they pleased, seek part-time employment – a practice encouraged by the army – or practise the arts of idleness. A good many of the often-cited problems of complying with the regulations governing one's uniform and personal appearance on duty seem to have been consequences of previous, avoidable sins of omission and commission regarding uniform, kit and grooming.

The Prussian army's culture of competence also fostered morale. Even under modern conditions, field service, let alone battle, takes up a limited part of a soldier's life. Far more important are issues involving everyday circumstances: food, clothing and shelter delivered with reasonable regularity and efficiency. An army able to meet such conditions will often survive flagrant mismanagement in combat. The Union's Army of the Potomac and the BEF of 1914–18 are two prime examples. In Prussia, the uniforms were durable and the pay regular. Old soldiers were not, as a matter of policy, cast adrift to end their days as beggars. As much to the point – and a point often overlooked by modern scholars – the precision drill that made such high demands on the parade ground could and did generate pride in performance. Drill was also directly linked to survival in combat. The unskilled or unwilling soldier in an eighteenth-century firing-line directly endangered his comrades as well as himself. A musket out of alignment when firing by ranks could mean a burst eardrum for the man in front of it. A man out of alignment in ranks could be the first step in the destruction of an entire battalion by a cavalry charge. In that context, service in the Prussian army meant joining the first team. And any recruit – cantonist or mercenary – who did not understand drill's practical importance was likely to become the subject of direct and uncomfortable enlightenment by the old soldiers of his company.[7]

None of these points made a soldier's lot happy – only acceptable in the context of reasonable alternatives. What made the system work, both generally and in a military context, was its reflection of a social contract no less solid for being unwritten and, indeed, unreflected upon. Social contract theory has been sufficiently intellectualized that it is easy to overlook the

---

7  Cf. in particular Christopher Duffy, *The Army of Frederick the Great* (Newton Abbot, 1976); and Showalter, *Wars of Frederick*, pp. 20ff.

fact that all state systems, even in a twentieth century characterized by ideologies calling for unlimited commitment, depend fundamentally on an if–then relationship based on the exchange of protection for service. *Ancien Régime* Prussia owed some of its character to an emerging official class whose bureaucratic orientation subsumed its social origins. It owed something to a Pietist religious revival stressing personal commitment to one's calling. It rested on patriarchal behaviours reinforced by Lutheran principles. But the kingdom was at pains, even during the worst stages of the Seven Years' War, to affirm and fulfil its side of the agreement, or at least to guarantee fulfilment as soon as possible.[8]

Frederick's system also gave society a direct stake in the most direct burden of service. The canton system may have made disproportionate demands on poor peasants and farm labourers. It also provided a generous spectrum of exemptions to almost everyone else – who in turn were expected to provide other forms of service. In that respect, cantonism prefigured the US Selective Service System of the 1950s and 1960s, which was based on the similar principle that those not conscripted directly were 'deferred' because they performed tasks of equal importance to a society geared in principle to total mobilization. Relative to the numbers available, peacetime call-up rates were low – fewer than 10 per cent of the eligible men for some districts in some years. Even when the Seven Years' War is included, fewer than half of the nearly nine million men actually registered ever donned a uniform. This degree of flexibility created ample opportunities for families and villages to assert control over their young men by deciding who went to the army and who stayed at home. On the other side of the coin, men doing military service were under military law, to which they could and did appeal against both communities and landlords. Since soldiers came disproportionately from the poorer classes, the result was a complicating of traditional patterns of authority, and sometimes of deference as well, in the Prussian countryside.[9]

The Seven Years' War thus did not directly challenge the parameters of the contract between Prussia and its soldiers. It did, however, confirm in Frederick's mind the vital importance to Prussia's state strategy of synthesizing technical procedures and willpower in a military system based on an endless capacity for taking pains. Frederick understood discipline and drill, not as ends in themselves, but as facilitators of war-fighting. The complex

---

8  Hubert C. Johnson, *Frederick the Great and His Officials* (New Haven, CT, 1975).
9  Hartmut Harnisch, 'Preussisches Kantonsystem und Laendliche Gesellschaft: Das Beispiel des mittleren Kammerdepartements', in B. Kroener and R. Proeve (eds), *Krieg und Frieden: Militaer und Gesellschaft in der Fruehen Neuzeit* (Paderborn, 1996), pp. 137–66, is the best recent overview.

evolutions developed after 1763 were designed to enable men to endure and units to manoeuvre under the worst foreseeable tactical conditions, against enemies who had long prepared to counter such battlefield tricks as the oblique order.[10] But with clockwork regularity, the order of the day drill movements grew exacting to the point of impossibility, even for experienced men. Standards of discipline and appearance became increasingly rigid, increasingly comprehensive in ways inviting comparison to the British Navy in the late age of sail, and for similar reasons. A smart ship and a smart regiment were both understood as possessing a certain deterrent effect by virtue of their respective grooming.[11]

As part of his programme to facilitate Prussia's economic recovery, Frederick also increasingly skimped on his army's infrastructure. The quality of uniforms steadily decreased – an important morale factor, and a significant financial burden on men required to make up loss and damage from their own pockets. Grain allowances for the cavalry were cut to the point where, in spring and summer, horses were expected to graze, with a corresponding decline in their strength and endurance. These kinds of institutional economies made it increasingly difficult to recruit and retain the foreign professionals whose presence kept peacetime draft calls low. As prices rose, moreover, foreign soldiers constrained to seek employment in the civilian economy found themselves at a significant disadvantage compared to their Prussian counterparts with better claims on garrison communities. Desertion was a logical consequence. It is not coincidental that most of the worst horror stories of preventive and punitive measures against 'French leave' in Frederick's army date from the period after the Seven Years' War.

Frederick's death in 1786 opened something like a window of opportunity for a rising generation of military theorists influenced by an *Aufklärung* suggesting that war, like literature, philosophy and art, was a human endeavour as well as the domain of reason. The new king, Frederick William II, supported policies calculated to restore pride as well as emphasize duty. Regimental schools, family allowances and soldiers' homes were accompanied by bans on the more extreme forms of physical punishment, and by the creation of a specialized light infantry, the fusiliers, whose mission was open warfare against irregulars and whose discipline was based heavily on appeals to professionalism and comradeship. Each line company as well was allotted ten 'sharpshooters', selected for physical fitness and mental

---

10  In the words of one critic, 'As [Frederick] always launches his attack against one of the two wings of the army he attacks, it is necessary simply to plan a suitable response.' Quoted in Jeremy Black, *European Warfare, 1660–1815* (New Haven, CT, 1994), p. 65.

11  John Lynn, *Giant of the Grand Siecle: The French Army, 1610–1715* (Cambridge, 1997), pp. 606–7, suggests as well the domestic uses of military display during the early modern period.

alertness, who provided a valuable source of efficient sergeants and a tangible vehicle for upward mobility.[12]

Implemented more systematically and with more enthusiasm, such policies might have given Prussia a more professionalized army, with foreigners easier to recruit and retain and Prussian natives making careers of military service. Even in their limited form, they were sufficient to keep desertion rates moderate during the 1790s, despite the appeal of French propaganda stressing the advantages of coat-turning in the name of liberty, equality and fraternity. The army's operational performance between 1792 and 1795 was also solid. Valmy was generally understood as a specific problem of command rather than a general indication of institutional decline. After some seasoning, Prussian line battalions combined well-controlled volleys and well-regulated local counter-attacks that matched, if they did not always master, French *élan* and *cran*. Prussian light infantry proved formidable opponents against French raiders and foragers, while on occasion teaching their opponents sharp lessons in the crafts of skirmishing and marksmanship.

Far from being hopelessly retrograde or terminally arteriosclerotic, in short, the Prussian army at the end of the eighteenth century was well able to support the Prussian state's strategy of prudent activism. It was, however, increasingly clear to the state's military professionals that the standards of warfare were now being set by France. It was equally clear that French human and material resources exponentially exceeded anything Prussia could hope to match. For almost a century, Prussia's military hole card had been a recruiting system that systematically tapped its indigenous manpower on a consensual basis. Now France, too, had begun mobilizing its lower classes systematically – and had many more of them. A decade of war and revolution had diminished the number of foreigners willing – or able – to don Prussian uniform. Increasing the domestic cadres was theoretically possible. Official figures gave over 2,000,000 cantonists available in 1799, 2,300,000 in 1805. Even if all the increasingly generous legal exemptions were continued, over 300,000 men could be conscripted in a given year without summoning the middle-ageing and the less physically capable. Matching France man for man in the long term was, however, impossible, apart from the risk that rapid increases in enrolments might gridlock an administrative system arguably already too finely tuned for the good of state and society.[13]

---

12  John E. Stine, 'King Frederick William II and the decline of the Prussian army, 1788–1797' (Ph.D. thesis, University of South Carolina, 1980), is a good English-language overview of this period.

13  Cf. Charles White, *The Enlightened Soldier: Scharnhorst and the Militaerische Gesellschaft in Berlin, 1801–1805* (New York, 1989); and Peter Paret, *Yorck and the Era of Prussian Reform* (Princeton, NJ, 1966).

Napoleon's army, moreover, was not a mass levy of armed patriots. Its regiments instead increasingly resembled those that had marched to glory with Frederick: strong cadres of professionals reinforced at intervals by conscripts little different in motivation from Prussia's own cantonists.[14] To match such an adversary required a 'quality army', able to counter French mass and skill with even greater fighting power of its own. Conceptualizing the specifics of that force was not easy in the context of rapid, continual changes in war-fighting combined with a state policy whose very success kept Prussian troops and officers from updating their operational experience. At least until 1793, the Prussian army had developed as a deterrent force in the context of a multipolar system. Suddenly, it was required to wage all-out war against a hegemonic empire. Nevertheless, and for all the short-comings so pitilessly exposed in the glare of hindsight, the Prussians fought well enough at Jena and Auerstedt to give their enemies more than a few bad quarters of an hour. Nor is it inappropriate to stress that the Prussian army faced in 1806 an opponent at the peak of its institutional effectiveness, commanded by one of history's great captains at the peak of his powers.

While these were explanations rather than excuses, the military reform movement did not begin *de novo* after the Peace of Tilsit. Since the turn of the new century, overlapping and lively debates on details had generated something like consensus on certain core issues. Officers and administrators, for example, agreed on replacing the canton system, with its elaborate structure of exemptions, by universal liability. Those conscripted, unlike their cantonist predecessors, would serve a limited time uninterrupted by extended furloughs. Those for whom places in the active ranks could not be found were to be assigned to the *Landwehr*, a citizen militia to be mobilized on the outbreak of war. Accompanying this fundamental restructuring was general acceptance of treating common soldiers with humanity, appealing to their goodwill and intelligence without moving too far in the direction of relying on enthusiasm and instinct – qualities that had time and again proved ephemeral in combat by comparison to training and discipline. Commissions were opened to merit as well as birth, at least in principle. Corporal punishment was abolished, except on active service and under extreme circumstances, also at least in principle. Revised drill regulations provided for training half the men in each infantry regiment as skirmishers, thereby eliminating the need for specialized corps of light infantry.

The ultimate intention of these changes was less to inculcate particular sets of skills and behaviours than to strengthen commitment and confidence.

---

14 John Elting, *Swords around a Throne: Napoleon's Grande Armée* (New York, 1988), is the best overview of Napoleon's army in English.

For conservatives, the soldier had to become an active subject of a revitalized state. For reformers, the soldier had to become a citizen whose military service epitomized his membership in the political community. In both contexts, it was no accident that the army's principal changes focused on the infantry: the arm of service best able to substitute enthusiasm for training, and the arm incorporating the largest number of conscripts. Cavalry and artillery were by comparison skill branches, depending on kinds and levels of competence impossible to acquire overnight and insusceptible to zeal. Both were correspondingly de-emphasized in the revised tables of organization, dispersed in peace and war by batteries and squadrons among the newly created permanent higher formations as opposed to being massed under central control in the style of the great Frederick – or of Napoleon. Prussian doctrine now stressed wearing down an enemy by extended firefights, then using small, flexible columns to determine weak spots, and finally developing opportunities through relatively small-scale attacks.

These were tactics for an army that was not intended to strike decisive, independent blows on any level. The Prussian army of the Wars of Liberation was essentially more the force of a *Kleinstaat* than of a great power. Operating within a coalition held together by the low common denominator of defeating Napoleon, it was at its tactical best in the war's early stages, between the battles of Lützen (2 May 1813) and Leipzig (16–19 October 1813), before its dilution by officers and men untrained in the new methods, or often in any methods at all. Rapid expansion after the Armistice of Pleiswitz (4 June 1813) meant too many units, themselves newly raised, were milked for cadres for even less experienced formations. The increasing tendency towards mass that characterized Prussian tactics from Dresden (26–7 August 1813) to Waterloo (18 June 1815) in good part reflected an inability at brigade and battalion levels to execute the sophisticated combination punches of the reformers' tactical system.[15]

The army that emerged from the Wars of Liberation also represented a high-risk option in the context of state policy. Hermann von Boyen, War Minister from 1815 to 1819, was convinced Prussia's strategic position continued to demand a strong standing army, able to take the field without waiting for its ranks to be filled by reservists. The Defence Law of 1814, developed under his auspices, required three years of active service and intended over half the men in the army's active battalions to be serving conscripts; Boyen hoped as well to have at least thirty 'career privates' in each company – native-born successors to the foreign professional soldiers so important to the eighteenth-century system. Establishing such a force,

---

15   Paret, *Yorck*, remains the best overview of the reforms in English.

however, meant concentrating the manpower of the line in a relatively small number of units – just over a hundred infantry battalions plus rifles, cavalry and artillery. Such a force, while about the same size as its Frederician predecessor, was no numerical match for post-Napoleonic French and Austrian armies that each had over 250 battalions, to say nothing of a tsarist Russia that counted over 700. Even the post-war British army, starved of funds and hidden away in the far corners of empire, stabilized at around a hundred battalions.

The possibility of developing the active army as a quality force whose efficiency performed a deterrent function was limited. The mystique destroyed at Jena had not been restored by Leipzig and Waterloo. Nor was the short-service force created after 1806 likely to master convincingly the skills that underlay the myth. An alternative approach, one never previously considered, involved developing technology as a combat multiplier. Instead, for twenty years after Waterloo, Prussian factories delivered smoothbore flintlocks, and Prussian cannon were so inaccurate that sentries had to be posted to warn passers-by during target practice. This lack of material progress reflected less a conservative distrust of innovation based on industrialization than a vitalist heritage common to both the reformers and their critics. The concept that men, rather than weapons, were the decisive element in war was reinforced by a continued association of firepower with mass and rigidity, the things the regulations of 1812 sought so strongly to avoid. Thus, when the first percussion muskets were introduced in 1839, their merits were debated in a context of skirmishing tactics: the theoretical accuracy of individual shots. The artillery system introduced in 1842 was tested not for hitting power, but for mobility. The breech-loading needle gun was criticized for lack of range and accuracy, for encouraging unaimed fire and thereby risking the soldier's decline into an unreasoning automaton unrestrained by even the artificial constructions of eighteenth-century discipline.[16]

Instead, the numerical gap between the Prussian army and its counterparts was projected to be filled by the *Landwehr*. Its creation during the war had been greeted by protests that in West Prussia and Silesia had included flight into Russian-occupied Poland. Eventually, the men brought into its ranks proved as generally willing and effective soldiers as their counterparts of the active regiments. The campaign of 1815, however, brought another wave of resistance in the western territories allocated to Prussia by the preliminary terms of the Congress of Vienna. Morale was so bad in some of the formations raised in the Rhineland that it was considered dangerous to

---

16 Dennis E. Showalter, 'Weapons and ideas in the Prussian army from Frederick the Great to Moltke the elder', in J. Lynn (ed.), *Tools of War: Instruments, Ideas, and Institutions of Warfare, 1445–1871* (Urbana, IL, 1990), pp. 193ff.

commit them in critical sectors or situations. Army rumour had it as well that not every officer casualty in those regiments fell victim to French steel or French lead.

This situation is usually interpreted in proto-nationalist terms, with the 'old Prussians' reluctant to change the status of subjects for that of citizens and the new additions influenced by decades of French governance. An alternative approach involves considering the implied social contract described earlier in the text. Under its terms, general military service, as opposed to particular military liability, was a revision too fundamental to be implemented unilaterally, particularly when the state was not obviously expanding its contributions to the bargain. Most accounts of *Ancien Régime* Europe emphasize the 'privileged orders', the clergy and the aristocracy. Societies as a whole, however, were structured around the concept of privilege as opposed to the concept of rights. It is only a slight exaggeration to say that almost everyone east of Britain, west of Russia and north of Vienna belonged to a 'privileged order'. For most, the privileges were extremely limited – but that made them correspondingly important.

Prussia's problem was exacerbated by the impossibility of inducting enough males annually to give the system a reasonable semblance of equity. Institutionally, the army did not have, and could not expect to receive, enough money both to implement anything resembling universal conscription and to maintain an infrastructure. At the same time, call-up rates were substantially higher than their Frederician predecessors, usually somewhere around 50 per cent, while, in principle, conscripts were kept in uniform and under discipline every day of every month of their active-service term.

The resulting imbalances would have challenged a society far more flexible than the 'well ordered police state' that emerged from the Congress of Vienna. Boyen, deeply committed to the principle of universal service, believed as well that reducing the active term would unacceptably diminish both the army's ability to respond to emergencies and the level of training of its reservists. Instead, he sought to square the circle by assigning men not conscripted for the active army directly into the *Landwehr*. Experience quickly indicated that these '*Landwehr* recruits' acquired no more than elementary skills during their brief and episodic periods of training. Of skirmishing, marksmanship and all the other skills demanded by the regulations of 1812, they remained ignorant. And the fact that they never spent a day in the active army was seldom lost upon those whose destiny was not only different, but determined by decisions made outside the influence of family and community.

Enthusiasm for *Landwehr* service of any kind declined so rapidly and so visibly that even the institution's staunchest supporters grew concerned. The army's solution, implemented in December 1819, was to incorporate the *Landwehr* formations directly into the active army, giving each division one line and one *Landwehr* brigade. This reorganization is usually interpreted politically, as part of a concerted conservative effort to emasculate a reform movement perceived as 'the organization of revolution'. It had military motives as well: the new structure was expected to improve the *Landwehr*'s training and administration within existing budget limits. Results were at best marginal, and arguably negative. The morale and effectiveness of the *Landwehr* did not improve significantly. That both its supporters and its critics regarded its new position as anomalous, and ultimately untenable, further diminished its status.[17]

While direct evidence is less comprehensive than in the Frederician era, the Prussian active army does not emerge as being much better off in terms of fighting spirit. Its conscripts were inclined to regard their term of active service less as proof of membership in the public community than as something to be endured pending return to real life. From a policy perspective, any attempt to use the army for any purpose beyond basic internal security required either the extensive mobilization of demonstrably unenthusiastic reservists – an initiative that itself was as likely to provoke war as deter it, even in the 1820s – or the complete disruption of every formation larger than a regiment in order to provide more than three active battalions in one place. Caught in a double-bind, the Prussian army of the Biedermeier era increasingly appeared to itself and its neighbours as a 'hollow deterrent', able neither to project power convincingly in a cabinet context nor to threaten effectively the apocalypse of people's war.[18] The consequences would become apparent after 1830 as Prussia's German and European policies became less cautious. That, however, is another story, for another volume.

---

17  Dennis E. Showalter, 'The Prussian Landwehr and its critics, 1813–1819', *Central European History* 4 (1971), 3–33.
18  Alf Luedtke, *Police and State in Prussia, 1815–1850*, tr. P. Burgess (Cambridge, 1989), establishes the domestic contexts of Prussia's military system in the Age of Metternich.

# PART FOUR

# Prussia, the French Revolution and Napoleon

CHAPTER ELEVEN

# Prussia during the French Revolutionary and Napoleonic Wars, 1786–1815

PHILIP G. DWYER

Contemporary observers all agreed – Prussia would not survive for very long the death of Frederick the Great.[1] It was considered an artificial power with a slender and precarious façade that had lasted as long as it did only because of the genius of its architect. One great king, in other words, did not make a great power. A battle lost, an incompetent king, an unfortunate set of foreign-political circumstances, and Prussia could not only be reduced in size and thrown back among the ranks of the minor German princes, but, as we shall see, could even be threatened with extinction. European history was full of such examples.

This view was based upon a particular political concept that was prevalent in the eighteenth century and which was commonly associated with absolutist states – namely, that everything revolved around the person of the king. True, the character of the Prussian monarch *was* important, but there are a number of other elements that need to be taken into consideration when examining Prussia's place in the European system: its geographical position in the heart of Europe; the scarce resources at its disposal; the structure of its decision-making process at the highest levels of government; and the given foreign-political conjuncture at any particular time, were all important factors that played a part in determining the course followed by the Prussian state.

During the French Revolutionary and Napoleonic wars, that course more often than not resembled a rollercoaster ride, with peaks and troughs that saw Prussia alternately rise to a dominant position in Europe (at the beginning

---

1  Albert Sorel, *L'Europe et la Révolution Française*, 8 vols (Paris, 1885–1911), i, pp. 92–3.
   My thanks to Brendan Simms and Rory Muir for their useful comments on drafts of
   this chapter.

of the revolutionary period), then come hurtling back down as it was reduced to a second-rate German power (as a result of war with France in
1806–7) and rise again during the Hundred Days when Prussia played an
important role in the alliance that brought Napoleon crashing down. The
peaks pointed the way and showed what could be done by a Prussia that
knew how to impose itself on Central Europe. The troughs were revealing
of just how precarious Prussia's position was as a middle state surrounded
by potentially hostile and more powerful neighbours. It was only at the end
of the Napoleonic period that the erratic ride came to an end and that
Prussia was able to find a degree of stability within the European system
that it had hitherto lacked. It is Prussia's search for a place in that system
that this chapter examines, and it begins with an event that made a splash
in contemporary diplomatic circles.

## Frederick William II and the search for territorial aggrandizement

On 28 June 1787, the Princess of Orange, who was in the unenvious
position of being both the wife of the Stadholder of Holland and the sister
of Frederick William II, was arrested on her way to The Hague by a
detachment of Free Corps, the paramilitary wing of the democratic 'Patriot
Party', and subjected to a number of 'indignities'.[2] The event was of no
great significance in itself. It was simply another episode in the power
struggle that had been going on since 1781 between the 'Patriot Party'
(backed by France), which wanted to limit the power of the Stadholder, and
the 'Orangists' (backed by Britain and eventually Prussia), who were, of
course, supporters of the Stadholder and his traditional rights. However,
the consequences of this act of *lèse-majesté* were to have a decisive impact on
the outcome of the struggle. Frederick William II used the supposed offence
committed against his sister as a pretext to intervene in Dutch domestic
affairs. After some hesitation and after making sure that France was not
going to act, the king sent in his troops and within the space of a few weeks
overran the country, either imprisoned or forced into flight France's Dutch
allies, and restored the Stadholder to his previous dominant position.

The conquest of the United Provinces was considered a remarkable feat
by contemporaries, and rightly so. Prussia had done something that both

---

2   For the conflict between 'Orangists' and 'Patriots', see Simon Schama, *Patriots and Liberators*
(London, 1977), ch. 3.

the Spanish armies after more than seventy years of fighting (between 1572 and 1648) and Louis XIV with over 200,000 troops (between 1672 and 1679) had failed to do. It proved, in the tradition of Rossbach, that Prussia was still a power to contend with,[3] and at the same time delivered a humiliating diplomatic defeat to France. And yet, historians consider the intervention in Holland a futile gesture, essentially because Prussia gained absolutely nothing from it, except an increase in political prestige.[4] True, Prussia did all the fighting while Britain reaped all the benefits – France was no longer influential in Holland, the Dutch navy was once again at the disposal of the British Admiralty, and the threat of French control of the Channel was overcome. What is revealing, however, is not so much what Prussia achieved as what it hoped to gain. As such, the invasion of Holland is, in many respects, characteristic of Prussian foreign policy; it was an attempt to consolidate its position in middle and northern Europe by building a 'system' that would give it a large dose of foreign-political security.

There were two possible ways of consolidating its position. One was through territorial expansion (this could be accomplished by either peaceful diplomatic means or overt aggression). As was pointed out in the Introduction, a 'rounding off' of Prussian territory, especially in the east, and a subsequent increase in population would bring with it the potential to better defend itself. The other means by which Prussia could consolidate its position was through an alliance system (neither approach, incidentally, was mutually exclusive). As things stood on the death of Frederick the Great, the European system was, to say the least, less than favourable to Prussia. Austria and Russia were allies; so, too, were France and Austria, at least nominally. Moreover, France was considering building a quadruple alliance system that would comprise Austria, Russia and Spain. This extremely dangerous foreign-political conjunction was to be countered by Prussia with a new triple alliance consisting of Britain and Holland, with the hope that Sweden and Poland would later join in (which they eventually did).

The Dutch intervention has to be understood, then, in the context of Prussia's search for regional security. If Prussia had let France get the upper hand in Holland, that is, if the French-backed Patriot Party had completely taken over the government, Prussia would have found itself facing three potentially hostile powers – France, Austria and Holland. The alternative was to join Britain, with a regenerated Stadholder in Holland, to form a 'northern system' behind which Prussia would find a degree of

---

3  See Dennis Showalter, 'Hubertusburg to Auerstaedt: the Prussian army in decline', *German History* 12 (1994), 318–19.
4  See, for example, T. C. W. Blanning, *The Origins of the French Revolutionary Wars* (London, 1994), pp. 51–2.

foreign-political security in the west, thus allowing it to pursue its expansionist plans in the east.

The objective was perfectly understandable, even if the means by which it was to be achieved were not particularly realistic. The overall scheme that was to enable Prussia to 'round off' its territories in the East is known as the 'Hertzberg Plan'.[5] It consisted of a multiple exchange of territories and was designed to bring Prussia significant gains without the need to go to war. The most important element in this plan, and indeed in Prussian foreign policy for most of Frederick William II's reign, was the acquisition of the Polish towns of Danzig and Thorn, which would consolidate the territories Prussia had obtained during the First Partition of Poland (1772). At the risk of simplifying too much, the Prussian Foreign Minister, Count Ewald von Hertzberg, was proposing a second partition of Poland, thinking it would be no more difficult than the first. Prussia was to eventually get what it desired, but not in the manner that Hertzberg had envisioned. Not only was Hertzberg's plan not particularly realistic, but from about 1788 onwards Prussian foreign policy was pursued in such an erratic, *ad hoc* manner as to compromise both its objectives and its position within the European system. This was as much a reflection of the personality of the king as of high-political intrigue at the court of Berlin; it was also the consequence of a particularly favourable foreign-political conjuncture.

When Frederick William II ascended the throne in 1786, he was already 42 years of age and had had to live in the shadow of Frederick the Great all his life. He had something to prove, namely, that he was a worthy successor to his great uncle, and there was really only one way of doing that – by pursuing a foreign policy that would bring glory to his name and add territories to his state. Frederick William II moved slowly towards military action, but once he had started, there was no holding him back. The success in Holland inflated his sorry ego and encouraged him to seek further opportunities in the quest for territorial gain and military glory.[6]

The result made Prussia appear as though it were suffering from the foreign-political equivalent of multiple personality disorder. That is, rather than build an alliance system that could be used to protect its regional interests, the Prussian government pursued more than one foreign policy at the same time and in so doing attempted to play off one great power against the other. This would not have been so bad, except that these policies were often fundamentally antagonistic and incompatible.

5  Andreas Theodor Preuß, *Ewald Friedrich Graf von Hertzberg* (Berlin, 1909), pp. 145–8.
6  This is what contemporaries referred to as the 'moral' quality of the prince. It was always a determining factor in the formulation of Prussian foreign policy. See T. C. W. Blanning, *The French Revolutionary Wars, 1787–1802* (London, 1996), p. 25.

For example, in the spring of 1790, Frederick William believed that the Habsburg monarchy was teetering on the brink of collapse and, wanting to pick up whatever territories he could, massed an army of 160,000 men in Silesia for that purpose. Poland and the Porte, it should be noted, were committed to joining the invasion after signing an alliance with Prussia earlier that year. In September 1790, however, Frederick William changed tack, essentially because Joseph II of Austria died and was replaced by his more pacific brother, Leopold, who was determined to avoid war at all costs, but also because Prussia received no support from Britain. He then sent out feelers to Vienna to explore the possibility of an alliance against the revolutionary government in France (which was fundamentally hostile to both Poland and the Porte) while, at the same time, his representatives in Paris were ordered to stir up hatred against Marie-Antoinette and Austria. After the Convention of Reichenbach (27 July 1790), which drew Prussia and Austria a step closer towards *rapprochement*, the king urged Britain to take vigorous measures against Russia while simultaneously making overtures to Catherine II for an alliance. In 1791, he was once again preparing to go to war, this time against Russia, and mobilized an army in East Prussia for that purpose. By 1792, however, Frederick William had come to terms with both Austria and Russia (remember, he was prepared to go to war against both only a short while before) and had instead opted for an aggressive policy against France and Poland.

After less than three years on the throne, the king had managed to spend over 40 million écus, almost exhausting the carefully saved treasury left by his predecessor, and had not one scrap of territory to show for it. In the eyes of diplomatic Europe, Prussia had fallen from the pedestal on which Frederick II had placed it; its prestige had evaporated and it was no longer taken seriously.[7] The blame for such an inconstant and unproductive foreign policy must be placed squarely at the feet of the king, although it is not difficult to see what he was attempting to do. Since Frederick William II was hell-bent on territorial expansion, the best he could do was to keep his options open, to keep putting out diplomatic feelers in all directions until, finding the soft underbelly of the European system, he could safely strike without fear of retaliation from a great-power alliance. This approach was eventually to pay off, but not until 1793, and again in 1795, with the Second and Third Partitions of Poland.[8] It was undoubtedly one of the reasons why Frederick William got involved in a war with revolutionary France.

---

7  Sorel, *L'Europe et la Révolution Française*, ii, p. 73.
8  For the Second and Third Partitions of Poland, see Robert Howard Lord, *The Second Partition of Poland. A Study in Diplomatic History* (Cambridge, MA, 1915) and id., 'The third partition of Poland', *The Slavonic Review* 3 (1924–5), pp. 481–98.

The origins of the War of the First Coalition against revolutionary France have been examined elsewhere.[9] Of all the participants, Prussia's motives for going to war were the least ambiguous. It was a question of putting the boot in while one of the great powers was down. That is, the war against revolutionary France was not fought for ideological reasons, but for blatant territorial gains. As early as September 1790, Prussia was promoting the annexation of French territory as recompense for the war that had not yet even begun.[10] By February 1792, a formal agreement had been signed between Austria and Prussia whereby Prussia would get the long-coveted territories of Jülich and Berg as compensation for its efforts in the war.

Frederick William II, however, bit off more than he could chew. The Prussians entered France in July 1792 under the command of the Duke of Brunswick, widely regarded as the finest soldier of his day, thinking that the Revolution had thrown the French army into disarray and that it would be a push-over. By 29 September, however, the retreat of the Austro-Prussian forces was already decided upon. The two events that marked the Prussian intervention in France in the first stages of the war were the battle of Valmy – in reality a non-event, but which was lent enormous significance by the revolutionaries – and the Brunswick 'manifesto', which had the opposite effect to that intended – that is, it galvanized rather than discouraged the revolutionaries. The Prussian army's performance at Valmy was not an indication that the army was in decline, but more an indication of how many unripe grapes it had eaten on its march through the fields of Champagne. Of the 42,000 Prussians who had entered France, less than 20,000 recrossed the frontier and more than half of those were sick. A Prussian soldier who was later to live through the horrors of the Russian campaign in 1812 wrote that the Prussian retreat from Champagne in 1792 was perhaps a more terrible sight than even the wreck of the Grand Army.[11]

Prussia stayed in the war another two years, but its heart was never in it. From 1793 on, quarrels over Poland eventually led to a falling out between Berlin and Vienna, but as they were such odd bedfellows, this was bound to happen sooner or later. The falling out reflects a changed perception of Prussia's own foreign-political interests.[12] A new partition of Poland was in

---

9  For Prussia's involvement in the war, see the excellent exposés by Blanning, *The Origins of the French Revolutionary Wars* and *The French Revolutionary Wars*, upon which most of the following analysis is based.

10  Adolf Beer (ed.), *Leopold II., Franz II. und Catharina. Ihre Correspondenz. Nebst einer Einleitung: Zur Geschichte der Politik Leopold's II.* (Leipzig, 1874), p. 37.

11  Arthur Chuquet, *Les Guerres de la Révolution*, 11 vols (Paris, 1886–96), iii, p. 209.

12  Brendan Simms, *The Impact of Napoleon: Prussian high politics, foreign policy and the crisis of the executive, 1797–1806* (Cambridge, 1996), p. 91.

the air and Frederick William wanted to be there for the kill. For a country the size of Prussia, this had practical resource implications. It meant that it could not fight a war on two fronts and that, consequently, the western theatre would have to be scaled down. Prussian statesmen had, in any event, become disillusioned about any benefits they might have gained from a war that was increasingly getting bogged down on the Rhine. In other words, Prussia liberated itself in the west in order to 'round off' its territories in the east.[13]

The treaty that saw Prussia officially withdraw from the War of the First Coalition was signed at Basle on 17 May 1795. It gave Prussia a unique opportunity to assert its domination of North Germany. Not only did Prussia withdraw, but it successfully negotiated a peace settlement on behalf of the North German states, thereby relieving Austria of its pre-eminent role in the Empire. It also introduced the concept of a Demarcation Line behind which all the participating North German states agreed to remain neutral in the continuing war between the allies and France. In return, France promised not to allow its armies to cross the line. Despite the fact that the treaty was violated on a number of occasions during the last half of 1795 and early 1796, the benefits accruing to North Germany and Prussia in particular were substantial – a decade of peace and prosperity during which time Prussia was able to recuperate from the war; this while the rest of Europe was ravaged by the continuing conflict. More importantly, at least for questions of Prussian prestige, Germany was effectively divided into two zones of influence – Prussia in the north, Austria in the south – thereby reinforcing the already-existent Austro-Prussian dualism, but this time in Prussia's favour; the North German states were decidedly smaller and easier to control than the much larger South German states.

The effective division of Germany into two zones of influence, however, was built upon shaky foundations. Increasingly, France, and to a lesser extent Russia, was to take an active interest in the affairs of the decrepit Holy Roman Empire. It is telling that the negotiations that led to the secularization of the German ecclesiastical states in 1803 were played out in Paris and St Petersburg, and not in Berlin and Vienna. Prussia, for reasons examined below, baulked at the idea of going to war to protect its own regional interests in North Germany, while Austria seems to have abandoned the concept of empire altogether. The void was quickly filled by an aggressive, newly remodelled French army that took the initiative, virtually dragging the French state along with it.

---

13   Edward Ingram regards the partition of Poland as 'an effective response to the imperialism of Revolutionary France' (*Commitment to Empire: Prophecies of the Great Game in Asia 1797–1800* [Oxford, 1981], p. 289).

After almost a decade of diplomatic bluff and blustering in which Frederick William II had been allied to almost every state in Europe (and had, by the same token, betrayed almost every one of them), and in spite of costly, badly led and badly fought campaigns, the balance sheet was remarkably in Prussia's favour. Prussia had asserted its position in Germany. Almost in spite of himself, Frederick William II had succeeded in acquiring more territory than any other Prussian monarch before him, increasing the size of the state by a third to over 300,000 square kilometres, in the course of which he made it a more 'coherent' kingdom. Prussia's population had also increased, from about 5.5 to about 8.7 million. Both of these additions were important factors in the consolidation of Prussia. They potentially translated into more money for the state and more men for the army.

However, Frederick William II also bequeathed problems that, up to a point, counteracted any immediate gains. They included the enormous strain placed upon the Prussian bureaucratic apparatus by the absorption of Polish lands,[14] an empty treasury and Prussia's virtual diplomatic isolation. Much more importantly, in terms of geopolitics the disappearance of Poland meant that Prussia no longer had a weak buffer state between itself and Russia. This had important implications for the future of Prussian foreign policy. It made Prussia, if not more dependent on Russia, then at least more accommodating. As for the policy of neutrality and the North German Demarcation Line, this was a sensible eighteenth-century foreign-political choice. It created a buffer zone in the middle of Europe between Austria and France. If it did not last more than ten years, it was not because the idea was unworkable, but because a new factor had come on the scene, completely upsetting traditional notions of great-power politics. That factor was Napoleon Bonaparte.

# Frederick William III and the Napoleonic threat

When Frederick William II died in November 1797, he was succeeded by a son as different from his father as the late king had been to Frederick the Great. Whereas Frederick William II had been a lazy, flamboyant

---

14  On the impact of the absorption of Polish territory on the Prussian state, see William W. Hagen, 'The partitions of Poland and the crisis of the old regime in Prussia, 1772–1806', *Central European History* 9 (1976), 115–28.

philanderer, a mystic and a spendthrift, his son was somewhat depressed,[15] a hard worker, monogamous, pious and frugal. One of the first things the new king did was to purge the court of undesirable elements by imprisoning one of his father's mistresses, the Countess von Lichtenau. The differences in character also meant a substantial change not only in the nature of the regime, but in approaches to foreign policy. Indeed, in stark contrast to his father, Frederick William III seemed reluctant to introduce any changes on the foreign-political scene at all. The neutrality that had been a means to an end under Frederick William II – that is, a disengagement from the west in order to take part in the Second and Third Partitions of Poland – became under Frederick William III an end in itself. In other words, he erected neutrality into a system and became so obsessed with maintaining it, even after it had become impractical, that he severely limited the foreign-political options open to Prussia.

As Frederick William II's chaotic search for aggrandizement was linked in part to his character, so, too, neutrality seemed to suit Frederick William III's natural disposition. In October 1798, almost a year after coming to the throne, he wrote to his uncle, Prince Henry, to say: 'Everybody knows that I abhor war and that I know of nothing greater on earth than the preservation of peace and tranquillity as the only system suited to the happiness of human kind.'[16] His foreign minister, Baron Hardenberg, once complained to a French envoy that 'all idea of glory or aggrandizement which would flatter or decide another Prince was far from the king's mind', and that this was absolutely due to his character.[17] Many more examples could be cited, but put simply Frederick William III had an ingrained dislike of what he called the *Raub- und Plündersystem* (the system of robbery and plunder) of the great powers.

In a sense, neutrality was not all that far removed from the policy advocated by Frederick the Great in the second half of his reign; it was simply a different means of acquiring the same goal – Prussian security within the European system. The decision to stay outside of the continental wars directed against France was a perfectly logical one as long as Prussia's regional security was in no way threatened, that is, as long as the French

---

15  Depression seems to have been an occupational hazard among Europe's kings throughout the early modern and modern period. See Elizabeth W. Marvick, 'Psychobiography and the early modern French court', *French Historical Studies* 19 (1996), 951; Thomas Stamm-Kuhlmann, 'Tätiges Leben und Melancholie im preußischen Königshaus: durch Charaktertypologie zum Epochenverständnis', in Hedwig Röckelein (ed.), *Biographie als Geschichte* (Tübingen, 1993), pp. 280–94; Evelyne Lever, *Louis XVI* (Paris, 1985), p. 48.

16  Paul Bailleu (ed.), *Preußen und Frankreich von 1795 bis 1807. Diplomatische Correspondenzen*, 2 vols (Leipzig, 1881–7) i, p. xlvii, note 2.

17  Duroc to Talleyrand, 19 September 1805: Bailleu, *Preußen und Frankreich*, ii, p. 387.

decided not to interfere with North Germany. There was little danger of that occurring with the French revolutionary governments, which on the whole respected North German neutrality. Things changed considerably, however, with the advent of Napoleon, who was prepared to strike at Britain wherever and whenever possible. As it happened, King George III of England was also the Elector of Hanover, which lay right in the middle of North Germany. As a result, and despite attempts by British statesmen to make a clear distinction between the two governments, Hanover was considered to be English territory by the French and hence fair game in a war between those two countries. Moreover, the northern sea ports of Danzig, Elbing and Königsberg were important not only from a strategic point of view, but also from a commercial one. By 1800, the amount of grain shipped from those ports, primarily to England, accounted for nearly one-third of the volume of the entire international grain trade. This meant that the region, which fell under Prussia's sphere of influence, would inevitably come under threat by a resumption of the Anglo-French conflict.

This is exactly what happened in 1803 when the resumption of the war between France and Britain brought the problems surrounding neutrality to a head. Frederick William III had to make some hard decisions: he could maintain neutrality and fight France to protect his regional interests (this implied that he would have great-power backing from either Russia, Britain or both); he could invade Hanover and either annex or 'hold it' for George III (which was likely to lead to open conflict with Britain); or he could do nothing. The choices were narrow and not particularly attractive, but are indicative of the dilemma Prussia faced as a middle power in the European states-system. Alone, it was no match against France and yet its regional security was threatened by a war that did not in the least concern it. One way around this dilemma was to try to galvanize international – that is, great-power – opinion in the hope that France would think twice about armed intervention in North Germany. This is what the Prussian government attempted to do in the months preceding the outbreak of war; it put out diplomatic feelers to both the courts of St James and St Petersburg asking for support against France and more or less asking for permission to occupy the Electorate. The response, however, was far from encouraging. George III could hardly condone an occupation of his own territory, even if it was in the name of preserving it from the French, while Alexander I, who had been on the throne only a short while and who was preoccupied with establishing his reign through domestic reforms, dithered about getting involved in a European conflict.

Consequently, when the French marched into Hanover at the end of May 1803, they did so virtually unopposed. Prussian diplomacy had been unable to move the great powers, but it is unlikely that anything could have done so at this stage of the game. Neutrality had failed to protect the smaller North German powers, but so, too, had the European system. For all intents and purposes, neutrality was now reduced to the sole territory of Prussia. This may have been a policy that was appropriate during the Revolutionary era, but once Napoleon's designs on Germany were clear, it was unsound and even dangerous. The problem was that Frederick William III took a long time to realize, or to admit to himself, the extent of that danger. In some ways, the king's persistence in maintaining neutrality is reminiscent of the story about a man who, having fallen off a fifty-storey building, repeats to himself as each floor goes by – 'So far, so good'. It is the impact that counts, and that impact took place at the twin battle of Jena-Auerstedt.

The events leading up to that battle represent the history of Prussia trying to accommodate both France and Russia, with a marked preference for the latter. If France threatened Prussia's position in Germany, and an alliance with Austria was unworkable, then Prussia's only alternative was to align itself with Russia, all the while trying to avoid the wrath of Napoleon. This policy resulted in the signing of a secret alliance in St Petersburg in May 1804. Frederick William III took things one step further when, on 3 November 1805, he signed a treaty at Potsdam with Austria and Russia, bringing Prussia into the Third Coalition.

The Treaty of Potsdam stipulated that Prussia was to declare war against France if a last bid at mediation failed. To this end, one of Prussia's leading statesmen, Count Christian von Haugwitz, was sent to Napoleon's head-quarters in Austria to present him with the terms of the Potsdam agreement. By the time Haugwitz caught up with Napoleon, however, he had already won the battle of Austerlitz (2 December 1805), crushing the combined Austro-Russian armies. More importantly for Prussia, both Austria and Russia started making separate peace agreements with France. What happened next put Prussia in an exceedingly difficult situation, but was much less worse than if it had fought Napoleon and lost.

In a preliminary convention that was drawn up in Vienna, Haugwitz was forced into signing a pact with France, aligning itself against Britain (15 December 1805). Prussia's possessions in southern and western Germany were surrendered to either France or Bavaria and, by way of compensation, Berlin was to receive the Electorate of Hanover and some territory around Bayreuth. When Haugwitz brought this treaty back to Berlin, the shock in high-political circles was profound and resulted in an attempt to renegotiate the treaty conditions; Haugwitz was sent to Paris for that purpose in

February 1806. Instead, he found Napoleon not only insisted on even further clauses stipulating the North German ports be closed to British shipping, but demanded the treaty be formalized, ratified and implemented immediately. The choice, as in 1803, was between accommodating Napoleon or war. Without great-power backing, Prussia could do little else other than resign itself and accept Napoleon's conditions.

Prussia's isolation on the international scene was complete at this stage. Like many other powers, it had been obliged to come to terms with French hegemony on the continent. It did so reluctantly, but it had gained signific-ant territorial benefits even if its reputation was damned by the British. In terms of *Realpolitik*, there was nothing that Prussia either could or necessarily should have done. The problem, however, was not Prussia, which would have been perfectly happy with a place in a French-dominated Europe. The problem was Napoleon.

Shortly after Prussia had been obliged to sign the Treaty of Paris in February 1806, rumours started to circulate that Napoleon was thinking of coming to terms with Britain and that he was even considering giving back Hanover in order to do so. On top of this came the proclamation of the Confederation of the Rhine (*Rheinbund*), completely reorganizing the hundreds of states comprising the Holy Roman Empire into around thirty more substantial states under French tutelage. In return for these new changes, Napoleon proposed the creation of a North German Confedera-tion under Frederick William III's auspices. He even suggested the king adopt the imperial title. Everything he did, however, gave the lie to his intentions. He insisted, for example, that the Hansestädte (Hamburg, Lübeck and Bremen) were to remain under French control, and he championed the causes of Saxony and Hesse-Kassel, both of which were opposed to Prussian domination.

All of this provoked indignation within Prussian society in general and within the army in particular. Frederick William and his entourage finally came to the realization that there was no coming to terms with Napoleon and that if they did not resist, Prussia would simply become another German client-state. Even the notoriously pro-French faction at the court of Berlin was disillusioned with Napoleon by this stage and advocated war. However, a more inauspicious time to declare war could not be found. Austria was exhausted after Austerlitz and was never, in any event, averse to seeing Prussia take a hiding from France. Britain was at war with Prussia and was not prepared to consider Prussia's demands for help until it had withdrawn from Hanover. Russia was Prussia's only ally, but it was far away and would take time to mobilize. Frederick William III wrote to Alexander I asking him to do so, but he simply could not wait. Napoleon had already amassed forces in South Germany, giving the impression that the threat was real and imminent. Given the Prussian king's past history – that is, his reluctance to get involved in war with France – and in order to show his determination to resist any further Napoleonic incursions in Germany, he had little choice other than to mobilize immediately. Consequently, the war against France was neither politically nor militarily well prepared. On 1 October 1806, the king delivered an ultimatum demanding the immediate withdrawal of all French forces beyond the Rhine, negotiations for the settlement of all outstanding points of dispute, and the return of key enclaves. Moreover, France was to refrain from interfering in Prussia's establishment of a North German Confederation. If France did not comply by 8 October, it would be at war with Prussia.[18]

Frederick William did not expect anything less. This was not taking into consideration, however, the rapidity with which the Napoleonic armies always fought. The climax of the campaign came at Jena-Auerstedt (14 October 1806) when the Prussian army under the command of the Duke of Brunswick and Prince Hohenlohe suffered what was probably the worst defeat of its history. Prussian resistance after that day was understandably desultory and most of the country was overrun within four weeks. The main contingents of the Prussian army surrendered. Most of the Prussian forts gave up, often without so much as a shot being fired (with the exceptions of Kolberg, Graudenz and Danzig).[19] The king and his advisers fled to Königsberg (and later Memel), and Napoleon marched into Berlin on 27 October. At the end of the year, only a tiny tip in the north-east of the country remained in government hands. The flight of the court of Berlin signalled the disintegration of central bureaucratic authority. Those officials who remained behind swore an oath of allegiance to Napoleon. Prussia, however, continued to fight on in alliance with the Russians, participating in another two major battles in 1807, Eylau (7 February) and Friedland (14 June). This was simply prolonging the inevitable. When Alexander I decided that he had had enough, he abandoned his ally in an agreement over Europe with Napoleon at Tilsit.

---

18  Leopold von Ranke (ed.), *Denkwürdigkeiten des Staatskanzlers Fürsten von Hordenberg*, 5 vols (Leipzig, 1877) ii, pp. 188–90.

19  Historians have been at pains to point this out, but it needs to be said that most Prussian forts probably surrendered for strategic reasons rather than reasons of bad morale. Forts depend on field armies for their survival and, with most of the Prussian army either destroyed or in retreat to the far north-east corner of the realm, relief of the besieged was hardly likely to be forthcoming. Under the circumstances, it is questionable whether resistance to the last man would have been either prudent or even honourable.

There, in a melodramatic staging that included a raft moored in the middle of the River Niemen, Alexander and Napoleon met to decide the fate of Europe. Significantly, Frederick William III was not included in the discussions; he was left standing alone in the pouring rain on the bank of the river to await the outcome of the meeting. When news of the results of their discussions came, it was catastrophic. The Peace of Tilsit, signed on 8 and 9 July 1807, reduced Prussia to a small territory east of the Elbe. Most of Prussia's Polish territories became part of Napoleon's Grand Duchy of Warsaw. All of Prussia's lands west of the Elbe were confiscated and joined to Hesse-Kassel, which became the new Kingdom of Westphalia under Jerome Bonaparte. Frederick William lost just under half of his territory and over half of his subjects (Prussia's population was reduced from about 10.5 to 4.5 million). What was left of Prussia was occupied by a French army of 150,000 men (whom Prussia had to feed). Prussia was, moreover, required to pay a war indemnity (which was left open at the time Prussia signed the treaty, but which was later set at 120 million francs, a sum equivalent to about sixteen times the Prussian government's annual revenue before the invasion), and compelled to join the Continental Blockade in an anti-British alliance with disastrous results for the North German grain trade. Its army was reduced from about 260,000 men to just 42,000. In the provinces occupied by the French, Prussian officials were left in charge only of the church, schools and the administration of justice; everything else fell directly under French jurisdiction. In short, Frederick William was reduced to the rank of a minor German prince. Worse, however, was that Prussia's future was left decidedly unclear – it was not really an ally of France, nor a member of the Rheinbund, nor a neutral; it was entirely subject to Napoleon's whim.

There was a lesson to be drawn from Tilsit: Prussia was dependent for its survival on the goodwill of at least one of its great-power neighbours. If one or more of those neighbours acquiesced in any partition plans or took part in an anti-Prussian alliance, its existence became precarious to say the least. If Prussia was to continue to exist, then, it had to find a place within a stable alliance system. If Prussia was not annihilated altogether at Tilsit, it was probably because Napoleon needed a strategic barrier against Russia. It is also possible, as Paul Schroeder speculates, that Napoleon did not really know what to do with Prussia. Eighteenth-century France had always had a Prussian policy, whether its statesmen were for or against Prussia. Napoleon, on the other hand, did not because he had no conception of what Europe should be.[20]

---

20  Paul Schroeder, *The Transformation of European Politics 1763–1848* (Oxford, 1994), p. 349.

Prussia is often pictured as responding to military defeat with a reform movement out of which the Wars of Liberation eventually emerged.[21] This characterization is correct, up to a point. The aim of reform was to strengthen the Prussian state – not, however, so that it could later fight Napoleon and win back lost territory, but first to increase Prussia's ability to pay the huge war indemnity and, second, to make Prussia an attractive ally to Napoleon, thereby securing more tolerable conditions for itself under French hegemony in Europe.[22] This was almost certainly the case for the two people most responsible for reform, Barons Hardenberg and Stein. This interpretation differs from the traditional notion, namely that Prussia reformed itself in order to better resist and eventually wreak revenge on the French. This may have been the objective of military reformers, like Scharnhorst and Gneisenau, but they had little or no influence in the political decision-making process. One could argue that there was a third objective: only by a thoroughgoing reform of the state and the army could Prussia hope to break out of its small-power client status and regain its rightful place in the European pentarchy.[23] In other words, the primary force behind domestic reform were foreign political considerations. This is the history of Prussia up to and including the Russian campaign of 1812. Officially, compliance and loyalty towards France, and not resistance, were the catchphrases of the Prussian government throughout that period. Unofficially, from about 1810 onwards, Prussia carried on secret negotiations with Russia after it realized that it would never be able to satisfy Napoleon, whose demands became increasingly severe (the negotiations with Russia, by the way, were kept ultra-secret and were known only to a few people at the court of Berlin).

The unofficial policy led to the signing of a convention for Russo-Prussian military co-operation in October 1811. The convention, however, clearly demonstrated that Russia, as on so many occasions in the past, was not in the least prepared to exert any effort to help its ally. It expected Prussia to be overrun before the two armies were to join forces when Napoleon reached the Vistula. Under these conditions, it is not surprising that the official policy culminated in a humiliating treaty with France on

---

21   The Reform Movement, it needs to be underlined, was a direct response to military defeat and the threat of Napoleonic hegemony in northern Europe. In other words, social and economic reforms were carried out under the primacy of foreign policy. Once the threat subsided with the fall of Napoleon in 1815, so too did the impetus for reform. A recent proponent of this view is Brendan Simms, *The Struggle for Mastery in Germany, 1779–1850* (London, 1998), pp. 75–90 and id., 'Reform in Britain and Prussia, 1797–1815: (confessional) fiscal-military state and military agrarian complex', *Proceedings of the British Academy* 100 (1999), 79–100.

22   Peter G. Thielen, *Karl August von Hardenberg, 1750–1822. Eine Biographie* (Berlin, 1967), p. 270.

23   Simms, *The Struggle for Mastery in Germany*, p. 75.

24 February 1812. Napoleon forced Prussia not only to put 20,000 troops at his disposal, but also to bear the burden of quartering and supplying the Grand Army that was being gathered in North Germany in preparation for the invasion of Russia. This, and the type of behaviour which accompanied any occupation army, led to a marked increase in indignation among the Prussian population that was one of the emotional preconditions for the uprising that was to take place the following year. However, Prussia's decision to enter into a 'servile alliance' with France in 1812 was the correct choice. As Paul Schroeder has pointed out, it was a 'delayed, slower form of death' but, since no other policy could have worked at this time, it was better than going into opposition only to be annihilated by France.[24] As long as Napoleon was victorious in Russia, the Prussians shut up and did as they were told. Even after it became clear the campaign was a catastrophe for Napoleon, the Prussian government did not dare endanger the little security the French alliance gave it. The chief actor in the reversal that occurred after Napoleon's defeat in Russia was not the king, nor his chancellor Hardenberg, but a little-known general by the name of Hans von Yorck von Wartenburg, who commanded the Prussian corps in the Grand Army. Acting entirely on his own impetus, Yorck defected and concluded an alliance with Russia at Tauroggen in December 1812.[25]

When news of Yorck's defection reached the king, he refused to ratify the treaty, relieved Yorck of his command and ordered his immediate arrest. Frederick William's condemnation was genuine. The king undoubtedly feared that Napoleon would bounce back after defeat in much the same way he bounced back after Egypt in 1799 and at Wagram in July 1809 after an Austrian victory at Aspern two months earlier. Hardenberg also condemned Yorck, but for tactical reasons. He needed time to mobilize Prussian troops and to conclude agreements with Russia, Austria and Britain. In order to do so, he continued to play a double game with Napoleon for a little while longer; he carried on negotiations with the Russians and Austrians while he held the French off with assurances that Prussia was still loyal and that it was obeying Napoleon's renewed call to arms. This was not simply a smokescreen. Frederick William III and many of his advisers were fearful of the risks involved about going over to the allied cause. It was only when the Estates in eastern Prussia had assembled without the king's permission in February 1813 in order to create a *Landwehr* based on universal conscription, and only after two-thirds of the Prussian army had risen in revolt against the French, that Hardenberg managed to persuade

---

24  Schroeder, *The Transformation of European Politics*, p. 411.
25  Peter Paret, *Yorck and the Era of Prussian Reform, 1807–1815* (Princeton, NJ, 1966), pp. 191–6.

the king to follow the lead shown to him by his people. He had little choice under the circumstances, but even then he hastened to secure Prussia's future by forming a treaty with Russia. The resulting Treaty of Kalisch (27–8 February 1813) guaranteed the restoration of Prussia to its former borders. A series of proclamations followed culminating in his most famous – referred to simply as 'An mein Volk' (17 March 1813) – in which the king appealed directly to his own people to resist. One should note, however, that despite subsequent nationalist mythology, Frederick William did not inspire a policy of national revolution. On the contrary, he dragged up the rear, well behind it. It was not a question of 'The king calling, and everyone answering', as nationalist historians would have it, but rather a question of 'Everyone calling and the king still not answering'.[26]

## A place in the European states-system

The degree of popular participation and the role of nationalist fervour in the 'War of Freedom', as it was known at the time, or the 'War of Liberation', as it was later called, have long been a subject for debate and need not be dwelt on here except to note that they played an important, albeit secondary role in the armed struggle to oust the French invader from German soil.[27] In terms of foreign policy, this last phase of the Revolutionary and Napoleonic Wars was necessarily the most important and was to set the political agenda that carried Prussia well into the nineteenth century. The two most important issues were Prussia's relations with Austria (hence Prussia's place in Germany) and Prussia's place within the European pentarchy. Both, of course, were directly related to Prussia's future security. The Foreign Minister, Hardenberg, attempted to achieve this, first, through negotiations and treaty alliances and then, when that did not work, through territorial acquisitions. Eventually, he was to achieve the security he desired, but not before the allies almost came to blows over the issue of compensations and not in the manner that Hardenberg had envisioned.

Once Prussia decided to fight the French, Hardenberg got busy trying to reach an agreement with the allies over compensations. This was perfectly in keeping with eighteenth-century conceptions of alliance politics. To this

---

26  Cited in Hans-Joachim Schoeps, *Preußen. Geschichte eines Staates* (Frankfurt/Berlin, 1966), p. 141.

27  Good starting-points are David Gates, *The Napoleonic Wars, 1803–1815* (London, 1997), pp. 221–54; Charles J. Esdaile, *The Wars of Napoleon* (London, 1995), pp. 261–76; and Michael Broers, *Europe under Napoleon 1799–1815* (London, 1996), pp. 237–43.

end, a series of treaties was concluded during the course of 1813 between Prussia, Russia and Austria – Kalisch on 27–8 February; Reichenbach on 27 June; and Teplitz on 9 September. They aimed at reshaping Central Europe in a post-Napoleonic world. The allied demands included restoring Prussia and Austria to their former territorial status; the abolition of the Rheinbund; the independence of the smaller German states; the partition of the Duchy of Warsaw; and the withdrawal of the French to the Rhine. Prussia renounced any annexationist aims on Hanover (essentially because it needed British subsidies) and instead came to an arrangement with Russia over Saxony. These treaties, then, were not based upon the disinterested willingness of the great powers to help each other defeat Napoleon, but rather on specific regional interests. As far as Prussia was concerned, they went part of the way to restoring it to its former limits and to solving its geopolitical dilemma by 'rounding off' Prussian territory, but there were no guarantees that it would not come under threat by a constellation of great-power alliances or even a regenerated France. In order to prevent this happening again, Hardenberg attempted to secure a place for Prussia through an alliance system, thereby obtaining implicit recognition as a great power.[28]

There was a problem, however. Prussia could realistically hope to do this only by associating itself with at least one other great power. Given the circumstances surrounding the campaign of 1812, that power had to be Russia. Austria did not decide to come into the fray against Napoleon immediately; indeed, Metternich took a lot of persuading and could not in any case be entirely trusted by Prussia. On the battlefield in 1813, Russia was a good choice to make. At the negotiating table at the Congress of Vienna in 1814, Prussia's reliance on it led only to a dead end.

The key issue at the Congress, at least as far as Prussia was concerned, quickly became the Saxon question. The details surrounding the negotiations are complex, but only two things need to be retained here: Prussia wanted all of it; and both Metternich and Castlereagh were prepared to cede it if Prussia agreed to support them in their opposition to the tsar's Polish plans.[29] This was not taking into account Frederick William's utter loyalty, not to say dependence, on the tsar; the king forbade Hardenberg to get involved in an anti-Russian combination. Once again, Prussia was to pay the price of remaining on Russia's side. Once Russia had gained what

---

28   For a discussion of the plans formulated by Hardenberg in the spring and summer of 1814, see Philip Dwyer, 'The two faces of Prussian foreign policy: Karl August von Hardenberg as minister for foreign affairs, 1805–1815', in Thomas-Stamm Kuhlmann (ed.), *Karl August von Hardenberg. Chancen und Grenzen der Reformpolitik* (Munich, forthcoming).

29   For details of the Polish–Saxon question see Schroeder, *The Transformation of European Politics*, pp. 523–38.

it wanted in Poland, Berlin found the tsar's support for Prussian territorial claims weakening by the hour. By late December 1814/early January 1815, three powers – France, Austria and Britain – confronted Prussia in its bid for Saxony and even formed a secret alliance to that end in January 1815 (they were soon joined by the Netherlands, Bavaria and Hanover). Hardenberg resisted this combined attack desperately, even threatening to annex Saxony and to go to war, but without Russian support Prussia could not have resisted this type of pressure for very long.

The Polish–Saxon question not only placed Prussia in an embarrassing diplomatic situation, it split the allies into two camps – Prussia with feeble Russian backing on the one side, Britain, Austria and France on the other. Neither side wanted war, however, and if push had come to shove, it is highly unlikely that Austria and Britain would have invited a French army to return to Central Europe to fight Prussia less than a year after the defeat of Napoleon. This temporary falling out over the Saxon question, which was probably far less serious than has been made out, was in any event quickly patched over upon Napoleon's egotistical return from Elba in March 1815. The allies found a renewed solidarity and a renewed determination to finish him off once and for all.

Prussia's role in defeating Napoleon at Waterloo strengthened its position at the negotiating table leading to the Second Peace of Paris (1815). Although it did not get all that it wanted, it nevertheless made substantial gains on two fronts. Both of these gains had enormous consequences for Prussia's future prosperity. First, Prussia's position in the European pentarchy was consolidated through two treaties – the Quadruple Alliance on 25 March 1815 (Austria, Russia, Britain and Prussia), and the Holy Alliance (Russia, Prussia and Austria) on 26 September 1815, designed to put an end to revolutionary unrest in Europe and inspired by a tsar who had found religion. In foreign-political terms, these treaties guaranteed Prussia's place in the European states-system and consolidated its status as a great power. For the first time in its history, Prussia did not have to be continually looking over its shoulder at potential enemies.

Secondly, not only was all of Prussia's former territory restored (no one at Vienna suggested a settlement at the expense of Prussia's territorial interests), but it also received a large chunk of Saxony for its role in defeating Napoleon. There were, however, new territories foisted upon Prussia, which were going to oblige it to adopt an entirely new role and which were going to have tremendous consequences for the future direction of Prussian foreign policy. Throughout the revolutionary period, Prussia had been preoccupied with consolidating its territory in eastern and northern Europe and had done its best, especially after 1795, to extricate itself from the west. Now Prussia received territory on the Rhine so that it could act as a bulwark against future French aggression in Germany. Accordingly, at the insistence of Britain and with the acquiescence of Frederick William III, Prussia was given territory it had not even asked for, nor, for that matter, coveted – the Rhineland and Westphalia. This was increasingly to drag Prussia's focus away from the east towards the west. Also, although Prussia's rulers were unaware of it at the time, the rich iron and coal deposits of the Rhineland were going to enable Prussia to industrialize in the course of the nineteenth century. In practical terms, Prussia faced many of the same geopolitical problems that had plagued it over the last century, but the Revolutionary Wars and Napoleon had shown the other great powers that Prussia had a role to play in the European system – to help contain France in central and northern Europe. It had taken more than half a century, but Prussia had at long last become a permanent member of the club of great powers.

# CHAPTER TWELVE

# The Prussian Reform Movement and the rise of enlightened nationalism

MATTHEW LEVINGER

The disaster of Jena-Auerstedt in 1806 lent new urgency to what had previously been a rather desultory debate within the country's ruling elite: how should Prussia respond to the political and social innovations of the French Revolution? Confronted by the potential prospect of the annihilation of the Prussian state, King Frederick William III was forced to seek assistance from an ambitious cadre of reform-minded officials, most of whom had served in middle-level positions within the civil service before 1806. The most prominent figures in this group were Karl Freiherr vom und zum Stein (1757–1831), who served as Prussia's first minister from October 1807 through November 1808, and Karl August von Hardenberg (1750–1822), who headed the government from 1810 until his death. Neither man was a native Prussian. Stein's family belonged to the imperial knights, owning estates in the Rhineland. Hardenberg was born to a wealthy landowning family in Hanover, and served as an official in Hanover and Brunswick before accepting an appointment in the Prussian civil service. At the respective ages of 50 and 57 in 1807, Stein and Hardenberg were two of the more senior members of this group. Most of their key supporters were in their thirties and early forties. These figures included Hardenberg's protégé Karl von Stein zum Altenstein (1770–1840), Heinrich Theodor von Schön (1773–1856) and Wilhelm von Humboldt (1767–1835).

The Prussian Reform Movement of 1806–15 was long the stuff of patriotic myth-making, especially for German historians writing before the Second World War. Stein, in particular, was often lauded as a forward-looking 'champion of national freedom and unity', whose fourteen-month ministry 'nurtured all of Prussian and German history in the nineteenth century'.[1] Scholars writing since 1945, however, have generally cast a more sceptical eye on the events of the Napoleonic era in Prussia. They have tended to focus not on how the Prussian reformers laid the foundation for Prussia-Germany's future greatness, but on how the events of the early nineteenth century reinforced an authoritarian political system in Prussia. Two classic interpretations are particularly worthy of note. Some historians, most notably Reinhart Koselleck, have argued that Prussian political leaders of the Napoleonic era attempted to establish a free market economy and liberal political institutions, but that the Prussian bourgeoisie was still too weak to sustain a viable system of parliamentary rule. Thus, these officials were forced to abandon their ambitions for political liberalization in order to achieve the implementation of their socio-economic reforms.[2] Other scholars have interpreted the motives of Prussia's leading civil servants in a less altruistic light. The early nineteenth century, argued Hans Rosenberg, witnessed a 'revolution from within' that resulted in a 'modified pattern' of aristocratic privilege and a political system based on 'bureaucratic absolutism'.[3]

This chapter reassesses both the motives and the consequences of the Prussian Reform Movement. Historians have often judged this movement according to *ex post facto* twentieth-century standards, depicting Prussia's political development as leading in one of two possible directions: either towards a liberal parliamentary system, such as those that now exist throughout Western Europe, or towards a dictatorial regime prefiguring the Nazi state. These twentieth-century political models, however, have limited relevance in characterizing the ambitions of the Prussian reformers. Rather, the Reform Movement is best understood in the context of the eighteenth-century philosophical and political traditions out of which it emerged. Stein, Hardenberg and their compatriots sincerely supported the establishment of parliamentary institutions of government – but they hoped that such institutions would enhance, rather than undermine, monarchical sovereignty.

The leading reformers were animated by a complex blend of motives. Their most pressing objective was to regain Prussia's status as a great power, and thus to defend the country against French domination. But they also

---

1  Gerhard Ritter, *Freiherr vom Stein: Eine politische Biographie*, 2nd edn (Stuttgart, 1958), title of Part II; Friedrich Meinecke, *The Age of German Liberation, 1795–1815* (Berkeley, CA, 1977), pp. 70, 71.

2  Reinhart Koselleck, *Preußen zwischen Reform und Revolution: Allgemeines Landrecht, Verwaltung und soziale Bewegung von 1791 bis 1848*, 3rd edn (Stuttgart, 1981).

3  Hans Rosenberg, *Bureaucracy, Aristocracy, Autocracy: The Prussian Experience, 1660–1815* (Cambridge, MA, 1958), pp. 203, 204, 226.

believed that this foreign-policy crisis presented a unique opportunity to enact far-reaching domestic social reforms, which were inspired partly by eighteenth-century philosophical ideals of universal freedom and equality. They anticipated that these new laws, by forging a cohesive and prosperous society, would help mobilize the full energies of the Prussian populace in the service of the state. In Hardenberg's formulation, 'democratic principles in a monarchical government' were 'the appropriate form for the spirit of our age'.[4] In other words, the king and his people must work in harmony for the attainment of the public good.

The reformers' political philosophy thus represented a hybrid of eighteenth-century theories of enlightened monarchy, as articulated both in Prussia and in other European states, and the new nationalist ideals of the revolutionary era. The phrase 'enlightened nationalism' (which may seem like an oxymoron) is meant to highlight this distinctive fusion between old and new political ideals. In imitation of earlier 'enlightened absolutists' such as Frederick the Great, the Prussian reformers hoped to *rationalize* the social order as a means of enhancing the prosperity and power of the monarchical state. Like the new generation of revolutionaries in France, they also sought to *mobilize* the energies of the 'nation'. Through this twin programme of social rationalization and popular political mobilization, these civil servants believed it would be possible to reconcile a sovereign monarch with a politically active citizenry.

This chapter consists of three parts. The first section examines the eighteenth-century theoretical traditions that informed Prussian political debate during the Napoleonic era, as well as the efforts of reform-minded civil servants to fuse these traditions with new nationalist ideals. Section two focuses on the leap from theory to practice. It explores two dimensions of the reformers' efforts to forge a rational and harmonious national community: their programme of social and economic reforms, and their plans for political and administrative reform. The final section discusses the mixed legacies of enlightened nationalism in Prussia. By striving to fuse the will of the king with the will of the nation, the Prussian reformers of the Napoleonic era succeeded (at least temporarily) in reinvigorating the monarchical state. They thereby helped make it possible for a strong monarchy to survive in Prussia and the German Empire through to the end of the First World War. At the same time, however, they unleashed volatile and

---

4   Hardenberg, Riga Memorandum, September 1807, in Georg Winter (ed.), *Die Reorganisation des Preußischen Staates unter Stein und Hardenberg. Erster Teil: Allgemeine Verwaltungs- und Behördenreform. Band I: Vom Beginn des Kampfes gegen die Kabinettsregierung bis zum Wiedereintritt des Ministers vom Stein* (Leipzig, 1931), p. 306.

unpredictable political forces that would haunt Prussia and Germany well into the twentieth century.

# Eighteenth-century traditions and nineteenth-century challenges

The culture of enlightened nationalism, which was central to the Prussian Reform Movement, represented an outgrowth of the older political tradition known as 'enlightened absolutism'. Frederick the Great (1740–86) expressed the essence of enlightened absolutist doctrine when he proclaimed himself to be the 'first servant of the state'. A prince's true purpose, Frederick argued, was to advance the good of his people, not his own private ends. According to this conception, the interests of the monarch were identical to those of the populace at large. Thus, absolute monarchy was the best form of government, because an enlightened prince could act rationally and efficiently on behalf of the common good.

Frederick the Great's arguments in favour of monarchical sovereignty reflected a long tradition of Prussian and European political thought. During the seventeenth and eighteenth centuries, German scholars and civil servants such as Johann Justi (1705?–1771) had developed a theory of public administration known as Cameralism. The purpose of government, Justi argued, was to achieve economic prosperity, social harmony and the 'perfection of our moral condition'. These goals were most likely to be attained by a rational monarch who was assisted by an enlightened bureaucracy.[5] This ideal of rational monarchical sovereignty was shared by social and political theorists outside of Prussia, such as the French physiocrats. In the words of one prominent physiocrat, Anne-Robert-Jacques Turgot (1727–1781), the king should seek to 'govern like God, by general laws'. This ideal political condition, he argued, could be attained through the rationalization of France's social and administrative institutions.[6]

In Prussia during the late eighteenth century, philosophers and legal theorists alike argued that absolute monarchs must serve the public good. Immanuel Kant, the most famous Prussian intellectual of his age, called on kings to govern in a 'republican' (*republikanisch*) manner, so as to advance the

---

5 Quoted in Mack Walker, *German Home Towns: Community, State, and General Estate, 1648–1871* (Ithaca, NY, 1971), p. 164.
6 Keith Michael Baker, *Inventing the French Revolution: Essays on French Political Culture in the Eighteenth Century* (Cambridge, 1990), p. 120.

'spirit of the laws of freedom'.[7] The jurist Carl Gottlieb Svarez, author of the Prussian Civil Code of 1794, presented a vigorous defence of the principle of 'unrestricted monarchy'. In a series of lectures to the Prussian crown prince held in 1791–2, Svarez argued: 'The regent can never, provided he has correct conceptions, possess an interest different from or hostile to the people.'[8] His pupil, the future Frederick William III, adopted this notion of sovereignty in an essay composed shortly before he ascended to the throne in 1797. Frederick William declared that princes must rule for the 'good of their land' and the 'true best of the state' (*besten des Staats*). Any monarch who failed to heed this principle, he warned, risked plunging his country into revolution – as, he argued, the recent events in France had shown.[9]

The upheavals of the French Revolution and the Napoleonic era proved a shock to Prussian leadership, as to other European *Ancien Régimes*. During the years leading up to 1806, certain officials appealed for broad reforms. One Prussian official, Johann Struensee, proclaimed the advent of a 'creative revolution . . . from above'. King Frederick William III displayed evidence of this new spirit by liberating the serfs on his own royal domains and by modifying Prussia's system of taxes and administration. Yet, in general, efforts at social and political reform proceeded only in fits and starts until the military catastrophe of 1806–7. Formally, the rump Prussian state became an ally of France in 1807 as a result of the Treaty of Tilsit. Behind the scenes, however, leading civil servants and publicists contemplated how best to resist French domination. In their view, Napoleon's might stemmed in large part from his ability to mobilize the French nation for a patriotic war. They argued that Prussia could recover its earlier vigour only by imitating its conqueror. In June 1807, four months before returning to head the Prussian ministry, Stein summarized his programme for reform in his famous Nassau Memorandum:

> The nation, despite all of its flaws, possesses a noble pride, energy, valour, and willingness to sacrifice itself for fatherland and freedom . . . [T]he government's purpose, in establishing new institutions and in forming a

---

7  Immanuel Kant, 'Der Streit der Facultäten in drey Abschnitten' (1798), in Wilhelm Weischedel (ed.), *Die Werke Immanuel Kants*, vol. 11, *Schriften zur Anthropologie, Geschichtsphilosophie, Politik und Pädagogik 1* (Frankfurt, 1977), pp. 364–5. See also Leonard Krieger, *The German Idea of Freedom: History of a Political Tradition* (Boston, 1957), pp. 122–3; and Matthew Levinger, 'Kant and the Origins of Prussian Constitutionalism', *History of Political Thought* 19 (1998), 241–63.
8  Carl Gottlieb Svarez, *Vorträge über Recht und Staat*, Hermann Conrad and Gerd Kleinheyer (eds), (Cologne, 1960), pp. 12, 475.
9  Max Lehmann, 'Ein Regierungsprogramm Friedrich Wilhelm's III', *Historische Zeitschrift* 61 (1889), 444.

constitution, will be to guide and direct these energies and convictions, not to suppress them. . . . If the nation is to be ennobled, the oppressed part of it must be given freedom, independence and property; and this oppressed part must be granted the protection of the laws.[10]

For Stein and his associates, universal freedom and at least some degree of civil equality were fundamental prerequisites for the forging of a national community. Altenstein put it succinctly when he wrote, 'the slave has no interest in the state'.[11] The citizenry, the reformers argued, could be bound together by a common spirit only if they existed under common legal conditions and were released from arbitrary rule.

Beyond reforming the social order, these members of Prussia's 'patriot party' considered it essential to engage the populace at large in public life. This project, they thought, required the reform of various public institutions. One critical public institution was the army. The efforts at military reform led by Gerhard von Scharnhorst and Neithardt von Gneisenau are discussed elsewhere in this volume and need not be addressed here.[12] Another such set of institutions were the schools. During the Napoleonic era, intellectuals such as Wilhelm von Humboldt and Johann Gottlieb Fichte worked for the establishment of a new system of public education. 'The means of salvation', proclaimed Fichte in his *Addresses to the German Nation* of 1807–8, 'lies . . . in the education of the nation – whose hitherto existing life has been extinguished under foreign influence – for an entirely new life.'[13] Finally, many of the new cadre of Prussian leaders demanded the creation of a 'national representation', which they believed would also help mobilize the populace politically. Only through the 'participation of the *Volk* in the operations of the state', wrote Stein's collaborator Theodor von Schön, could 'national spirit be positively aroused and animated'.[14]

In calling for the political mobilization of the nation, however, the Prussian reformers confronted certain basic challenges. First, it was far from clear what 'nation' they had in mind. Was it 'Prussia' or 'Germany'? Was it an egalitarian fellowship of free citizens or a hierarchical community led by the landed aristocracy? Some of these questions became the subjects of heated

---

10  Stein, Nassau Memorandum, June 1807, in Walther Hubatsch and Erich Botzenhart (eds), *Briefe und amtliche Schriften* (Stuttgart, 1957–74), ii, p. 397.
11  Altenstein, Riga Memorandum, 1807, in Winter, *Reorganisation*, pp. 403–4.
12  See Chapter 10.
13  Johann Gottlieb Fichte, 'Reden an die deutsche Nation', in J. H. Fichte (ed.), *Johann Gottlieb Fichte's Sämmtliche Werke* (Berlin, 1846), vii, p. 274.
14  Stein's 'Political Testament', 24 November 1808, in Heinrich Scheel and Doris Schmidt (eds), *Das Reformministerium Stein: Akten zur Verfassungs- und Verwaltungsgeschichte aus den Jahren 1807/08* (Berlin, 1968), iii, pp. 1136–8.

debate during the Napoleonic era. Others became taboo for discussion. For example, most of the leading reformers during this era consistently shied away from stipulating whether the 'nation' comprised Prussia alone or all of German-speaking Europe. They may have maintained this ambiguity in order to avoid prematurely antagonizing Napoleon or the rulers of the other German states, all of whom might have been threatened by explicit demands for German national unification.

A second challenge was related to the mixed legacy of France's recent history. Prussia's leaders urgently wanted to find a way of harnessing the power of the French Revolution without incurring what they considered to be the Revolution's disastrous side-effects. Between 1789 and 1794, many leading French revolutionaries had employed appeals to the 'nation' as a catalyst for further radicalizing the struggle against internal enemies. The Prussian reformers, by contrast, sought to develop a form of nationalism that would dampen, rather than radicalize, internal conflicts. Instead of setting commoners against aristocrats, and subjects against the king, they wanted to mobilize the nation in a manner that would *enhance* the internal harmony of Prussian society and the political solidarity of its people. Only by achieving domestic harmony, they believed, would it become possible to direct the full energies of their populace against the foreign foe. It is worth examining, then, how the reformers attempted to translate their ideals into practice, and some of the pitfalls that accompanied this transition.

## The project of nation-building in Napoleonic Prussia

The Prussian reformers may be labelled 'enlightened nationalists' because they believed that the rationalization of social and political institutions was an indispensable prerequisite for the formation of a patriotic citizenry. They believed that both of these goals would be served through the adoption of enlightened legislation and through the education of the people. Their faith in the powers of reason, however, was sorely tested by the political conflicts of the Napoleonic era. This section explores some of the dilemmas confronted by Prussian leaders as they sought to realize their vision of a rational and harmonious national community. First, I discuss their project of social reform, exploring the tensions between hierarchical and egalitarian principles in Stein and Hardenberg's legislative proposals. Second, I examine their efforts at political reform, analysing their attempts to reconcile the principles of monarchical sovereignty and national representation. This discussion will provide a clearer sense both of the nature of the reformers' political vision and of the gap between their ideals and their achievements.

## The project of social reform: equality and its limits

Though the leading reformers all professed faith in the Enlightenment ideal of universal freedom, they proceeded gingerly in challenging the traditional privileges of Prussia's social elites. The proposals of Stein and Hardenberg reflected an uneasy compromise between the older principles of the particularistic, hierarchical social order and the newer, egalitarian and universalistic principles of the Enlightenment and the French Revolution. Though these leaders portrayed the nation as a community of equals, they also emphasized the importance of preserving elements of the traditional corporate order. Stein, in particular, was devoted to reinvigorating, rather than annihilating, what he saw as old organic institutions. These conflicting tendencies may be illustrated through an examination of three key reform measures: Stein's October Edict of 1807, which emancipated the serfs and abolished many of the traditional barriers between the bourgeoisie and the aristocracy; Stein's municipal ordinance of October 1808; and Hardenberg's economic reforms of 1810.

The first great reform measure adopted during Stein's ministry was the edict of 9 October 1807, which declared momentously, 'After 11 November 1810, there will be only free people' throughout the Prussian realm.[15] In keeping with the language of Stein's memorandum, the provisions of this edict were directed towards two goals: first, to forge a liberal economic order that would allow each individual to achieve prosperity 'according to the measure of his energies';[16] and second, to create a legal system under which all inhabitants of Prussia would become 'citizens of the state' (*Staatsbürger*), and all citizens would be considered equal before the law.

The movement to abolish serfdom in Prussia had begun already in the late eighteenth century. Between 1799 and 1806, Frederick William III had abolished the feudal obligations of the peasants who lived on the royal domains (about one-seventh of Prussia's agricultural population). In 1803, the king had also expressed support for a proposal that would have gradually eliminated hereditary servitude throughout the realm, but he had withheld

---

15  Edict of 9 October 1807, quoted in James J. Sheehan, *German History, 1770–1866* (Oxford, 1989), pp. 299–300.
16  'Edikt den erleichterten Besitz und den freien Gebrauch des Grundeigentums sowie die persönlichen Verhältnisse der Landbewohner betreffend', 9 October 1807, in Hubatsch and Botzenhart, *Stein*, ii, part 1, p. 458. See also Ritter, *Stein*, p. 220.

his final approval for this measure out of fear of provoking a conflict with the nobility.

The October Edict not only abolished all hereditary servitude in Prussia, but also eliminated certain traditional restrictions on the bourgeoisie and the nobility. Commoners obtained the right to purchase landed estates (*Rittergüter*), a privilege that had previously been reserved to the nobility. Conversely, nobles received the right to practise bourgeois professions without incurring any penalty to their status. Stein also favoured other reforms, not included in the initial edict, that would have fundamentally transformed the relationship between lord and peasants. For example, he wanted to eliminate the nobility's traditional exemption from property taxes; even more importantly, he sought to abolish the nobles' police and judicial powers over their estates, placing the entire realm directly under the legal authority of the state. These proposals foundered against bitter opposition from the landholding nobility. Ultimately, the Prussian nobles preserved their exemption from property taxes until 1861, and they kept their police powers until 1872.

At one level, the theory behind Stein's plans was simple. He spoke of the need to secure the 'original and inalienable rights of mankind' by establishing a social order based on the principles of freedom and the rule of law.[17] Yet the October Edict left many questions unresolved. For example, even though the serfs became officially free, the law did not abolish their compulsory labour obligations to their former masters. Nor did it grant them any ownership rights over the lands that they had farmed. Not until 1816 did the government finally settle the questions of how Prussian estate owners should be compensated for their loss of peasant labour and how their lands should be distributed between them and their former peasants. This settlement worked largely to the advantage of the nobility, so that many of Prussia's peasants ended up living under worse material conditions than they had before 1807.

A more fundamental ambiguity in Stein's political theory involved the status and function of the traditional estates. On the one hand, Stein wanted to abolish the nobility's hereditary exclusivity as well as most of its privileges. Yet Stein also hoped to *restore* the nobility to the position of political pre-eminence that it had enjoyed prior to the eighteenth century. As a class consisting of Prussia's largest landowners, the nobility would play a leading role in the new representative assemblies that Stein planned to establish. Stein believed that a politically active nobility would support, rather than undermine, monarchical authority. In other words, rather than establishing

---

17  Quoted in Ritter, *Stein*, p. 227.

full civil equality, Stein wanted to reinvigorate what he saw as Prussia's traditional hierarchical institutions. He favoured increasing the degree of mobility between estates, rather than abolishing outright the legal distinctions between different categories of the population.

The second great reform measure, the municipal ordinance (*Städteordnung*), enacted near the end of Stein's ministry in November 1808, revealed a similar ambivalence toward the traditional social institutions of Prussia's municipalities. Traditionally, the status of 'citizen' (*Bürger*) had been extended to only a small minority of urban residents: to qualify, one needed to be a self-sufficient practitioner of a 'bourgeois trade'. Under this system, only the leading figures in the guilds and other corporate bodies had been entitled to participate in the political life of the towns. The municipal ordinance significantly expanded the class of *Bürger*, and it also created new municipal assemblies in many towns where no representative institutions had previously existed. The law stipulated that any male resident of a town, as well as any unmarried female, could qualify for citizenship either by practising a 'municipal trade' or by owning a house in the town. All male citizens who met certain property qualifications were permitted both to vote and to hold office in the town council, an assembly that was responsible for administering local institutions such as the police, schools and poor relief.

Stein hoped that his municipal ordinance would produce a vigorous public spirit in Prussia's towns while still preserving their particularistic institutions. In the words of one historian, Stein's political theory stood 'on the border between the old and the new constitutional thought'.[18] Though he wanted to maintain the traditional estates as discrete corporate entities, Stein perceived their character in an entirely new way. No longer did he view the estates as 'beneficiaries of rights' that sought to defend their private privileges against encroachment by the monarchy. Rather he saw the estates as institutions that derived their legitimacy from their performance of a public function, and which were bound to serve the public good.

The third great reform measure was Hardenberg's economic programme, most of which was promulgated in a series of laws of October and November 1810. Hardenberg showed less deference than Stein towards traditional social hierarchies. Influenced by the economic theories of Adam Smith, he argued that the adoption of liberal economic and social principles was an essential precondition for Prussia's economic growth, as well as a catalyst for the moral improvement of the people. His legislation went a long way towards abolishing the remnants of aristocratic privilege in Prussia, and liberalized

---

18　Herbert Obenaus, 'Verwaltung und ständische Repräsentation in den Reformen des Freiherrn vom Stein', *Jahrbuch für die Geschichte Mittel- und Ostdeutschlands* 18 (1969), 135–6.

the economies of the towns as well. The Finance Edict of 27 October declared the state's intention to equalize tax burdens, reform the tariff and toll system, create freedom of enterprise, and secularize land belonging to the Catholic and Protestant churches.

In the countryside, Hardenberg's programme contributed to levelling the social status of the different estates. The peasants, who had been formally freed by Stein's October Edict, were now to be released from their economic obligations to the estate owners, and to be granted ownership of part of the land they occupied. In the towns, Hardenberg's programme provided an equally forceful challenge to the position of the guilds. Though the guilds were permitted to remain in existence, they lost their exclusive rights to practise particular trades. The *Gewerbesteueredikt* of 2 November 1810 stipulated that anyone, whether a resident of the countryside or the towns, could begin practising a trade simply by paying an annual 'tax on enterprises' (*Gewerbesteuer*). This law, combined with the decree of October 1807, which had opened all professions to both nobles and bourgeois, constituted a significant step towards the creation of a fully free labour market in Prussia. It also enhanced the administrative powers of the central state by shifting the authority to regulate economic activity away from the guilds and towns.

While some of Stein's reforms – notably his attacks on the aristocracy's tax exemptions, as well as on their police and judicial powers – met with opposition from Prussia's social elites, these groups accommodated themselves to much of the new legislation, often finding ways to turn it to their own economic advantage. Many nobles, for example, capitalized on the edict emancipating the serfs as a means of absorbing peasant lands into their estates. Hardenberg's legislation, which represented a more radical assault on the traditional social order, provoked a storm of outrage that forced the government to retreat from many of its bolder plans. For example, Hardenberg's tax reforms remained incomplete, and the Gendarmerie Edict of July 1812, which sought to diminish the administrative powers of the nobility by creating a bureaucratic rural government in the French style, was ultimately revoked because of the vehement protests of the Prussian aristocracy.

Historians have often judged Stein's reforms in a more favourable light than Hardenberg's – though increasingly sympathetic interpretations of Hardenberg have appeared in recent years. While Stein sought to instil 'national consciousness' in Prussia's subjects, scholars have argued, Hardenberg's primary goal was the 'augmentation of national income'.[19] This portrait

---

19 Ernst Walter Zeeden, *Hardenberg und der Gedanke einer Volksvertretung in Preußen 1807–1812* (Berlin, 1940), pp. 88–9.

of Hardenberg as a bloodless technocrat, devoid of patriotic spirit, is unjust. It is indisputable that financial concerns were of paramount importance in driving Hardenberg's reform agenda. But Hardenberg and his allies also viewed the rationalization of Prussia's economy as intimately intertwined with the broader project of national renewal. Hardenberg sought not just to consolidate state power, but to 'establish a common national interest, in which the financial engagement and political participation of all property owners would grow together'.[20] By eliminating the social barriers that pitted the estates against each other, and by founding a new order based on rational, egalitarian principles, he hoped to create a more productive and harmonious national community, thus stimulating the formation of patriotism within the Prussian population. At the same time, however, Hardenberg sometimes backed down in the face of protests by the Prussian nobility. He, like Stein, believed that some degree of established hierarchy was essential to preserve the stability of the social order.

## The project of political reform: the quest for a 'democratic monarchy'

Just as the Prussian reformers sought to reconcile hierarchical and egalitarian social principles, they also attempted to harmonize the principles of monarchical and democratic sovereignty. The actual word 'democracy' appeared quite rarely in their writings: only Hardenberg explicitly called for the establishment of 'democratic principles in a monarchical government'. But the writings of many of the reformers expressed the desire to establish a popular foundation for monarchical sovereignty. A typical example is found in Stein's 'Political Testament', which was drafted by Stein's associate Theodor von Schön in December 1808. Calling for the establishment of a 'general national representation' (*allgemeine Nationalrepräsentation*), the Testament declared:

> The right (*Recht*) and the unlimited authority of our king was sacrosanct to me, and remains so to us! But in order for this right and this unlimited power to achieve the good that lies within it, it seemed to me necessary to give the highest power a means through which it can become acquainted with the wishes of the *Volk* and through which it can give life to their determinations.[21]

---

20  Koselleck, *Preußen*, p. 185.
21  Stein's 'Political Testament', 24 November 1808, in Scheel and Schmidt, *Das Reformministerium Stein*, iii, pp. 1136–8.

According to this formula, the monarchy functioned as an organ for expressing and achieving the wishes of the entire Prussian people.

To the twentieth-century observer, the notion of fusing 'unlimited' monarchical sovereignty with popular representation may appear absurd. But this project was far more plausible from the perspective of eighteenth-century political thought. Stein and Hardenberg drew on the theories of physiocrats such as Turgot, enlightened jurists such as Svarez, and philosophers such as Kant. All of these authors had postulated an underlying harmony between the interests of the king and his subjects. Yet, in order for this harmony to manifest itself in practice, they argued that the political process must be reformed both from above and from below. From above, the state apparatus must be rationalized and new representative institutions forged. From below, the Prussian people must educate themselves politically so that they could recognize and express the true national interest, elevating the good of the country as a whole above their own private benefit. Twentieth-century Western theorists generally discuss democratic politics as a *contestatory* process that pits competing interests against each other. The Prussian reformers, however, based their efforts on the premise that representative institutions would help forge a *consensus* between the monarch and his people.

Plans for administrative rationalization met with only partial success during the Napoleonic era. In 1806, Stein proposed abolishing the Prussian Cabinet (a council of the king's cronies that existed independently from the rest of the Prussian administration), and replacing it with a Council of State of five ministers, made up of the heads of each of the Prussian administrative departments, who would deliberate with the king concerning legislative proposals. Any new decree, he argued, should be valid only if signed both by the king and by the members of the ministerial council. Laws would thus obtain their legitimacy not from the person of the monarch, but from the duly constituted administrative authorities of the state.[22] This scheme failed to win Frederick William III's sanction. Ultimately, however, the king agreed to a plan for a Council of State developed by Hardenberg in 1817. This plan created a larger council, which officially served in a purely advisory capacity. Other proposals for administrative reform met with similarly uneven results: Stein's municipal ordinance successfully reorganized the government of the towns while other measures, such as Hardenberg's Gendarmerie Edict of 1812, were blocked by aristocratic opposition.

More successful than these attempts at administrative reorganization were the efforts to create a new system of public education in Prussia. The leading

---

22   Ritter, *Stein*, pp. 145–55; Sheehan, *German History*, pp. 233–4, 297–8.

reformers held a highly idealistic vision of the potential of educational institutions to foster public-spiritedness and the capacity for self-rule among the Prussian populace. Stein, for example, argued in 1808 that the schools' mission should be to provide a 'uniform national education' (*Nationalbildung*), which would reinvigorate the state.[23] Johann Wilhelm Süvern, who designed the new system of Prussian primary schools (*Volksschulen*), argued that universal public schooling would help form Prussia into 'an organism (*Organismus*) in which each of society's components, province, nobleman, vassal, or locality, is allowed to develop its life [while] allowing at the same time these components to grow together into a unified whole'.[24] The schools, he argued, should foster the 'general education of humanity' (*allgemeinen Bildung des Menschen*) through the 'education of the nation and the youth'.[25] This goal was to be attained not through narrow occupational training, but rather through a broader programme of humanistic learning. Up through the 1820s, the methods of the Swiss educational reformer, Pestalozzi, served as the pedagogical model for the Prussian elementary schools. Pestalozzi, whose work was applauded by Stein, Süvern and other leading reformers, encouraged spontaneous and independent enquiry by students, and emphasized the intimate link between the formation of intellect and character.

Ultimately, the results of public education were more prosaic than anticipated by the high-flown rhetoric of these memoranda: it is questionable to what extent the public schools of this era contributed to the formation of patriotism and generosity of spirit among their pupils. Moreover, beginning in the 1820s, the government mandated a more conservative pedagogical approach that was intended to reinforce class barriers, rather than to forge a unified nation. None the less, the reformers' commitment to the project of 'national education' had important consequences for nineteenth-century Prussia. During the Napoleonic era, for example, Wilhelm von Humboldt designed plans for the new University of Berlin, as well as for a system of academic high schools (*Gymnasien*) to train the country's intellectual elite. Prussia was among the first European countries to develop a centralized, state-run network of schools for its youth, and during the nineteenth century its educational system became a model for the Western world. By the 1840s, over 80 per cent of Prussian children between the ages of 6 and 14

---

23  'Proklamation an sämtliche Bewohner des preußischen Staates', 21 October 1808; quoted in Franzjörg Baumgart, *Zwischen Reform und Reaktion: Preußische Schulpolitik 1806–1859* (Darmstadt, 1990), p. 35.

24  'Promemoria' to Süvern's draft of an educational reform bill, 1819; quoted in Karl A. Schleunes, 'Enlightenment, reform, reaction: the schooling revolution in Prussia', *Central European History* 12 (1979), 315–42.

25  Draft of the School Reform Bill of 1819, quoted in Baumgart, *Preußische Schulpolitik*, p. 79.

were attending primary schools – a figure greater than for any other contemporary society, with the exception of Saxony and parts of Scotland and New England.

For Stein, Hardenberg and their compatriots, the linchpin of the Reform Movement was intended to be the establishment of a constitution. By creating a 'national representation', they hoped to forge an indissoluble bond between the nation and its king, thus encouraging the formation of patriotic spirit and social harmony. Their vision of the precise character of the new representative institutions, however, evolved only gradually during the Napoleonic era. For both Stein and Hardenberg, Prussia's fiscal crisis provided the immediate motivation for developing plans for parliamentary institutions. Under the terms of the Treaty of Tilsit of 1807, Prussia risked losing its independence if it fell behind in its war-tribute payments to France. This condition created tremendous pressure for the mobilization of the financial resources of the Prussian monarchy. Already in 1808, Stein convened a representative assembly in the province of East Prussia in order to secure approval for a new income tax, as well as to guarantee mortgages on lands from the royal domains. Stein's immediate successors, Altenstein and Dohna, (who headed the Prussian ministry for eighteen months after Stein's resignation in 1808) subsequently convened representative assemblies in the provinces of Brandenburg and Pomerania as well. The record of these assemblies was mixed: while the East Prussian representatives approved both the income tax and the mortgage guarantees, the delegates from Brandenburg's Kurmark fiercely resisted each of these measures. Ultimately, the government was forced to implement some of its new financial measures against the objections of the provincial assemblies. Other plans, such as the creation of an income tax throughout the Prussian realm, were simply abandoned.

The leading reformers initially viewed the role of popular representation in highly restrictive terms. In a letter to the king of 1810, for example, Hardenberg advocated establishing a new central representative assembly that would serve 'as an organ of Your Royal Majesty': it would 'communicate the results of Your resolutions to the estates, representing those plans . . . as acceptable and as capable of fulfilling the goal; thus awakening patriotism and zeal for the salvation of the Fatherland'.[26] The king himself would appoint the delegates, and they would serve in a purely advisory role. This assembly, in other words, was not intended to represent the people to the king, but rather to represent the king's policies to the people, thus facilitating their execution.

---

26 'Auszug aus dem Finanzplan Hardenbergs', 28 May 1810, in Hubatsch and Botzenhart, *Stein*, iii, p. 376.

Ironically, even though the experimental representative assemblies Hardenberg created during the Napoleonic era obstructed many of his plans for social reform, he steadily broadened his vision of the rightful role of popular representation. During his last years as chancellor, from 1815 until his death in 1822, Hardenberg argued increasingly stridently for the establishment of a constitution in Prussia. He by now favoured not only the formation of an elective central representative assembly, but one which would have a deciding vote over legislation involving taxation and government debt. Indeed, Hardenberg backed his pro-constitutional rhetoric with actions: one of his last major legislative accomplishments, the State Debt Law of January 1820, ultimately contributed to the outbreak of the Prussian Revolution of 1848. This law required the monarch to obtain the consent of the estates of the realm (*Reichsstände*) in order to contract any new state debts. Thus in 1847, seeking funds to build a Berlin–Königsberg railway, Frederick William IV was forced to convene the estates of the realm.

Hardenberg's arguments on behalf of a constitution were among the clearest expressions of enlightened nationalist thought by a Prussian statesman. His proposed constitution, he claimed in a letter of 1820 to the king, would be '*truly* liberal, and yet would fully safeguard the monarchical principle and the power of the sovereign'.[27] In other words, Hardenberg envisioned a fundamentally harmonious relationship between the monarch and the representative assembly. Because the representatives and the king would co-operate in serving the public good, he argued, a parliamentary assembly need not infringe on the political supremacy of the monarch.[28]

The king's reactions to Hardenberg, on the other hand, demonstrated the limits of enlightened nationalism in Prussia. Though Hardenberg was long the most trusted adviser of Frederick William III, the king never overcame his suspicions toward parliamentary institutions. In October 1810, Frederick William published an edict promising to give 'the nation an appropriately arranged representation, both in the provinces and for the whole, whose counsel we will gladly use'.[29] Though the king would repeat this promise several times – in decrees published in 1811, 1815 and 1820 – he ultimately decided that such a plan was ill-advised. In his view, and in the

---

27 Hardenberg to Frederick William III, 10 October 1820, Geheimes Staatsarchiv Preußischer Kulturbesitz, Brandenburg-Preußisches Hausarchiv, Rep. 192, Wittgenstein, V, 6, Nr 4, Bl. 82.

28 On the evolution of Hardenberg's constitutional theory, see Matthew Levinger, 'Hardenberg, Wittgenstein, and the constitutional question in Prussia, 1815–22', *German History* 8 (1990), 257–77.

29 Ernst Rudolf Huber (ed.), *Dokumente zur deutschen Verfassungsgeschichte*, 3rd edn (Stuttgart, 1978), i, p. 46.

view of an increasingly vocal conservative faction within the Prussian court, a central representative assembly would be more likely to jeopardize than to enhance the authority of the monarch. Fearing that the establishment of such an assembly would open the floodgates of revolution, Frederick William III rejected his chancellor's pleas on behalf of a Prussian constitution.

## Legacies of enlightened nationalism

In discussing the power of myths in history, the cultural critic Roland Barthes once wrote:

> Myth does not deny things, on the contrary, its function is to talk about them . . . it gives them a natural and eternal justification, it gives them a clarity which is not that of an explanation but that of a statement of fact . . . . In passing from history to nature, myth acts economically: it abolishes the complexity of human acts, it gives them the simplicity of essences.[30]

For many Prussians during the Napoleonic era, the idea of the 'nation' became just such a myth, in Barthes' sense of the word. Members of Prussia's political elite came to see the nation as a natural and obvious form of political community. Moreover, they attributed to the nation certain distinctive characteristics, which reflected both Prussia's eighteenth-century cultural heritage and the particular challenges of the struggle against Napoleon. The nation, they argued, was an ideally harmonious and rational community; it was a band of citizens striving, in concert with the king, for the attainment of the common good.

As a myth, the 'nation' also became a rallying-point for political action. The reformers agreed that an enlightened national community did not yet exist in Prussia, and that it still needed to be forged. (They generally avoided specifying whether the 'nation' should comprise all of German-speaking Europe rather than Prussia alone, partly because they wanted to pitch their appeals as broadly as possible without openly challenging the autonomy of the other German states.) The present chapter has explored various dimensions of the programme by which these figures sought to realize this ideal. For example, the Stein–Hardenberg party agreed that universal freedom was an indispensable prerequisite for the creation of a patriotic citizenry. Measures such as Stein's October Edict and Hardenberg's free trade

---

30  Roland Barthes, *Mythologies* (New York, 1972), p. 143.

legislation enshrined into law the principles of legal and economic freedom. (In practice, however, these decrees had mixed effects: for example, the unfavourable terms of the legislation liberating Prussia's serfs contributed to the growth of a class of landless and impoverished agricultural labourers.) The reformers' social legislation also weakened the hereditary boundaries between Prussia's traditional corporate groups, for example by allowing commoners to purchase aristocratic properties. But these laws stopped short of establishing full civil equality in Prussia, which would have required the abolition of the aristocracy and the other traditional estates. Stein and Hardenberg, in other words, sought to balance old hierarchical social principles with the new egalitarian ideals of the revolutionary era. They strove to redefine the foundations of the Prussian social order without provoking any sudden social upheaval – and to a great extent, they succeeded in these efforts.

Stein and Hardenberg's attempts at political reform proved more problematic than their social legislation. King Frederick William III rejected Stein's initial proposals for restructuring the Prussian administration, believing that it would excessively restrict monarchical authority. Likewise, the king remained sceptical towards Hardenberg's claims that it would be possible to infuse 'democratic' elements into the monarchical state without undermining royal power. Frederick William's fears about the destabilizing potential of parliamentary institutions escalated during the decade after Napoleon's final defeat in 1815. He and his conservative advisers were troubled by the spread of a boisterous movement for national unification among German students, as well as by the outbreak of a wave of revolutions across Southern Europe during the year 1820. Frederick William became convinced that the establishment of a constitution would result in irresistible revolutionary pressures in Prussia as well.

Even though Hardenberg's efforts on behalf of a Prussian constitution ended in failure, the torch of enlightened nationalism was carried on by subsequent liberal intellectuals and political activists. In large part, the political conflicts between 'progressives' and 'reactionaries' in Prussia after 1815 reflected the clash between two myths: on the one hand, the liberal myth of the enlightened nation, and on the other hand, the conservative myth of the revolutionary nation. According to the supporters of constitutional rule, the establishment of parliamentary institutions would result in harmonious co-operation between a sovereign nation and a sovereign king. According to opponents of a constitution, a politically active nation would inevitably unleash chaos, overthrowing the king and destroying the existing social order.

Thus, during the early nineteenth century in Prussia, both liberals and conservatives came to harbour highly exaggerated visions of the potentialities of 'national' politics: the liberal vision was excessively utopian, while the conservative vision was excessively apocalyptic. Almost wholly missing from the rhetoric of both liberals and conservatives was a realistic assessment of the practical workings of power within the parliamentary state.[31] By proclaiming the inviolability of monarchical sovereignty, liberals in particular found themselves in a rhetorical bind. They found it difficult to justify the formation of a 'loyal opposition', as was traditional in England and elsewhere. The ideal of political harmony also may have inhibited the formation of a pluralistic system of party politics in Prussia, by reducing political activists' tolerance for frank differences of opinion.

The rise of enlightened nationalism had both positive and negative consequences for Prussian political culture. On the one hand, it encouraged an admirable commitment to forging 'public spirit' through the liberalization of social institutions, the establishment of national schooling and the rationalization of government. On the other hand, it resulted in a marked tendency to *avoid* or *suppress* internal political conflict. The demand for consensus and harmony between the nation and its rulers contributed to the rigidification of Prussian political life. The expectation of harmony may also have encouraged the search for scapegoats who could be held responsible for any existing disharmony within the national community – witness, for example, Bismarck's blistering diatribes against the 'red menace' and the Jews later in the nineteenth century.[32] A viable system of parliamentary rule depends on a healthy measure of tolerance for imperfection and internal strife. The Prussian reformers of the Napoleonic era, for the most part, lacked this tolerance. Ironically, their very optimism about the perfectibility of the nation may have become a key obstacle to the establishment of effective institutions for popular self-rule.

---

31  On this point, see James J. Sheehan, *German Liberalism in the Nineteenth Century* (Chicago, 1978), pp. 59–78, 95–118.
32  See, for example, Hans-Ulrich Wehler, *The German Empire 1871–1918* (Leamington Spa, 1985), pp. 95–6.

Wherever possible, prominence is given to works in English, though foreign-language books and articles are cited when they are of particular importance or where no titles in English can be given.

# 1. Prussia in history and historiography from the eighteenth to the nineteenth century

On the burgher identity of early modern Prussians in Royal Prussia, see Karin Friedrich, *The Other Prussia. Royal Prussia, Poland and Liberty, 1569–1772* (Cambridge, 2000). Specifically on the historiography of Gottfried Lengnich, see David Bell, Ludmila Pimenova and Stephane Pujol (eds), *Eighteenth Century Research. Universal Reason and National Culture During the Enlightenment* (Paris, 1999), pp. 11–29. On eighteenth-century Prussian historiography, see Johannes Schultze, *Die Mark Brandenburg*, vol. 1 (Berlin, 1961), pp. 7–13, as well as Reinhold Koser, 'Umschau auf dem Gebiet der brandenburgisch-preußischen Geschichtsforschung', *Forschungen zur Brandenburgischen und Preußischen Geschichte* 1 (1888), 1–56. Specifically on Berlin historiography, see Reimer Hansen and Wolfgang Ribbe (eds), *Geschichtswissenschaft in Berlin im 19. und 20. Jahrhundert: Persönlichkeiten und Institutionen* (Berlin, 1992). Of seminal importance on the changing perceptions of Prussia and Prussian history is Otto Büsch and Wolfgang Neugebauer (eds), *Moderne Preußische Geschichte 1648–1947. Eine Anthologie*, 3 vols (Berlin, 1981). See also Otto Büsch (ed.), *Das Preußenbild in der Geschichte. Protokoll eines Symposiums* (Berlin, 1981); Dirk Blasius (ed.), *Preußen in der deutschen Geschichte* (Königstein/Ts., 1980). On the nationality conflict in Prussia starting with Frederick II's anti-Polish measures, see W. W. Hagen, *Germans, Poles and Jews. The Nationality Conflict in the Prussian East 1772–1914* (Chicago, IL, 1981). Also Gerard Labuda, 'The Slavs in Nineteenth-Century German Historiography', *Polish Western Affairs* 10 (1969), 177–234. On the reception of the French Revolution in mainstream Prussian historiography, see Monika Voelker, *Die Auseinandersetzung mit der französischen Revolution in der Geschichtsschreibung der 'kleindeutschen Schule'* (Egelsbach, 1993). On Droysen, see Robert Southard, *Droysen and the Prussian School of History* (Lexington, KY, 1995).

# 2. Frederick William I and the beginnings of Prussian absolutism, 1713–1740

In contrast to the abundant literature on Frederick William I's son and successor, Frederick the Great, there are a limited number of studies in English dealing with Frederick William I. Most promote the traditional view that Brandenburg-Prussia is the prime example of a strong early modern state typifying the kind of professional government that reached its peak in the enlightened absolutist eighteenth century. Such studies conclude that Frederick William I's attempts to establish his authority were successful. In other words, the king won a notable victory over the selfish and blinkered territorial elites that was a natural consequence of the struggle between central government pitched against provincial authority. This view contends that because Frederick William I believed he needed to establish order and thus increase Hohenzollern authority in the territories, he in turn reduced the scope of provincial authority and interests. On Frederick William I, there currently exists only one biography, a popular and overly simplistic account, Robert Reinhold Ergang's *The Potsdam Führer: Frederick William I, Father of Prussian Militarism* (New York, 1941).

Nevertheless, one is able to piece together a more comprehensive (but mostly traditional) account of Frederick William I using more specialized studies that have been published in the English language. The attention to formal structures, a trademark of the traditional interpretations, is exemplified by Reinhold Dorwart, whose studies primarily cover the administrative history of Frederick William I: Reinhold August Dorwart, *The Administrative Reforms of Frederick William I of Prussia* (Cambridge, MA, 1953) and *The Prussian Welfare State before 1740* (Cambridge, MA, 1971). Dorwart's studies are, in reality, a summation of the traditional German literature and uncritically incorporate its perspectives. Dorwart's work, in particular his first book, remains among the most comprehensive examinations of this period of Brandenburg-Prussian history in any language and is certainly the best-known to an English-language readership. Another influential historian, Hans Rosenberg, has also placed particular emphasis upon the formal structures of government and power as they relate to the social composition of administrators. Rosenberg's *Bureaucracy, Aristocracy and Autocracy: The Prussian Experience 1660–1815* (Cambridge, MA, 1958) has contributed greatly to the debate surrounding the notion of Germany's unique development, or

*Sonderweg.* Rosenberg differs from the work of Dorwart in that he suggests that officials continued to dominate the administration and operation of Hohenzollern government throughout the eighteenth century, rather than being subsumed in a bureaucratic Leviathan.

For Frederick William I and the military, see the recently translated study, Otto Büsch, *Military System and Social Life in Old Regime Prussia, 1713– 1807: The Beginnings of the Social Militarization of Prusso-German Society* (New Jersey, 1997). Büsch demonstrates the impact of the elite and the military as a significant component in the operation of government in this period and an important dimension of the development of society in the Brandenburg-Prussian state.

A recent study of the territorial elite, which breaks from the traditional interpretation, is found in Edgar Melton's chapter, 'The Prussian Junkers, 1600–1786', in H. M. Scott (ed.), *The European Nobilities in the Seventeenth and Eighteenth Centuries. Volume Two: Northern, Central and Eastern Europe* (New York/ London, 1995), pp. 71–109. A more traditional study is Francis Ludwig Carsten's *A History of the Prussian Junkers* (Aldershot, 1989). Carsten has also written a more general article on Frederick William I, 'Prussian Despotism at its Height', *History* 40 (1955), 42–67.

On the peasantry, see Edgar Melton's chapter in this volume as well as the following: William W. Hagen, 'Working for the Junker: The Standard of Living of Manorial Laborers in Brandenburg, 1584–1810', *Journal of Modern History* 58 (1986), 143–58 as well as [id.,] 'Seventeenth-Century Crisis in Brandenburg: The Thirty Years' War, the Destabilization of Serfdom, and the Rise of Absolutism', *American Historical Review* 94 (1989), 302–35.

In addition to Christopher Clark's chapter on Pietism in this volume, the following studies emphasize religion: Mary Fulbrook, *Piety and Politics: Religion and the Rise of Absolutism in England, Württemberg and Prussia* (Cambridge, 1983); Richard L. Gawthrop, *Pietism and the Making of Eighteenth-Century Prussia* (Cambridge, 1993); and Mack Walker, *The Salzburg Transaction: Expulsion and Redemption in Eighteenth-Century Germany* (Ithaca, NY, 1992).

A study of education and its relationship to Hohenzollern absolutism in this period can be found in James Van Horn Melton's book, *Absolutism and the Eighteenth-Century Origins of Compulsory Schooling in Prussia and Austria* (Cambridge, 1988). Finally, two case studies that emphasize the more informal structures of government include: Rodney Gothelf, 'Absolutism in Action: Frederick William I and the Government of East Prussia, 1709– 1730' (Ph.D. dissertation, University of St Andrews, 1998); and James Leonard Roth, 'The East Prussian *Domänenpächter* in the Eighteenth Century: A Study of Collective Social Mobility' (Ph.D. dissertation, University of California, 1979).

# 3. Piety, politics and society: Pietism in eighteenth-century Prussia

R. L. Gawthrop, *Pietism and the Making of Eighteenth-Century Prussia* (Cambridge, 1993) offers a stimulating outline history of the movement's Prussian variant and links it with key transformations in state policy and structure during the reigns of Frederick III/I and Frederick William I. The central thesis is controversial, but this is the best English-language account of the movement in Prussia and contains an excellent bibliography. Also important is M. Fulbrook, *Piety and Politics. Religion and the Rise of Absolutism in England, Württemberg and Prussia* (Cambridge, 1983); this study sets Prussian Pietism within a comparative framework and draws out some of its distinctive characteristics. F. E. Stoeffler, *Pietism in Germany During the Eighteenth Century* (Leiden, 1973) is still of some use as a general introduction to the Pietist movement in the German states. For the neo-Pietist revival in Prussia, readers are referred to R. M. Bigler, *The Politics of Prussian Protestantism. The Rise of the Protestant Church Elite in Prussia 1815–1848* (Berkeley, CA, 1972); H. Lehmann, 'Pietism and Nationalism: the relationship between Protestant Revivalism and National Renewal in nineteenth-century Germany', *Church History* 51 (1982), 39–53; C. M. Clark, 'The Politics of Revival. Pietists, Aristocrats and the State Church in Early Nineteenth-Century Prussia', in J. Retallack and L. E. Jones (eds), *Between Reform, Reaction and Resistance. Studies in the History of German Conservatism from 1789 to 1945* (Providence, RI/Oxford, 1993), pp. 31–60.

The German-language historiography on the Pietist movement is vast. For general orientation, readers are referred to the periodical *Pietismus und Neuzeit*, which publishes recent work on the movement and reviews a sample of current publications. Among the many works on Pietism in Prussia, the most important include: C. Hinrichs, *Preußentum und Pietismus. Der Pietismus in Brandenburg-Preußen als religiös-soziale Reformbewegung* (Göttingen, 1971) – this classic study is packed with arresting insights and continues to stimulate new research; K. Deppermann, *Der Hallesche Pietismus und der preußische Staat unter Friedrich III. (I.)* (Göttingen, 1961); id., 'Die politischen Voraussetzungen für die Etablierung des Pietismus in Brandenburg-Preußen', *Pietismus und Neuzeit* 12 (1986), 38–53 – Deppermann has done more than any other scholar to reconstruct the political context of Halle Pietism. On Philipp Jakob Spener, see especially J. Wallmann, *Philipp Jakob Spener und die Anfänge des Pietismus* (Tübingen, 1970); an excellent outline of the historiography on Spener (with a useful bibliography) is M. Brecht, 'Philipp Jakob Spener. Sein programm und dessen Auswirkungen', in id. (ed.), *Geschichte des Pietismus*, vol. 1, *Der Pietismus vom 17. bis zum frühen 18. Jahrhundert* (Göttingen, 1993).

For a similar survey of the specialist literature on Francke and the Halle Orphanage, see M. Brecht, 'August Hermann Francke und der Hallesche Pietismus', in id. and K. Deppermann (eds), *Geschichte des Pietismus*, vol. 2, *Der Pietismus im 18. Jahrhundert* (Göttingen, 1995). On the Pietist mission to the Jews, see C. M. Clark, *The Politics of Conversion. Missionary Protestantism and the Jews in Prussia 1728–1941* (Oxford, 1995). A sample of recent research on this aspect of the Pietist movement and a helpful bibliography (compiled by Christoph Bochinger) may be found in W. Beltz (ed.), *Biographie und Religion – III. Internationales Callenberg-Kolloquium* (Hallesche Beiträge zur Orientwissenschaft, 24; Halle, 1997). On the impact of Pietism on schooling, see J. Van Horn Melton, *Absolutism and the Eighteenth-Century Origins of Compulsory Schooling in Prussia and Austria* (Cambridge, 1988), pp. 23–50 – the most important German works on the subject are listed in Melton's bibliography.

# 4. Prussia and the Enlightenment

Most of the literature deals with the Enlightenment in Germany, not specifically in Prussia; it seldom deals with the early Enlightenment, little of it is in English, and there is no one work that deals exclusively with the Enlightenment in Prussia. With these restrictions in mind, the following bibliography may be of some use.

Horst Möller, *Vernunft und Kritik. Deutsche Aufklärung im 17. und 18. Jahrhundert* (Frankfurt-am-Main, 1986) is an introduction to the Enlightenment in Germany as a whole with discussions about its origins, goals and institutions. It incorporates parts of Möller's earlier essay 'Wie aufgeklärt war Preußen?', in H. J. Puhle and H. U. Wehler (eds) *Preußen im Rückblick* (Göttingen, 1980), 176–200, which sees enlightened political consciousness anticipating the reform era in Prussia. The older, very readable work by Werner Schneiders, *Die wahre Aufklärung. Zur Selbstverständnis der deutschen Aufklärung* (Freiburg/ Munich, 1974), is philosophically oriented, discussing a series of Enlightenment thinkers and their major publications. Basic for the new, cultural interpretation of the Enlightenment is Hans Erich Bödeker, 'Aufklärung als Kommunikationsprozeß', *Aufklärung* 2, Heft 2 (1988), 89–111.

On the social stratum that mostly carried the Enlightenment, see the extensive discussion by Hans Erich Bödeker, 'Die "Gebildeten Stände" im späten 18. und frühen 19. Jahrhundert: Zugehörigkeit und Abgrenzungen, Mentalitäten und Handlungspotentiale', in Jürgen Kocka (ed.), *Deutsches Bildungsbürgertum im 19. Jahrhundert*, 4 vols (Stuttgart, 1989), iv, pp. 21–52. Another valuable essay on the authors of the Enlightenment is Rudolf

Vierhaus, 'Die aufgeklärten Schriftsteller: Zur sozialen Charakteristik einer selbsternannten Elite', in Hans Bödeker and Ulrich Hermann (eds), *Über den Prozeß der Aufklärung in Deutschland im 18. Jahrhundert* (Göttingen, 1987), pp. 53–65. Günter Birtsch highlights the role of the enlightened theologians in 'The Christian as Subject: The Worldly Mind of Prussian Protestant Theologians in the Late Enlightenment Period', in Eckhart Hellmuth (ed.), *The Transformation of Political Culture: England and Germany in the Late Eighteenth Century* (London, 1990), pp. 309–26. Insightful also is Anthony J. La Vopa, 'The Politics of Enlightenment: Friedrich Gedike and German Professional Ideology', *Journal of Modern History* 62 (1990), 34–56.

On the problem of the relationship between absolutism and Enlightenment, especially under Frederick II, see Günter Birtsch, 'Friedrich der Große und die Aufklärung', in Oswald Hauser (ed.), *Friedrich der Große in seiner Zeit* (Cologne/Vienna, 1987), pp. 31–46. Although critical of the concept of enlightened despotism, Birtsch is intrigued about the enlightened motivation of some of Frederick II's policies, especially in regard to his legal reforms. In another article, Birtsch described the 'ideal type' of the enlightened ruler: 'Der Idealtyp des aufgeklärten Herrschers', *Aufklärung* 2, Heft 1 (1987), 9–47. Birtsch now dismisses the term as conceptually flawed: 'Aufgeklärter Absolutismus oder Reformabsolutismus', *Aufklärung* 9, Heft 1 (1996), 101–9. Other historians still tend to accept the term unquestioningly. In his contribution to a volume on enlightened absolutism, the British historian Blanning conveniently lists the many arguments against the enlightened character of Frederick II's rule before defending the king's record on this score: T. C. W. Blanning, 'Frederick the Great and Enlightened Absolutism', in H. M. Scott (ed.), *Enlightened Absolutism. Reform and Reformers in Later Eighteenth-Century Europe* (Ann Arbor, MI, 1990), pp. 265–88, 367–72. In the introduction to this volume (pp. 1–35), the editor admits the limited explanatory power of the concept of enlightened absolutism for the reforming initiatives of this period but, like Blanning, still sees the use of it. C. B. A. Behrens, *Society, Government, and the Enlightenment. The Experience of Eighteenth-Century France and Prussia* (New York, 1985) is valuable for the comparison between France and Prussia. The author argues in the third part of the book that in neither country was the Enlightenment revolutionary, but that in fact it did undermine the existing political and social order.

Science and philosophy in the eighteenth century are discussed in Rudolf Vierhaus (ed.), *Wissenschaften im Zeitalter der Aufklärung* (Göttingen, 1985), with notable contributions on history, theology, medicine and mathematics, among others. There is no biography on Thomasius. The older English-language essay by Frederick M. Barnard, 'The "Practical Philosophy" of Christian Thomasius', *Journal of the History of Ideas* 32 (1971), 221–46 is a good introduction. A more recent volume discussing many aspects of

Thomasius's thought is Werner Schneiders (ed.), *Christian Thomasius (1655–1728). Interpretationen zu Werk und Wirkung* (Hamburg, 1989). The thought of Wolff can be accessed in another volume edited by Schneiders, *Christian Wolff (1679–1754). Interpretationen zu seiner Philosophie und derer Wirkung* (Hamburg, 1983). For both volumes, some background in German history and philosophy of the eighteenth century is recommended. Paul Guyer (ed.), *The Cambridge Companion to Kant* (Cambridge, 1992) offers convenient overviews of aspects of Kant's philosophy; for his moral philosophy, see J. B. Schneewind's contribution, 'Autonomy, Obligation and Virtue: An Overview of Kant's Ethics', pp. 309–41. For the historical context of Kant's moral and political philosophy in the 1780s and 1790s, see Steven Lestition, 'Kant and the End of the Enlightenment in Prussia', *Journal of Modern History* 65 (1993), 57–112.

Popular philosophy is thematized by Johan van der Zande, 'In the Image of Cicero: German Philosophy Between Wolff and Kant', *Journal of the History of Ideas* 56 (1995), 419–42. Horst Möller wrote an extensive volume on a central figure of the Prussian Enlightenment with much on the Enlightenment besides: *Aufklärung in Preußen: der Verleger, Publizist und Geschichtsschreiber Friedrich Nicolai* (Berlin, 1974). The recent monograph by David Sorkin, *Moses Mendelssohn and the Religious Enlightenment* (Berkeley, CA, 1996), is an excellent work on Mendelssohn's person and thought. The Enlightenment from a religious (Jewish, Protestant and Catholic) perspective is covered by Karlfried Gründer and Nathan Rotenstreich (eds), *Aufklärung und Haskalah in jüdischer und nichtjüdischer Sicht* (Heidelberg, 1990).

Enlightenment sociability is a new theme in the historiography on the Enlightenment. For an overview of the many different societies, see Ulrich Im Hof, *Das Gesellige Jahrhundert: Gesellschaft und Gesellschaften im Zeitalter der Aufklärung* (Munich, 1982). A fine essay that shows the importance of the coffee house for Enlightenment sociability is Hans Erich Bödeker's 'Das Kaffeehaus als Institution aufklärerischer Geselligkeit', in Etienne François (ed.), *Sociabilité et société bourgeoise en France, Allemagne et en Suisse, 1750–1850* (Paris, 1987), pp. 65–80. The ambiguous relationship between Freemasonry and the Enlightenment is discussed by Rudolf Vierhaus, 'Aufklärung und Freimauerei in Deutschland', in Helmut Reinalter (ed.), *Freimaurer und Geheimbünde in 18. Jahrhundert in Mitteleuropa* (Frankfurt-am-Main, 1983), pp. 115–39.

The emergence of a public sphere as the main product of the Enlightenment is increasingly discussed, both on a general level and on that of individual thinkers. The basic theoretical study is Jürgen Habermas, *The Structural Transformation of the Public Sphere*, tr. Thomas Bürger (Cambridge, MA, 1989). Hans Erich Bödeker, besides his article mentioned in the second paragraph of this section ('Aufklärung als Kommunikationsprozeß'), has written more specifically on this theme in his 'Journal and Public Opinion: The Politicization of the German Enlightenment in the Second Half of the Eighteenth Century'. In his 'Enlightened Societies in the Metropolis: The Case of Berlin', Horst Möller describes some of the societies mentioned in this chapter and their fashioning of public opinion. Both essays appeared in Eckhart Hellmuth (ed.), *The Transformation of Political Culture. England and Germany in the Late Eighteenth Century* (London, 1990), pp. 423–45 and 219–33 respectively. For Kant's thought on public opinion and its possible politically subversive implications, see John C. Laursen, 'Kant's Politics of Publicity', *History of Political Thought* 10 (1989), 99–133. The popular philosopher Thomas Abbt envisioned the public not as readers, but as belonging to a fatherland or as those who contributed to the common good, as explained by Benjamin W. Redekop, 'Thomas Abbt and the Formation of an Enlightened German "Public"', *Journal of the History of Ideas* 58 (1997), 81–104.

The debate on 'What is Enlightenment?' is now available in the English anthology by James Schmidt (ed.), *What is Enlightenment? Eighteenth-Century Answers and Twentieth-Century Questions* (Berkeley & Los Angeles, CA/ London, 1996) with English translations of (among others) Kant's and Mendelssohn's answers and many other contributions by present-day historians and philosophers; the volume has a select bibliography for further reading. Eckhart Hellmuth gives a good picture of the debates in the Wednesday Club in his 'Aufklärung und Pressefreiheit: Zur Debatte der Berliner Mittwochgesellschaft während der Jahre 1783 und 1784', *Zeitschrift für historische Forschung* 9 (1982), 316–45. Günter Birtsch weighs some of the arguments of the debate in his 'Religions- und Gewissensfreiheit in Preussen von 1780 bis 1817', *Zeitschrift für historische Forschung* 11 (1984), 177–204.

# 5. The transformation of the rural economy in East Elbian Prussia, 1750–1830

The primary goal of this section is to direct the reader to important works in English that deal with Prussian agrarian history in our period. Since, however, footnotes have been kept to a minimum, it is appropriate to begin with a few comments on the most important works in German. Georg Friedrich Knapp's *Die Bauernbefreiung und der Ursprung der Landarbeiter in den älteren Teilen Preußens*, 2 vols (Leipzig, 1887) remains the most influential work on Prussian agrarian history in the eighteenth century and the agrarian reforms of the early nineteenth century. Although still indispensable for any serious study of these themes, Knapp's study, by focusing on the most disadvantaged part of the peasantry – the 25 per cent who did not own their own farmsteads – presented a negative assessment of the Prussian agrarian reforms that persists today. Fortunately, several recent studies have corrected Knapp's overly negative assessment. Most important here is the work by Hartmut Harnisch, *Kapitalistische Agrarreform und industrielle Revolution* (Weimar, 1984), a major achievement. Also important are two shorter studies: Hanna Schissler, *Preußische Agrargesellschaft im Wandel* (Göttingen, 1978); and Rudolph Berthold, 'Die Veränderungen im Bodeneigentum und in der Zahl der Bauernstellen, der Kleinstellen und der Rittergüter in der preußischen Provinzen Sachsen, Brandenburg, und Pommern während der Durchführung der Agrarreform des 19. Jahrhunderts', in *Studien zu den Agrarreformen des 19. Jahrhunderts in Preußen und Rußland* (Jahrbuch für Wirtschaftsgeschichte, Sonderband) (Berlin, 1978), pp. 7–116.

The following discussion of works in English does not attempt a comprehensive review of the literature, but rather directs the reader to recent works that I found essential in writing this chapter. On the problem of *Gutsherrschaft*, the most important work is William Hagen's 'Seventeenth Century Crisis in Brandenburg: the Thirty Years' War, the Destabilization of Serfdom, and the Rise of Absolutism', *American Historical Review* 94 (1989), 302–35. Also useful are three articles by Edgar Melton: 'Gutsherrschaft in East Elbian Germany and Livonia, 1500–1800', *Central European History* 21 (1988), 315–49; 'The Decline of Prussian Gutsherrschaft and the Rise of the Junker as Rural Patron, 1750–1806', *German History* 12 (1994), 334–50; and 'Population Structure, the Market Economy, and the Transformation of Gutsherrschaft in East Central Europe, 1650–1800', *German History* 16 (1998), 297–327.

On the Prussian nobility, there is a survey by Edgar Melton, 'The Prussian Junkers, 1600–1786', in Hamish Scott (ed.), *The European Nobilities in the Seventeenth and Eighteenth Century*, 2 vols (London, 1995), ii, pp. 71–111. The most important monograph on the nobility is Robert M. Berdahl's *The Politics of the Prussian Nobility. The Development of a Conservative Ideology, 1770–1848* (Princeton, NJ, 1988), especially pp. 107–57 for an excellent discussion of the Prussian agrarian reforms.

On the Prussian peasants and agricultural labourers, the following works by William Hagen are unsurpassed: 'Village Life in East-Elbian Germany and Poland, 1400–1800: Subjection, Self-Defence, Survival', in Tom Scott (ed.), *The Peasantries of Europe from the Fourteenth to the Eighteenth Centuries* (London, 1998), pp. 227–68; 'The Junkers' Faithless Servants: Peasant Insubordination and the Breakdown of Serfdom in Brandenburg-Prussia, 1763–1811', in Richard J. Evans and W. R. Lee (eds), *The German Peasantry: Conflict and Community in Rural Society from the Eighteenth to the Twentieth Century* (London, 1986), pp. 71–101; and, finally, 'Working for the Junker: the Standard of Living of Manorial Workers in Brandenburg, 1584–1810', *Journal of Modern*

*History* 58 (1986), 143–58. Also useful is Robert A. Dickler, 'Organization and Change in Productivity in East Prussia', in William Parker and Eric Jones (eds), *European Peasants and their Markets* (Princeton, NJ, 1973), pp. 273–89.

In addition to the above-mentioned work by Robert Berdahl, two other studies offer useful perspectives on the agrarian reforms. Jerome Blum's *The End of the Old Order in Rural Europe* (Princeton, NJ, 1978) is a comparative study that devotes considerable attention to Prussia. John Gagliardo's *From Pariah to Patriot: The Changing Image of the German Peasant, 1770–1840* (Lexington, KY, 1969) also devotes considerable attention to the Prussian peasants in his study of the transformation of elite perceptions of the rural population.

# 6. The development of the Prussian town, 1720–1815

There are no recent comprehensive treatments of this topic, and there is little that is useful in English. Comparative studies on German urban history usually focus on the south-western Holy Roman Empire, although some include chapters on Brandenburg or Prussian towns, such as Volker Press (ed.), *Städtewesen und Merkantilismus in Mitteleuropa* (Cologne/Vienna, 1983), Walter Rausch (ed.), *Die Städte Mitteleuropas im 17. und 18. Jahrhundert* (Linz, 1981), and Wilfried Ehbrecht (ed.), *Verwaltung und Politik in den Städten Mitteleuropas* (Cologne/Vienna/Weimar, 1994). The best and most recent survey of literature on Brandenburg towns is provided by Brigitte Meier in Ralf Pröve and Bernd Kölling (eds), *Leben und Arbeiten auf märkischem Sand; Wege in die Gesellschaftsgeschichte Brandenburgs, 1700–1914* (Bielefeld, 1999). The history of Brandenburg towns is set in a wider territorial context in Ingrid Materna and Wolfgang Ribbe, *Brandenburgische Geschichte* (Berlin, 1995). A useful Polish survey of the development of towns and cities in Polish Prussia (West Prussia), Ducal Prussia and Western and Eastern Pomerania is given in G. Labuda *et al.* (eds), *Historia Pomorza*, vol. II (2): 1675–1815 (Poznań, 1984).

A more specific focus on Polish Prussia and East Prussia is provided in the detailed demographic and economic analysis of East and West Prussian towns by Thomas Lewerenz, *Die Größenentwicklung der Kleinstädte in Ost- und Westpreußen bis zm Ende des 18. Jahrhunderts im Rahmen der Stadtgrößen in Ostdeutschland* (Marburg, 1976). Max Bär's *Westpreußen unter Friedrich dem Großen*, 2 vols (Leipzig, 1907), on the integration of Polish Prussia into the Prussian state under Frederick II, is still a classic, mainly because it includes a volume with primary sources. Although there is a large body of older German and recent Polish literature on Polish Prussian towns, the only works on the eighteenth century in English are Edmund Cieślak's *History of Gdańsk* (Gdańsk, 1995) and Karin Friedrich's *The Other Prussia. Royal Prussia, Poland and Liberty, 1569–1772* (Cambridge, 2000), which focuses on Danzig, Thorn and Elbing. Histories of specific cities in the Hohenzollern territories in this period are numerous, but again, not available in English (see footnotes in the chapter). The only recent history of Königsberg is a work in Polish by Janusz Jasiński, *Historia Królewca. Szkice z XIII–XX stulecia* (Olsztyn, 1994). Good comprehensive treatments of the history of Berlin are provided by Wolfgang Ribbe's *Geschichte Berlins*, 2 vols (Berlin, 1988) and Helga Schultz, *Berlin 1650–1800. Sozialgeschichte einer Residenz* (Berlin, 1987). The problems of the garrison town of Potsdam are discussed in the collection of articles by Bernhard Kröner (ed.), *Potsdam. Stadt, Armee, Residenz in der preußisch-deutschen Militärgeschichte* (Frankfurt-am-Main/Berlin, 1993).

Excellent recent contributions on the reform period in Brandenburg-Prussia are Ralf Pröve's article on the Städteordnung of 1808 in W. Neugebauer and R. Pröve (eds), *Agrarische Verfassung und politische Struktur. Studien zur Gesellschaftsgeschichte Preußens 1700–1918* (Berlin, 1998) and a piece by Ilja Mieck in Bernd Sösemann (ed.), *Gemeingeist und Bürgersinn. Die preußischen Reformen* (Berlin, 1993).

The development of industries in some of the border territories of the Hohenzollern state is covered by Hans Kisch, 'The Textile Industries in Silesia and the Rhineland: a comparative study in industrialisation', in Peter Kriedte, Hanns Medick and Jürgen Schlumbohm (eds), *Industrialisation before Industrialisation* (Cambridge, 1981) and William O. Henderson, *The State and the Industrial Revolution in Prussia, 1740–1870* (Liverpool, 1958). Silesian towns have not yet been studied comprehensively, but there are several case-studies, and useful information can be gleaned from Peter Baumgart's article on the 1740 annexation of Silesia, in Mark Greengrass (ed.), *Conquest and Coalescence: the shaping of the state in early modern Europe* (London, 1991), even though it follows a rather old-fashioned model of 'absolutism'.

# 7. Prussia's emergence as a European great power, 1740–1763

The wider context is provided by chs 1, 7 and 8 of the vintage study of W. L. Dorn, *Competition for Empire, 1740–1763* (New York, 1940), still the best portrait of Europe at mid-century, and by Derek McKay and H. M. Scott, *The Rise of the Great Powers, 1648–1815* (London, 1983), ch. 6. An up-to-date military introduction can be found in ch. 8 of Peter H. Wilson, *German Armies: War and German Politics 1648–1815* (London, 1998). H. M. Scott,

'Prussia's Royal Foreign Minister: Frederick the Great and the administration of Prussian diplomacy', in Robert Oresko, G. C. Gibbs and H. M. Scott (eds), *Royal and Republican Sovereignty in early modern Europe* (Cambridge, 1997) examines the creation of absolute royal control over diplomacy and its operation throughout the reign. The most authoritative modern biography, written in 'structural' style, is Theodor Schieder, *Frederick the Great* (London, 2000), which provides a penetrating commentary on Prussia's emergence as a great power, while a convincing study of Frederick's personality is provided by Gerhard Ritter, *Frederick the Great* (Engl. trans. London, 1968). The introduction by D. B. Horn, *Frederick the Great and the Rise of Prussia* (London, 1964) remains a clear and fair-minded account of Prussia's diplomatic impact upon Europe. Two studies of the 1740s have recently appeared: M. S. Anderson, *The War of the Austrian Succession, 1740–1748* (London, 1995) is more wide-ranging and authoritative, while Reed Browning, *The War of the Austrian Succession* (New York, 1993) contains much important detail. The best study of Prussian government, despite its Prussophilic tone, is Walther Hubatsch, *Frederick the Great: Absolutism and Administration* (London, 1975), while there is a valuable article by Peter Baumgart, 'The Annexation and Integration of Silesia into the Prussian State of Frederick the Great', in Mark Greengrass (ed.), *Conquest and Coalescence: the shaping of the state in early modern Europe* (London, 1991). W. Mediger, 'Great Britain, Hanover and the Rise of Prussia', in Ragnhild Hatton and M. S. Anderson (eds), *Studies in Diplomatic History* (London, 1970) examines one reaction to Prussia's rise during the 1740s. Frederick's own analysis of the emergence of his state and its implications is contained in his 1752 Political Testament, an English translation of parts of which can be found in C. A. Macartney (ed.), *The Habsburg and Hohenzollern Dynasties in the seventeenth and eighteenth centuries* (London, 1970). The best introduction to the international realignment of the 1750s is still D. B. Horn, 'The Diplomatic Revolution', in J. O. Lindsay (ed.), *The New Cambridge Modern History*, vol. vii: *The Old Regime, 1713–1763* (Cambridge, 1957), while Kaunitz's efforts to foster this are examined in two articles: W. J. McGill, 'The Roots of Policy: Kaunitz in Vienna and Versailles, 1749–1753', *Journal of Modern History* 43 (1971), 228–44; and R. Browning, 'The British Orientation of Austrian Foreign Policy, 1749–1754', *Central European History* 1 (1968), 299–323. A lively and large-scale study of Prussia's wars between 1740 and 1763 is provided by Dennis Showalter, *The Wars of Frederick the Great* (London, 1995), while an informative anatomy of the army is contained in Christopher Duffy, *The Army of Frederick the Great*, 2nd edn (Chicago, IL, 1996); the same author has written a sprightly military biography: *Frederick the Great: a military life* (London, 1985). The best brief introduction to the king as military commander is still R. R. Palmer, 'Frederick the Great, Guibert, Bülow: From Dynastic to

National War', reprinted in Peter Paret (ed.), *Makers of Modern Strategy: from Machiavelli to the Nuclear Age* (Princeton, NJ, 1986). Two authoritative studies of the wartime partnership have appeared: P. F. Doran, *Andrew Mitchell and Anglo-Prussian Diplomatic Relations during the Seven Years' War* (New York, 1986); and Karl W. Schweitzer, *Frederick the Great, William Pitt, and Lord Bute: the Anglo-Prussian Alliance, 1756–1763* (New York, 1991). The war's military legacies and particularly the consequences of Rossbach are set out in the first chapter of T. C. W. Blanning's lively *The French Revolutionary Wars, 1787–1802* (London, 1996). Finally, Christopher Duffy has provided Austrian and Russian military perspectives on the rise of Prussia in *The Army of Maria Theresa: the armed forces of Imperial Austria* (Newton Abbot, 1977) and *Russia's Military Way to the West: Origins and Nature of Russian Military Power, 1700–1800* (London, 1981).

# 8.  The 'Second Reign' of Frederick the Great, 1763–1786

The material available in English on Frederick's second reign is less than for the period 1740–63. Biographical studies of the king devote a chapter or two to these decades: see Gerhard Ritter, *Frederick the Great* (London, 1968), chs 9 and 10, and T. Schieder, *Frederick the Great* (London, 2000), chs 6, 7 and 8, while the second half of Chester V. Easum's sturdy and neglected biography of the king's brother, *Prince Henry of Prussia* (Madison, WI, 1942), provides an interesting perspective on the later reign. Though the book's Prussophilic tone, dense style and defective organization make it difficult to use, the best guide to the structures of government is still Walther Hubatsch, *Frederick the Great* (London, 1975). Hubert C. Johnson, *Frederick the Great and his Officials* (New Haven, CT, 1975) offers a contrasting and less convincing view. The old article by Walter L. Dorn, 'The Prussian Bureaucracy in the eighteenth century', *Political Science Quarterly* 46 (1931), 403–23, and 47 (1932), 75–94 and 259–73, is a convenient introduction to the older German literature and contains some original material on this period. The king's later foreign policy is surveyed by H. M. Scott, 'Aping the Great Powers: Frederick the Great and the Defence of Prussia's International Position, 1763–86', *German History* 12 (1994), 286–307, while the same author's 'Frederick II, the Ottoman Empire and the Origins of the Russo-Prussian Alliance of April 1764', *European Studies Review* 7 (1977), 153–77, examines the making of the key treaty. The loss of that alliance can be viewed from an Austro-Russian perspective in Harvey L. Dyck, 'Pondering the Russian Fact: Kaunitz and the Catherinian Empire in the 1770s',

*Canadian Slavonic Papers* 22 (1981), 451–69; in Isabel de Madariaga, 'The Secret Austro-Russian Treaty of 1781', *Slavonic and East European Review* 38 (1959–60), 114–45, and in her major political biography, *Russia in the Age of Catherine the Great* (London, 1981), chs 12–15 and 24; and in the outstanding life of another of Frederick's fellow monarchs, Derek Beales, *Joseph II*, vol. i: *In the Shadow of Maria Theresa 1741–80* (Cambridge, 1987), chs 9 and 13. European international relations are examined in the seminal Paul W. Schroeder, *The Transformation of European Politics, 1763–1848* (Oxford, 1994), ch. 1, and by Derek McKay and H. M. Scott, *The Rise of the Great Powers, 1648–1815* (London, 1983), ch. 8. There are informative and up-to-date studies of the army and military policy by Dennis E. Showalter, 'Hubertusburg to Auerstaedt: the Prussian Army in Decline?', *German History* 12 (1994), pp. 308–33, and his *The Wars of Frederick the Great* (London, 1995), ch. 7, and by Christopher Duffy, *The Army of Frederick the Great*, 2nd edn (New York, 1996). The most elusive dimension in English is the actual domestic policies pursued during the second reign. The question of whether Frederick was or was not an 'enlightened absolutist' is decisively settled by T. C. W. Blanning, 'Frederick the Great and Enlightened Absolutism', in H. M. Scott (ed.), *Enlightened Absolutism: reform and reformers in the later eighteenth century* (London, 1990), pp. 265–88. Royal policy towards the nobility is examined in ch. 3 of Robert M. Berdahl, *The Politics of the Prussian Nobility: The Development of a Conservative Ideology 1770–1848* (Princeton, NJ, 1988). The incorporation of West Prussia after 1772 is examined in ch. 2 of William W. Hagen, *Germans, Poles and Jews: The Nationality Conflict in the Prussian East, 1772–1914* (Chicago, IL, 1980), while the same author's 'The Partitions of Poland and the Crisis of the Old Regime in Prussia, 1772–1806', *Central European History* 9 (1976), 115–28, highlights the problems of governing the new province. W. O. Henderson, *Studies in the Economic Policy of Frederick the Great* (London, 1963) is a shrewd guide to the older German literature and is focused on the second half of the king's reign, while James Van Horn Melton, *Absolutism and the eighteenth-century origins of compulsory schooling in Prussia and Austria* (Cambridge, 1988), ch. 7, provides a brief account of the educational initiatives. Finally, Christina Rathgeber, 'The Reception of Brandenburg-Prussia's New Lutheran Hymnal of 1781', *Historical Journal* 36 (1993), 115–36, is an interesting sidelight.

# 9.   The Prussian military state, 1763–1806

English literature on the Prussian military state in the eighteenth and nineteenth centuries is not abundant. The fundamental work, Otto Büsch, *Military System and Social Life in Old Regime Prussia, 1713–1807: The Beginnings of the*

*Social Militarization of Prusso-German Society* (New Jersey, 1997) has recently been translated. In addition, as an introduction to the subject, one can consult, despite being out of date in parts, Sidney B. Fay, *The Rise of Brandenburg-Prussia to 1786* (rev. edn New York, 1981), a short, well-written overview up to the death of Frederick the Great. The latest overview of the research can be found in Stanislaw Salmonowicz, 'The State and Requirement of Research into Prussia's History 1701–1871', *Polish Western Affairs* 27/1 (1986), 111–32. A recent general survey of German history in the seventeenth and eighteenth centuries in which Prussia is treated in a comparative perspective is John G. Gagliardo, *Germany under the Old Regime, 1600–1790* (London, 1991). The particularly bureaucratic character of Prussia in the eighteenth century is analysed in the classic work by Hans Rosenberg, *Bureaucracy, Aristocracy, and Autocracy: the Prussian Experience, 1660–1815* (rev. edn Boston, 1966). C. B. A. Behrens points out that Prussia in the eighteenth century was not only a military and a police state, but also a successful model of the Enlightenment: *Society, Government, and the Enlightenment: the Experience of Eighteenth-Century France and Prussia* (New York, 1985).

A useful introduction is Margaret Shennan's *The Rise of Brandenburg-Prussia* (London/New York, 1995), with a bibliography. The history of Prussia in the eighteenth century is generally associated with the reign of Frederick II. The myth of the great Prussian king attracted Anglo-Saxon biographers early on, as with Thomas Carlyle's hero cult. Nor is there any lack of modern biographies. Especially worth mentioning are: Christopher Duffy, *Frederick the Great: A Military Life* (London, 1985) and Robert B. Asprey's *Frederick the Great: The Magnificent Enigma* (New York, 1986). The biographies complement each other; while Duffy emphasizes the military genius of the Prussian king (at the same time underestimating Frederick's dangerous tendency to take incredible risks), Asprey portrays the king within the larger context of Prussian history and does not as a result leave out the often-underestimated father, Frederick William I. A good introduction for students can be found in the small volume by Thomas M. Berker (ed.), *Frederick the Great and the Making of Prussia* (New York, 1972), which also contains a bibliography. Richard Gawthrop, *Pietism and the Making of Eighteenth-Century Prussia* (New York, 1993) points out that the particular character of the Prussian state possessed a religious component.

The Prussia of Frederick the Great and his army were almost identical; nor is there a lack of material on this subject. The classic account, despite more recent research that has not overtaken its essential traits, is Gordon A. Craig, *The Politics of the Prussian Army, 1640–1945* (Oxford/New York, 1956). It has the advantage of offering a long-term interpretation in which the Frederician era is a key element and in which the thesis of a Prussian–German *Sonderweg* is described within the context of European history. A more modern, even if more difficult to read, counterpart to Craig's work is Jonathan R. White, *The Prussian Army, 1640–1871* (Lanham, 1996). To date, there is no work in English on the social history of the Prussian middle classes, nobility and officer corps, with the exception of Robert M. Berdahl, *The Politics of the Prussian Nobility: The Development of a Conservative Ideology 1770–1848* (Princeton, NJ, 1988). Even more pressing is a comparative analysis of Prussia's social and military structures within a European context. It is possible that as a result certain ideas about a Prussian *Sonderweg* would have to be qualified.

# 10. Prussia's army: continuity and change, 1713–1830

A full biography intended for general readers and which is the best work of its kind in English is Robert B. Asprey's *Frederick the Great: The Magnificent Enigma* (New York, 1986). C. B. A. Behrens, *Society, Government, and Enlightenment: The Experiences of Eighteenth-Century France and Prussia* (London, 1985) is a comparative analysis of the developed *dirigiste* state by a distinguished scholar of early modern Europe. A generally favourable analysis of Frederick's way of war is Christopher Duffy, *Frederick the Great: A Military Life* (London, 1985), who also presents details of Frederick's organization, tactics and mentality in *The Army of Frederick the Great* (New York, 1974). An excellent analysis of the religious and spiritual elements in the Prussian ethos can be found in Richard Gawthrop's *Pietism and the Making of Eighteenth-Century Prussia* (New York, 1993). Anthony Moore's *The Army of Brandenburg-Prussia, 1685 to 1715* (Upton, 1992) is a straightforward narrative overview with a limited analytical dimension. Behind the somewhat deceptive title of Peter Paret's *Yorck and the Era of Prussian Reform, 1807–1815* (Princeton, NJ, 1966) lies a superb analysis of the army's reconstruction in the general context of the Reform Movement. Ferdinando Salleo, 'Mirabeau in Prussia, 1786–87: Parallel Diplomat or Secret Agent?', *Revue d'Histoire Diplomatique* 91 (1977), 346–56, is significant less for its subject-matter than for its insight into the most familiar contemporary foreign commentator on Prussia. Dennis Showalter's 'Hubertusberg to Auerstaedt: The Prussian Army in Decline?', *German History* 12 (1994), 308–33, is a revisionist interpretation of Prussia's military effectiveness in the period from 1763 to 1806. An overview of Prussia's military performance in a general European context can be found in Dennis Showalter, *The Wars of Frederick the Great* (London, 1995). R. Steven Turner, 'The *Bildungsbuergertum* and the Learned Professions in Prussia, 1770–1830: The Origins of a Class', *Social History* 13/25 (1980),

105–35, analyses the integration of the bourgeoisie into public service. Charles Edward White, *The Enlightened Soldier: Scharnhorst and the Militärische Gesellschaft in Berlin, 1801–1805* (New York, 1989) presents the intellectual matrix of the military reform movement. Emilio Willems, *A Way of Life and Death: Three Centuries of Prussian–German Militarism: An Anthropological Approach* (Nashville, TN, 1986) is frequently wrongheaded and sometimes muddle-headed, but a useful alternative perspective if approached with caution. Otto Büsch, *Military System and Social Life in Old Regime Prussia, 1713–1807: The Beginnings of the Social Militarization of Prusso-German Society* (New Jersey, 1997) is a welcome translation of a long-standard work (whose title is self-explanatory) by the leading authority on the subject. Peter H. Wilson, *German Armies: War and German Politics 1648–1815* (London, 1998) is an indispensable analytical overview. John E. Stine, 'King Frederick William II and the Decline of the Prussian Army, 1786–1797' (Ph.D., University of South Carolina, 1980) is more useful for its data than its analysis, but is nevertheless a solid narrative of the conventional wisdom on Prussia's military problems. Hagen Schulze, *The Course of German Nationalism. From Frederick the Great to Bismarck, 1763–1867* (Cambridge, 1991) surveys the social and political, as well as the military, elements of nationalism and its co-option by Prussia.

# 11. Prussia during the French Revolutionary and Napoleonic wars, 1786–1815

There are no general histories of Prussia for the period. For general histories of Germany, see Matthew Levinger's suggestions below. One can include Brendan Simms, *The Struggle for Mastery in Germany, 1779–1850* (London, 1998).

For the diplomatic context of the 1780s and 1790s leading to the War of the First Coalition, see T. C. W. Blanning, *The Origins of the French Revolutionary Wars, 1787–1802* (London, 1986); and id., *The French Revolutionary Wars, 1787–1802* (London, 1996). Paul Schroeder's *The Transformation of European Politics, 1763–1848* (Oxford, 1994) is a masterly account of international relations throughout the period, even if Prussia generally receives short shrift. Many important diplomatic documents are to be found in Paul Bailleu (ed.), *Preußen und Frankreich von 1795 bis 1807. Diplomatische Correspondenzen*, 2 vols (Leipzig, 1881–7).

There are no scholarly studies of Frederick William II, although David Barclay is in the process of preparing one. In the meantime, one can consult Wilhelm Moritz Bissing, *Friedrich Wilhelm II. König von Preußen: Ein Leben* (Berlin, 1967). His foreign minister, Hertzberg, has fared better: Andreas

Thedor Preuss, *Ewald Friedrich Graf von Hertzberg* (Berlin, 1909). The diplomatic monographs for his reign are dated, but the following works are nevertheless still worth consulting: on the Prussian invasion of the Dutch Republic, see Friedrich Carl Wittichen, *Preußen und England in der europäischen Politik 1785–1788* (Heidelberg, 1902). For the Second and Third Partitions of Poland, the work of Robert Howard Lord, *The Second Partition of Poland. A Study in Diplomatic History* (Cambridge, MA, 1915) and id., 'The third partition of Poland', *The Slavonic Review* 3 (1924–5), 481–98, is still indispensable. On the impact of the absorption of Polish territory on the Prussian state, see William W. Hagen, 'The Partitions of Poland and the Crisis of the Old Regime in Prussia, 1772–1806', *Central European History* 9 (1976), 115–28.

The reign of Frederick William III has recently been the focus of new studies. The most recent and most thorough biography of the king is Thomas Stamm-Kuhlmann, *König in Preussens grosser Zeit: Friedrich Wilhelm III, der Melancholiker auf dem Thron* (Berlin, 1992). Brendan Simms's *The Impact of Napoleon: Prussian high politics, foreign policy and the crisis of the executive, 1797–1806* (Cambridge, 1996) is a detailed account of Prussia's foreign-political response to the French threat during the revolutionary era. It should be supplemented by the following articles: by Brendan Simms, 'The road to Jena: Prussian high politics, 1804–1806', *German History* 12 (1994), 374–94, and '"An odd question enough". Charles James Fox, the crown and British policy during the Hanoverian crisis of 1806', *Historical Journal* 38 (1995), 567–96; and by Philip Dwyer, 'Prussia and the Armed Neutrality: the decision to invade Hanover in 1801', *International History Review* 15 (1993), 661–87, 'The politics of Prussian neutrality, 1795–1805', *German History* 12 (1994), 351–73, and 'Two definitions of neutrality: Prussia, the European states-system and the French invasion of Hanover in 1803', *International History Review* 19 (1997), 522–40. Dennis Showalter, 'Hubertusberg to Auerstaedt: the Prussian Army in Decline?', *German History* 12 (1994), 308–33, questions traditional notions of whether the Prussian army really was as bad as all that.

Most of the biographical material on the leading Prussian political figures of the Napoleonic era is in German – Gerhard Ritter, *Freiherr vom Stein: Eine politische Biographie*, 2nd edn (Stuttgart, 1958); Peter Gerrit Thielen, *Karl August von Hardenberg 1750–1822: Eine Biographie* (Cologne, 1967); the most recent work on Hardenberg is Thomas Stamm-Kuhlmann, '"Man vertraute doch der Administration!" Staatsverständnis und Regierungshandlen des preußischen Staatskanzlers Karl August von Hardenberg', *Historische Zeitschrift* 264 (1997), 613–54. Stamm-Kuhlmann has also edited Hardenberg's papers, *Tagebücher und autobiographische Aufzeichnungen des Staatskanzlers Karl August von Hardenberg, 1750–1822* (Munich, forthcoming).

For the Reform Movement, see Matthew Levinger's suggestions below. There is a general lack of English material available for the diplomatic history of the period after 1807. Philip Dwyer, 'The two faces of Prussian foreign policy: Karl August von Hardenberg as minister for foreign affairs, 1805–1815', in Thomas Stamm-Kuhlmann (ed.), *Karl August von Hardenberg. Chancen und Grenzen der Reformpolitik* (Munich, 2000), looks at Hardenberg's role in the formulation of foreign policy *vis-à-vis* France and Russia. There is no modern synthesis of the Wars of Liberation, although Rudolf Ibbeken, *Preußen 1807–1813. Staat und Volk als Idee und in Wirklichkeit. Darstellung und Dokumentation* (Stuttgart, 1970) is worth consulting. Similarly, there is a lack of recent material on Prussia's role during the Congress of Vienna, although a good starting-point is Schroeder's *Transformation of Europe*.

# 12. The Prussian Reform Movement and the rise of enlightened nationalism

Excellent general treatments of the Napoleonic era, both in Prussia and in the other German states, are found in Thomas Nipperdey, *Germany from Napoleon to Bismarck, 1800–1866* (Princeton, NJ, 1996), and James J. Sheehan, *German History 1770–1866* (Oxford, 1989); Hans-Ulrich Wehler, *Deutsche Gesellschaftsgeschichte*, vols 1 and 2 (Munich, 1987).

The arguments in this essay are elaborated further in Matthew Levinger, *Enlightened Nationalism: The Transformation of Prussian Political Culture, 1804–1848* (New York, 2000). Important synthetic interpretations of the Prussian Reform Movement include Hans Rosenberg, *Bureaucracy, Aristocracy, Autocracy: The Prussian Experience, 1660–1815* (Cambridge, MA, 1958); Reinhart Koselleck, *Preußen zwischen Reform und Revolution: Allgemeines Landrecht, Verwaltung und soziale Bewegung von 1791 bis 1848*, 3rd edn (Stuttgart, 1981); Herbert Obenaus, *Anfänge des Parlamentarismus in Preußen bis 1848* (Düsseldorf, 1984); and Bernd Sösemann (ed.), *Gemeingeist und Bürgersinn: Die Preußische Reformen, Forschungen zur Brandenburgischen und Preußischen Geschichte*, n.s., Beiheft 2 (Berlin, 1993). Several other works available in English are Friedrich Meinecke, *The Age of German Liberation, 1795–1815*, tr. Peter Paret (Berkeley, CA, 1977); Walter Simon, *The Failure of the Prussian Reform Movement 1807–1819* (Ithaca, NY, 1955); and Marion Gray, 'Prussia in Transition: Society and Politics under the Stein Reform Ministry of 1808', *Transactions of the American Philosophical Society*, vol. 76 (Philadelphia, PA, 1986).

On the events leading up to the reform period, see C. B. A. Behrens, *Society, Government, and the Enlightenment: The Experiences of Eighteenth-Century France and Prussia* (New York, 1985); Eckhart Hellmuth (ed.), *The Transformation of Political Culture: England and Germany in the Late Eighteenth Century* (Oxford, 1990); and Brendan Simms, *The Impact of Napoleon: Prussian high politics, foreign policy and the crisis of the executive, 1797–1806* (Cambridge, 1997). A sophisticated treatment of the intellectual antecedents of the Reform Movement is found in Frederick C. Beiser, *Enlightenment, Revolution, and Romanticism: The Genesis of Modern German Political Thought, 1790–1800* (Cambridge, MA, 1992).

The idea of nationhood, as found in the writings of Prussians during the Napoleonic era, is discussed in Friedrich Meinecke's classic *Cosmopolitanism and the National State*, tr. Robert B. Kimber (Princeton, NJ, 1970); as well as in Jörg Echternkamp, *Der Aufstieg der deutschen Nationalismus 1770–1840* (Frankfurt, 1997); Bernhard Giessen, *Intellectuals and the Nation: Collective Identity in an Axial Age*, tr. Nicolas Levis and Amosz Weisz (Cambridge, 1998); Dirk Alexander Reder, *Frauenbewegung und Nation: Patriotische Frauenvereine in Deutschland im frühen 19. Jahrhundert (1813–1830)* (Cologne, 1998); and Hagen Schulze, *States, Nations and Nationalism from the Middle Ages to the Present* (Oxford, 1996). Liah Greenfeld's *Nationalism: Five Roads to Modernity* (Cambridge, MA, 1992) offers an interesting perspective on the emergence of nationalist ideology in Germany, focusing on bourgeois intellectuals rather than on the bureaucratic elite.

The economic plans of the Prussian reformers are discussed in Barbara Vogel, *Allgemeine Gewerbefreiheit: Die Reformpolitik des preußischen Staatskanzlers Hardenberg (1810–1820)* (Göttingen, 1983); and in Eric Dorn Brose, *The Politics of Technological Change in Prussia: Out of the Shadow of Antiquity, 1809–1848* (Princeton, NJ, 1993). On aristocratic responses to the Reform Movement, see Robert Berdahl, *The Politics of the Prussian Nobility: The Development of a Conservative Ideology, 1770–1848* (Princeton, NJ, 1988), as well as Hanna Schissler, *Preußische Agrargesellschaft im Wandel: Wirtschaftliche, gesellschaftliche und politische Transformationsprozesse von 1763 bis 1847* (Göttingen, 1978).

# A NOTE ON FURTHER RESEARCH POSSIBILITIES

The ideas for further research possibilities compiled below are the result of suggestions made by the contributors.

## 1. Prussia in history and historiography from the eighteenth to the nineteenth century

It is of paramount importance to set Prussian historiography in a comparative context. Comparisons with other European historiographies in the eighteenth and nineteenth centuries would be especially helpful. Furthermore, following in the footsteps of Klaus Zernack and Karin Friedrich, more on the Polish historiography of Prussia would be welcome.

So far, the eighteenth-century historiography of Prussia has not been systematically researched. Micro-studies on individual historians might shed new light on the historical writings of seventeenth- and eighteenth-century historiography. The strong influence of Protestantism and of religion more generally on the writing of history has also often been neglected. Once again, comparisons with other Protestant-influenced north-west European historiographies would be rewarding.

While we are well informed about the institutional beginnings of academic history-writing in Prussia in the late eighteenth and early nineteenth centuries, it would be beneficial to give more attention to the question of how historical knowledge was shaped by the development of a particular scientific style. Studies on historical texts that make the language of those texts the object of historical enquiry are the most promising way ahead in this area.

Much needs to be done to deconstruct the social institution of academic history-writing. At the same time, we need to explore the impact of non-academic history-writing (for example by Theodor Fontane and Gustav Freytag) on perceptions of Prussia and the interplay between academic and non-academic history-writing. Given the popularity of local historical associations in Prussia in the nineteenth century, more work could be done on the relationship between local, Prussian and German national identity-building through the writing of history.

Finally, both the Social Democratic and the Catholic historiographies of Prussia need to be explored further, in particular through closer analysis of key works and writers as well as through the exploration of historical perceptions carried forward in the Social Democratic and Catholic press. So far, research is very largely restricted to a few 'key' persons such as Franz Mehring, Karl Kautsky, Ono Klopp and Franz Schnabel. The challenges of the dominant Prussian–German tradition of historiography are still a rich seam for future works on Prussian historiography.

## 2.  Frederick William I and the beginnings of Prussian absolutism, 1713–1740

The reign of Frederick William I is one of the areas for research in Prussian history that remains wide open. Clearly, since one cannot generalize about the way in which absolutism was implemented throughout all the Brandenburg-Prussian territories, more case-studies would be helpful to fully appreciate the experience of territories during the early eighteenth century. In particular, a study of Brandenburg and the western provinces that utilizes newly available research sources would go far to help explain this complex reign. In addition, an updated biography of Frederick William I that incorporates recent research about his reign is greatly needed.

## 3.  Piety, politics and society: Pietism in eighteenth-century Prussia

The Pietist movement has been a privileged object of research interest among German church historians since the Second World War. Research into the history of the movement in Prussia has flourished particularly since 1989, when the reunification of Germany opened access to the crucial Halle archives and libraries. Funding has been made available for the modernization of library and archive facilities and the production of scholarly editions of important documents and rare printed texts. However, it must be said that the recent published work on Prussian Pietism has only very rarely achieved the breadth and suggestiveness of the classic studies by

Hinrichs and Deppermann. The historiography is fragmented, parochial and highly specialized, lacks comparative scope and is generally uninterested in the broader social and political context. To a certain extent, these weaknesses reflect the continuing prominence in this field of a traditional and antiquarian style of *Kirchengeschichte*. There is no contemporary study of the Prussian movement that could compete with Hartmut Lehmann's authoritative survey of Württemberg Pietism, *Pietismus und weltliche Ordnung in Württemberg vom 17. bis zum 20. Jahrhundert* (Stuttgart, 1969). The relevant chapters in M. Brecht's multi-volume *Geschichte des Pietismus* provide a useful point of departure, but a new synthesis is needed that will integrate the results of specialized research over the last few decades with a nuanced social and political history of religion in the Prussian provinces.

# 4.   Prussia and the Enlightenment

Although interest in the Enlightenment has surged in the last thirty years, several areas are in need of further investigation. On one level, there is a simple lack of biographical information on many adherents of the Enlightenment. Not even Thomasius has found a biographer, although he has received more attention recently. The material on many others often has not been updated since the *Allgemeine deutsche Biographie* published a century ago. It certainly would be worthwhile to have intellectual biographies of, for instance, notable Enlightenment theologians such as J. J. Spalding or W. A. Teller. Because most of them were in one way or another involved in the workings of the government, a political setting and the rich source of information that comes with that are a given. This is also the easiest way to start because of the relatively easy access to their writings. Many works of authors at the end of the eighteenth century have been reprinted in the 1970s in the series *Aetas Kantiana*.

Something similar is true for other high government officials. In this chapter, the validity of the notion of enlightened absolutism for Prussia is questioned, but since other historians continue to employ the term it would be profitable to have studies on state ministers who implemented 'enlightened' policy. There is a recent monograph by Peter Mainka on the Minister of Education and Cultural Affairs, *K. A. von Zedlitz* (1995). A suitable candidate for such a study would be the Minister for Mining, F. A. von Heinitz.

So far, studies on the Enlightenment in Prussia have tended to concentrate on Berlin. Much more work needs to be done on the Enlightenment in the provinces. On Halle and Königsbergen, a beginning has been made with the series *Zentren der Aufklärung* in the *Wolfenbütteler Studien zur Aufklärung*, but on Breslau and Silesia there is nothing. Not only provincial authors could be examined, but also Enlightenment societies. Some provincial Masonic lodges have been studied, but other societies should be researched as well, along the same lines as for the Wednesday Club in Berlin. On a different level than the biographical approach, this demands a combination of intellectual and social history.

Finally, the public sphere that the late Enlightenment fostered has to be further scrutinized. Who were included, who excluded from the public as it was fashioned in the writings of Enlightenment authors? Did women belong to it? Was there ideally only one, or were there more than one public – one of educated readers, another of entertainment readers, for instance – and what were the relationships between them? The answers to these and other questions determine our historical appreciation of Prussian society as it emerged during the Enlightenment. Here, too, intellectual and social history should be combined.

## 5.  The transformation of the rural economy in East Elbian Prussia, 1750–1830

The agrarian history of Brandenburg-Prussia in the late eighteenth and early nineteenth centuries is a researcher's dream, with largely untouched archival and published sources, on the one hand, and a very small, but high-quality, body of recent scholarship, on the other. Thus, for example, studies by Lieselott Enders, William Hagen and Jan Peters (all cited in the text) provide imaginative models for regional history (Enders), estate studies (Hagen) and anthropological approaches (Peters). In addition, there are entire regions and topics that are virtually untouched. Thus, while the agrarian history of Brandenburg and East Prussia has received considerable attention, other regions, especially Silesia and Pomerania, remain neglected save by Polish historians, whose studies are accessible only to scholars who can read Polish.

Fortunately, political changes in East Central Europe since 1989 have created much greater opportunities for research on these areas, whose regional archives are located in the Polish cities of Wrocław and Szezecin, and in the German city of Greifswald. For a useful overview of new research perspectives on the history of Prussia, see Wolfgang Neugebauer, 'Brandenburg-Preußische Geschichte nach der deutschen Einheit', *Jahrbuch für brandenburgische Landesgeschichte* 43 (1992).

Research on the agrarian history of East Elbian Prussia has focused primarily on social and economic issues, leaving other areas, like demographic and cultural history, almost untouched. Several topics within these latter areas deserve urgent attention. One of the major demographic problems, for example, concerns the landless and semi-landless population. Although the landless and semi-landless accounted for most of the rural population of East Elbian Prussia by the late eighteenth century, we know very little about their origins, the conditions of their lives, or the reasons for their rapid population growth in the eighteenth century. Fortunately, this topic has an excellent starting-point – the ground-breaking article by Jan Peters, 'Ostelbische Landarmut: Sozialökonomische über landarme und landlose Agrarproduzenten im Spätfeudalismus', *Jahrbuch für Wirtschaftsgeschichte* 3 (1967).

*Preußische Adelskultur*, the culture of the Prussian nobility, presents yet another problem that deserves special attention. Did the Prussian nobility, despite its regional particularisms, share a coherent world-view? How did the men and women of this rural elite live their daily lives? How did they educate their children? What was the local or regional political culture? Several recent studies provide starting-points for some of these problems: Dieter and Renate Sinn, *Der Alltag im Preußen* (Frankfurt, 1991); Shearer Bowman, *Masters and Lords: Mid-19th Century U.S. Planters and Prussian Junkers* (New York, 1993); Peter-Michael Hahn, *Formen der Visualisierung von Herrschaft: Studien zu Adel, Fürst und Schlossbau vom 16. bis zum 18. Jahrhundert* (Berlin, 1996); and Wolfgang Neugebauer, *Politische Wandel im Osten. Ost- und Westpreußen von den alten Ständen zum Konstitutionalismus* (Stuttgart, 1992).

# 6. The development of the Prussian town, 1720–1815

The traditional historiographical focus on Prussian diplomatic and political history, and on the relationship between the monarchy and the landed nobility, as well as the dogma of the 'decline' of the Prussian medieval cities, has left Prussian urban history – with a few exceptions – for a long time in the hands of local patriotic amateurs. The tide has turned mainly during the last decade, and an increasing number of social, economic and cultural case-studies, particularly of Brandenburg towns and the court cities of Berlin and Potsdam, have helped to paint a fuller picture of Prussian urban development in the eighteenth century. Yet large gaps are still waiting to be filled. There are no comparative and synthetic works which look at the great diversity of social, economic, cultural, religious and con- stitutional conditions of all the Hohenzollern territories, let alone Polish Prussia and other annexed Polish provinces, or the Pomeranian towns under Swedish domination until 1815. At the same time, more case-studies are needed beyond the core Brandenburg territories, especially of towns in East Prussia, Silesia, Pomerania, the Netzedistrikt, 'New East Prussia' and 'South Prussia'. This omission is not least due to the lack of knowledge of Polish sources and secondary literature of most German and Anglo-Saxon historians of Prussia of this period.

In contrast to the well-developed tradition of social research and 'history from below' applied to south and west German cities, this approach has been neglected by historians of Brandenburg-Prussia. There is great need for studies of the poor, vagrants and other marginal groups of urban soci- ety, as well as prosopographic studies of urban elites. So far, little has been done on Brandenburg-Prussia to compare with the rich research on other German cities in the Reformation period, on the role of women, on popular culture and literacy, on social disciplining and witchcraft.

There has been little systematic research on the responses of urban elites in the various provinces and regions to attempts at political centralization and administrative unification. How did Prussian burghers react to the institution of the *Steuerrat* and other interference by state officials, and what strategies did they develop to defend their traditional status, constitutions and local identities? Although there has been a large number of studies on proto-industrialization, mercantilism and the development of manufac- turing industries and trade, our knowledge of burgher mentality, popular beliefs and social behaviour remains poor. There has been little research to challenge some of the older assumptions about the alleged 'tolerance' of Prussian rulers, especially towards Jews or Catholics in the annexed Polish territories. Despite Hans-Jürgen Bömelburg's findings that the Jewish urban population of the towns annexed from Poland between 1772 and 1795 was expelled into great misery, few historians have responded to his appeal to extend this line of enquiry. Little is known about migratory movements during periods of war and annexation, both in Silesia from 1740, and within the Polish territories in 1772–95.

Further research is also needed on the effect of garrisons and the canton system, despite several excellent studies of the cohabitation of the milit- ary and civilians in Potsdam, Berlin and Frankfurt-an-der-Oder. How did the strategies vary by which the urban population in different provinces integrated or rejected military interference in everyday life, and was the 'militarization' of urban society successful?

# 7.  Prussia's emergence as a European great power, 1740–1763 *and*

# 8.  The 'Second Reign' of Frederick the Great, 1763–1786

For the Frederician period, the areas most in need of research are the royal courts, government and government policy in just about every field after 1763, and the provincial dimension of Prussian absolutism. Most studies tend to focus on and assume the effectiveness of central directives, but these need to be tested by an examination of their effectiveness on the ground.

# 9.  The Prussian military state, 1763–1806

The canton system and the Prussian army in the Age of Metternich are likely possibilities for further research. Both depend heavily on conventional wisdoms and generalizations and both will repay further investigation along the lines developed by the 'new' social history.

# 10.  Prussia's army: continuity and change, 1713–1830

The main desideratum since the appearance of Otto Büsch's seminal work, *Military System and Social Life in Old Regime Prussia, 1713–1807*, tr. John G. Gagliardo (New Jersey, 1997) is that we have an idea of the general picture, but nearly none about the reality of the military system at the bottom. It would be highly welcome if we knew more about the real functioning at the level of the *Gutshöfe* and the differentiations between regions and the provinces.

# 11.  Prussia during the French Revolutionary and Napoleonic wars, 1786–1815

There is no work in English that covers the whole French Revolutionary and Napoleonic period. Prussia's involvement in the revolution in Liège and Belgium in 1789–90 has received little attention from modern historians and would probably repay another look from the foreign-political perspective.

As far as political figures are concerned, a biography on Frederick William II is long overdue, but David Barclay is thankfully in the process of filling that lacuna. Up to now, historians have had to rely on traditional interpretations, which see Frederick William II's foreign policy as erratic and lacking in direction. This needs to be re-examined in the light of the high-political manoeuvrings and the contest for power that took place at the court and which led to Hertzberg's demise. In the same vein, biographical treatments of both Hertzberg and Haugwitz in terms of foreign policy would be useful. The latter especially has been badly treated by German and Anglo-Saxon historians, but, in general terms, a reappraisal of foreign policy and high politics for most of the reign of Frederick William II and III is long overdue (the exception of course is Brendan Simms's work). The conflict between Woellner and Hertzberg, for example, would undoubtedly throw light on the decision-making process at the court of Berlin. An up-to-date work on Hardenberg's foreign policy would also be worthwhile. Most of the material dealing with Hardenberg concentrates on his involvement in the Reform Movement, and does so to the neglect of foreign policy. The same can be said for most of the high-political figures at the court of Berlin during the revolutionary era. The material on many of them has not been updated since the *Allgemeine deutsche Biographie* published a century ago.

Prussian foreign policy after 1806 also needs detailed modern treatment; Prussia's role in the Congress of Vienna especially could do with a reassessment. The political and diplomatic manoeuvrings that preceded the *Befreiungskriege* remain to be adequately explored. The *Freiwilligen-Bewegung* (the volunteer movement) of 1813 needs to be looked at, especially in relation to the impact the Reform Movement may have had on it. In this context, work on the *Landsturm* and the *Landwehr* might be revealing. So, too, might an examination of the *Tugendbund* movement.

# 12. The Prussian Reform Movement and the rise of enlightened nationalism

While the Prussian Reform Movement has long been among the most intensively studied topics in modern German history, there is room for further research on a variety of questions. One important issue is the relationship between Prussia and the international system: to what extent were the reforms of the Napoleonic era motivated by foreign-policy concerns (for example, the desire to return Prussia to great-power status), and how were the legislative innovations in Prussia linked to concurrent social and political changes elsewhere in Europe, such as in the other German states, as well as in Britain, France and Russia? A second broad area for additional research is on the relationship between the Prussian central state and the individual regions within Prussia. One theme that was constantly emphasized by the Prussian reformers was the need to overcome the fragmented cultural and political identities that existed within Prussia and to forge a common 'national' spirit. Thus, a tension emerged between the competing desires for regional uniqueness and cultural uniformity. How did the central state grapple with the issue of cultural and political diversity (for example, between ethnic Germans and Poles in the East Elbian provinces, or between the predominantly Protestant old provinces and the predominantly Catholic Rhenish territories annexed in 1815)? Conversely, how did individual regions seek to preserve their individual identities in the face of assaults by the centralizing state?

Over recent decades, there has been little systematic research on the relationship between church and state in Prussia at the beginning of the nineteenth century, or on the relationship between Protestant revivalism and the emergence of new ideas of nationhood and civil society. While the origins of nationalism in the German states have been extensively studied, there is a need for further research on how precisely nationalist rhetoric *worked* in mobilizing various groups – for example, in recruiting and motivating troops for the War of Liberation. The shifting ways in which citizenship was defined on the basis of class, gender and religion also merit further study. To what extent, and with what success, did women, workers and members of religious minorities stake claims to citizenship in the 'nation'?

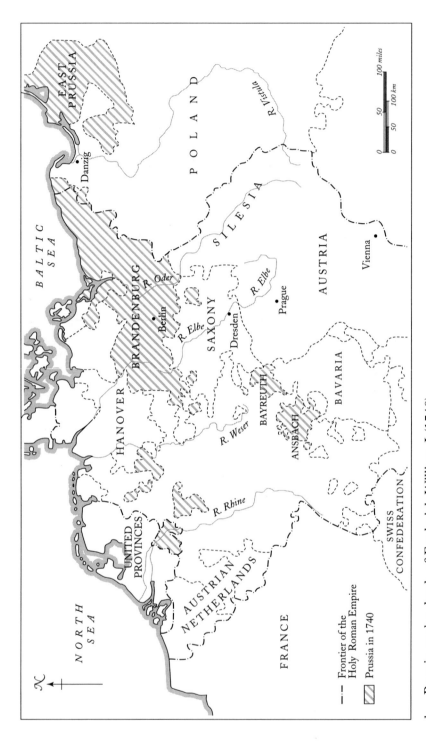

1. Prussia at the death of Frederick William I (1740)
*Source:* adapted from H. W. Koch 1978.

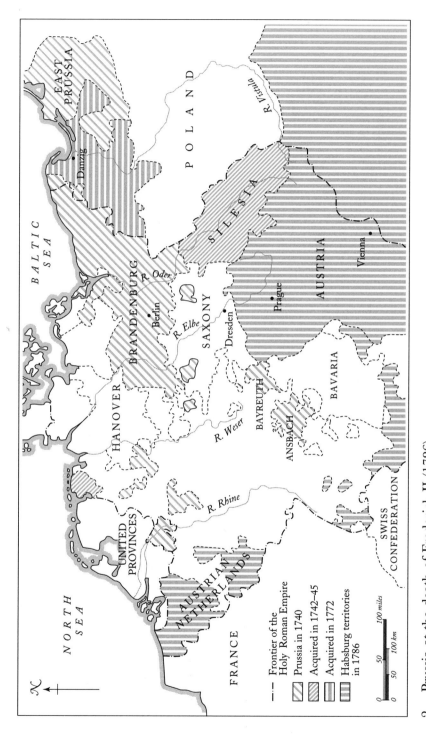

2. Prussia at the death of Frederick II (1786)
*Source:* adapted from H. W. Koch 1978.

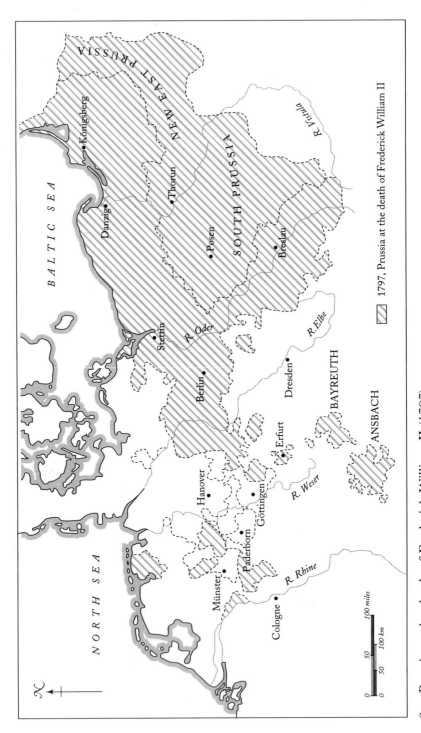

3. Prussia at the death of Frederick William II (1797)
*Source:* adapted from H. W. Koch 1978.

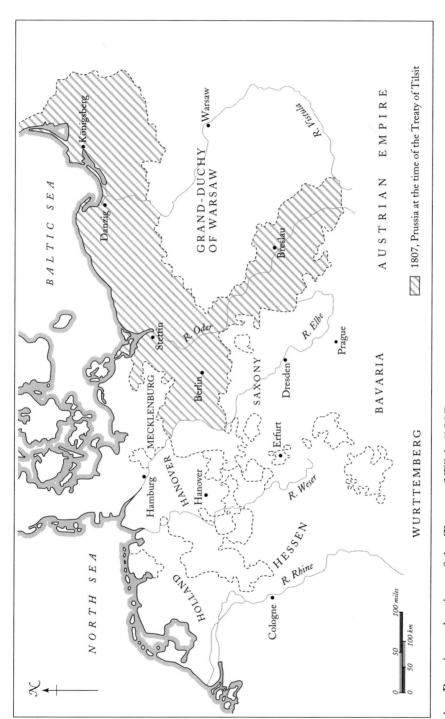

4. Prussia at the time of the Treaty of Tilsit (1807)
*Source:* adapted from H. W. Koch 1978.

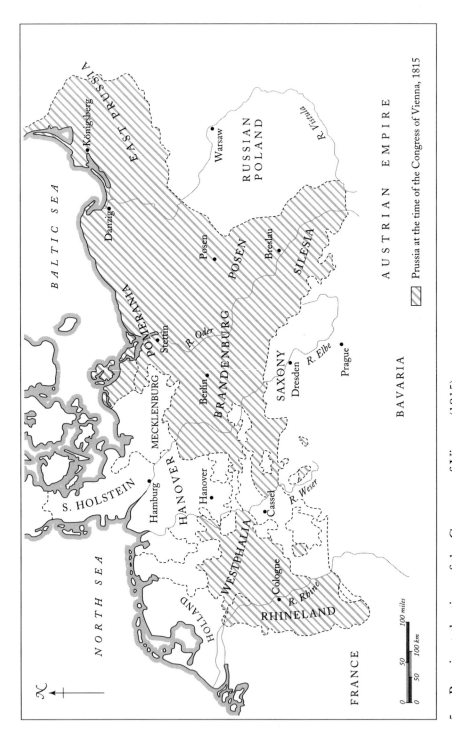

5.  Prussia at the time of the Congress of Vienna (1815)
*Source*: adapted from H. W. Koch 1978.

# INDEX